Duluth's Historic Parks

THEIR FIRST 160 YEARS

NANCY S. NELSON & TONY DIERCKINS

ZENITH CITY PRESS
DULUTH, MINNESOTA

Zenith City Press
Duluth, Minnesota
www.zenithcity.com
218-310-6541

Duluth's historic parks: their first 160 years

Text by Nancy S. Nelson and Tony Dierckins
Copyedit and index by Scott Pearson
Design, layout, and maps by Tony Dierckins

Portions of this book were previously published by the authors (see page 243 for more information).

First Edition, May 2017

Library of Congress Control Number: 2016958792

ISBNs: 978-1-887317-45-0 (softcover); 978-1-887317-47-4 (hardcover)

Printed in Minnesota, USA, by JS Print Group

Cover: Lithographic postcard of the pavilion in Lincoln Park, ca. 1900. [Image: Zenith City Press]

Title Page: Sketch of a scene in Garfield (Chester) Park, ca. 1895. [Image: Duluth Public Library]

Copyright Page: Sketch of the bridge carrying Terrace Parkway over Chester Creek, ca. 1895. [Image: Duluth Public Library]

Acknowledgments Page: Sketch of the bridge carrying Terrace Parkway over Chester Creek, ca. 1895. [Image: Duluth Public Library]

Page iv: Lithographic postcard of Gem Lakes, ca. 1900. [Image: Zenith City Press]

Contents Page: Sketch of Rogers Boulevard and Gem Lakes, ca. 1895. [Image: Duluth Public Library]

Page vi: Lithographic postcard of Cascade Park, ca. 1900. [Image: Zenith City Press]

Pages vii & ix: Sketches showing portions of Terrace Parkway, ca. 1893. [Image: Duluth Public Library]

Page xi: Lithographic postcard of Lincoln Park Drive within Lincoln Park, ca. 1900. [Image: Zenith City Press]

For all those who have donated time, energy, property, and funding to help create and care for Duluth's city parks.

The authors and publisher would like to thank:

Mark Atkinson, Kris Aho, Heidi Bakk-Hansen, Kathy Bergen, Erik Birkeland, David Blazevic, Millissa Brooks-Ojibway, Dawn Buck, Anthony Bush, Christine Carlson, Sam Cook, Dwight "Deacon" Nelson, Kraig Decker, Herb Dillon, Ellen Dunlop, Lindsay Dean, Jim J. Denney, Andrew Ebling, Randy Ellestad, Gladys Eral, Jim Filby-Williams, Mike Flaherty, Kelly Fleissner, Jerry Fryberger, Daniel Hartman, Jim Heffernan, Ronald House, Tim Howard, Dave Johnson, Tom Kasper, Andrew Krueger, Emily Larson, Tim Lee, Jeff Lemke, Brandee Lian, Sam Luoma, Paul Lundgren, Ryan Marshick, Captain Tom McKay, Grant Merritt, Hollis Norman, Maryanne C. Norton, Bob Norstrom, Jan Olson, Tom O'Rourke, David Ouse, Jerry Paulson, Marsha Patelke, Jill Peterman, Scott Pearson, Dan Proctor, Suzanne Rauvola, Tari Rayala, Robert Rodriguez, Mark Ryan, Dave Schaeffer, Dr. Margaret Scheibe, Cheryl Skafte, Peter Spooner, Kinnan Stauber, Thom Storm, Bob Swanson, Walter N. Trennery, Daniel Turner, Lynn Wagner, Erin Walsburg, and Matthew Waterhouse; Mags David and Pat Maus of the University of Minnesota Duluth Kathryn A. Martin Library Archives and Special Collections; and the entire Reference Department staff of the Duluth Public Library, active and retired, without whose invaluable help this book would not have been possible.

Special thanks to Tobbi Stager and the staff of JS Print Group of Duluth.

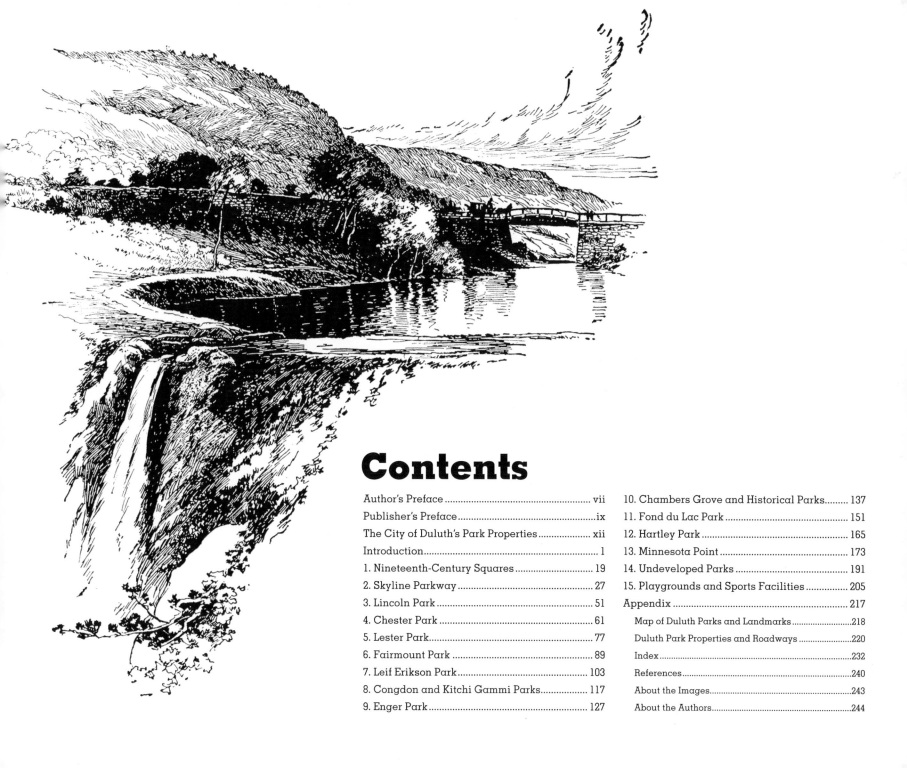

Contents

SCENE ON THE TERRACE DRIVE

Author's Preface

Our Rich Legacy

The story of Duluth's parks is really a story about people. The foundation for our amazing park system was created by a five-member Board of Park Commissioners between 1889 and 1913, but while I was researching the history of this rich legacy it quickly became clear to me that—although the park board guided the development of the parks—citizens have always played a crucial role. For over 160 years, the residents of Duluth have donated their time, money, and land to improve the parks, develop and maintain playgrounds, skating rinks, and trails, and create community resources such as Hartley Nature Center. Uncovering their stories has been a fascinating journey for me.

People often ask how I got involved in writing about Duluth's historic parks. I grew up in northern Illinois where most of the parks were just manicured blocks of grass with a few trees. Then in the 1970s my friends Olive and Fred Anderson invited me to visit their cabin in Michigan's Upper Peninsula where they introduced me to Lake Superior and the Pictured Rocks National Lakeshore. Over the next few years Olive and I spent many hours hiking and exploring the forest, dunes, and beaches of Pictured Rocks as she worked on writing a trail guide for the park. It was there, on the south shore of Lake Superior, that my love of the North Woods and my interest in geology was awakened.

I moved to Duluth in 1987 to earn a master's degree in geology at the University of Minnesota Duluth (UMD). Before classes started that fall, the professors took new graduate students on a field trip to familiarize us with the local landscape. The area that stuck in my mind most clearly was Bardon's Peak and the Magney-Snively forest. It was there, on the far end of West Skyline Parkway, that my interest in Duluth's parks was born. I am grateful to these professors, and especially my advisor Dr. John C. Green, for introducing me to this special area.

After completing my degree, I found a job in Duluth and settled into an old house on a tree-lined street near Chester Park. By 1996 I had left my job in environmental consulting and was working as a freelance technical writer when I learned that developers were proposing to build a golf course at Spirit Mountain, adjacent to Magney-Snively Park. As I worked with other concerned Duluthians to protect this magnificent old-growth hardwood forest, we realized that it is just one piece of the larger landscape of the western hillside, and that Skyline Parkway connects it to the city's other greenspaces. We created the West Skyline Planning and Preservation Alliance to bring attention to this scenic and historic section of the parkway. As public support for our efforts grew, we expanded our mission to include all of Skyline Parkway, and I began to search for information about its history. This led me to Pat Maus and the archives at the UMD library (at that time called the Northeast Minnesota Historical Center), where my research on the city parks began.

In 2005, Tom Kasper and Tony Dierckins began discussing the idea of publishing a book about the history of the city's parks. Tom was already immersed in many projects besides his full-time job as city gardener and had little time for writing, so in 2007 they invited me to help. I agreed, not realizing that it would become a decade-long commitment. Tom had already photocopied numerous historical documents about the parks, and he generously shared all of this material with me. Mark Ryan, who has written extensively about William K. Rogers, Sam Snively, and Skyline Parkway, also graciously shared the results of his research. When Tom eventually bowed out of the project, I became the chief researcher and writer.

My most important sources of information included meeting minutes of the Board of Park Commissioners, annual reports prepared by the park board and the park department, and hundreds of newspaper articles. The Duluth Public Library's reference librarians, newspapers on microfilm, local history collection, and clippings files were all essential to my research. When GenealogyBank.com came online with a searchable database of newspapers, it became possible to locate even more articles, many of which I would never have found by scanning through microfilm. When I ventured out to explore the lesser-known parks or field-check details, I was often accompanied by my good friend and fellow historian Maggie Scheibe. Our adventures and discussions provided me with a broader understanding of the history of the Duluth-Superior area and the time period during which most of our parks were created.

As I wrote about each park, my goal was to go beyond a simple timeline of events and share some of the wonderful stories that I discovered. I included many quotes taken directly from the old newspaper articles to try to evoke a sense of what life was like during this period of rapid development and social change. One of my favorite discoveries is Henry Cleveland, who served as park superintendent from 1909 to 1925. He played a huge role in the early days of the parks and was beloved by friends and coworkers, but his name has been forgotten. I hope this book helps to restore his place in the history of our parks. And the homecrofting movement—Tom Kasper's files contained many newspaper articles about gardening, and in these stories I encountered references to "homecrofting." I decided to spend some time following this story, and it turned out to be fascinating. In 1911 Duluth was christened the "Homecroft City" by the national leader of the movement—I am amazed that we have forgotten this part of Duluth's history! Another favorite is the story of Mina Merrill Prindle who donated forty acres for a park that she named after her mother, Janette Pollay. Mina was one of the few women who played a public role related to the parks. I'm sure many women privately influenced the men making decisions, but women were never included in newspaper reports. Not only did the newspapers mention Mina, they used her name instead of referring to her as Mrs. W. M. Prindle.

My main interest is the early history of the parks, and I chose to end my research at the point in 1956 when a revision to the city charter transformed Duluth's government from the commission system to a mayor/council system. That's when Mayor Eugene Lambert changed the park department to the Department of Public Recreation. For me, that was the end of the story. But of course, it was not the end of the parks, so Tony took over and added information about what happened after 1956. He also put together the appendix that includes information about every area that the city lists as a park. And, as with all of his publishing ventures, he found the fantastic images that bring the stories to life. Tony's creativity, dedication, and incredible energy made this book a reality.

In 1894, describing "Duluth and Her Beautiful Park System," the members of the park board wrote, "And while her enterprising citizens are putting forth every effort to increase her present greatness in a commercial point of view, they are nevertheless not living for to-day alone, but are laying a foundation upon which to build the superstructure that will be the envy of any city upon the continent, and which will gain in appreciation as the years go by and will not be fully appreciated until those who were instrumental in the great work shall have passed away." This book is dedicated to all those Duluthians who have been instrumental in creating and caring for this rich legacy.

— Nancy Nelson, January 2017

SCENE ON THE TERRACE DRIVE.

Publisher's Preface

A Long Walk in the Park

In the summer of 2005, then Duluth city gardener Tom Kasper visited my office to propose the idea of a book on the history of Duluth's parks. Zenith City Press, then known as X-Communication, was not yet focused on regional history as we are today. Our most popular book to date, *Will to Murder: The True Story Behind the Crimes and Trials Surrounding the Glensheen Killings*, was more true crime than history. But I was working on my first history book, *Zenith: A Postcard Perspective of Historic Duluth*, and was impressed by Tom's collection of vintage lithographic postcards featuring Duluth's parks. So we agreed to at least explore the idea. I went back to work on the postcard book and Tom began researching at the main branch of the Duluth Public Library with the help of his friend Bob Norstrom, and as always the library's fabulous reference staff provided additional help.

Two years later I had published Chuck Frederick's *Leatherheads of the North*—a history of the NFL's 1926–1927 Duluth Eskimos—and was writing *Crossing the Canal: An Illustrated History of Duluth's Aerial Bridge*. X-Communication was indeed becoming a publisher of local history, but while Tom continued his research, he didn't have the time to begin writing. He also didn't consider himself a writer.

At the suggestion of Duluth historian Maryanne C. Norton, Tom and I asked Nancy S. Nelson—a writer and geologist who had helped establish the Skyline Planning and Preservation Alliance—if she wanted to come on board as the book's author, using Tom's research. As often happens, reviewing that research led to more questions, which led to more research by Nancy—leaving little time for writing. Tom had essentially completed his end of the project at this point, and his contributions to it are incalculable. This book simply would not exist if not for Tom Kasper.

By 2009 Nancy was still researching, and to expedite matters we spoke with Mark Ryan about becoming the book's coauthor. Mark is best known for his work on William K. Rogers, who first conceived of a park system anchored by a great boulevard, and Samuel F. Snively, the driving force behind the completion and expansion of Rogers's vision, which resulted in today's Skyline Parkway. Mark agreed and shared much of his research with Nancy.

Three years later, however, little of the book had been written. In May 2012 X-Communication changed its name to Zenith City Press and released *Lost Duluth: Landmarks, Industries, Buildings, Homes, and the Neighborhoods in Which They Stood*, written by myself and Maryanne C. Norton. At the same time we launched *Zenith City Online*, an internet publication celebrating historic Duluth, Western Lake Superior, and Minnesota's Arrowhead region. Mark provided *Zenith City*'s first feature story—a biography of William K. Rogers—and would contribute three other features in the next few years. Meanwhile Nancy began writing monthly installments on the development of Duluth's parks for *Zenith City Online*; those stories became the basis for the chapters in this book.

During this time I was receiving a crash course in Duluth history from Nancy, Mark, and other contributors to *Zenith City*, including Heidi Bakk-Hansen, whose focus on the origins of local place names (streets, streams, parks, etc.) taught me much about our pioneers and the development of Duluth's neighborhoods; David Ouse, who introduced me to Duluthians whom history had forgotten; Jim Heffernan, who made me nostalgic for a time and place I never knew; Anthony Bush, who showed me how sports played an important role in shaping Duluth; and Jeff Lemke, who illustrated how the railroads connected everything, both figuratively and literally, during the city's early years. Meanwhile, Maryanne and I continued to explore Duluth's historic architecture and learned even more about the city's past while answering reader questions. (Maryanne also provided invaluable research for this book.)

As Nancy produced more stories about Duluth's parks for *Zenith City Online,* it became clear that capturing the entire history of Duluth's park system would be an overwhelming if not impossible task. Duluth owns nearly 150 properties and roadways considered part of the parks system, some established as early as 1856 and others as recent as 2016. We decided to focus this book on the years during which our major historic parks and William K. Rogers's boulevard idea were initially developed—from 1889 when our first park board was established and we began work on the boulevard to 1941 when Hartley Park was established and work on the Minnesota Point Recreation Center was complete (and, sadly, about the time parks became a very low priority for the city). While the book also covers the periods from 1856 to 1888 and 1941 to today, it remains focused on the creation and development of today's Skyline Parkway and Duluth's major historic parks—Lincoln Park, Chester Park, Lester Park, Fairmount Park, Leif Erikson Park, Congdon Park, Kitchi Gammi Park, Enger Park, Chambers Grove, Fond du Lac Park, Hartley Park, and parks located on Minnesota Point—as well as the city's undeveloped parks, playgrounds, and sports venues. And just so we didn't overlook someone's favorite park property, we also created an appendix that provides information on all of Duluth's park properties as of 2016.

By fall 2015 Nancy had nearly completed the manuscript for the this book. But when we tried to weave her stories with Mark's, we recognized that his work was too expansive for this project—and none of us wanted to chop it up to force it to blend with Nancy's. So Mark graciously stepped away from the project as a coauthor, but his work is still here; much of this book is informed by his research, and his articles are referenced frequently.

This change in authorship forced Nancy to create chapters we had thought Mark would write, and in the meantime we recognized that there were ancillary stories to tell about subjects related to the history of each park that did not fit within each park's narrative. I volunteered to write these sidebar stories, as I had written about many of their subjects in previous books and articles. I also took on a portion of the work expanding Nancy's chapters to cover important aspects of the past fifty years and developed the appendix. By the time we had finished, I had essentially become her coauthor—but I recognize my contribution is mere window dressing to hers.

I received a lot of help with my end of things, as did Nancy, and we have listed everyone we could remember to thank on the book's acknowledgments page. Many of those listed went far beyond what I requested or expected. Randy Ellestad taught me a great deal about the history of the *Leif Erikson* replica Viking vessel. Mark Atkinson tutored me on the history of Lakeside and Lester Park. Lake Superior Zoo experts Matthew Waterhouse and Erin Walsburg provided information for passages about the zoo within Fairmount Park. The legendary Jim J. Denney and Thom Storm helped us get the stories of the Duluth Ski Club and Chester Park right. Fond du Lac historian Christine Carlson's research enlightened our work on the parks in the Fond du Lac neighborhood. Current Parks and Recreation director Lindsay Dean and her predecessor, Kathy Bergen, met with me to help complete the book's expansive appendix. At their suggestion I turned to Tim Howard, retired from Duluth's Facilities Management Department, who not only reviewed the appendix but also spent a great deal of time helping me track down vital information from the files he created during his long career with the city.

Just like Duluth's parks, this book is the result of the efforts of a great many people over a long period of time. Tom Kasper and I started this long walk through the history of Duluth's parks twelve years ago, and many have joined along the way. Nancy's and my name might be on the cover, but we alone did not create this book, just as the city of Duluth could not have created its remarkable park system without the help of private citizens.

— Tony Dierckins, January 2017

Duluth's Historic Parks

1856–2016

The City of Duluth's Park Properties

A larger version of the map below appears on pages 218 and 219. See the Appendix starting on page 220 for more information about the properties listed below.

Amity Park
Arena Waterfront Park
Arlington Athletic Complex
Bayfront Festival Park
Bellevue Park
Birchwood Park
Blackmer Park
Boy Scout Landing
Brewer Park
Brighton Beach (at Kitchi Gammi Park)
Bristol Beach Park
Buffalo Park
Canal Park
Carson Park
Cascade Square
Central Entrance Triangle
Central Park
Central Hillside Park
Chambers Grove Park
Chester Park
Civic Center Plaza
Clover Hill Triangle (aka Granitoid Memorial Park)
Cobb Park
Como Park (aka Glen Avon)
Congdon Boulevard

Congdon Park
Corner of the Lake Park
Downer Park
Duluth Heights Park
Endion Ledges Park
Endion Park
Enger Park
Enger Park Golf Course
Ericson Place
Evergreen Memorial Plaza
Fairmount Park
Fairmount Park Triangle
Fifth Ave. W. Mall
Fifty-ninth Ave. W. Mall
Fond du Lac Park
Fond du Lac Square
Fortieth Ave. East and Jay Street Park
Forty-second Ave. East Lake Access
Forty-seventh Ave. E. & London Rd. & Regent St. Triangle
Forty-third Avenue East Lake Access
Franklin Square
Fremont Point Park
Fryberger Arena

Gary–New Duluth Park
Gasser Park
Gateway Plaza
Grant Park
Grassy Point Park
Greysolon Block Triangle
Greysolon Farms Park
Grosvenor Square
Harrison Park
Hartley Field
Hartley Park
Hartman Park
Hawk Ridge
Hazelwood Triangle
Heritage Park
Hillside Sport Court
Hilltop Park
Historical Park
Indian Park
Indian Point Campground (at Fairmount Park)
Irving Park
Janette Pollay Park
Jay Cooke Plaza
Johnson Park
Jollystone Park
Keene Creek Park

Kelso Park
Klang Memorial Park
Kitchi Gammi Park
Lafayette Square
Lake Park Athletic Complex
Lake Place Park
Lake Place Plaza
Lake Superior Plaza (aka Minnesota Power Plaza)
Lake Superior Zoo (at Fairmount Park)
Lakeside Court Park
Lakeview Park
Lakeview Manor Park
Lakewalk
Leif Erikson Park
Lester Park
Lester Park Golf Course
Lester Park Library Triangle
Lilliput Park
Lincoln Park
Lincoln Park Drive
Longview Tennis Courts
Lost Park
Lower Chester Park Playground
Lyman Park
Magney-Snively Park

Manchester Square
Memorial Park
Merritt Park
Mesaba Ave. & Central Entrance Triangle
Michael Colalillo Medal of Honor Park
Midtowne Park
Miller Creek Disc Golf Course
Minnesota Point Pine Forest Scientific and Natural Area
Minnesota Point Recreation Area
Mira M. Southworth Lake Superior Wetlands Preserve
Moose Hill Park
Morgan Park
Morley Heights Park
Morningside Park
Munger Landing
Munger Park
New Park
Norton Park
Observation Park
Occidental Boulevard
Old Main Park
Oneota Park
Ordean Court
Ordean Park

Pennell Park
Piedmont Heights Park
Playfront Park (at Bayfront Festival Park)
Pleasant View Park
Point of Rocks Park
Portland Square
Portman Square
Quarry Park
Rail Park
Reverend L. F. Merritt Memorial Park
Rice's Point Landing
Riverside Park
Riverside Playground
Rose Garden (at Leif Erikson Park)
Rose Park
Russell Square
Second Ave. E. & Tenth St. Triangle
Seven Bridges Road
Sister Cities Park
Skyline Parkway
Smithville Park
Spirit Mountain Recreation Area
Stanley Park
Stoney Point
Strickland Park

Thirtieth Ave. E. & Greysolon Rd. Triangle
Thirty-eighth Ave. E. & Greysolon Rd. Triangle
Thirty-first Ave. E. & Greysolon Rd. Triangle
Twenty-seventh Ave. W. & Winnipeg Ave. Triangle
Twin Ponds
Unnamed Dog Park
Unnamed Park
Unity Park
University Park
Vermilion Trail Triangle
Wade Stadium Athletic Complex
Wallace Triangle
Wallace Ave. & Vermilion Rd. Triangle
Wallbank's Park
Washington Park
Washington Square
Waverly Park
Web Woods
Wheeler Athletic Complex
Woodland Ave. & Eighth St. Triangle
Woodland Ave. & Fifth St. Triangle
Woodland Ave., Wallace Ave. & Victoria St. Triangle
Woodland Park

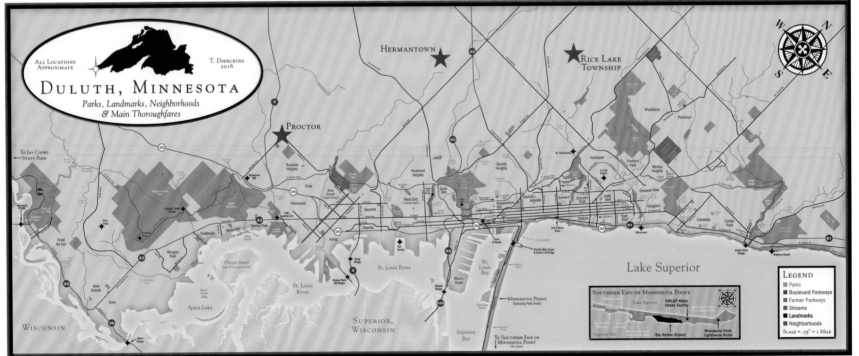

Introduction

Developing Duluth's Park System

Rock, water, and ice: These forces of nature inspired Duluth's park system. Eleven thousand years ago a massive layer of glacial ice melted away slowly as the climate warmed. Meltwater collected in the huge basin we now call Lake Superior. Much deeper than today, the shoreline of this lake stood at an elevation of about 1,100 feet—nearly 500 feet above today's lakeshore. For thousands of years the waters of the glacial lake washed up against the rock, creating gravel beaches and wave-cut cliffs.

As the ice melted away to the north, exposing more land and new outlets, the water began flowing out to the east through the St. Mary's River at Sault Ste. Marie. The water level in the lake dropped, leaving the old shoreline sitting high and dry, perched on the hillside above the newly exposed rocky land that would one day become Duluth.

Before 1854, the land on the western side of the St. Louis River was "Indian Territory." Ojibwe lived in scattered villages, and an all-but-abandoned fur trading post at Fond du Lac still housed a handful of white traders and missionaries.

The 1854 Treaty of La Pointe changed everything. The Ojibwe ceded a large block of land on the western shore of Lake Superior to the United States. They retained the right to hunt, fish, and gather in the ceded territory, but the treaty opened the land to American settlement and speculators wasted no time staking their claims. Between 1856 and 1859, settlers laid out eleven separate townsites in what is now Duluth. In addition to Fond du Lac, the townsites included Oneota, Rice's Point, Fremont, Duluth, North Duluth, Cowell's Addition (much of today's Canal Park business district), Middleton (most of today's Park Point), Portland, Endion, and Belville. The area encompassed by the townships of Duluth, North Duluth, and Cowell's Addition later became known as Upper Duluth and Lower Duluth.

The Nineteenth-Century Squares

As the early settlers carved their towns out of the northern wilderness, they also created the city's first parks or "squares"—one or two city blocks designated as public open space. The squares were set

LITHOGRAPHIC POSTCARD, CA. 1910, OF TISCHER CREEK FLOWING THROUGH CONGDON PARK; MOST OF DULUTH'S HISTORIC PARKS WERE PLANNED ALONG THE CREEKS AND RIVERS THAT RUN THROUGH DULUTH ON THEIR WAY TO LAKE SUPERIOR OR THE ST. LOUIS RIVER.

[IMAGE: ZENITH CITY PRESS]

aside from development when the townsites were platted, the process followed when a tract of undeveloped land was divided into smaller parcels connected by streets, alleys, and parks.

Reflecting the role of urban parks in mid-nineteenth-century America, Duluth's platted squares represented a remnant of the old English system of the commons—unimproved tracts of land in a central area used by the community as a public gathering place. In agricultural England, people also used the commons for grazing their cows and sheep. In America, these urban squares simply provided undeveloped public spaces.

The founders of the Duluth townsite set aside two platted parks: Cascade Square, a four-acre parcel in the heart of downtown, and Central Park (sometimes called Zenith Park), a thirty-acre parcel high on the rocky hillside west of downtown. The developers of several other townsites also set aside platted parks: Lafayette Square and Franklin Square in Middleton (1856), Fond du Lac Square (1856), Portland Square in Portland Township (1856, now the East Hillside), and five squares in New London (1871, now Lakeside): Washington,

Russell, Manchester, Portman, and Grosvenor. (See Chapter 1, "Nineteenth-Century Squares," for more information.)

Several of the original townsites joined together in 1870 to form the City of Duluth: Middleton, Upper and Lower Duluth, Portland, Endion, Rice's Point, and Fond du Lac. When these towns merged, the new city became responsible for all the platted parks.

But the role of urban parks in America was already changing. Thousands of people were leaving their farms and moving to cities to work in factories. Reformers began to advocate for large public parks with manicured greenspaces that would allow people a chance to escape from long, dreary days of factory work. Frederick Law Olmsted, America's most famous landscape architect, led the movement to design elaborate urban park systems that included pastoral landscapes with picturesque elements. Olmsted designed his parks to provide residents relief from their noisy, man-made surroundings. Parkways—broad, landscaped boulevards with separate roadways for pedestrians, bicyclists, equestrians, and horse carriages—were an important component of Olmsted's designs.

DULUTH HARBOR

LAKE SUPERIOR

DRAWN BY H.WELLGE

The Roots of Duluth's Modern Park System

Duluth's promoters believed the city would one day rival Chicago, and they knew such a city had to contain this new type of urban park. William K. Rogers is credited with proposing a park system for Duluth that included a scenic hillside parkway connected by stream corridor parks to a boulevard along the shore of Lake Superior. Rogers presented his ideas to the Duluth Common Council (similar to today's city council), which officially adopted his plan in February 1888.

It's relatively easy to set aside parks by platting before the land is sold to private individuals. But to carry out Rogers's plan for a connected park system meant the city had to purchase many acres of land already in the hands of private landowners. Led by Rogers, Duluth's leaders petitioned the state legislature to create a citizen commission with the authority to develop the park system. In March 1889 the State Legislature approved "An Act Providing for a System of Public Grounds for the City of Duluth." This legislation created Duluth's first Board of Park Commissioners and gave it broad powers to acquire

land, make improvements, and adopt regulations to guide the use of parks. Along with the power to condemn and take land, the board could issue bonds to borrow money for purchasing land. It could also levy special assessments on nearby property that benefited from the development of the parks and parkways.

Made up of William K. Rogers (president), John H. Upham (vice president), Frederic W. Paine (secretary-treasurer), Roger S. Munger, and Mayor J. B. Sutphin (as an *ex officio* member) the park board members met for the first time on May 22, 1889. They prepared a list of the land they intended to acquire, namely a narrow strip along the lakeshore and a corridor of land for a parkway (referred to then as Terrace Parkway, later Rogers Boulevard, and today as Skyline Parkway) that would extend from Chester Creek across the hillside to Miller Creek.

With the enthusiastic Rogers at the helm, the park board went to work immediately on the hillside road, hiring appraisers to determine the value of the land and seeking bids from contractors. They

A PANORAMIC BIRD'S-EYE VIEW OF DULUTH IN 1887. (ETCHING BY HENRY WELLGE.)

[IMAGE: ZENITH CITY PRESS]

DULUTH'S FIRST PARK BOARD

Led by President William K. Rogers (see page 30) and with Mayor J. B. Sutphin as *ex officio*, the men that made up Duluth's first park board (1889 to 1891) were some of Duluth's most remarkable pioneers.

Major John H. Upham, the board's vice president, earned his rank during the Civil War. He enlisted in the 149th New York Infantry in 1862, served in the Army of the Potomac, and was wounded three times at Gettysburg, losing a finger in the process. In 1864 he became captain of the 107th U.S. Colored Infantry. Born in Fayetteville, New York, in 1841, Upham came to Duluth following the war, contracting with the federal government on river and harbor improvements at the Head of the Lakes. Upham was behind the wheel of the dredging tug *Ishpeming* when the vessel cut the Duluth Ship Canal in 1870 to 1871. Upham was called "the submarine diver of Duluth," as in 1871 he surveyed portions of the St. Louis River by donning diving gear and walking along the river bottom. In 1872 he wed Libbie A. Banks, also of Fayetteville, and together they had two children. Major Upham died in a sanitarium in Lawrenceburg, Tennessee, in November 1920.

The park board members selected **Frederic W. Paine**, one of the city's most respected bankers, as their secretary/treasurer. Born in 1856 in Niles, Michigan, Paine (pictured, left) began his career in 1875 in the Grand Rapids, Michigan, law firm of Taggart, Simonds and Fletcher, which sent him to Duluth in 1880 to look after its interests in the Graff, Little and Co. sawmill. In 1882 he and Luther Mendenhall established the Duluth National Bank, and Paine worked as its cashier for five years until he and Henry Lardner—father of humorist Ring Lardner—established the house of Paine & Lardner, later the Security Bank, which failed in 1896. Paine then left banking and invested in life insurance and real estate companies. Besides the park board, he served on the board of education and committed his time to the community fund, the symphony association, St. Paul's Episcopal Church, St. Luke's Hospital, and several welfare and charitable societies. In 1928 Paine became the fourth person elected to the Duluth Hall of Fame. He died in February 1940. Paine's son, F. Rodney Paine, served as Duluth's superintendent of parks from 1926 to 1937.

Roger S. Munger was born in North Madison, Connecticut, in 1830 and married Olive Gray in Maine in 1858, a year after he and two of his brothers opened a music store in St. Paul. The siblings built St. Paul's first opera house and performed as the Munger Brothers Orchestra. Roger (pictured, right) and Olive Munger were just the twelfth family in Duluth Township when they arrived in the late 1860s. Partnering with other Duluth settlers, Munger built Duluth's first sawmill, first flour mill, first coal dock, and, as in St. Paul, its first opera house. He was also a founding member of Duluth's Board of Trade and established the Lake Superior Elevator Company, Imperial Mill, and the Duluth Iron & Steel Company. While he only held one elected office (register of deeds, 1898), he also served on the first school board and first city council. It was Munger who, in 1870, hired the dredging tug his fellow park board member Upham used to dig the ship canal. In the 1890s Munger started the tall tale that the ship canal was dug by hand in less than two days by "one hundred stout men." He died in 1913.

secured a loan from the city for $5,000 at 8 percent interest, and construction began on Tenth Street at Lake Avenue.

By early August 1889, President Rogers reported that the first section of the parkway was being used and appreciated by citizens of Duluth and visitors to the city. He also reported that considerable rock blasting was required from Seventeenth Avenue West to Eighteenth Avenue West, significantly increasing the cost of construction. The board members authorized the additional expenditure even though they did not yet have the money to cover it.

Over the next few months, money flowed out as the park board purchased land, rented office space, and hired a clerk to assist the appraisers and engineers. Expenditures on the parkway added up to $5,810.54 by the end of 1889. The following year the board members continued to purchase land, and they estimated that expenses for 1891 would be $24,000.

The park board's attempts to issue bonds for the needed money met with numerous roadblocks. In August 1889 they asked Mayor Sutphin to hold a special election on the question of issuing park bonds. The mayor designated September 23, 1889, for the special election, but the common council neglected to appoint election judges. When the board repeated the request for a special election, the mayor set October 23, 1889, as the new date; once again the council failed to appoint election judges far enough in advance. The special election finally took place on October 29, 1889, and Duluth's citizens overwhelmingly gave their approval. However, problems with the New York firm hired to handle the bonds resulted in cancellation of the entire deal, and no money was raised.

The bills continued to mount. On April 23, 1891, the *Duluth Daily Tribune* reported that "Orders having been issued from time to time to workmen who have had to wait unduly for their pay, and other parties who contracted to sell property to the board have not received their money as promised. There have been some unfortunate results from attempts to float the park bonds that, in the opinion of city authorities, have tended to hurt the credit of the city.... The park commission should be reorganized upon a firm basis with men of recognized financial ability at its head."

City officials realized changes had to be made. They requested revisions to the legislation, and state legislators approved these revisions on April 6, 1891. The new act narrowed the park board's powers. The board could no longer have its own treasurer; all money had to remain in the hands of the city treasurer. The board also had to prepare a map and a statement showing how much money it had or could raise to pay for land it intended to buy, and the council had to approve each purchase.

Mayor M. J. Davis promptly appointed three new park commissioners: Luther Mendenhall, Bernard Silberstein, and Henry Clay Helm, all successful businessmen who were widely respected in the community. William K. Rogers remained a member of the board; when straws were drawn, he received a one-year term.

Mendenhall, president of what would become the First National Bank of Duluth, was elected president. An April 23 *Daily Tribune* article assured the public, "With Mr. Mendenhall as president the commission ought to have first class standing in financial circles."

The Parkway and Five Parks

After Rogers left the board, the mayor appointed businessman Arthur B. Chapin as his replacement. But even under the competent guidance of Mendenhall, Silberstein, Helm, and Chapin, the minutes of park board meetings paint a picture of a city whose enthusiasm and desire for parks always outstripped its ability to pay for them.

Because of financial constraints, the board found it necessary to trim back the original plans for the city's park system. In their first annual report, published in February 1892, the board members wrote:

> "There was included in the system of parks and parkways, as planned by the former board, and put under condemnation by them, land to the amount of about $700,000. This amount was considered by the present board as being out of proportion with the amount of funds available for the purchase of land, and it was deemed best by them to revise and reduce the system to such proportions as would make it practicable in the end to acquire what remained. This, after due consideration, they proceeded to do, and finally agreed upon and formulated a plan and system which is estimated to cost, for the acquirement of the land, from $400,000 to $450,000."

The new board spent most of its resources during the first three years (1891 to 1893) on the parkway, which extended from Miller Creek at Third Street across the hillside to Chester Creek at Fourth Street. Board members spent many hours overseeing construction, reviewing maps, and deliberating over the alignment of the road, even shifting sections of the constructed roadway from "temporary"

LUTHER MENDENHALL: BOARD PRESIDENT, 1891–1913

Martin Luther Mendenhall (who went by his middle name) was appointed to the Duluth Board of Park Commissioners following its reorganization in 1891. He remained on the board as its president until it was eliminated in 1913. In 1910 the board decided to make each board member responsible for three or four specific parks in Duluth's growing system; Mendenhall was assigned Lakeshore and Fairmount Parks.

Born on a farm in Chester, Pennsylvania, Mendenhall attended the University of Michigan and served as a quartermaster in the Union Army throughout the Civil War, taking part in several battles, including Gettysburg. Following the war he moved to Philadelphia to study law. In the late 1860s he became involved with Jay Cooke's Lake Superior & Mississippi Railroad; Mendenhall was part of a team Cooke sent to Duluth to complete the railroad, set up banking houses and hotels, and oversee other Cooke investments. Mendenhall made investments of his own and, with other pioneers, financed Duluth's first blast furnace and established First Methodist Church. After the Panic of 1873 left Cooke penniless, Mendenhall—instead of leaving bankrupt Duluth—doubled down on the Zenith City and stayed. When Duluth lost its city charter in 1877, Mendenhall acted as treasurer of the reforming community and was, along with Andreas M. Miller and Judge Ozora P. Stearns, instrumental in salvaging Duluth's financial future. In 1882 he organized the Duluth National Bank, which by 1889 had evolved into Duluth's First National Bank. Mendenhall invested in other enterprises as well. He and Guilford Hartley together owned much of the Duluth Street Railway Company and incorporated Duluth Dry Goods and the Duluth Shoe Company. Mendenhall also served as the first president of the Duluth Library Association.

When he retired from business in 1912, Mendenhall was honored with a celebration at Duluth's exclusive Kitchi Gammi Club (he had been a member since 1882). Fellow park board member Bishop James McGolrick praised Mendenhall for his philanthropy while another board member, John Jenswold, called Mendenhall a "promoter of the City Beautiful," responsible for developing "the city's beauty spots." His friend Guilford Hartley said Mendenhall was "a man that has never been known to speak ill of his neighbor, and he always is to be counted on to help when help is needed, whether it is for any direct benefit to him or not." When it was Mendenhall's turn to speak, he noted that while he and his fellow pioneers had begun the work, others "must take up the work and complete it." He then added, "I hope to live to see the day that this empire will be a garden spot. We are building, not only for our own satisfaction and possible profit, but for prosperity."

Mendenhall's reputation was sullied in the 1890s when his relationship with Kate Hardy led to a scandalous divorce from his wife, Ella. Hardy was the headmistress and namesake of Hardy Hall, a private girls prep school that Mendenhall had constructed along Woodland Avenue. Following his divorce, Mendenhall married Hardy in 1898. The school, renamed Craggencroft, closed in 1902. Unable to find a buyer for the property, Mendenhall had the entire structure disassembled, then built three houses on the property reusing the original building's field stones. Luther and Kate Mendenhall lived in one of the houses until his death in 1929 at age ninety-three. He ascribed his long life and health to the fact that he was from a Quaker family and had led a Quaker's calm and temperate life.

BERNARD SILBERSTEIN: BOARD VICE PRESIDENT, 1891–1911

Bernard Silberstein, along with Luther Mendenhall, was appointed to the Duluth Board of Park Commissioners in 1891. Fellow board members elected him vice president, an office he held until he resigned from the board in April 1911. Between 1910 and his retirement he was responsible for Portland Square, Chester Park, and Lincoln Park.

In 1866, eighteen-year-old Hungarian-born Silberstein left Vienna, where he had been educated, to immigrate to the United States. He eventually landed in Detroit, but soon after headed to Duluth, as he often said, "only to look around." Silberstein must have liked what he saw. He returned to Detroit to marry Ernestine "Nettie" Rose Weiss, a native of Budapest, then took his bride to the Zenith City for their honeymoon. The Silbersteins stayed, helping to establish its first synagogue, Temple Emanuel. Bernard and Nettie, along with brothers Asa and Henry Leopold, are considered Duluth's first Jewish residents.

Silberstein began his career in Duluth selling items from house to house before he and William Farrell opened what is thought to be Duluth's first dry-goods store, which, according to his obituary, sold "everything imaginable." (Dry goods described anything not considered hardware or groceries.) Before the year was out, the pair had joined forces with a man named Whitcher to form Whitcher, Silberstein & Company, referred to in newspapers as Whitcher & Silberstein's Fancy Furnishings Store. The partnership was short-lived. By 1872 Silberstein was working with Isaac Bondy under the name B. Silberstein Company. Bondy, who lived and worked in New York City, acted as the company's purchasing agent. In 1881 they organized the Silberstein & Bondy Company; the firm's 1884 building still stands at 9–11 West Superior Street.

In 1912 the Silbersteins moved into High Point, an eight-thousand-square-foot Georgian Revival home at 21 North Twenty-first Avenue East designed by Frederick German. In 1913 Silberstein ran for mayor but was defeated by William I. Prince in one of the wildest political contests in the history of Duluth. Two years later he ran for city commissioner. Both he and James Farrell, who had also lost the mayoral race in 1913, were elected by wide margins; Farrell was the nephew of William Farrell, Silberstein's first business partner in Duluth. Silberstein held the office of commissioner of public safety until 1919, when he refused to run for another term.

The high point of public recognition for Silberstein came in 1920. Recently retired from politics, he celebrated the golden anniversaries of his marriage, his business, and his membership in Covenant Lodge, an Independent Order of B'nai B'rith, which held a golden jubilee banquet and ball in honor of Mr. Silberstein. The event was described as "the most brilliant ever staged by the Jews of Duluth, Superior and Northern Minnesota and, in a small measure, indicated the esteem with which he was held by the people of his faith everywhere." That esteem was again on display in Duluth newspapers two years later, when Bernard Silberstein passed away on September 3, 1922. The flag over city hall flew at half mast, and both the Palestine Lodge and Covenant Lodge held services. In his obituary, the *Duluth News Tribune* recognized his major contributions to the city's park system: "With great foresight and optimistic as to the future of Duluth, he often advanced the money to the city for the purchase of park property. It was the cash that brought the best deals and in those early days the city had very little money with which to do any high financing. But he took a chance and advanced the money that Duluth might have a park system to be proud of."

——— **IMAGE: DULUTH PUBLIC LIBRARY** ———

to what they hoped would be "permanent" locations. Where they could not acquire land by willing purchase, they acquired it through eminent domain.

By 1892 the board reported that they controlled 145 acres, including the right-of-way for the parkway, along Miller Creek and Chester Creek, Central Park, Portland Square, and Cascade Square.

Duluthians loved the parks immediately, and they soon began asking for improvements. Residents west of Miller Creek requested a foot bridge over the creek at or near Tenth Street. The common council encouraged the board to improve the public squares.

Board members wanted to comply with these requests, but they did not have enough money to acquire land and carry out all the desired improvements. In June 1892 they reported that the balance due on property under condemnation was $41,379.23. After evaluating all available funds, they estimated a shortage of $20,000 to $25,000. They requested a temporary loan from the city and proposed to repay it with money raised through an assessment.

Unfortunately, everything came to a screeching halt a little more than a year later—and several months after a stock market crash that caused the nationwide Financial Panic of 1893—when, at their August 8, 1893, meeting, "the financial condition of the board was considered, and owing to a lack of funds it was deemed advisable to stop all improvements and to lay off all but two men on August 12." The board did not meet again until eight months later, in April 1894.

The meeting minutes shed little light on where the board found the money to resume work, but it is clear that the financial problems continued. In May 1894 Leonidas Merritt, whose family had suffered huge financial losses in the Panic of 1893, requested repayment of money he had loaned four years earlier (at Rogers's request) for building an extension of the parkway west of Miller Creek. And in July 1896, contractors A. & D. Sang requested $3,663.58 that had not yet been reimbursed for work done in 1890 on construction of the parkway—also at Rogers's request.

Despite the constant struggle for funding, the board members moved ahead on several projects. In June 1894 they used a $2,000 loan to improve Portland Square. Although they specified that the cost of the improvements should not exceed $2,000, the final total reached nearly $6,000. To cover the extra cost, the board requested that the city levy an assessment on nearby properties that benefited from the improvements. The board also began a major tree planting effort, authorizing the purchase of $2,000 worth of trees and shrubbery.

As board members began to better understand the task of creating a park system, they realized that their own processes needed to be more formalized. In November 1894, Commissioner Helm introduced a resolution that "the park in the west end of the city, and now known as Cascade or Millers Creek Park, be designated and hereafter known as Lincoln Park."

During the discussion of this resolution, the question arose as to whether any of the park grounds of the city had been formally named or designated. After looking back through the minutes, Secretary Helm reported that no formal action had ever been taken.

As a result, in December 1894, the board officially designated "Lincoln Park" in the West End, "Central Park," located below today's Enger Park, and the eastern hillside's "Garfield Park," later renamed Chester Park. The board also officially named the parkway "Rogers Boulevard...in recognition of the valuable services rendered the city by the late Col. Wm. K. Rogers former President of this board in planning and supervising the construction of the Parkway connecting the above system of parks."

Citizens Help Create Parks

Duluth's park board began to make real progress on the park system in the late 1890s. Taxes, assessments, and short-term loans provided a relatively steady flow of funds to work with, and board members spent the money cautiously. They continued to acquire land for the permanent alignment of Rogers Boulevard and worked on expanding it to the west while adding more land to the park system, including forty acres in West Duluth, which they named Fairmount Park. They hired park policemen, built skating rinks throughout the city, and began to subsidize music in the parks. They also planted and maintained trees in the parks and along the city streets.

As a result of the increased activity, in 1899 the park board created the position of superintendent of parks and hired Henry C. Helm—who had served as secretary of the board since 1891—to fill the position at a salary of $75 per month. This arrangement worked out so well that in 1900 the board members continued Helm's contract. In 1901 they combined the positions of secretary and park superintendent, and in 1903 Helm resigned from the board to devote all his time to the job.

The citizens of Duluth not only loved and used the parks, they also helped to acquire land, make improvements, and maintain facilities. In 1904 Chester Congdon, owner of the Glensheen estate,

donated land and money to create a linear park along Tischer Creek, later named Congdon Park in his honor.

In October 1906 a group of citizens led by F. A. Patrick (who later became a member of the park board) offered to furnish money to construct a better connection to the eastern end of Rogers Boulevard near the Chester Creek bridge. The board accepted their offer, and construction of the new road was completed within a year.

Public donations helped purchase fourteen acres of land from the Northern Pacific Railroad in 1907, which became known informally as Lake Shore Park (now Leif Erikson Park). Of the $20,000 paid for the land, $8,000 was raised by subscriptions from "public spirited citizens" while the remainder came from the park fund.

In 1909 Sam Snively (Duluth's mayor from 1921 to 1937) offered to find buyers for $10,000 of park bonds, provided the money would be used for the restoration of the roadway he had built for public use along Amity Creek. Work on the "Snively Highway"—now called Seven Bridges Road—began in 1910, with the official opening in July 1912.

Youngsters pitched in as well. Neighborhood boys and girls, along with numerous organized clubs, helped maintain skating rinks in the parks. A petition from 121 boys and girls of the West End resulted in permission for them to create a skating rink in Lincoln Park—as long as there was no expense to the park fund. The board also appropriated $200 for a warming house at Portman Square with the requirement that the Lakeside Club take care of it throughout the year. In 1910 the board reported fifteen free skating rinks in the city, eight of which were "wholly furnished by the park board, and seven furnished by private subscriptions."

THE COVER OF THE DULUTH BOARD OF PARK COMMISSIONERS 1896 ANNUAL REPORT.

[IMAGE: DULUTH PUBLIC LIBRARY]

DULUTH'S BOARD OF PARK COMMISSIONERS, 1891–1913

From its reorganization in 1891 to its dissolution in 1913, some of Duluth's most prominent citizens served on Duluth's Board of Park Commissioners. The board was led by president Luther Mendenhall (see page 5), longtime vice-president Bernard Silberstein (see page 6), and secretary Henry Helm, who also served as the first park superintendent (see page 54). Other members included a true pioneer, a physician, a Catholic bishop, an attorney, and several executives from Duluth's jobbing houses, predecessors to today's wholesale distributors. All had one thing in common: a passion for Duluth and the quality of life of its citizens.

ARTHUR B. CHAPIN (1892 to 1900)

William K. Rogers was the only board member who remained in office following the reorganization of the Duluth Board of Park Commissioners in 1891. When Rogers resigned from the board due to poor health and left Duluth in 1892, Arthur B. Chapin took his place on the park board, serving until 1900. A native of Ohio, Chapin came to Duluth by way of Saginaw, Michigan, where he worked as a lumberman after fighting with the First Ohio Cavalry during the Civil War. In 1886 he and his wife Electa moved to Duluth to help his nephew G. C. Greenwood run his retail hardware company, which was reorganized as A. B. Chapin & Co. By 1890 Chapin & Co. had merged with the hardware department of Wells-Stone to become Chapin-Wells. In 1892 another Saginaw man, Albert M. Marshall, purchased the firm, which he renamed Marshall-Wells, and turned it into the largest hardware wholesaler in the world. Chapin later organized the St. Louis Lumber Company, which he sold in 1906. His wife Electa died in 1904; in 1907 he married Florence C. Greenwood and the couple moved to Pasadena, California. Chapin died in Los Angeles in 1913.

IRVIN T. BURNSIDE (1900 to 1908)

Dr. Irvin "Ira" T. Burnside replaced Chapin on the park board in 1900 and served until 1908. Little is known about Burnside, who was born in Berlin, Wisconsin, in 1857. Burnside, his wife Clara, and their daughter Anna moved to West Duluth sometime in the 1890s, where they joined the Holy Apostle Episcopal Church. A son, Harlan, was born in 1901. In 1912 Dr. Burnside accidentally killed a ten-year-old boy in Lester Park after the boy, according to witnesses, jumped in front of Burnside's car as it was passing a streetcar. The doctor was later acquitted of negligence. That same year he and his fellow members of the West Duluth Commercial Club led the effort to extend Fairmount Park to the St. Louis River. Burnside also served as director of Oneota Cemetery Association. In 1919 he sold his property, including an eighty-acre tract in Proctor—some of which he set aside as a public park—and moved to Minneapolis where he lived until his death in 1929.

REVEREND JAMES McGOLRICK (1901 to 1913)

From 1891 to 1900, Duluth's mayor sat on the park board as an ex officio member—first M. J. Davis (1890 to 1891), Charles d'Autremont Jr. (1892 to 1893), Ray T. Lewis (1894 to 1895), and Henry Truelson (1896 to 1900). After 1900, a rule change eliminated the mayor as a board member, and Reverend James McGolrick—the first bishop of the Diocese of Duluth, serving from 1889 until his death in 1918—occupied the open seat until its 1913 dissolution. McGolrick was born in Ireland's County Tipperary in 1841 and received his education at Dublin's All Hallows College before coming to St. Paul, Minnesota, in 1867 to assist Father John Ireland, who later became archbishop of that city. From 1868 to 1889 McGolrick served as the pastor of Minneapolis's Church of the Immaculate Conception; he built the church's first temporary facility, a simple wood-frame building, by himself. While McGolrick was bishop, the Duluth Diocese built Sacred Heart Cathedral, St. Mary's Hospital, St. James Orphanage, and Cathedral School, which was funded in part with a $30,000 gift from the bishop himself. Known for his extensive personal library, McGolrick also served on Duluth's library board. While on the park board he was responsible for Cascade Square, Twin Lakes, Hilltop Park, and the city's playgrounds.

FRANCIS A. CLARKSON (1903 to 1907)

In 1903 the park board combined the roles of board secretary and park superintendent into one paid position. Henry Helm, who had already been serving as secretary/superintendent, resigned from the board to continue in this role as paid staff. Francis A. Clarkson was appointed to fill Helm's seat, serving until 1907. Clarkson first arrived in Duluth in 1887 when he was forty-four years old, relocating from Perry Mills, New York, to help establish Wells-Stone Mercantile, a grocery and hardware wholesaler. The firm's grocery division was absorbed by Stone-Ordean in 1896, creating Stone-Ordean-Wells. That same year Clarkson withdrew from the company to establish the Clarkson-Wright Mercantile. In 1904 the company began manufacturing syrups, packaged teas, vinegar, extracts, and ammonia and distributed its products throughout Minnesota, Michigan, Wisconsin, the Dakotas, and Canada. Clarkson died in 1913 after being confined to bed for nearly three years while suffering from "a disease of the arteries." That same year Clarkson-Wright merged with the Gowan-Peyton-Congdon Company to create Gowan-Lenning-Brown, considered Duluth's premier wholesale grocer. The firm's 1913 headquarters at 525 Lake Avenue South is known today as the Paulucci Building.

JOHN JENSWOLD (1907 to 1913)

Attorney and respected civic leader John Jenswold replaced Clarkson in 1907, serving until the board was eliminated in 1913. As a member of the park board, Jenswold was responsible for Lester Park, Snively Boulevard, and the squares in Lakeside. Born to Norwegian immigrants in 1857 in Albany, Wisconsin, Jenswold was the eldest of eight children. His family relocated to a farm in northwestern Iowa in 1865, with eight-year-old John driving the family's team of oxen. He eventually earned a law degree from the University of Iowa and started practice in Emmetsburg, Iowa, and Sioux Falls, South Dakota, before establishing himself in Duluth in 1888. During his career he argued more than 240 cases before the Minnesota Supreme Court. In 1908 Jenswold's fellow Democrats tried to convince him to run for Minnesota governor, but he declined. He retired from practice in 1936 and died on June 2, 1940.

FREDERICK A. PATRICK (1908 to 1913)

In 1908 Frederick A. Patrick replaced Dr. Burnside and in 1911, after Bernard Silberstein resigned, Patrick became the board's vice president, serving until it was eliminated in 1913, and was responsible for Congdon Park and Rogers Boulevard. Born in 1857, Patrick came to Duluth in 1891 from his hometown of Marengo, Illinois, where his father found success in banking, manufacturing, and merchandising. In Duluth, Patrick worked as the treasurer of Stone-Ordean-Wells until 1901, when he and J. E. Granger formed Patrick-Granger Drygoods. The firm eventually became the F. A. Patrick Company, which in 1904 began manufacturing shirts and overalls. By 1924 the company, under the name Patrick Duluth Knitting Mills, owned several mills throughout the state and distributed nationally a wide range of garments including overcoats, shirts, and sportswear. Its most popular product was the Mackinaw jacket, a short wool coat which was warm but light in weight. In 1902 Patrick spearheaded a movement to revive Duluth's dormant Chamber of Commerce, creating the Duluth Commercial Club—predecessor to today's Chamber of Commerce—in the process. Patrick died in 1931, two years after he sold his company, from injuries suffered in an automobile accident.

LEONIDAS MERRITT (1911 to 1913)

While Patrick replaced Silberstein as vice president, Leonidas Merritt filled his seat and served until the board's 1913 elimination. As a board member, he was responsible for Chester Park, Lincoln Park, and Portland Square. Merritt was twelve years old when he arrived at the Head of the Lakes with his family in 1856 and helped establish Oneota Township (now part of West Duluth). Merritt worked a variety of jobs until 1890, when he and several of his brothers opened the Mesabi Iron Range. Leonidas Merritt remained connected with the mining industry. He married fellow Oneota pioneer Elizabeth Wheeler in 1873, and together they raised three children. Merritt served as the first president of the West Duluth Village Council and represented northeastern Minnesota in the 1893 to 1894 Minnesota legislative session. A former alderman, he became Duluth's first commissioner of public utilities (1914 to 1917) and later commissioner of finance (1921 to 1925). He retired from business thirteen days before his death in 1927, remarking that "if I've learned one thing it's this—don't give up an idea that you're satisfied is correct, when the 'experts' say it can't be so."

Henry Cleveland Becomes Park Superintendent

November 1909 brought the first major change in park personnel. After having served the board in various capacities for over eighteen years, Henry Helm's failing health forced him to retire as park superintendent. Henry Cleveland, a professional landscape architect who had worked for the city since 1900, became the new superintendent. Even with Cleveland in charge of day-to-day operations, the park system had grown so large that board members were having difficulty managing it, and in 1910 they decided to divide up the responsibilities, giving each board member three or four specific parks to oversee.

By 1911 the board once again ran short of funds. In early August, in the midst of many ambitious projects, they asked the city to sell $50,000 in bonds to raise money for acquiring and improving land for the park system. To save money, the secretary was also ordered to "lay off all the night keepers except Cascade and Lincoln Parks" starting on August 15, 1911.

Despite this setback, the board resumed work the next year, proposing to acquire land for the extension of several parks. Unfortunately, even Duluth's beloved park system was subject to the whims of the people. Politics have always played a crucial role in fulfilling (and sometimes interfering with) the implementation of Duluth's vision for a park system. In spite of the successes of the board and the overwhelming public support for the park system, politics brought an abrupt end to Duluth's park board in 1913.

Duluth Park Board Eliminated

By 1910 urban areas throughout the country were expanding rapidly as immigrants poured into the United States and people from rural areas moved to cities to find jobs in expanding industries. Local governments were widely viewed as corrupt, and reformers advocated for greater accountability at all levels of government. In Duluth, citizens agitated for enforcing the closing laws for saloons and cleaning up the city's red light district, located in what is now the Canal Park Business District.

In the spirit of progressive reform, a new model for city government swept across the country. It reached Duluth in December 1912, when citizens voted to replace the ward and boss system of government, which it had been using since before the city regained its charter in 1887. Under this old system, the mayor held a great deal of power, and aldermen representing wards for one- and two-year terms served as the city's Common Council. As a result of the 1913 charter

Duluth's Parks

Report of the
Board of Park Commissioners

Duluth, Minnesota
1911

change, a new commission form of government was adopted, which placed five commissioners in charge of five city departments: public affairs, public works, public safety, public utilities, and finance. The mayor served as commissioner of the public affairs department, which included the park system.

The *Duluth News Tribune* of December 4, 1912, reduced this astounding reorganization of city government to one simple sentence: "Under the provisions of the new charter, all the present city officers will be thrown out of office April 14."

Perhaps most citizens did not realize that voting for the new charter would mean the elimination of all citizen boards and commissions, but when the charter change took effect, the Duluth Board of Park Commissioners was dissolved. The city would never again have a group of citizens with the dedication and power to create and maintain the park system. The minutes from the last meeting of the park board on April 7, 1913, ended with a sense of resignation: "Meeting then adjourned subject to provisions of the Commission Charter legislating all present officials out of office on April 14, 1913 at 12 o'clock noon. *Finis*."

Duluth's park board, under the leadership of Luther Mendenhall and Bernard Silberstein from 1891 to 1913, had created a system of parks that, in their words, expressed "the concept of the soul of the city." They had worked hard to achieve a grand vision, which they described in their 1911 annual report: "The park system of a modern city is not only a series of grounds dedicated to park purposes, but a related and connected plan in which all the members are articulated into one unit. The park system of a modern city not only concerns itself that every neighborhood shall have its appropriate ornaments of lawns and shrubbery and glimpses of loveliness, but also that all these fragments shall compose parts of one harmonious whole. The park system of a modern city not only aims at beauty, but strives to express the concept of the soul of the city. The parks of a modern city bear witness that its people are members of one great family. They are the concrete expression of civic consciousness in its highest visible form."

The Magney-Snively Era

Following the reorganization of city government, Duluth no longer had a group of citizens dedicated to providing leadership for the park system. Instead, the mayor, as commissioner of public affairs, was in charge of the city's parks. As a result, support for the parks became a political issue, changing with every new administration.

In April 1913, newly elected mayor William Prince took over control of the city's parks. Prince retained Henry Cleveland as park superintendent but announced that he would not re-establish the park board. As the *Duluth Herald* reported, all the new commissioners felt that "the whole theory of the commission form is centralization of responsibility and the appointment of advisory boards is not in keeping with that spirit."

Although he supported acquiring additional land for park purposes and developing playgrounds throughout the city, Mayor Prince said he intended to abandon "the policy of spending thousands upon thousands of dollars for roadways." Despite Prince's claims of support, parks were not a priority as the new commissioners focused on reorganizing city government and cleaning up old problems. Annual reports prepared by Henry Cleveland for the years 1914 and 1915 indicate that most of his work focused on maintenance and repair of existing parks.

Prince's term as mayor expired in April 1917. He ran for re-election but was eliminated in the primary. The city charter required candidates to limit their spending to $500, forcing a relatively low-key campaign between John Armistead and Clarence Magney. The city, and indeed the nation, faced far bigger concerns than Duluth's park system. Europe had already been at war for more than two years, and on the day before Duluth's mayoral election President Woodrow Wilson asked Congress for a Declaration of War against Germany. Four days later the United States officially joined World War I. On the home front, the Prohibition movement was gaining steam, and Duluth's ballot included an ordinance to prohibit alcohol in the city. When the votes were counted, Clarence Magney became the new mayor of a "dry" Duluth.

During his three years as mayor, Magney witnessed more than his share of significant events: World War I ended, women gained the right to vote, automobiles became available to the middle class and auto touring became popular, the massive fire of October 1918 caused over $700,000 in damages to the city, and an angry crowd lynched three young black men in Duluth. Despite these challenges, Magney understood the value of parks and is credited with adding 1,433 acres to Duluth's park system, including the upper portion of Chester Park (aka "Chester Bowl"), Enger Park, Memorial Park, and the Magney and Fond du Lac municipal forests.

Magney did not serve out his full four-year term as mayor; he resigned in September 1920 to campaign for election as a district judge. Duluth's remaining commissioners appointed Trevanion W. Hugo, who had served as Duluth's mayor from 1900 to 1904, to finish out the final six months of Magney's term. Whatever contributions Hugo made to the city's park system went unrecorded, but they were likely minimal at best. Two days after he took office, the commissioners

released their proposed budget for 1921. Although the total budget increased by over $108,000 and funding increased for nearly every department, the park department budget was cut by $6,000.

In the spring of 1921, Duluthians elected Sam Snively as their new mayor. Snively loved the city's parks and had worked with the park board a decade earlier to build his scenic roadway along Amity Creek. In 1917, when campaigning for a seat as commissioner, his advertisements emphasized re-establishment of citizen advisory boards, especially the park board. As mayor, Snively made the city's park system a high priority.

When Henry Cleveland retired in 1926, Mayor Snively appointed F. Rodney Paine as the new park superintendent. Paine was a native of Duluth; he had earned a master of forestry degree from Yale University, and he came to the Duluth Park Department after serving as manager of Jay Cooke State Park and superintendent of parks for the State of Minnesota. Paine and Snively became a powerful team with a vision for the park system and the political will to carry out that vision.

EMPLOYEES OF DULUTH'S PARK DEPARTMENT GATHERED AT CHAMBER'S GROVE FOR A PICNIC IN 1927. (PHOTO BY F. R. PAINE.)
[IMAGE: UMD MARTIN LIBRARY]

Their progress was slowed, however, after 1929 when the entire country was affected by the onset of the Great Depression. Significant budget cuts meant the park department lost many employees. Paine took advantage of all the government work relief programs to keep his department functioning; eventually the Works Progress Administration (WPA) provided funds and manpower for most of the work accomplished during the Depression.

According to calculations completed by the Duluth Department of Research and Planning in 1975, "During its seven-year existence, more than $10.5 million was spent on 459 WPA projects in Duluth, with project sponsors contributing $2.6 million. In 1938 alone, more than 12,000 families in the county looked to WPA for their income. Included in the program were the construction of new buildings at the zoo, fieldhouses at several playgrounds, winter sports facilities, and a major rehabilitation of the Skyline Parkway. The annual reports of the Park Board [sic] during these Depression years reveal that nearly all park improvements were funded through the WPA and related agencies." Many of the projects initiated by Snively and Paine through the WPA were completed by later administrations.

In spite of the hard times, Snively and Paine are credited with many improvements to the park system during the sixteen years Snively served as mayor, including the extension of the parkway west to Jay Cooke State Park and east along Hawk Ridge, the acquisition of 326 acres of parkland by purchase and 163 acres by donation,

construction of the Lester Park and Enger Park golf courses, construction of the fieldhouse and athletic field at Chester Bowl, establishment of the municipal zoo at Fairmount Park, improvements to Lake Shore Park (renamed Leif Erikson Park during Snively's administration), and the development of tourist camps at Chester Bowl, Indian Point, and Brighton Beach. Many of these projects reflected a shift in the park department's priorities, toward developing more recreational and revenue-producing activities. In the words of Rodney Paine, "These improvements provided a much larger recreational use of the park property and, in several cases, provided income towards their support. The park receipts have jumped from $3,169.00 in 1925 to $40,724.00 in 1931."

Deterioration of the Parks

After Sam Snively's tenure as mayor ended in 1937, support of the park system varied with every change in leadership, and for the next two decades each mayor appointed his own park superintendent. The problems caused by the Depression and the war continued to mount, creating increasing challenges for the park department.

When Rudolph Berghult replaced Snively in 1937, he appointed Earl H. Sherman as park superintendent. Sherman continued many of the projects started by Paine, including development of the ski center at Fond du Lac and the recreation area on Minnesota Point. Sherman also created the arboretum adjacent to the municipal nursery. In his 1940 report Sherman stated, "Properties which have

deteriorated through neglect, due to lack of funds for maintenance, are examples of temporary economy resulting in the need for reconstruction which demands a large single annual outlay of funds. This necessary reconstruction of deteriorated properties amounts to accumulated maintenance."

In 1941, Mayor Edward Hatch chose John V. Hoene as his park superintendent. The park department's financial challenges continued. In his first annual report Hoene wrote that "the receipts were very poor, due to a very rainy fall season. The department, therefore, ended the year being overdrawn approximately $4,000.00."

Hoene's yearly reports regularly acknowledged his gratitude to the citizen volunteers and organizations that helped with park programs, and to his employees, who did their best to keep up with maintenance needs. He wrote, "Although our 1942 budget for operation and maintenance was approximately 16% lower than it was in 1941, we attempted to keep the most essential facilities and grounds in good condition. ... The employees worked as they have never worked before, many of them putting in longer hours than are required. At the same time they took on their shoulders the responsibilities of the tasks that they were performing and as much as possible tried to solve their own problems without referring to the office."

The federal government eliminated the WPA in 1943, and the Duluth Park Department did not have the resources to maintain all the new facilities that had been created with its help. That year Hoene

wrote, "It is interesting to note that the Park system, since 1929, has more than doubled in its size and scope, yet less money is available to the Park Department in order to operate and maintain its facilities. ... The total estimated valuation of the park system is $6,739,451.88 and the tax monies spent in 1943 totalled $90,299.69, which figures less than 1½% spent for upkeep."

George W. Johnson took over as mayor in 1945 and hired Gust A. Johnson as park superintendent. The eight-year Johnson administration included the final months of World War II and the early postwar years. No annual reports are available from this period, but a 1946 study of public recreation in Duluth by L. H. Weir, field secretary of the National Recreation Association, reflected how completely recreation had taken over the park system. Weir's report stated: "It cannot be too strongly emphasized that the Park Department is a *primary recreation agency*. It exists for no other purpose than to provide recreation opportunities for all ages and both sexes of the population."

George D. Johnson served as mayor from 1953 to 1956 with former mayor Edward H. Hatch as his park superintendent. In his annual report for 1955, Hatch tried to sound optimistic, but he didn't have much good news to report. He wrote, "Although our budget was again substantially reduced we managed to keep all our equipment working and [made] a few worth while improvements. This was accomplished by the cooperation of civic minded citizens, city and

WHEN RUDY BERGHULT BECAME MAYOR IN 1937, HE IMMEDIATELY REPLACED PARK SUPERINTENDENT F. RODNEY PAINE AND DULUTH ZOO DIRECTOR AND FOUNDER BERT ONSGARD.

[IMAGE: DULUTH PUBLIC LIBRARY]

county employees." Hatch resigned at the end of October 1956 after Duluthians once again voted in favor of a major change to the city charter and reorganization of city government.

This time the city transformed from the commission form of government to a strong mayor and nine-member city council system. Eugene R. Lambert, publisher of the *News Tribune*, was the first mayor elected under the new system. Sigurd I. Duclett served as acting park superintendent from November 1, 1956, until the end of the year, after which Mayor Lambert renamed the park department as the department of public recreation and Duclett became director of public recreation. Before Duclett retired on August 1, 1957, he recommended the establishment of a citizen advisory board as a way to divorce park management from politics. Duclett was replaced by Lauren J. Ogston.

E. Clifford Mork became mayor in 1959, and Ogston stayed on until he retired in early 1960. In July 1960, Mayor Mork appointed Harry Nash as the new director of the department of public recreation. Nash remained with the department for fifteen years, serving under three different administrations. When Nash took over in 1960, the parks were a mess, but conditions gradually began to improve. Many civic organizations, individual citizens, and members of the business community stepped in as volunteers, donating time to beautify the parks and enrich the recreation program. In 1960 the Arrowhead Civic Club's City-wide City Pride Campaign helped inspire many organizations to adopt a park and work on cleaning it up.

In 1961 the mayor appointed a nine-member Recreation Advisory Board, which met for the first time on February 23, 1961. In 1962 Mork put the word "park" back into the department's name, making it the "Park and Recreation Advisory Board."

After George D. Johnson became mayor for the second time in 1963, Nash, as director of the parks and recreation department, wrote in his report for 1964 that "for the first time in many years, the women and girls of our community were given a chance to participate in recreational activities designed especially for them. This was brought about by the additional funds received from the Duluth Board of Education."

But finances were still tight, and some city councilors wanted to sell park land because they believed the city had too many parks. In May 1964 Duluth City Council President Clifford W. Johnson told the *Herald*, "We should get rid of our surplus land and thoroughly develop about six good parks where people will use them...not attempt to keep up many areas which are seldom used." According to researcher Charles Aguar, Johnson had the support of many Duluthians who "considered the greenbelt a wasted resource that might better be sold to real estate developers. George E. Dizard, president of the Duluth Park and Recreation Advisory Board, agreed, saying, "We are badly in need of revenue to prevent the collapse of our park and recreation program. Maybe the sale of some of this land would be the answer to our problem." Fortunately, very little park land was sold to developers.

At the end of 1966, Nash wrote, "It is also unfortunate that so many of the Department's facilities are deteriorating because of the lack of financing.... I believe that the time is drawing near when much more money will have to be spent on capital improvements and programming, or many of our Department's facilities will deteriorate beyond repair."

Citizen volunteers continued to support the park system. In the mid 1960s, as the concept of "urban renewal" reached Duluth, Julia and Caroline Marshall and Dorothy Congdon formed the Duluth Improvement Company. They privately financed the Fifth Avenue West Mall, a greenspace that linked the Civic Center with the waterfront near the Duluth Entertainment and Convention Center. And in 1967 the Duluth Rose Society began transforming a portion of Leif Erikson Park into a spectacular rose garden.

A New Environmental Consciousness

Things began to improve between 1967 and 1975, the years Ben Boo served as mayor. The environmental movement was growing across the country, bringing a renewed interest in the parks. But at the same time, Duluth's largest employer—United States Steel's Minnesota Steel plant in Morgan Park—shut down, leaving many people without jobs and bringing economic hard times to all of Duluth. According to Nash, the first year of Boo's term (1967) was "one of the most trying for the Parks and Recreation Department because of the fact that our Program Budget was eliminated from June 1st to December 1st, during which time we had to operate our softball, playgrounds, and playfield programs by using volunteer help, Neighborhood Youth Corp, and Work Study personnel as employees. Not only did it set our Program back, but many of our capital facilities were damaged by vandalism because we were unable to have full-time personnel in charge of them."

By 1968 Nash was able to report that the program was back to form after the drastic cutback of 1967. But he also warned, "Although

we continue to cut costs wherever possible, inflation has caught up. The Department needs added revenue in order to stop its backward movement and advance in the future."

To try to stabilize the department's budget, the advisory board helped develop and lobby for passage of what they called "the Permanent Plan," asking voters to approve a $12 million special levy for improving and maintaining the parks. In 1969 voters said "no" to the special levy, despite the plea that "Duluth's parks have been left to deteriorate and are now in overall disrepair!"

Nevertheless, in his 1970 annual report Nash wrote, "A successful and comprehensive Capital Improvement Program, which encompassed both new construction and major remodeling, was carried out during the year. In fact more improvements were accomplished in 1970 than in the previous thirty years combined." These improvements included a new pavilion at Chambers Grove, pavilion work at Fairmount and Lincoln parks, remodeling at Memorial, Portman, and Lafayette fieldhouses, and the purchase of grooming equipment for Chester Park.

Challenges for the department in the early 1970s included the loss of thousands of trees to Dutch elm disease and extensive damage to the parks as the result of major flooding in late summer 1972. Improvements included a cooperative project with the Junior League of Duluth to renovate and publicize many of the park trails and opening of the Spirit Mountain Recreation Area in 1974.

Ben Boo resigned as mayor in January 1975 to become director of the Western Lake Superior Sanitary District. City council president Robert Beaudin finished out the last year of Boo's term. Following Beaudin's election to a four-year term as mayor, Harry Nash resigned

PRILEY FOUNTAIN AT THE CENTER OF DULUTH'S CIVIC CENTER, 1970. THE FOUNTAIN, AND THE DRIVE THAT SURROUNDS IT, ARE NAMED FOR JOSEPH PRILEY, AKA "PETUNIA JOE," A MUSICIAN AND ST. LOUIS COUNTY COMMISSIONER WHO INSTITUTED A CIVIC BEAUTIFICATION PROGRAM IN DULUTH WHICH RECEIVED NATIONAL ATTENTION. (PHOTO BY LYMAN NYLANDER.)
[IMAGE: UMD MARTIN LIBRARY]

in February 1976 as director of parks and recreation, replaced by Mary K. Schroeder. As the Atlas Cement plant—the last remaining section of the steel plant—shut down, Mayor Beaudin, himself a former steel plant worker, focused his efforts on economic development and job creation.

John Fedo became mayor in 1979 and appointed Ray E. Carson director of the parks and recreation department; James McCord replaced Carson in 1983. Fedo is credited with launching the renaissance of Duluth's lakefront and the development of Canal Park in the 1980s. He converted Duluth's industrial waterfront into a tourist attraction, was active in the design and beautification of downtown Duluth, and expanded the golf courses. Additional support came from Gerald Kimball, director of the Department of Research & Planning, who promoted the idea of surrounding the central urban area with a "greenbelt" composed of connected parks and undeveloped tax forfeited land. In 1989 Fedo selected Carl Seehus as McCord's successor.

Turning Challenges into Opportunities

As always, citizens continued to play an important role in developing and maintaining the park system. With the help of a citizen advisory committee, one of Duluth's major controversies was resolved in the 1980s; construction of Interstate 35 from Thompson Hill to Mesaba Avenue in the 1960s and early 1970s had destroyed neighborhoods in West Duluth and the West End. (It also created two small parks. Keene Creek Park and Midtowne Park, both located under highway overpasses.) Many Duluthians were appalled by the results of the initial expansion, and they weren't happy with the plan to continue the highway eastward through downtown and then elevate it on stilts over the Lake Superior shoreline.

Public outcry brought a halt to the project until a more acceptable design could be developed. The Citizens Advisory Committee, working with the Minnesota Department of Transportation, created

THE EXPANSION OF INTERSTATE 35 THROUGH DULUTH, UNDERWAY IN THIS 1986 PHOTO, CREATED LAKE PLACE PARK, GATEWAY PLAZA, JAY COOKE PLAZA, AND RAIL PARK AS WELL AS A REVISIONING OF LEIF ERIKSON PARK. (PHOTO BY CHARLES CURTIS.)

[IMAGE: DULUTH NEWS TRIBUNE]

a more sensitive plan that utilized the existing railroad corridor, added tunnels to carry the roadway under Leif Erikson Park and downtown streets, and preserved public access to the lakeshore. Duluth landscape architect Kent Worley proposed a landscaping design that included Lake Place Park on top of a highway tunnel and the Lakewalk, a walking and biking path along the shoreline. Duluth's Lakewalk was officially dedicated and opened in 1990 with what the park department called "a very festive and memorable event." Gateway Plaza, Jay Cooke Plaza, Lake Place Park, and Rail Park were all created during this portion of highway expansion as well. Also in 1990, the Junior League of Duluth built Playfront, a playground within Bayfront Park.

Mayor Gary Doty served from 1992 to 2004. He replaced Seehus with Suzanne Moyer as director of the Parks and Recreation Department; she served until 1999 when Doty made the uprecedented move of reappointing Carl Seehus. Doty focused primarily on economic development and infrastructure improvements, mainly streets and sewers. After many years of conflicting plans for the bayfront, in 1999 Lois Paulucci, wife of frozen-food magnate Jeno Paulucci, donated $3 million to improve Bayfront Festival Park. A permanent stage, named the Lois M. Paulucci Pavilion, was completed and opened on July 26, 2001. And in 2003 the Hartley Nature Center opened, the culmination of an effort begun by a volunteer group in the 1980s. The Park and Recreation Advisory Board became the Parks and Recreation Commission.

After taking office in 2004, Mayor Herb Bergson retained Seehus as director of the parks and recreation department. The department focused its efforts on the Lake Superior Zoo, the municipal golf courses, senior and after-school programs, music in the parks, and recreational opportunities.

During the administration of Mayor Don Ness (2008 to 2016), Kathy Bergen succeeded Seehus. The Ness administration's record in regard to Duluth's parks might best be described as inconsistent. State budget cuts to local government aid in 2009 forced tough decisions; the public library's hours of operation were severely reduced, as was park maintenance.

In 2010 the Ness administration hired the Hoisington Kaogler Group, Minneapolis-based planning consultants, who advised that Duluth take drastic measures to reduce its park inventory. According to the *News Tribune*, on the firm's advice the parks division proposed "the demolition of 40 percent of the city's recreation centers" and

Lucas Kramer scales the icy cliffs of Quarry Park during the winter of 2015–2016. The newest addition to Duluth's park system, Quarry Park was established in 2016. (Photo by Kraig Decker.)

[IMAGE: CLIMB DULUTH]

the sale of much of its undeveloped park land. Nine of the city's twenty-two recreation centers were on the chopping block, including those at Hillside Sport Court, Observation Park, Piedmont Park, Lincoln Park, Merritt Park, Memorial Park, Riverside Park, Gary–New Duluth Park, and Fond du Lac Park—all in the western part of the city. Also in the west, the plan called for selling off portions of Bayview School Forest and Brewery Park. To the east, park properties threatened for sale included Lower Chester Park Playground and Lakeside's Portman Playground, Manchester Square, Russell Square, and Scott Keenan Park (aka Fortieth Avenue East & Jay Street Park).

Many Duluthians, particularly those west of Mesaba Avenue, did not like the plan. At the very least it failed to consider that Duluth is a city of neighborhoods, and each neighborhood has a certain amount of sentimentality and pride in its parks and schools—especially in the city's western half. Duluthians flooded the email inboxes of city councilors with complaints about the proposed plan. More than fifty concerned citizens showed up at a master plan meeting in November, most expressing their desire to retain neighborhood community centers.

Thanks to community efforts, only a few of the plan's recommendations were carried out. In Lakeside, tiny Scott Keenan Park was sold, and in West Duluth the historic fieldhouses at Irving Park and Memorial Park—damaged by the 2012 flood—were demolished. The parks and recreation commission helped to develop new master plans for many of the parks, and voters approved a 2011 referendum that created a property tax fund dedicated specifically to support the park system and public library.

Ness again faced strong public reaction when in 2014 he proposed selling all or some of the Lester Park Golf Course to housing developers; the course was not sold. Ness received a much better reaction to his plans for the St. Louis River Corridor Initiative, an $18 million plan with the goal of investing in public park and trail improvements from Lincoln Park to the Fond du Lac neighborhood. Included in the plans were improvements to Chambers Grove Park, the Gary–New Duluth Recreation Area, Irving Park, Lincoln Park, and Memorial Park. A new chalet for Spirit Mountain was built at the base of the ski hill with access from Grand Avenue, and Wade Stadium was refurbished. With public input a radical new plan was devised for Fairmount Park and the Lake Superior Zoo, and

enthusiastic ice climbers helped establish Quarry Park. As of 2016 many of the initiative's projects are yet to be implemented, including work at Piedmont, Harrison, Merritt, Irving, Grassy Point, Keene Creek, Norton, Riverside, Smithville, Morgan Park, Blackmer, Fond du Lac, and Historical parks.

While Ness was in office the city also cooperated with the Cyclists of Gitchee Gumee Shores (COGGS) to create the Duluth Traverse, a multiuse, single-track trail purpose-built for mountain biking; the Superior Hiking Trail was extended through the city; and in 2012 an effort by the Duluth City Council created the F. Rodney Paine Forest Preserve.

Director Bergen retired in the fall of 2015, shortly before Ness left office, and was replaced by Lindsay Dean. In January 2016 Emily Larson took over as mayor of Duluth. Larson was a very strong and vocal supporter of the 2011 referendum, and as a city councilor (2011–2015) she served as chairperson for the council's Recreation, Libraries & Authorities Committee. Her support for the city's park system is clearly expressed in her 2016 statement that "The history of land, and who has access to it, tells an enormous amount about the values and priorities of a community. Duluth's story is based on a resounding value for our green space, open space, wild space and free space. Parks are where people gather, families play, and memories are made. And the best part is that parks are for everyone: all neighbors, all neighborhoods. No one needs to pay admission or a membership fee. Everyone already belongs."

Following Bergen's retirement, the *News Tribune* wrote that as a result of major budget deficits in 2008 and 2009 that forced cuts in staff and resources, the parks and recreation department had increasingly turned to volunteers and service groups for help with facilities and programming. Calling this a "new model," Mayor Ness said, "What we've moved to is a model in which the city prioritizes maintenance of our public space and then works with community organizations to use those spaces well."

In reality, this is not a new model at all. For over 125 years Duluth's park system has been built, improved, maintained, and sustained by a partnership between city government and the generous and dedicated citizens of this city. Throughout the years Duluthians have confirmed what the Board of Park Commissioners wrote in 1911: "The parks of a modern city bear witness that its people are members of one great family. They are the concrete expression of civic consciousness in its highest visible form."

1. Nineteenth-Century Squares

The Zenith City's First Parks

When the first settlers in the 1850s platted the townships that later joined to become Duluth, they set aside land for public squares—open spaces in the heart of the townsite that could be used for community gatherings. This pattern of development soon fell out of favor as the work of Frederick Law Olmsted, designer of New York's Central Park, gave rise to the new concept of "landscape architecture." Olmsted believed that "the greatest counterpoint to urban form was pure wilderness," an idea Duluth's park board would embrace when it began establishing the city park system in the 1890s. Over the next one hundred years, some of Duluth's public squares were left undeveloped, some were used for purposes other than parks, and others became the central feature of the neighborhoods that surround them.

Cascade Square

Located above Fifth Street between Lake Avenue and Second Avenue West, Cascade Square is one of Duluth's oldest parks. Originally a four-acre parcel bisected by Clarkhouse Creek, Cascade Square was set aside as public open space when the land was platted in the 1850s as part of Duluth Township.

In 1889 the newly created Duluth Board of Park Commissioners took over responsibility for Cascade Square, but board members focused their resources on developing the scenic park system proposed by William K. Rogers. They described Cascade Square as "the most unsightly and unmanageable land in the entire city. In a block of about five acres there was a fall of 100 feet in 300. It was cut by an ugly gully and broken by rocks whose roughness lacked picturesque qualities." In October 1891 the board gave a local contractor permission to dump "refuse rock and earth in Cascade Square," illustrating its lack of interest in the park.

But in late 1892 the city council officially requested that the park board make improvements to the city's public squares. Because of Cascade Square's prime location in the heart of the city, the board decided to intentionally create the picturesque qualities that the land

LITHOGRAPHIC POSTCARD, CA. 1905, SHOWING CLARKHOUSE CREEK FLOWING THROUGH CASCADE PARK.

[IMAGE: ZENITH CITY PRESS]

of poplar. Erected on the pinnacle of this park is a substantial and artistic brownstone observatory surmounted by a pagoda shaped wood and iron canopy. Splendid views are here obtained of the downtown section of the city, harbor, and lake, Park Point and Superior beyond, as well as the new government ship canal, piers and lighthouses, with the vessels passing to and fro.

Unfortunately, the park board soon learned that maintaining the elaborate improvements at Cascade Square required a high level of investment. Heavy rainstorms often resulted in flash floods along the channels of Duluth's many streams, including Clarkhouse Creek. A heavy downpour in July 1897 caused major damage at Cascade Square. The day after the storm newspapers reported that "Cascade Square is a sight to make the park commissioners and the frequenters of that popular resort weep. The pavilion is badly wrecked, the walks are badly damaged, the stone steps were torn up, an incandescent light pole in the center of the park washed out and fell across a path, gorges are cut through the property, the flower beds and grass are wrecked and things have been torn up ruthlessly."

The board moved quickly to repair the damage, but just twelve years later, in July 1909, another major storm hit the city. The newspaper reported that "at Cascade Park the principal disaster was wrought. The main channel for the creek was quickly choked up, allowing an immense torrent of water to sweep over the place. This carried away with it masonry and shrubs, and left the beauty spot in a very bedraggled condition. Work will commence as soon as possible to clear the channel and restore the park to its former condition."

The park board once again restored Cascade Square, but by this time the park system included many parks and playgrounds

lacked. In 1895 a crew of fifty men went to work on improvements that cost a total of $16,807. They built a stone-lined channel to contain Clarkhouse Creek (so named because it once flowed close to Duluth's first major hotel, the Clark House) and created a charming waterfall to justify the name Cascade. The improvements also included a large covered pavilion, walkways, benches, trees, flowers, and grass.

As a result of this transformation, Cascade Square rapidly became one of the city's most beloved parks. The *Duluth News Tribune* described it in flowery terms:

This park, although but a square in extent is well worth visiting and is, it may be said, in the heart of the city. Cascade Square contains a fine display of flowers and plants as well as many beautiful and ornamental shade trees such as maple, willow, box elder, mountain ash and four kinds that required attention. In addition, the automobile was becoming affordable, providing more people with the option of traveling greater distances to visit the larger parks on the outskirts of town. Maintenance of Cascade Square slipped lower and lower on the city's priority list.

By the end of World War II, nearly every family in Duluth had an automobile and the increased traffic downtown made street improvements a necessity. When preparing a plan for widening Mesaba Avenue, the Minnesota Department of Transportation proposed cutting straight through Cascade Square instead of going around it. Inevitably yielding to the demands of the automobile, in the early 1950s workmen tore down the park's remaining structures, covered over the channel of Clarkhouse Creek, and sacrificed the western half of the park to Mesaba Avenue. This small but lovely public square that once exhibited the best in landscape design and park planning became an eyesore.

When it entered its second century as a park, Cascade Square consisted of

about two and a half acres of land, providing some much-needed (but poorly maintained) greenspace in the densely developed Central Hillside neighborhood. In 1966 the *News Tribune* printed a short article about Cascade Square, lamenting its neglect and urging restoration. "The grass is almost knee-high; tansy, dock and ragweed ring the perimeter of the area, and the poisonous nightshade plant greets visitors.... For all practical purposes it is being returned to wilderness, except no self-respecting wilderness has so much garbage and litter strewn about."

Another major flood in August 1972 sent Clarkhouse Creek cascading down First Avenue West, carrying much of the street's pavement along with it. Cleanup following this flood included a limited restoration of Cascade Park, during which the city installed walkways and picnic tables. When Mesaba Avenue was widened in 1975

to accommodate traffic heading toward Miller Hill Mall and the surrounding retail developments, more of the park was sacrificed. The city demolished the remaining sandstone structures and sent Clarkhouse Creek completely underground. The city then built a concrete towerlike structure on the pavilion's old sandstone foundation. The words "Cascade Park" are still visible, carved into the original sandstone. That foundation and portions of the rock wall supporting Mesaba Avenue are all that remain of the original structures. Rededication of the park took place on July 1, 1975.

In the late 1990s, neighbors and other concerned citizens began to care for the park. The League of Women Voters, the Central Hillside Garden Club, and students from nearby Nettleton School adopted Cascade Park and worked to beautify it by planting and maintaining flower beds.

CASCADE PARK CA. 1908.
(PHOTO BY THE DETROIT
PUBLISHING COMPANY.)

[IMAGE: LIBRARY OF CONGRESS]

PORTLAND SQUARE, DULUTH, MINN.

No. 1321. V. O. Hammon Pub. Co., Minneapolis and Chicago

Portland Square

Portland Square, located between Tenth and Eleventh Avenues East from Fourth Street to Fifth Street in Duluth's East Hillside, holds a clue to Duluth's early development. Its name comes from Portland Township, established in 1856 by a group of men including James D. Ray, Clinton Markell (Duluth's second mayor), and Judge Josiah D. Ensign. The township itself occupied the space from Third Avenue East to Chester Creek, from the lakeshore to approximately the location of today's Skyline Parkway.

Duluth's park board first turned its attention to Portland Square in June 1894 when board member Bernard Silberstein pushed for its improvement. The board had to clear a small hurdle first: Carl Eskelson, who the *News Tribune* described as "an old man who lives on Fourth street adjoining the property," claimed he owned the square. Eskelson even staked out his property and built a fence around it and "served notice on the mayor." The newspaper reported that "no attention will be paid to the notice and if Eskelson attempts to interfere with the work he will be arrested." There were no further reports on the issue.

Work began that summer, with the *News Tribune* acting as cheerleader, claiming the square would soon become "the garden spot of Duluth." Its central feature was a fountain, described as a "shell and dolphin design, of cast iron, handsomely bronzed. It throws seven sprays, and is said to present a very pretty appearance when in operation." The fountain, which cost $400, was surrounded by a concrete pool which itself was encompassed by a sixteen-foot diameter concrete basin. During the summer the pool was planted with water lilies and stocked with goldfish. Sidewalks lined with concrete benches led from each of the square's four corners to the fountain at its center. The borders of the square were lined with trees, and its interior spaces filled with shrubs, flower gardens, and a circular promenade.

By 1896, according to the *News Tribune*, Portland Square had become a popular gathering place for "the ladies and little ones," particularly because it sat along the streetcar line, making it easily accessible to everyone. In 1908 the square helped Duluth launch the local playground movement, but noise complaints by local residents ended the experiment after just three days. In 1927 the park department chose Portland Square as one of five sites throughout the city to build ramps to serve as "snow slides."

As of 2016, a small modern playground and a few scattered benches and picnic tables give nearby residents a reason to visit. But for those who do not know the history of Cascade Square, the park appears rather formless and puzzling. What is left of the old stone retaining wall ends awkwardly, cut off by the concrete barricade that supports four lanes of traffic on Mesaba Avenue. The characterless concrete pavilion contains nothing but a mysterious round concrete plinth that serves no apparent purpose. The pavilion still provides an impressive view of downtown and Lake Superior, but no benches or other amenities invite visitors to linger. An attempt to beautify the park with public art became a highly controversial issue in 2011, and the project's many critics consider the effort a failure.

Most curious of all today is the name Cascade Park. Except when Clarkhouse Creek breaks free of its concrete prison following a major rainstorm, as it did once again in June 2012, no evidence remains of the small stream that once cascaded through the park. Visitors who listen carefully, however, can hear the stream flowing underground. Those who follow the sound can peer down through a small sewer grate and see the glimmer of moving water, now cascading secretly through the heart of the city.

Like most Duluth parks, Portland Square eventually fell into a state of neglect, particularly following World War II. The fountain and its surrounding pool are gone, with no record of what became of them, but the original layout of the park's 1894 concrete elements is relatively intact. While the flower beds no longer exist, trees still line the walkways, and playground equipment offers neighborhood children a place to play without anyone complaining about the noise.

Fond du Lac Square

When the founders of Fond du Lac Township platted its streets in 1856, they set aside a square block of public open space between today's West Third Street (State Highway 23) and Fourth Street from 130th to 131st Avenues West. In the late 1860s when the Lake Superior & Mississippi Railroad was built along the St. Louis River, connecting Duluth to the Twin Cities, the railroad tracks were laid straight through Fond du Lac Square. Then in the 1930s the State of Minnesota took additional land from the square for Highway 23. In 1956 the St. Louis County Historical Society, along with the Minnesota Highway Department, erected a historical marker at the center of the square along the highway, but the square remains otherwise undeveloped.

Lakeside's Squares

According to historian Warren Upham, when Jay Cooke's business associate Hugh McCulloch platted New London in 1871 he included five public squares each measuring "two and seven tenths acres" (two square blocks) and named all but one of them after public squares in London, England. The squares became part of the Village of Lakeside in 1889, which became the City of Lakeside in 1891, which was annexed by Duluth in 1893, at which point the squares became part of Duluth's park system.

Located between Forty-ninth and Fiftieth Avenues East from McCulloch Street to Gladstone Street, **Grosvenor Square** is likely named after Grosvenor Square in London's upscale Mayfair district, which takes its name from Hugh Grosvenor, named the first Duke of Westminster in 1874. Lakeside's Grosvenor Square retains its original two-block size and is mostly wooded, except for a few pieces of playground equipment and a large field in the southwest quadrant.

Manchester Square, between Forty-sixth and Forty-seventh Avenues East from Peabody Street to Colorado Street, takes its name from an eighteenth-century garden square in London's once-fashionable

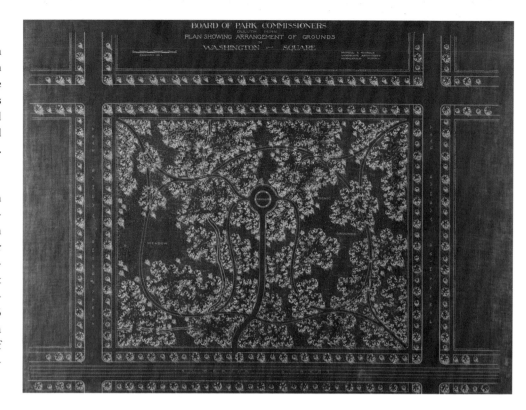

Marylebone neighborhood. Lakeside's Manchester Square has been reduced to one square block and is entirely covered with trees. Its northern border, Colorado Street, was originally named Summit Street, which served as the northern boundary of the New London township.

Situated between Forty-sixth and Forty-seventh Avenues East from McCulloch Street to Gladstone Street, **Portman Square** became a public playground in 1910 following plans developed by landscape architects Anthony U. Morell and Arthur R. Nichols. The square was named after London's Portman Square, once part of the nearby estate of England's aristocratic Portman Family (Edward Berkeley Portman became the first Viscount of Portman in 1873). Lakeside's Portman Square today is still two blocks in size and, as it has for over one hundred years, serves as a public playground with a fieldhouse, a baseball diamond, and three hockey rinks in the winter. The fieldhouse was built in 1940 as part of a Works Progress Administration improvement effort.

Russell Square lies between Forty-second and Forty-third Avenues East from Pitt Street to Jay Street. Like Manchester Square it has

BLUEPRINT FOR THE LANDSCAPING OF WASHINGTON SQUARE, DRAWN IN 1911 BY LANDSCAPE ARCHITECTS MORELL & NICHOLS. THE PARK BOARD WAS ELIMINATED IN 1913, AND THE PLANS WERE NEVER IMPLEMENTED.

[IMAGE: CITY OF DULUTH]

been reduced to one square block in size and, except for the stretch along Jay Street, it is entirely wooded. The Russell surname is famous in England as the family name of the Duke and Earl of Bedford, including John Russell, who became the First Earl of Russell in 1861 and briefly served as England's Prime Minister from 1865 to 1866. England's Russell Square is located in the London borough of Camden, near the University of London and the British Museum.

The only square in Lakeside not named for a London square, **Washington Square** sits between Forty-second and Forty-third Avenues East from Superior Street to Regent Street. In 1911 Morell & Nichols offered two different plans for the park. One, shown on the previous page, featured a pavilion in the center, surrounded by groves of trees, picnic grounds, and a meadow. The other plan included a baseball diamond that could be flooded and used as a skating rink in the winter. Today the square is partially wooded and includes playground equipment. It is named not after New York City's famous Washington Square—also established in 1871—but rather for Philadelphia's long-established Washington Square, located just four blocks from Jay Cooke's bank, where McCulloch once worked.

The Public Squares of Minnesota Point

Minnesota Point's original two parks, Franklin Square and Lafayette Square, were set aside when the land was platted in 1856. These small squares, less than two acres each, became city parks when the Village of Park Point joined Duluth in 1889. Despite Minnesota Point's popularity as a summer resort, the park board never developed amenities at either location. Instead, these parks housed other public facilities for most of their histories.

Franklin Square, named in honor of Benjamin Franklin, originally included the land between Lake Avenue South and Minnesota Avenue from Twelfth Street to Thirteenth Street. The site—then the northern border of Middleton Township (predecessor to the Village of Park Point)—contained an early cemetery used for burials of European pioneers, which may be the reason it was left undeveloped. Shifting sand dunes do not provide stable ground for a cemetery, and in 1883 the human remains, along with remains from two other burial sites on Minnesota Point, were moved to Forest Hill Cemetery.

The city deeded the Franklin Square property to the federal government in 1894 to be used by the U.S. Life Saving Service—predecessor to the U.S. Coast Guard—as the location for the Duluth Life Saving Station, which opened in June 1895. The Coast Guard built a new facility in 1959, and ownership of the Franklin Square parcel reverted to the City of Duluth. Within a few years the Public Works Department had demolished the old Lifeboat Station, constructed the S curve connecting Lake and Minnesota avenues, and provided a parking lot with access to the lakeshore. The Tot Lot playground opened in 1971, paid for with funds raised by the Park Point Community Club and assistance from the Coast Guard, the American Legion, and the Duluth Parks and Recreation Department.

Located on the lake side of Minnesota Avenue between Thirtieth and Thirty-first Streets South, **Lafayette Square** was named in honor of Gilbert Motier, Marquis de Lafayette, the young French aristocrat who helped the fledgling United States defeat the British in the War of Independence. Biographies of Lafayette have often reported that "no other foreign dignitary has ever had so many places named after him as Lafayette"; apparently in 1856 Middleton Township simply followed the lead of other U.S. communities.

The square never received any attention from the park board, and in 1905 the city gave the Independent Duluth School District permission to build a school on a portion of the land. Named Radisson Elementary in honor of another historic Frenchman, explorer Pierre-Esprit Radisson, the two-room school served residents on the southern end of Park Point. In 1910 the Duluth Board of Education proposed closing the Radisson School, primarily because the building was small, drafty, and heated only by a wood stove. Residents objected, and while the debate raged a story in the *News Tribune* asked, "What will the park board do with the property on which stands the abandoned Radisson School?" According to the newspaper, the response from the board indicated that "some of them did not seem to be aware that the school was on park property."

When the school finally closed in 1919, Park Superintendent Henry Cleveland requested that the building be sold to the city for one dollar for use as a community center. Instead, in 1921 the board of education gave the building to the Duluth Department of Public Welfare. The former school became a gathering place for the Park Point Community Club, a function it still serves.

U.S. LIFE SAVING STATION AT FRANKLIN SQUARE

In 1894 the City of Duluth deeded Franklin Square on Minnesota Point to the federal government for the location of the Duluth Life Saving Station of the U.S. Life Saving Service. Designed by federal architect George R. Tolman, the station opened in June 1895. Tolman's design for the main building (below), with its distinctive watch tower, was called the Duluth style. It soon became one of the standard models for life-saving stations built along the East Coast of the United States. Donald McKenzie was appointed the station's first keeper, with Captain Murdoch McLennan taking over when McKenzie died of cancer three years later.

The Duluth Life Saving Station crews maintained a visual watch of Lake Superior and the Duluth harbor from the station's tower and also by regularly walking the beach all the way to the southern end of the point. Always ready to launch their boats to assist any ship that appeared to be in trouble, crew members followed a regular schedule of daily practice exercises, including gun and beach apparatus practice (right) on Mondays and Thursdays, boat practice on Tuesdays, signal practice on Wednesdays, and "resuscitation of the apparently drowned" on Fridays. According to U.S. Coast Guard records, during its first six years the Duluth station assisted in sixty-five rescue operations, nearly eleven each year.

Unfortunately, during Duluth's most tragic storm the crew of the station stood helplessly onshore. The nor'easter of November 28, 1905, aka the *Mataafa* Storm, wrecked or damaged twenty-six vessels on Lake Superior and stranded seventeen others; thirty-three men died, nine of them just outside the Duluth Ship Canal. The steamer *Mataafa* had struck the canal's north pier broadside and broke in two about 150 yards offshore. At the time the life-saving

Firing the Life-line.   At Duluth, Minn.

crew was assisting the *R. W. England*, which was beached about two miles south of the canal. By the time the lifesavers could get to their boats at the station—nearly three hours later—the seas were so rough that McLennan and his crew could not even launch their rescue vessels. They were forced to wait until the next day. By then, the sailors trapped in the *Mataafa's* aft section had frozen to death.

Outside of the *Mataafa* storm, between 1901 and 1915, the station was called to assist only ten times. In 1915 the U.S. Congress merged the U.S. Life Saving Service and the U.S. Revenue Cutter Service to form the U.S. Coast Guard, and the Minnesota Point facility became the Duluth Lifeboat Station. McLennan continued as its keeper until 1924.

In 1938 the Duluth Port Authority announced plans to construct a maritime center on Minnesota Point that would extend from the lakeshore to the harbor between Twelfth and Thirteenth Streets, including the Franklin Square land. The plan called for drill grounds and new quarters for the coast guard, the Duluth's naval reserve, and the lighthouse service; the old lifeboat station was to be abandoned and Franklin Square restored as a city park and extended to the lakeshore to include a supervised bathing beach. A paved road would cut diagonally through the square to connect Lake Avenue and Minnesota Avenue (prior to that Twelfth Street South was used as the connector). Supporters of the maritime center project applied for funding from the federal Public Works Administration, but the funds did not materialize and the project was put on hold.

Money finally became available in 1949 for a new Coast Guard station, essentially a scaled-back version of the maritime center idea. Located on the harbor shoreline west of Minnesota Avenue between Twelfth and Thirteenth Streets South, the building opened in 1953. Ownership of the Franklin Square parcel reverted to the City of Duluth, and within a few years the Public Works Department had demolished the old lifeboat station. Following construction of a playground west of the bathing beach in 1971, the square became known as the Franklin Tot Lot.

U.S. LIFE SAVING STATION.

THE PARK POINT COMMUNITY CLUB AT LAFAYETTE SQUARE

Lafayette Square, named for the French hero of the American Revolution, sat undeveloped and ignored from its creation in 1856 until 1905, when the Independent Duluth School District asked the city for permission to build a school on a portion of the park to serve students living in the lower half of Minnesota Point (those living closer to the canal attended the 1892 Whittier School along Minnesota Avenue at Twelfth Street South). Permission was granted for a two-room frame building at the cost of $1,808—just over $5,000 in today's money. The school district named the building for another Frenchman, explorer and fur trader Pierre-Esprit Radisson. Radisson and his brother-in-law Médard Chouart des Groseilliers are thought to be the first men of European descent to visit the Head of the Lakes; in 1765 they reached at least as far as Chequamegon Bay at the site of today's Ashland, Wisconsin.

Two teachers taught grades five through eight at Radisson Elementary. Records indicate that no more than fifty students attended the school at any time during the twenty-four years it served Minnesota Point residents. It closed along with Whittier in 1919 when Park Point Elementary opened at 2400 Minnesota Avenue to serve all students living south of the canal.

After the closing of Radisson School, the Duluth Board of Education gave the building to the city to use as the Park Point Community Center and, in part, as the headquarters of the Park Point Community Club. In the 1920s the club and its president Samuel Clark Dick (pictured) led the charge to convert the famous Duluth Aerial Bridge from a transfer bridge to a lift bridge, even putting forth the idea that Park Point landowners would pay for a portion of that work. The club's efforts included finding the company that executed the conversion.

In 1922 club members asked Mayor Sam Snively to improve Lafayette Square with landscaping, benches and tables, fire grates for cooking, and a wooden walkway across the sand from the clubhouse to Lake Superior. Members of the community club volunteered to paint the old school. Many of the club's requests for improvements were probably not honored, as in following years mention was often made of the building's unsatisfactory condition.

By 1933 demands for improvements in the park and clubhouse had increased. Depression-era efforts by the Works Progress Administration (WPA) included remodeling and expanding the clubhouse following a design (pictured) by Duluth architect A. Reinhold Melander. His design called for a two-story building with a warming room for the skating rink, playground headquarters, a large community room with fireplace, and a branch of the Duluth Public Library that would open only on evenings and Friday afternoons. Initially the WPA funded $20,000 for the plan, but the 1938 Duluth Park Department Annual Report indicates that funds spent on the clubhouse and park totaled $40,000, nearly $650,000 today.

The renovation involved moving the school building northeast from its original location and raising it to serve as part of the new building's second story. A full first floor was built as a warming house and playroom, and a wing was added on the north side for restrooms.

Dedication of the Park Point Community Center took place in September 1936. Dignitaries providing speeches included club president Dick, Mayor Samuel F. Snively, and Duluth author Margaret Culkin Banning, then president of the Duluth Library Board.

For decades Lafayette Square supported skating and hockey rinks and fielded summer baseball and softball teams. Today much of the square is dedicated to a community garden, and the center remains the home of the community club, which organizes the annual Park Point Rummage Sale and Park Point Art Fair and is also involved in the care of the point's natural resources and other issues that affect its residents. The club has never relinquished its concerns for crossing the canal and has made several efforts—some temporarily implemented—to reduce or schedule bridge raisings so that residents wouldn't get "bridged"—stuck on one side of the bridge trying to get to the other side while the center span is up—nearly as often.

— IMAGE: ZENITH CITY PRESS —

— IMAGE: WALTER N. TRENNERY —

2. Skyline Parkway

Backbone of the Modern Park System

Visitors to Duluth in the summer of 1890 may have expected to find a rough frontier settlement surrounded by wilderness. Instead they discovered a beautiful modern city with over 30,000 residents and a busy harbor filled with cargo ships. Tourists could dine in the elegant Palm Room of the magnificent seven-story brick and brownstone Spalding Hotel, enjoy a trip up the St. Louis River on a steam-driven excursion boat, or take a carriage ride along Duluth's new scenic parkway, described by the *Duluth Herald* as "winding along on the brow of our hillside...the terrace drive forever to be linked with the fame and glory of Duluth.... No where in our much-loved land can there be found a drive the peer of this alike in sylvan beauty and lofty grandeur."

The role of urban parks was changing in the late 1800s, and cities throughout the country were designing elaborate urban park systems that included parkways—broad landscaped roadways built expressly for pleasure excursions. Duluth's developers embraced this new trend, and in 1889 they started creating a parkway perched nearly five hundred feet above Lake Superior. An ancient beach terrace left behind by Glacial Lake Duluth—formed by meltwater as glaciers retreated thousands of years ago—provided a natural pathway across the hillside and gave rise to the road's first name: Terrace Parkway.

The *Herald* declared that after driving over the parkway, visitors "were enraptured and could not express their praise in language strong enough for the occasion." Of course, in 1890 the road provided a spectacular unobstructed view of the city and lake below because the central hillside had been clearcut to make way for businesses, churches, schools, and homes built from the native white pines.

The parkway's construction involved many people, but two men—William K. Rogers and Samuel Frisbee Snively—were instrumental. Without Rogers and Snively the parkway would not exist.

LITHOGRAPHIC POSTCARD, CA. 1904, OF A COACHING OR "TALLYHO" PARTY TOURING ROGERS BOULEVARD, TODAY'S SKYLINE PARKWAY.

[IMAGE: ZENITH CITY PRESS]

Rogers Boulevard

The idea of a scenic parkway across the hillside came from William K. Rogers, who first arrived in Duluth around 1870 as the new town was being established. Rogers's plan included more than just a parkway. He envisioned a park system made up of the Terrace Parkway high on the hillside, a stream corridor park at each end (Miller Creek and Chester Creek), and a parkway along the shore of Lake Superior from Chester Creek to the corporate boundary at Fortieth Avenue East.

Rogers, in his enthusiasm, may have started work on the road as soon as the common council approved his plan in February 1888—a year before the state legislature officially created the Duluth Board of Park Commissioners and gave them the authority to build a system of parks and parkways. Years later the board members would write, "When the Park Board organized in 1889 it had little property in its control and a floating debt of $67,000 to meet, incurred by the enthusiasm of Mr. Rogers in his voluntary proceedings."

The historical record does not reveal what Rogers accomplished on his own. The park board's minutes indicate that at the first meeting in April 1889, the members decided to officially start construction of the road on Tenth Street at Lake Avenue, continuing east and west as rapidly as possible. They agreed that work would be carried out "under the personal supervision" of Rogers and that "competent foreman, laborers, and teams" would be employed by the day. Rogers moved quickly, hiring appraisers to determine the value of the land to be purchased and an engineer to lay out the road, as well as renting rooms in the Stenson Block at $38 per month for them to use as offices.

Just four months later—in early August 1889—people were using the parkway. Rogers reported to the board, "The road is now for some distance in public use and is evidently appreciated by the citizens of Duluth and visitors to the city." Work was still underway west of Lake Avenue, where bridges were being built over Buckingham and Coffee (aka Coffey) Creeks and the massive rock outcrops around Seventeenth Avenue West required extra blasting. Duluthians confirmed their support in October when 740 out of 822 voted in favor of selling city bonds to finance the park system. The park board needed that support—at the end of 1889 they calculated that the money

TWO DULUTHIANS ON HORSEBACK, CA. 1893, ENJOY A REST WHILE TOURING TERRACE PARKWAY, THE ORIGINAL SECTION OF TODAY'S SKYLINE PARKWAY, NAMED ROGERS BOULEVARD IN 1894.

[IMAGE: UMD MARTIN LIBRARY]

spent that year on the Terrace Parkway totaled $5,810.54. Following the successful vote, board members authorized a bond for $312,000, the amount they calculated would be needed to cover the debt and acquire the necessary land.

By the end of 1890, with spending exceeding the available funds, city leaders realized the powers of the park board needed to be redefined. After consulting with other major cities that had a Board of Park Commissioners, the state legislature revised the board's rules and in April 1891 Mayor Davis appointed new commissioners. Although William K. Rogers remained on the board, he was no longer the driving force. He attended meetings for a few months, then left the board, apparently due to ill health. Responsibility for completing the parkway shifted to the other three prominent businessmen who made up the new board: Luther Mendenhall, Bernard Silberstein, and Henry Helm. The following year they were joined by Arthur Chapin, appointed by the mayor to replace Rogers.

Shortly after being appointed in 1891, the new board members began meeting frequently, working to pick up where the previous board had left off, deciding on a more permanent route for the parkway, looking for funds, and establishing operating procedures. They wanted the parkway to be "finished and made safe" by June 1; the date was later pushed back to June 15. They met their goal, but they did not hold a formal opening ceremony to mark the occasion. The road had already been in use for nearly two years, and even as they reached the June 15 deadline, board members continued to make changes to the right-of-way. In their annual report for 1891 they wrote, "At the present time we have a drive that is the pride of our city and one that for its picturesque and varied scenery, is second to none in the world." They reported that they had spent $25,954.67 to acquire land for the right-of-way, and they calculated that by the end of 1891 the total amount spent on building the road was $102,737.15 (equivalent to at least $3 million in 2016 dollars).

Visits to Duluth had to include a trip on the parkway, as indicated by this May 1891 statement in the *Duluth News Tribune*: "It goes without saying that one must drive over the boulevard. On foot the lover of the picturesque would consume several days in viewing its charms, but he could easily see them all at his leisure behind a good horse in the space of several hours." All forms of transportation were

TERRACE PARKWAY WEST OF GRAND MOUNTAIN, THE SITE OF TODAY'S ENGER PARK, CA. 1893; THE STREAM SHOWN IS LIKELY MILLER CREEK.

[IMAGE: UMD MARTIN LIBRARY]

DULUTH PARKS VISIONARY WILLIAM K. ROGERS

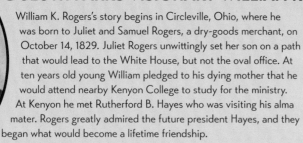

William K. Rogers's story begins in Circleville, Ohio, where he was born to Juliet and Samuel Rogers, a dry-goods merchant, on October 14, 1829. Juliet Rogers unwittingly set her son on a path that would lead to the White House, but not the oval office. At ten years old young William pledged to his dying mother that he would attend nearby Kenyon College to study for the ministry. At Kenyon he met Rutherford B. Hayes who was visiting his alma mater. Rogers greatly admired the future president Hayes, and they began what would become a lifetime friendship.

Rogers graduated Kenyon in 1848, but within two years poor health forced him to give up the ministry—the first of many times sickness would force him to relocate or change careers. His next stop was Boston, where he—like Hayes—earned a law degree at Harvard. He then returned to Ohio in 1854 where he joined Hayes and Richard M. Corwine to create the Cincinnati firm of Corwine, Hayes & Rogers.

While Hayes had faith in Rogers, he also recognized his weaknesses. Rogers biographer Mark Ryan points out that while Hayes counted Rogers among his closest companions, considering him a "true friend" whom he loved "better than most brothers are loved," Hayes also "fretted over the younger man's easy-going manner" and noted his dear friend's "extreme anxiety to do as others are pleased to have him." This mix of poor physical health and anxiety, Ryan explains, "hounded Rogers throughout his life." By 1856, Rogers had left Cincinnati "for his health." He ended up in Hastings, Minnesota, acquiring land and helping to settle the community. When Minnesota was granted statehood in 1858, Rogers became one of its first attorneys and a Hastings alderman. He returned to Ohio briefly in 1862 to wed Mary Lord Andrews; they returned to Hastings, and the following year Mary gave birth to William K. Rogers Jr.

Rogers's poor health had kept him out of service during the Civil War, but although he avoided combat he soon found himself in legal trouble after cosigning a questionable loan for his brother. A year after the war ended, William and Mary Rogers added daughter Phoebe to their growing family. About this same time they relocated to Chicago and invested in the Andrews Block; the building, near Lincoln Park, served as both the family's home and its chief source of income. In 1870 Hayes asked Rogers to visit the Head of the Lakes, where Jay Cooke was building his Northern Pacific Railroad, which would eventually reach the west coast at Puget Sound. Believing that real estate in the fledgling northern Minnesota community might prove a worthy investment, Rogers and Hayes together purchased 160 acres "along the hilltop" and two lots in downtown Duluth at First Avenue East and Superior Street.

Rogers returned to Duluth the following year to arrange for construction of the Hayes Block (pictured, facing page) on Superior Street, which the *Duluth Minnesotian* promised would be "a substantial ornament to Duluth." He and his family took up summer residence in Oneota, and he began hiring contractors. Work was well underway in October when Hayes learned that his Chicago home, the Andrews Block, had been destroyed in the Great Chicago Fire. His family was safe, but he had lost everything else, including his chief income stream. The

Minnesotian expressed mixed emotions when it learned the Rogers family would be forced to remain in Duluth for the winter: "We are glad, and yet sorry, to hear that his stay will be prolonged, and perhaps he will remain among us permanently." Hayes wasn't the only one who found Rogers likable. "Mr. Rogers is a fine lawyer," the newspaper gushed, "and a gentleman: and his continued residence amongst us as a citizen would be a valuable and acceptable acquisition." Rogers not only stayed, but in March 1872 he was elected to the Oneota Town Board of Supervisors and selected as a justice of the peace.

Later that month Hayes, now the former governor of Ohio, visited his friend in the Zenith City to see his building; Rogers's losses had forced Hayes to support the entire investment. The next year the Rogers family visited Ohio where their third child, Andrew, was born. This happy event was followed quickly by a national tragedy—the Financial Panic of 1873—which temporarily put a halt to all development in Duluth.

Rogers likely moved back to Ohio at this point, as there is no mention of him in Duluth newspapers until 1877, when he landed a job with his old friend Hayes, who had just been elected president of the United States. "Our half-adopted worthy townsman, William K. Rogers, Esq., whom everybody in Duluth is familiar with, has been appointed Private Secretary to President Hayes," the *Minnesotian* reported. "This appointment is as wise as was that of the election of the President himself." Presidential scholar Shirley Anne Warsaw writes that Hayes "reluctantly" chose Rogers after two other Ohioans declined the offer.

Hayes restricted Rogers' authority and his main role was "to serve as friend and cheerleader for presidential decisions rather than manage the internal workings of the White House." In Washington Rogers also busied himself answering the president's mail, and even this was interrupted by bouts with illnesses that, as Ryan explains, "could keep him prone for weeks at a time, sometimes unable to walk short distances or even sit up." His illnesses weren't enough to prevent him from fathering a child while working in the White House. He named the new baby boy Rutherford Hayes Rogers.

When Rogers's name was raised as a potential governor of Dakota Territory in 1880, Duluth's *Lake Superior News* eagerly got behind the idea, calling Rogers "a man of integrity, a lawyer of high ability, [and] a statesman rather than a politician." But Hayes instead appointed Jeremiah Ordway, who was later removed from office due to corruption. The next year, unemployed after Hayes left office, Rogers sought to fill a seat on the Illinois Court of Claims. The *Chicago Inter-Ocean* didn't like the idea: "While he may possess the abilities necessary for judgeship, he has failed to show them. That he is a good man no one doubts, but his warmest admirers would hesitate before claiming him eminent for legal learning." Apparently, outside of Hayes, Rogers's warmest admirers were all in Duluth.

After his duties at the White House ended, Rogers opened a Washington, D.C., law practice with Quinton Corwine, his former partner's son, but less than a year later he returned to Ohio. When his father-in-law died in 1886, Rogers took over management of his investments. That same year a booming Duluth regained its city charter and a new business, the Duluth State Bank, moved into the Hayes Block. Rogers was named the bank's president as well as one of its directors, and he soon relocated to Duluth. A month before he left for the Zenith City, Rogers wrote his old Duluth friend Judge O. P. Stearns, raving about the fine park system in Chicago. The letter was reprinted in the *Duluth Weekly Tribune* under the headline

"We Must Have Parks!" Once back in Duluth, Rogers proposed to the common council his idea for a park system, which, according to lore, he first envisioned while walking the city's hills in the early 1870s. The council adopted his plan in February 1888, and soon thereafter the state legislature created the Duluth Board of Park Commissioners. Duluth mayor John B. Sutphin selected Rogers as a member of the new park board; at the board's first meeting he was appointed president.

In 1889 Rogers again convinced Hayes to invest in Duluth, this time with the Highland Improvement Company, a development group whose plans for Duluth Heights included building the Seventh Avenue West Incline Railway and the Highland Park Tramway, which met at the top of the Incline near Rogers's newly constructed scenic boulevard.

In March 1891 the *Duluth News Tribune* again gushed with praise for Rogers: "Duluth will honor itself by trusting Mr. Rogers, for no city ever had a more loyal and capable promoter of its true progress in all directions, especially as regard to parks." But apparently Rogers and the first park board had too much enthusiasm and too much power (and not enough oversight) when it came to spending money. The state legislature soon revised and narrowed the board's powers, particularly those pertaining to finances. Three new board members were appointed. Rogers was the only member reappointed, but within a year he resigned from the park board, once again due to health concerns. He returned to Ohio and died there two years later.

A story from the 1916 *News Tribune* summed up Rogers's tenure as the park board's president: "Once upon a time the parks were run blindly. That was the Rogers regime. When they gave him a dollar he spent ten. When he was authorized to acquire a foot he took an acre. He drove his boulevard across city property if he could get it and slapped it across private property if he couldn't. He was so perniciously active that they wanted a park board and made him secretary [sic] so they could hold him down. Whereupon he began expanding the park system as though he owned the whole city."

Seventeen years after Rogers's death, the Democratic *Duluth Herald* got behind an idea suggested by park commissioner F. A. Patrick, who pointed out that the road, known popularly as just "the boulevard," needed an official name. Different segments of the road were known as Carriage Drive, Terrace Parkway, and Rogers Boulevard. Moreover, Patrick felt the word "boulevard" was a French derivative of "bulwark" and an "awkward, uncouth, mouthful, difficult to spell and pronounce." He preferred strong Anglo-Saxon words like "parkway, drive or road." The Republican *News Tribune* surprisingly agreed with the *Herald* and suggested "Rogers Drive." The *Herald* didn't like the idea and said it would reject any names that included Rogers's name, though it did concede that Rogers had "made the boulevard possible." The *News Tribune* retorted firmly, stating that "he did more than this. He located it, solved, himself, the engineering problems, superintended its building, hired the labor and forced the city, much against its will, to pay the bills."

Luther Mendenhall, who had replaced Rogers as park board president, put the matter to rest by producing a document dated December 27, 1894, which

read, "Resolved: That in recognition of the valuable services rendered the city by the late Col. [sic] Wm. K. Rogers, former President of this board, in planning and supervising the construction of the Parkway connecting the above system of parks, that the same be named Rogers Boulevard."

In 1921 local Rotary, Kiwanis, and Lions groups wanted to change the parkway's name to "Armistice Memorial Boulevard." Mayor Snively promised if that happened, "the name of W. K. Rogers shall not be wholly lost" and that he expected to have a memorial to Rogers erected somewhere along the boulevard. In 1929 the road was renamed Skyline Parkway, but to date the city has not erected a memorial to William K. Rogers. The Hayes Block, altered many times (and pictured below), still stands.

available for hire: a horse, a horse and buggy with driver, or a bicycle (known then as a wheel). The newspaper claimed that H. C. Kendall & Co. on Second Avenue West maintained the best equipped barns in the city of Duluth. "They have a large number of excellent and speedy horses and teams.... Careful and experienced drivers are in the employ of the firm and they are quite familiar with the beauties of the boulevard. A certain number of gentle and gaited horses for riding are also to be had for hire."

Prior to 1894 the road had no official name. The park board referred to it as the Terrace Parkway or the Boulevard Drive. Newspapers called it "the Boulevard." The Roe Atlas of 1890 labeled the eastern section Lake View Terrace, which included the circle drive around the Grand View Mountain, now the location of Enger Tower. West of the "mountain," the road was labeled Bay View Terrace. Finally, in December 1894, the park board members unanimously voted to call the road Rogers Boulevard in honor of William K. Rogers, who had died the previous year in his home state of Ohio.

The board also created two small lakes on the northeastern side of Grand View Mountain by damming Buckingham Creek. Called

Twin Lakes or Gem Lakes (and currently Twin Ponds), the parkway crossed over the creek between the two lakes.

The parkway brought welcome attention to the booming city. On July 7, 1895, the *News Tribune* wrote, "Today scarcely a tourist leaves Duluth without taking the ride and view on Rogers Boulevard and it already has almost a national fame. ...People who have traveled the world over will spend time and money to see Duluth's parks and driveways and the matchless views connected therewith."

The men of the park board at first seemed to view the park system as something that could be "completed." They intended to purchase the necessary land and build the parkway. However, they soon realized that this would be an ongoing project—that the system would continue to expand and the road would require ongoing maintenance. In 1900 they reported that it had already become necessary to replace the original wooden bridges on the road because "the condition of the old timber structures that had been in use for about ten years had become such as to make them unsafe for further traffic." In 1903 the old bridge at Fourth Avenue East was replaced—the last of the original wooden bridges.

TERRACE PARKWAY WINDS BETWEEN THE NEWLY CREATED GEM LAKES SOMETIME IN THE EARLY 1890S. KNOWN TODAY AS TWIN PONDS, THE PONDS WERE FORMED BY EXCAVATING BASINS AND DAMMING THE FLOW OF BUCKINGHAM CREEK.

[IMAGE: UMD MARTIN LIBRARY]

The Western Extension

Although the park board apparently did not have plans for extending the parkway beyond the original section, newspaper editorials soon began to predict that the road would someday reach all the way to the Dalles of the St. Louis River and along the North Shore of Lake Superior beyond the Lester River.

William K. Rogers had actually roughed out an extension of the road from Miller Creek to Fortieth Avenue West by 1890, using money he borrowed from Leonidas Merritt, a prominent West Duluth businessman. Most of this roadway remained in a "state of nature" according to board secretary Henry Helm, and in September 1903 members of the West Duluth Commercial Club began lobbying the park board to finish the western extension. In 1904 the board agreed to start work on extending the road from Lincoln Park to Fortieth Avenue West.

At the end of that year, secretary Helm reported that "a large amount of work was required...to put the roadway in passable condition from Twenty-eighth Avenue to the westerly terminus," the section that had been partially constructed fourteen years earlier. Three extensive ravines had been encountered, delaying work and adding to the cost. In addition, "in some instances the work of former years

was found to be a hindrance rather than a benefit; since it had become necessary to tear down before building up in a more permanent and lasting manner."

In 1905 the board acquired the right-of-way to extend the parkway from Fortieth Avenue West to approximately Sixty-fourth Avenue West. During 1906 and 1907, laborers worked on filling the deep ravine at Fortieth Avenue West, which the board reported was the slowest and most expensive part of the whole job. When hiring a contractor, the *News Tribune* reported that the park board hoped to find a large firm that would keep the men and teams on the project until it was completed, because "it is pointed out that the distance from the car lines is so great that the men employed on the job would consume much time daily in going and coming. If they camp on the spot much time will be saved."

Secretary Helm announced in October 1908 that the parkway extension to the Oneota Cemetery was complete, and the *News Tribune* reported that on October 17 "about sixty men and women, mostly from West Duluth, made a trip over the new boulevard extension yesterday afternoon in automobiles, tallyhos, and carriages.... The work was done at a cost of $4,000, including the purchase of the right of way."

A SURVEY CREW, CA. 1905, WORKING ON THE WESTERN EXTENSION OF ROGERS BOULEVARD.

[IMAGE: UMD MARTIN LIBRARY]

HILLTOP PARK AND THE SEVENTH AVENUE WEST INCLINE RAILWAY

William K. Rogers, Duluth's original park board president and the man who first envisioned today's Skyline Parkway, was also an investor in the Highland Improvement Company, which developed the Duluth Heights neighborhood. The company, whose investors included former U.S. president Rutherford B. Hayes, controlled over one thousand acres of land along today's Skyline Parkway adjacent to Duluth's downtown business district. The company had grand plans for this choice property, which it would develop into the first phase of the Duluth Heights neighborhood.

The Highland Improvement Company's prospectus, quoted in the March 22, 1889, *Duluth Daily News*, claimed that "skillful landscape artists and topographical engineers have platted [Duluth Heights] to conform with nature's suggestions and realize the most pleasing effects. Streets and avenues will wind about in delightful disregard of the points of the compass, and the lots and blocks upon which elegant houses are to be built will be of a size and shape which aid in giving to each home a distinctive yet harmonious individuality." It called the hillside parkway "one of the most wonderfully picturesque and unique boulevards in the world, with a view of transcendent beauty and grandeur."

To provide the future citizens of Duluth Heights access to their hilltop property, the company constructed an incline, or funicular, railway running from Superior Street five hundred feet up the hillside along Seventh Avenue West to the top of what was called Beacon Hill. Beyond that they built the Highland Park Tramway, a short-line streetcar system to serve Duluth Heights. The incline allowed those living in Duluth Heights to get to and from downtown, where they could transfer to streetcars to reach other portions of the city. Once complete, the Duluth Street Railway Company took over operation of both railways.

The Seventh Avenue West Incline consisted of two tracks built into a 2,975-foot superstructure. Two specially designed streetcars, each weighing twenty-nine tons, were pulled along cables by a hoisting engine driven by several four-hundred-horsepower boilers in a powerhouse located at the top of the railway. The cars—which carried both people and horses—were positioned on the track to provide counterbalance: when one car was at the top of the railway, the other was at the bottom. They passed at precisely the middle.

The incline opened in October 1891. Among the passengers in the first test ride was Luther Mendenhall, an investor in the Street Railway Company who had recently replaced William K. Rogers as president of the Duluth Board of Park Commissioners. Conductors called out "East car clear!" and "West car clear!" before the cars were engaged in operation. Both going up and coming down, the railway offered spectacular views of downtown, the harbor, Minnesota Point, and (after 1905) the aerial lift bridge. Along Superior Street the company built a small depot.

Duluthians immediately embraced the incline, many riding to the top just to enjoy the stunning view. The company decided that a pavilion adjacent to the powerhouse would bring even more people (and potential home owners) to the Heights. Designed by Oliver Traphagen and Francis Fitzpatrick, Duluth's premier architects at the time, the $20,000 Beacon Hill Pavilion made the top of the incline a destination. The large Shingle-style building measured one hundred by three hundred feet and featured a square tower. Twenty windows across the building's front façade offered views of the harbor.

The Beacon Hill Pavilion, called simply the Incline Pavilion by most, opened in July 1892, just in time to host a huge community Fourth of July celebration that featured $500 worth of fireworks. The street railway company reported that 14,716 passengers rode the incline that day. The pavilion quickly became the most fashionable place in Duluth. Open from May until late autumn, it included restaurants, an amusement center, and the Pavilion Theatre, which sat two-thousand spectators who paid twenty-five cents to see dramatic works and vaudeville acts "suitable for ladies and children as well." Diners enjoyed the Palm Garden, a restaurant operated by pavilion manager J. L. Travers. Orchestral and military bands provided music for dances, while the grounds were used for picnics and hot air balloon flights by Professor Baldwin, a "daring aeronaut" whose acts included a hot-air balloon.

By early 1893 the park board came under pressure to create a public park adjacent to the pavilion. An editorial in the *Duluth News Tribune* claimed that the spot was "already settled upon by the people as a pleasure and recreation ground, it is already half park...one thousand can pay the 5 cents each to take them to the Pavilion....The Pavilion park would be the rest and breathing spot of the whole city." The park board responded favorably. In January 1893 members voted to acquire four blocks of land located below the pavilion for a "hilltop park."

Unfortunately, due to the Financial Panic of 1893, the board was so short of money that in August 1893 it stopped all park improvements and laid off all but two men. In June 1895 the board members again resolved to create the hilltop park, but it wasn't until 1907 that they finally acquired just one of the four parcels—a square block between Sixth and Seventh Avenues West and Eighth and Ninth Streets. Duluthians would have their Hilltop Park, but by then the Beacon Hill Pavilion was already just a memory.

On May 28, 1901, a fire had broken out in the incline's powerhouse and quickly spread to the pavilion. The east car sat just outside the powerhouse while the west car waited at the bottom of the hill. The intense heat of the fire literally melted the rail system's cables, releasing the flaming east car, sending it racing down toward Superior Street. Luckily the Superior Street station attendants anticipated the situation and did as much as they could to get people, horses, and streetcars out of the way. The car smashed through the station, crossed Superior Street, and came to a halt in the rail yards near the Union Depot. The car was destroyed; amazingly no one was injured. The pavilion, heavily damaged in the fire, was never rebuilt. The incline was hastily reconfigured with just the west car operating and a counterweight taking the place of the east car. An electric engine replaced the steam boilers, but the railway did not receive a proper overhaul and new cars until 1911. The incline returned to two-car operation in 1912.

The Seventh Avenue West Incline served Duluth until Labor Day 1939, the last of Duluth's streetcar system to be dismantled and sold for scrap. The park board never added any more land to Hilltop Park, nor did they make any improvements to the area. After 1939 Hilltop Park was all but forgotten, remaining just a small unmarked parcel of public greenspace on the hillside above Skyline Parkway, seldom visited by anyone other than nearby residents.

A coaching party (also called a "tallyho"), ca. 1900, stopped along Rogers Boulevard to pose for a picture. (Photo by Hugh McKenzie.)

[Image: UMD Martin Library]

By this time many people owned automobiles, and the new road became such a popular place for driving that in July 1909 the board members decided it was necessary to regulate travel on the western extension. They adopted the following regulations: "1. All vehicles must be driven east to west, only. 2. Automobiles must not be driven at a speed greater than twelve miles per hour, and must slow down to six miles per hour or less at short turns or narrow spaces in the roadway where signs will be displayed for the guidance of all drivers."

In the spring of 1912, the park board began work on adding three more miles from Sixty-fourth Avenue West to the upper end of Fairmount Park near Thompson Hill. The *News Tribune* wrote enthusiastically, "This will give Duluth a boulevard driveway 18 miles long, the most picturesque highway in the world, whose scenic beauties are unequaled anywhere, and an attraction that should of itself bring thousands of visitors each summer."

Work on this final segment proceeded relatively fast, and by 1913 the work was completed. The park board's 1912 annual report indicated that $6,253.03 had been spent on construction of the western extension of the boulevard from Oneota Cemetery to Earl Street (now called Proctor Road).

A 1904 COACHING PARTY ON ROGERS BOULEVARD. THE FAINT VERTICAL LINES INDICATE WHERE THE IMAGE WAS CROPPED WHEN IT WAS USED TO CREATE THE LITHOGRAPHIC POSTCARD ON PAGE 27. (PHOTO BY THE DETROIT PUBLISHING CO.)

[IMAGE: LIBRARY OF CONGRESS]

The Eastern End of the Parkway

The park board made no effort to extend Rogers Boulevard east of Chester Creek. To access the eastern end of the parkway from London Road, a horse and buggy had to make the steep uphill climb on Fifteenth Avenue East and Chester Park Drive. (At this time there was no bridge across Chester Creek between Fourth Street and the parkway; the Eighth Street bridge over the creek was not built until 1920.)

In September 1906, a number of prominent residents of the East End, including future park commissioner F. A. Patrick, approached the board with a request to establish a new connection to the eastern end of the parkway that would provide access with an easier (less steep) grade. Patrick described the existing approach as "very hard on horses, as you know if you have ever ridden up it, and I know that I hesitate to drive my horses over it owing to the exceedingly hard character of the pull." The proposed connection followed Eighth Street west from Woodland Avenue, then up the "partially improved" Nineteenth Avenue approximately four blocks, "to a point where it was required to construct another stretch of new roadway for the remaining distance of some four hundred feet." The citizens offered to pay for the improvement, and the park board agreed to oversee the work. The new connection, known as the "cut-off," was completed in the summer of 1907. The new four hundred foot long stretch later became part of West Kent Road.

Snively Boulevard

Although the park board did not extend the parkway to the east, one ambitious citizen—Samuel Frisbee Snively—decided to do it on his own. In 1899, perhaps inspired by the work of the park board, Snively started building a scenic road at the far eastern end of the city. He later recounted that he "felt that the city should possess a right of way along this stream [Amity Creek], so varied in interest and scenery...to a junction with the contemplated easterly extension of the Rogers boulevard."

Snively's road began at the junction of Lester Park's carriage paths—Oriental and Occidental boulevards—and followed Amity Creek up the hill for about two-and-a-half miles to his farm. Snively walked the hillside to find the most scenic route, "without regard to the ease of construction," as he later explained. He contacted landowners along his proposed path and convinced many of them to donate the strip of land he needed for the right-of-way, then he asked those same landowners to donate money for road construction. He managed to raise $1,200 from landowners, $400 from the Lakeside Land Company, and a pledge of $1,500 from the city.

Snively described the road as very costly and difficult to build. Many trees and stumps had to be removed, and the stream crossings required long, high bridges over Amity Creek. Snively spent over $7,000 of his own in addition to what had been contributed by other sources. After building about half the length of the planned roadway, he ran out of money and launched a new fundraising effort.

AN UNIDENTIFIED WOMAN DRIVES A HORSE AND CARRIAGE OVER ONE OF THE RUSTIC BRIDGES ALONG SNIVELY BOULEVARD, CA. 1909. TODAY THE DRIVE IS KNOWN AS SEVEN BRIDGES ROAD.

[IMAGE: UMD MARTIN LIBRARY]

SAMUEL FRISBEE SNIVELY: MAYOR, ROAD BUILDER, LOVER OF PARKS

When Samuel Frisbee Snively, Duluth's longest-serving mayor, died in 1952, the *Duluth Herald* reported that "friends often said of him that no man ever had a greater love for his city than Mr. Snively." As a result of his dedication to Duluth, love of nature, and passion for road building, Sam Snively left behind a rich legacy of parks and boulevards.

Snively was born November 14, 1859, on a farm in the Cumberland Valley of Pennsylvania. His parents, Jacob Snively and Margaret Snyder, both came from families that had lived in Pennsylvania since the time of William Penn. In fact, Snively's ancestors, who worked for Penn as surveyors, received two entire counties when Penn died in 1718. By the time Sam Snively was born, most of the land had become small family farms, like his father's. Snively's own brief sketch of his parents does a fine job of describing Snively himself: "My mother was a woman of restless energy, a lover of all that was grand and beautiful in nature and an influential representative of that which was most ennobling and uplifting in life; my father being of rather an easy-going nature, always jovial and possessing a trait of subtle humor that quickly made friends of all with whom he came in contact."

Snively attended Dickinson University, earning his bachelor's degree in 1882. He stayed on to earn his master's degree while gaining some teaching experience, but within a year he opted for a career in law. In Philadelphia he received on-the-job training in the law offices of Benjamin Harris Brewster, who at the time was the attorney general of the United States; he also attended classes at the University of Philadelphia. By 1885 he had been admitted to the Philadelphia bar.

Snively left Philadelphia to seek his fortune farther west, arriving in the Zenith City on March 21, 1886. He would later tell friends he had just fifteen dollars in his pocket and was wearing two sets of long underwear in anticipation of Duluth's reputed weather (it was a mild day, and he spent his first few minutes in town trying to remove one layer of long johns). Another favorite tale displayed Snively's tenacity. During his first day in a Duluth courtroom, Snively lost a case to a veteran attorney who mocked his inexperience. Undaunted, the young lawyer returned to court that afternoon, made a counterclaim, and won. Snively later told the *Herald* that his payment, a twenty dollar gold piece, was "the start of his first fortune."

Snively was soon joined by Charles P. Craig, a college chum and fellow Philadelphia lawyer. Together they established Snively & Craig and set up practice in Duluth's Metropolitan Block. Business must have been good, as the following year they moved into the third floor of the brand new Duluth National Bank, a prominent address for such a young firm. On their wall hung a portrait of Attorney General Brewster—sent to them by Brewster himself. Besides practicing law, both men also invested in real estate, purchasing property in the developing communities of Lakeside and Lester Park.

Newspapers would later describe Snively as a "plunger" when it came to business, meaning that he approached his decisions with a certain recklessness, plunging in feet first. One move that must have baffled his friends came when the lifelong Republican purchased an interest in the Democratic-leaning *Herald* in 1892. Snively also invested in iron mining, incorporating

the Snively Iron Mining Company in April 1893. It was terrible timing. A month later the nation was struck by the Financial Panic of 1893, and suddenly no one was buying iron ore or real estate. At the same time, he and Craig ended their law partnership. "We somehow got separated in the financial massacre of 1893," Snively would later recall.

Snively stayed in Duluth until 1898, participating heavily in the St. Louis County Republican Club, which he chaired or presided over for several terms. He also remained active in real estate, becoming a director of the East Superior Development Company. A trip to the Pacific Northwest in 1898, however, took him away from Duluth. Upon his return the *Duluth News Tribune* reported on his travels, with Snively announcing, "I am going back to Seattle, certainly, and probably to Alaska."

Snively indeed ended up in Alaska, but the venture did not reward him as he had expected. He and several companions searched the Klondike for gold but found nothing. (Some say he found a great deal, but was swindled out of it in Nome.) Their return walk to Juneau included crossing seventy miles of glacier while encountering giant clouds of mosquitoes. Once in Juneau, he and his friends found brief work unloading steel from a freighter, all the while verbally abused by one of the ship's mates who demanded they work faster. When finished, the group stowed away on the same vessel to get back to Seattle and upon arrival gave their former taskmaster "the beating of his swashbuckling life." In Seattle Snively was forced to pawn his watch to pay for lodging while he waited for friends to wire money from Duluth for his return trip. Back when saloons gave away free lunch with the purchase of a beer, Snively took to frequenting drinking establishments to sneak a bite to eat.

He managed to make it back to Duluth in 1900 where, according to Snively himself, he "drifted into the farm land development business" with Jed Washburn and John G. Williams. Together they purchased over 200,000 acres of surplus land from Northern Pacific Railway, and Snively took charge of selling the land. At about the same time he bought a farm for himself, approximately 1,200 acres of property near Jean Duluth Road and Amity Creek. He may have been inspired to go into farming by his old law partner, as Craig was by this time heavily involved in the local agricultural movement, part owner of the four-thousand-acre Jean Duluth Stock Farm and promoter of the local Homecroft movement. Snively built a small dairy farm on his land, including a house and barn made of field stones cleared from the property; the barn was thought to be the largest in northern Minnesota at the time. According to researcher Mike Bayer, Snively maintained about 150 head of Jersey and Guernsey cows on the farm.

It was during this time that Snively built Seven Bridges Road (originally called Snively Boulevard or Snively Road), which followed Amity Creek uphill from Superior Street to his farm. The *News Tribune* characterized the project as bordering on reckless: "He spent almost every cent he had on the venture...most of the money [spent building] was his own." When construction was complete, Snively gave his road to the city. He also purchased 150,000 acres along the south shore of Lake Superior between Superior and Bayfield, Wisconsin, that he helped develop into today's Highway 2. Most of his money, however, went into his projects in Duluth.

One of the great ironies of Snively's life is that although he is considered a great road builder, he never learned to drive. According to Snively biographer Mark Ryan, "he'd prefer to walk, but when driving was necessary he'd enlist others to chauffeur him to and from boulevard projects and other city business.... This fear was probably compounded by Snively's involvement in several auto accidents, both as a pedestrian and a passenger, and by the fact that he was blind in one eye."

Snively's time on the farm ended when the 1918 Cloquet Fire tore through his property, leaving nothing behind but the stone house. Snively moved into the city, just east of downtown near Thirteenth Avenue East and Second Street, and later sold his farm to Albert M. Marshall of Duluth's Marshall-Wells Hardware, then the largest hardware distributor in the world.

In 1919 Snively plunged into politics as the first person to throw his hat in the ring to fill one of two open city commissioner seats. Snively lost, but his friend Clarence Magney was elected mayor. Magney resigned in the fall of 1920 to become a district court judge, and former mayor Trevanion Hugo served out his term. Hugo had no desire to run for reelection in 1921, so Snively became the Republican candidate. He won the 1921 mayoral election and was reelected in 1925, 1929, and 1933. "In each of the elections," the News Tribune reported, "he gained a greater majority than in each preceding contest."

The job of mayor suited Snively well. Under Duluth's commission form of government (1913 to 1956), the mayor served as commissioner of public affairs, which included responsibility for the city's parks. By all accounts he spent most of his energy on this aspect of the job, and Snively's efforts on behalf of Duluth's parks and boulevards are outlined throughout this book. In other aspects of politics, Snively could be unorthodox. During the 1928 debate over converting Duluth's aerial transfer bridge into a lift bridge, Snively twice abruptly adjourned council meetings when he felt the issue had reached a deadlock—once by simply walking out of a meeting.

Fairmount Park became one of Mayor Snively's favorite spots. While he never married, Snively—called "Duluth's grand old man" by the News Tribune—had a great affection for children, and during the Depression he hosted an annual day at the zoo in Fairmount Park for the city's orphans. Thanks to public contributions of food, transportation, and services, the mayor was able to take over the zoo for a day and treat as many as five hundred children from the city's orphanages to an afternoon of fun. The News Tribune called these events one of Snively's "happiest days of the year" and reported that he "loved to prepare their food and take a troupe of them for an inspection tour of the zoo animals."

Snively was seventy-eight years old when he lost the 1937 mayoral election to Rudy Berghult. Over 350 guests honored Snively with a testimonial dinner at the Hotel Duluth during which Magney stated that Snively "retires with a clear conscience—no one in sixteen years has accused him of dishonesty; no one has ever thought it of him; no inference has ever been given of it." Snively himself declared that "nothing in a political nature could part me with the desire to help build this city." He then promised to help Berghult "in every way."

The next year Snively became the fourteenth inductee in the Duluth Hall of Fame and Berghult tried to get Snively back to work on Duluth's parks by creating a "Department of Boulevards" and making Snively its superintendent. The measure did not pass, but a similar resolution in 1941 succeeded, and at age eighty-two Snively went back to work at city hall, assisted by longtime-secretery Alta Marie Johnson (pictured). It is not clear when he gave up his office.

Snively eventually moved in with his niece Zelda Overland and her husband William at their modest home in Duluth's East Hillside neighborhood. The ex-mayor was particularly proud of his grandnephew, Douglas Snively Overland. A photo of the pair taken on Snively's ninetieth

birthday shows them playing chess. Snively died three years later on November 6, 1952, in the Overland home.

In 1923 he wrote a simple statement that remained true for the rest of his days: "My life here in Duluth, like that of many of my contemporaries, has had its success and its disappointments, but always [has been] lived in support of measures I believe designed for the common good of this city and its people." A fairly modest statement for a man who accomplished so much. His grave in Hermantown's Sunrise Memorial Cemetery contains an epitaph that is a kinder, more accurate version of the News Tribune's name for Snively: "Duluth's Grand Old Dad."

In 1934 a bandstand/pavilion was constructed in Lincoln Park, and the Swedish American League had a plaque made in honor of Snively that was affixed to the building. It read in part, "Mayor S. F. Snively / Reciprocated Popular Affection of Noble Ideas / Promoted Parks, Blvds, Libraries / Long Time Mayor." The plaque is gone, and while just a faint concrete outline of Snively's face can be seen on the pavilion, his legacy is visible in just about every Duluth park and parkway.

— PHOTO: M. RYAN COLLECTION —

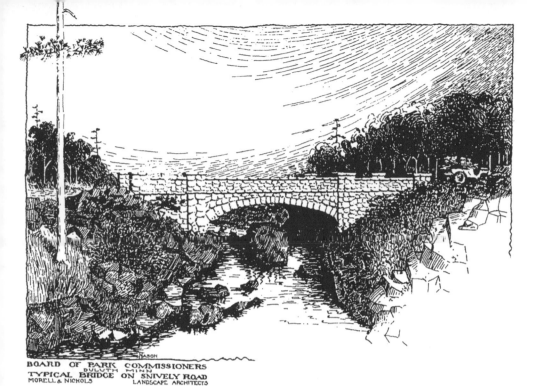

BOARD OF PARK COMMISSIONERS
DULUTH MINN
TYPICAL BRIDGE ON SNIVELY ROAD
MORELL & NICHOLS   LANDSCAPE ARCHITECTS

LESTER PARK ABOUNDS WITH BEAUTY SPOTS

He convinced a number of prominent Duluthians, including Chester Congdon, G. G. Hartley, F. A. Patrick, and park board president Luther Mendenhall, to contribute $50 each. This additional funding made it possible for him to complete construction as far as Jean Duluth Road.

Snively opened his road for public use in 1901 and continued to seek financial support from every source he could think of to extend it. In 1903, acknowledging the importance of the road, which "affords access to the city...from a large suburban and farming country which is rapidly building up," Duluth's common council pledged to reimburse Snively $1,000, but not until there was enough money in the city's permanent improvement fund. The county board promised an additional $750. How he used this money is not clear; he apparently continued construction west from Jean Duluth Road to Vermilion Road north of Park Hill Cemetery.

Snively succeeded in building his road, but he struggled to maintain it. The wooden bridges deteriorated after a few years, leaving the road unsafe for vehicles. Editorials in the *News Tribune* soon began calling on the city to fix the road, but the resources were not available.

In July 1909 Snively approached the park board and promised to find investors to purchase $10,000 of a proposed park bond issue "provided proceeds of same would be expended for the restoration of the Snively Road." As a result, in 1910 the park board was given control of Snively Road with the intent to turn it into a boulevard that would eventually be connected to the parkway system. The board appointed Snively to work with an engineer to refine the right-of-way and acquire additional land along the route that was suitable for dedication as a park. In May 1910, Snively reported to the board that "he had influenced several abutting owners to offer to dedicate lands in aid of proposed extension of Snively Road and Parkway."

TOP: A sketch by Morell & Nichols, commissioned by Duluth's Board of Park Commissioners, of a design for the stone arch bridges of Snively Boulevard, today's Seven Bridges Road.
[IMAGE: M. RYAN COLLECTION]

BOTTOM: Lithographic postcard made between 1915 and 1925, mislabelled as a scene in Lester Park, of one of the stone arch bridges built along Seven Bridges Road.
[IMAGE: ZENITH CITY PRESS]

The park board hired the landscaping firm of Morell & Nichols to design stone arch bridges to replace the old wooden structures. Local stonemasons constructed the bridges, which they faced with stone collected from the creek or quarried from nearby outcrops. Special pink granite purchased from quarries in St. Cloud, Minnesota, topped the bridge walls and piers.

The newly rebuilt Snively Boulevard, later renamed Seven Bridges Road, opened in July 1912 with the announcement that "while no formalities are to be observed today in connection with the opening to traffic the public is urged by members of the park board to drive over the road and enjoy its likeness to a trip through wonderland."

The following year saw the end of the Duluth Board of Park Commissioners after citizens approved a major change to the city charter and adopted a commission form of government, which placed five commissioners in charge of five city departments. The new charter eliminated all citizen boards and shifted responsibility for the parks to the mayor as commissioner of public affairs. William Prince, first mayor under the new charter, announced that he supported the park system but he intended to abandon "the policy of spending thousands upon thousands of dollars for roadways." Mayor Prince chose instead to focus his efforts on creating playgrounds. During Prince's administration, from 1913 to 1917, the parkway was maintained but not expanded.

After the loss of the park board, Snively became the primary supporter of the city's parkway. As the *News Tribune* later explained, "Although the winding road atop the hill overlooking Duluth had been laid out before Mr. Snively came into public office, he was largely instrumental in its very existence as a private citizen. But it was not until he was elected mayor that the present Skyline parkway, which is commonly called the boulevard, began to take on its scenic beauty. Under Mr. Snively's personal direction this boulevard was extended westerly and easterly," finally reaching a length of more than twenty-five miles.

ONE OF THE BRIDGES ALONG SNIVELY BOULEVARD, DATE UNKNOWN. (PHOTO BY HUGH MCKENZIE.)
[IMAGE: T. KASPER COLLECTION]

Bardon's Peak Boulevard

When Sam Snively took over as Duluth's mayor in 1921, he had a grand vision for "a combined park and boulevard system" that included: 1) extending and connecting the boulevards from Jay Cooke State Park along the brow of the hill all the way to Lester Park and Brighton Beach; 2) creating parks along the ravines and creek basins; and 3) linking the parks together by the boulevard and building driveways through the parks from the hillside down to the lake. He intended that the parkway would be part of a "great interstate and international highway" leading from the Mississippi Valley through Duluth and along the lakeshore to Canada.

Snively went to work immediately to make his vision a reality. His first project was to carry on the work that one of his predecessors, Mayor Clarence Magney, had started. In 1920 Magney had begun to work on connecting the parkway to the newly created Jay Cooke State Park. He planned to extend the road across the western hillside from Thompson Hill to Beck's Road and then south along Mission Creek to the St. Louis River and the state park. Magney took the first steps to acquire land for the road, but he resigned as mayor in late 1920 to become a district court judge. (Trevanion Hugo, who served as Duluth's mayor from 1900 to 1904, finished Magney's mayoral term before Snively took office; see chapter 14, "Undeveloped Parks," for more about Magney.)

In May 1921, Snively completed the purchase of 330 acres surrounding a high rocky outcrop overlooking Morgan Park, Smithville, Gary, and New Duluth. The natural landmark was known

as Bardon's Peak for Superior, Wisconsin, pioneer James Bardon, who once owned the land. Snively named the new park land after Magney in recognition of his contributions to the Duluth park system, and went to work building the road. Bardon's Peak Boulevard, which Snively opened to traffic in 1925, included an impressive overlook at Bardon's Peak with dramatic views of Lake Superior and the St. Louis River estuary. The overlook was outlined by a rough stone wall built of the same type of local rock as the picturesque bridge over Stewart Creek. In 1927, on the east side of the Stewart Creek bridge, the city built a memorial to Sam Snively. It consisted of a small reflecting pool surrounded by flagstones; a small stream of water cascaded over a rough stone wall into the reflecting pool (see page 195 for a photograph of the memorial).

Mission Creek Boulevard

Snively also purchased several hundred acres of forested land along Mission Creek near Fond du Lac, where he planned to construct the final leg of the linking road to the state park. City engineers built the road along Mission Creek in the summer of 1926. The Mission Creek Boulevard included five stone bridges, similar in design to those on Snively Boulevard at the eastern end of the city, and two railroad bridges built by the Northern Pacific and the Duluth, Missabe & Northern railroads. Snively also raised the funds and personally helped to build a branch road into Fond du Lac he had promised the neighborhood's residents, who complained that the parkway bypassed their community. Thanks to his efforts, the Mission Creek

SNOW COVERS STEWART CREEK BRIDGE ALONG BARDON'S PEAK BOULEVARD, NOW WEST SKYLINE PARKWAY, IN 1927. (PHOTO BY F. R. PAINE.)

[IMAGE: UMD MARTIN LIBRARY]

Boulevard, including the branch road, was completed by the fall of 1927. On November 5 residents of Fond du Lac hosted an opening ceremony at the city nursery; Judge Magney gave a short speech to celebrate the occasion, which was attended by several hundred people. (More about Mission Creek Boulevard can be found in chapter 11, "Fond du Lac Park.")

At the same time, laborers working for Duluth contractor C. R. McLean were building the state road along the St. Louis River that led to Jay Cooke State Park. When their work was finished in January 1928, the link was complete. Automobiles could travel on Duluth's scenic parkway from the St. Louis River to the North Shore of Lake Superior.

At this time, each segment of the parkway was known by a different name—Rogers Boulevard for the oldest segment, Amity Creek or Snively Boulevard for the eastern segment, and the very awkward Bardon's Peak–Mission Creek–Fond du Lac–Jay Cooke State Park Boulevard for the newest segment.

Once the state road to Jay Cooke Park opened, Mayor Snively declared the parkway complete, and in July 1929, he and the *News Tribune* sponsored a contest to christen the entire length of the scenic drive with one new name. The mayor received over 3,500 entries, and six people suggested the winning name of "Skyline Parkway." The judges voted unanimously to split the prize of $25 among the six winners: Jennie Kesty of Cloquet; H. A. Sanders of Two Harbors; and Frances George, Ella Hatch, M. E. Thorpe, and George Baxter of Duluth. They each received an award of $5, donated by the *News Tribune*. Road signs designed by Duluth artist N. A. Long, featuring a pine tree silhouetted against the full moon, were installed along the entire length of the parkway.

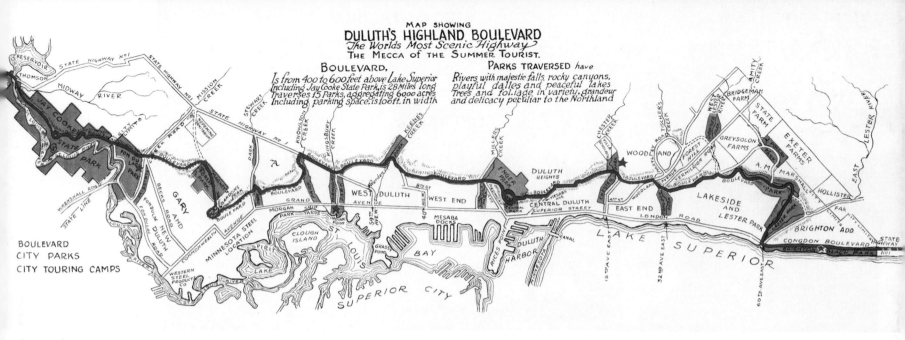

MAP SHOWING
DULUTH'S HIGHLAND BOULEVARD
The Worlds Most Scenic Highway
THE MECCA OF THE SUMMER TOURIST.

BOULEVARD.
Is from 400 to 600 feet above Lake Superior
Including Jay Cooke State Park, is 28 Miles long
Traverses 15 Parks, aggregating 6000 acres
Including parking space, is 100 ft. in width

PARKS TRAVERSED have
Rivers with majestic falls, rocky canyons,
playful dalles and peaceful lakes
Trees and foliage in variety, grandeur
and delicacy peculiar to the Northland

BOULEVARD
CITY PARKS
CITY TOURING CAMPS

At last, on August 3, 1929, "beneath the towering pines of Jay Cooke park, where only 15 years ago a wood-trodden trail existed, a gathering of state, county, and municipal officials and civic leaders... dedicated the driveway leading from the boulevard system of Duluth to the park." The *News Tribune* reported that Otto Swanstrom, president of the Minnesota Good Roads Association and founder of Duluth's Diamond Tools, headed the auto caravan that left city hall at eleven in the morning to drive over the new road for the formal ceremony at Jay Cooke State Park. Judge Magney, one of the pioneers in the movement to create the state park, was the principal speaker. Other speakers included Lieutenant Governor Charles E. Adams and Mayor Snively. Minneapolis Mayor W. F. Kunze and members of the Minneapolis Park Board also attended the ceremony that officially opened Skyline Parkway.

"Complete"—But Not Finished

Although Mayor Snively declared the parkway to be "complete" in 1929, he continued to build roads as part of his grand vision for a combined park and boulevard system. Residents of the western part of the city wanted a connection to Skyline Parkway, and in 1929 Snively began assembling land for a road that would run west from Fairmount Park (home of the municipal zoo), then uphill along the Knowlton

Creek valley to join the main parkway. Built during the Depression, the road project served partly as an unemployment relief measure.

According to the park department annual report, Snively personally raised money for the construction, aided by an appropriation from the council. The mayor also personally supervised the work and "deserves a great deal of credit for his energy in putting this project through." Snively opened the Knowlton Creek Boulevard in 1931, creating an important link between Fairmount Park and the western section of the parkway near what later became the Spirit Mountain Recreation Area. A *News Tribune* article from December 1932 called it "a new scenic entrance to Duluth." Motorists coming into town over Bardon's Peak could now follow the new road downhill to Grand Avenue and West Duluth.

Despite his love of road building, Snively never satisfactorily filled the eastern gap between Chester Park and Snively Boulevard. Park superintendent Rodney Paine wrote in his 1928 annual report, "At the east, the boulevard has no well defined beginning or end. There is no fitting approach and there is no boulevard at all between Fifteenth Avenue East and the Snively Boulevard.... Owing to the fact that the district just east of Fifteenth Avenue has been platted and built up with no provision for any boulevard connection the problem is a difficult one."

THIS STYLIZED MAP CALLING TODAY'S SKYLINE PARKWAY "HIGHLAND BOULEVARD" WAS PRODUCED IN THE 1920S BY THE DULUTH CHAMBER OF COMMERCE AND THE MAYOR'S OFFICE, DESIGNED TO BE HANDED OUT AT DULUTH'S AUTOTOURIST CAMPS. NOTE THAT IT INCLUDES NONEXISTENT UNNAMED PARKS ALONG STEWART CREEK AND KNOWLTON CREEK AS WELL AS A MUNICIPAL TOURING CAMP IN FOND DU LAC THAT WAS NEVER BUILT, PERHAPS INDICATIONS OF SAMUEL SNIVELY'S AND/OR F. RODNEY PAINE'S UNREALIZED VISION FOR THE FUTURE OF DULUTH'S PARKS.

[IMAGE: UMD MARTIN LIBRARY]

Over the years, the city designated various connecting routes to guide motorists through this gap. During the 1920s, the favored route was from the east side of Chester Creek, down Kent Road to Eighth Street, then along Vermilion Road to Tischer Creek (at the north end of Congdon Park), then on Lakeview Drive to Snively Road. In fact, a map produced by the city in 1929 shows this route as the path of Skyline Parkway. Later signs were installed that led those cruising Skyline to take Kent Road to Woodland Avenue, then Woodland north to Snively Road. (Traffic in 2016 is routed from Kent Road, up Nineteenth Avenue East, around the University of Minnesota Duluth campus on St. Marie Street, and then along Woodland Avenue to Snively Road.)

In 1934 Snively Boulevard on the eastern end of the city followed Amity Creek from Lester Park to Jean Duluth Road. Because a high ridge hid the road from Lake Superior, it lacked the scenic views that made Skyline Parkway famous. Near the end of that year, Mayor Snively announced his plan to construct a new road that would follow the highest part of the ridge from Amity Creek to Morley Heights, providing spectacular views of Lake Superior and the neighborhoods of Lakeside and Lester Park. According to the *News Tribune,* "Mayor Snively has had this parkway in mind for a great many years and it is through his efforts that the donations of necessary right-of-ways were obtained, surveys completed and the work on the road started. ...The development of the natural beauties of this easterly section of the city has been the life work of Mayor Snively."

Once again, Snively personally supervised construction. WPA crews completed rough grading on about half of the road in 1936, but their work was suspended in June 1937 when they were called away to work on the Civic Center in downtown Duluth. They resumed work on the parkway in November, but according to historian Mark Ryan, "finishing touches were delayed until the summer of 1939." By that time Sam Snively was no longer mayor of Duluth, but his days of working on the parkway were not over. Four years after his final term as mayor ended, the Duluth City Council created a Department of Public Boulevards and appointed Snively as Superintendent of Boulevards.

Snively's final road segment later became known as Hawk Ridge, because the area had always been a place where large numbers of hawks could be observed as they migrated south each fall. Local hunters had often used the birds for target practice. To protect the migrating birds, in 1950 members of the Duluth Bird Club (now the Duluth Audubon Society) successfully petitioned the city to enforce the prohibition against shooting within the city limits.

The Bird Club organized the first "hawk watch" in 1951, and twenty years later, in 1972, the Duluth Audubon Society, with a loan from the Minnesota Chapter of The Nature Conservancy, donated funds to the City of Duluth to purchase the highest part of the ridge and create a nature reserve. The city acquired approximately 250 adjacent acres in 1973 to serve as a buffer area. Under a trust agreement with the city, the Hawk Ridge Bird Observatory now manages the 365-acre reserve, which is open to the public for study and enjoyment. Each fall thousands of people gather on Skyline Parkway at Hawk Ridge to see this amazing migration and learn more about the lives of raptors.

Skyline Parkway in the Twenty-first Century

Following the Snively era, maintenance of Skyline Parkway was inconsistent, depending on the priorities of whomever held the mayor's office. Mission Creek Boulevard was permanently closed in 1958 because of serious erosion following a major rainstorm, cutting off that all-important link to Fond du Lac and Jay Cooke State Park. When the Spirit Mountain Recreation Area was constructed in the 1970s, a section of the parkway immediately south of Interstate 35 was moved

higher on the hillside to accommodate the ski hill. The city abandoned the Knowlton Creek Boulevard at the same time, turning the old roadbed into a hiking trail.

These changes triggered a renewal of public interest in the historic roadway, and in 1988 the Stewart Creek bridge on the western hillside was added to the National Register of Historic Places. In 1995 the Duluth Heritage Preservation Commission, using funds made available by the National Park Service through the Minnesota Historical Society, hired consultants to conduct a study of the historical significance of the parkway system. Historian Patrick Nunnally completed his report, "A Historic Landscape Evaluation Study," in 1997, and this detailed study provided the necessary information for Jill Fisher of the city planning department to nominate Skyline Parkway as a State Scenic

Byway. In 1998 the byway designation was approved, making the road eligible for funding from various state and federal sources.

The West Skyline Planning and Preservation Alliance, a grassroots citizen advocacy group, formed in 1999 to bring attention to the need for cleanup and maintenance on the western section of the parkway. A few years later the group expanded their mission to include the entire length of the road and changed their name to the Skyline Planning and Preservation Alliance (SPPA). For the next decade, members of the SPPA sponsored annual cleanup days at Bardon's Peak, led hikes through parks located along the corridor, participated in planning sessions, lobbied for increased maintenance, and supported the city's efforts to obtain grant funding for improvements to the parkway.

A GREYHOUND BUS STOPPED ALONG WEST SKYLINE PARKWAY, LIKELY AT THE SCENIC OVERLOOK AT THOMPSON HILL, WHICH PROVIDES AN IMPRESSIVE VIEW OF CLOUGH ISLAND IN THE ST. LOUIS RIVER, CA. 1930S.

[IMAGE: UMD MARTIN LIBRARY]

The bridges on Seven Bridges Road were rebuilt over a period of eleven years, from 1996 to 2007. With the assistance of a Citizens' Task Force, URS Corporation cooperated with the city to prepare a Corridor Management Plan, which was completed in 2003 and updated in 2015. New wayfinding signs were installed along the entire route in 2011, and much of the roadway was resurfaced. The Snively Memorial and the Stewart Creek Bridge were rehabilitated by the City of Duluth in 2012 to 2013.

One of the most consistent complaints over the years has been the lack of vegetation maintenance along the parkway, as trees continue to grow tall on the lower side of the road, blocking the once-spectacular views. The 2003 Skyline Parkway Corridor Management Plan called for the creation and implementation of a vegetation management plan. Following continued lobbying by citizens and SPPA members, along with support from city councilors Sharla Gardner and Joel Sipress, in 2015 the city administration formed a task force to address this issue. As a result, in early 2016 the administration hired SAS + Associates Landscape Architects and Levy Tree Care to prepare a plan to manage vegetation along the parkway. Work was scheduled to begin in summer 2016.

One hundred and twenty-five years after the original section of Rogers Boulevard was built, Skyline Parkway—the backbone of Duluth's park system, is once again recognized as one of Duluth's most unique and valuable resources.

3. Lincoln Park

'So Rich in Beauty'

Duluth's park board members spent much of their time, energy, and resources from 1889 to 1913 creating the parkway. Lincoln Park and Chester Park formed the bookends of the scenic roadway and were the first parks created intentionally by the park board.

To establish the western end of the parkway, in 1889 the board started purchasing land along Miller Creek between Twenty-fifth and Twenty-sixth Avenues West. According to Duluth historian Heidi Bakk-Hansen, the creek was named for pioneer Robert P. Miller, a native of Pennsylvania who came here in the late 1850s and built a cabin and small farm on the east side of the stream. Miller left his farm to fight for the Union in the Civil War. He never returned to Duluth, as he died from dysentery in Vicksburg on June 21, 1864. Newspaper stories from the 1890s mention "the ruins of an old mill with still and silent water wheel," within the park, but it is not known if this was built by Robert Miller.

The board referred to the area as "Millers Creek Park" and sometimes as "Cascade Park" (creating confusion with Cascade Square in downtown Duluth) until 1894 when they officially named it "Lincoln Park." The board members gave no reason for the choice of name. Perhaps they were copying their rival city, Chicago, which already had a Lincoln Park, named for Abraham Lincoln, who had been assassinated in 1865. At the same time they changed the name of Chester Park to Garfield Park, after President James Garfield, assassinated in 1881. Dozens of American cities have (or once had) parks named in honor of these fallen presidents.

Lincoln Park Takes Shape

Minimal work was required to make Lincoln Park an appealing place for families to spend time. In the words of the board, "the ravine is so rich in beauty that little had to be done in the way of formal treatment." The board ordered the construction of rustic benches, a small

LITHOGRAPHIC POSTCARD, CA. 1905, SHOWING MILLER CREEK FLOWING THROUGH LINCOLN PARK.

[IMAGE: ZENITH CITY PRESS]

pavilion, sidewalks, bridges, ponds, and Lincoln Park Drive, a drive-way along Miller Creek from Third Street up the hill to Sixth Street. On July 4, 1896, the board formally dedicated Lincoln Park during what the *Duluth News Tribune* described as a "grand celebration of the National Birthday." Festivities included music by the West End Band and Glee Club, a New England dinner served by "the ladies," and a variety of speakers.

Just one year later a major storm on July 3 damaged most of the city's parks, including Lincoln, where water from the rain-swollen Miller Creek washed away bridges and embankments and strong winds blew over trees. The board had planned a huge Independence Day celebration for Lincoln Park, so Secretary Henry Helm hired every man he could find to help with clean up. The *News Tribune* re-ported that "the park looked like a beehive along toward night, with men working everywhere." They succeeded in getting Lincoln Park re-stored well enough for the July 4 celebration to take place as planned.

Located in the heavily populated West End and easily accessible by street car, Lincoln Park quickly became a favorite place for family picnics and outings. Newspapers soon began to report that "every pleasant day the park is almost crowded with ladies and children who take their lunches and spend hours in the favored retreat. On Sundays thousands visit the spot if only for the pleasure of a brief stroll through the secluded paths and to listen to the music of the stream as it tears over the rocks on its way to the great Gitchi Gummee."

In the winter of 1896, the park became home to one of the first public skating rinks in the city when the park board agreed to flood about an acre of land adjacent to the creek and to temporarily convert the pavilion into a warming house for skaters. But for the most part, Lincoln Park remained in a relatively wild state; in the words of the *News Tribune*, it was "almost as nature left it."

Unfortunately young people soon found Lincoln Park to be a convenient place to congregate late at night. Newspaper reports of the arrest of young hoodlums, drunks, and trespassers became all too common. As the park system grew and public use increased, the

board members realized they needed to hire men to watch over the parks. David Vaugh was sworn in as Lincoln Park's first park policeman in 1890; by 1902, Civil War veteran and former city alderman Ambrose Cox filled the position. Cox also built a pavilion on land he owned adjacent to the west side of Lincoln Park on Fifth Street, between Twenty-sixth and Twenty-seventh Avenues West, and operated it as a dance hall.

Sadly, Cox was not long on the job. In November two workmen were repairing a sewer at Twenty-seventh Avenue West and needed help to shift a pipe. Cox descended into the pit to help and was quickly overcome by sewer gas. He was pulled out by the workmen and neighbors, and although he briefly regained consciousness, he later fell into a coma and died three days later. His wife Mabel was left alone to raise their four daughters and one son.

Mabel Cox continued to own and rent out the pavilion, which became her source of income. But the facility also precipitated a community debate over dance halls and liquor in the parks. By 1903 neighbors considered the pavilion, which was still used as a dance hall, to be a nuisance and a disgrace to the neighborhood. The

Duluth, Minnesota. Lincoln Park, looking down the Canon

Duluth, Minn. View in Lincoln Park.

HENRY C. HELM: DULUTH'S FIRST PARK SUPERINTENDENT

Henry Clay Helm served as a member of Duluth's Board of Park Commissioners from 1891 to 1903 and became the Zenith City's first park superintendent in 1899. Helm was born in 1844 in Logansport, Indiana. Not much is known about his early years, but when the Civil War broke out he was living in Monticello, Minnesota. He enlisted with the 8th Minnesota Volunteer Infantry Regiment in August 1862, and rose to the rank of sergeant before mustering out in June 1865. The 8th spent most of the war battling Native Americans in the Dakota and Montana territories, but later participated in battles in Tennessee and North Carolina. By the time the war ended, the 8th Minnesota had travelled more miles than any other regiment of the Union Army.

Helm returned to Monticello following the war and in 1881 married Emma Rozelia Kreis, a Monticello resident who was born in Baltimore in 1854. The Helms came to Duluth in 1884 and settled in the West End. Helm was involved in real estate and founded the West End Building and Loan Association. He purchased what became known as the Helm Addition, between Twenty-sixth and Thirtieth Avenues West along the northern edge of the Northern Pacific Railroad tracks between Twenty-seventh and Twenty-eighth Avenues West just north of Michigan Street. Helm built his home at 2702 Huron Street. During the lumber boom of the 1890s, sawmills surrounded the area, and the Helm Addition became part of Slabtown, so named because its working-class residents used discarded slabs of bark from the sawmills to heat their modest homes. (Much of Helm Street was lost to the expansion of Interstate 35 through Duluth.)

Helm, a Republican, ran for alderman of Duluth's Sixth Ward in 1889 but failed to get his party's nomination. Two years later he was appointed to the brand new Board of Park Commissioners and elected the board's secretary. By 1899 Helm was receiving a salary of $25 per month for his work as secretary when the board decided to also employ him as the first superintendent of parks. In 1903 Helm resigned as a member of the board to devote all his time to the job of park secretary/superintendent.

In 1898 Helm found himself at the center of controversy when members of the West End Commercial Club objected to the construction of a stone wall in Lincoln Park, which they claimed was a project directed by Helm. The club members saw the wall—estimated to cost $5,000—as an unnecessary expense that would injure local property values and spoil the looks of the park. Construction was stopped, but the issue led to accusations of favoritism by residents of West Duluth who thought a park in their neighborhood was long overdue. According to the *Duluth News Tribune* they claimed that Lincoln Park—located in the West End, where Helm lived—had been "constantly improved... through the influence of Secretary Helm...while all requests for West Duluth's proposed park [were] met with a deaf ear." The group also expressed their belief that Helm, as secretary and superintendent, was "practically the entire board. He is said to audit, approve, and pay all bills for the board, and to generally control the park system affairs." Further, the entire board was "avowedly against West Duluth." West Duluth residents would finally get their park, Fairmount, in 1901.

In March 1909 the Duluth Commercial Club endorsed a petition signed by many leading citizens requesting the park board to provide band music in the city parks. The *News Tribune* reported that Helm gave a cold reception to the petition. "There is no money for that purpose, and I am not sure that we would use it if we had it. We are not much stuck on band concerts."

That same year Henry Helm resigned as park superintendent, reportedly due to failing health, and moved to the West Coast to eventually become a fruit farmer in Forest Grove, Oregon, where he died on February 1, 1920. His brief obituary credited him as being instrumental in the improvement of Cascade, Lincoln, Fairmount, and Lester Parks.

building burned to the ground in the summer of 1904, and three hundred neighbors petitioned the board to purchase the land so the pavilion would not be rebuilt. The petitioners stated that the building had "greatly depreciated the value of their property and deprived them of the enjoyment of their home life." The board first voted to move ahead with the purchase, but when dance hall manager John Moore threatened to reopen it on another lot adjacent to the park, the board members quickly realized that purchasing property to prevent a nuisance was not a practical solution and abandoned the idea.

Instead, in February 1905 the city council unanimously passed an ordinance that would prevent "noisy amusement" within five hundred feet of any park. The ordinance prohibited any business, calling or vocation, either for amusement or profit, in the conduct of which any dancing, disorderly conduct, noisy demonstration, shows, theatrical exhibitions, concerts, merry-go-rounds, or any other act or thing is permitted which will, in the opinion of the Board of Park Commissioners of the City of Duluth be likely to result in disturbing the quiet, orderly, and suitable use and enjoyment of the public park or parkways situated within five hundred feet thereof, without having first obtained from the Board of Park Commissioners a permit in writing.

At about the same time, Mrs. Cox leased the property to W. J. Chestock who intended to rebuild the pavilion and use it for dancing, skating, indoor ball games, and musical entertainment. But when Chestock applied for a license to serve liquor, the neighbors strongly objected. They claimed that it was not so much the dancing they were opposed to, but rather the liquor. They feared that the park as a "family fresh air ground" would suffer from the introduction of liquor. On May 30 the city council turned down the application, but Chestock persevered, and in May 1906 the council finally granted him a license to operate a dancing, concert, and amusement pavilion on the condition that it did not violate any city ordinances.

In November 1916, fire once again destroyed the pavilion, but the controversy that had been ignited by the dance hall continued to burn for many years.

Home of Duluth's First Playground

When the park board began developing the city's park system in the 1890s, the idea of creating urban parks for public use was still relatively new. Initially these urban parks were viewed primarily as

"breathing spots" and a place for families to get outdoors to enjoy a picnic or a stroll along the tree-lined paths.

But this was a time of great social change throughout the country as millions of farm families and immigrants moved into urban areas that were not prepared to handle them. Many people looking for a better life instead found themselves living in poverty in overcrowded neighborhoods with poor sanitation and uncontrolled crime. As conditions in the larger cities deteriorated, many social reform movements sprang up, agitating for changes that would improve the lives of the urban masses. Even the role of the parks began to change, and as a result of one national reform movement, Lincoln Park became the site of the city's first official playground, thanks to the efforts of the Duluth Playground Association.

Opened on July 17, 1908, the Lincoln Park playground consisted of little more than swings and sand piles, but two supervisors were on hand to control the children. The *News Tribune* reported that on the beautiful sunny day of July 19, people flocked to all the city parks "as though they had never before in their lives seen a park," and at Lincoln Park the children loved the new playground. While standing in line to try the swing, "the children were orderly and patient, as a rule, in waiting for their turns to come, some of them never did get a turn all day, so long were the lines of waiting youngsters."

At the end of the 1908 summer season, the Playground Association members decided to close the playground for the winter. They removed the equipment and stored it for future use. Mayor Roland B. Haven reported that "the Lincoln Park playground was more an experiment than anything else, but its success has been greater than we expected...the playground scheme next year will be handled on a much larger scale."

The following year the Lincoln Park site was deemed too small and the playground was not rebuilt, but the Park Board and the Playground Association did, indeed, expand their efforts and began to add playground equipment to existing parks and acquire land throughout the city specifically for the purpose of creating supervised playgrounds for the children of Duluth. (See chapter 15, "Playgrounds and Sports Facilities," for more about Duluth's playgrounds.)

A Community Gathering Place

By the early 1900s, community groups of every kind were holding summer picnics and gatherings in all the city parks. While improvements to Lincoln Park were at first quite minimal, around 1906 the park board added an artificial lake 150 feet long by 100 feet wide, fed by pipes that brought water from the creek. A wading pool was added a few years later, located adjacent to the stream near Sixth Street. For many years a fountain, highlighted by colored lights, rose from the

CHILDREN PLAYING IN MILLER CREEK WITHIN LINCOLN PARK, CA. 1900. (PHOTO BY L. PERRY GALLAGHER SR.)

[IMAGE: UMD MARTIN LIBRARY]

A bridge carrying Lincoln Park Drive over Miller Creek within Lincoln Park, ca. 1900.
Note Lincoln Park Elementary School in the background.

[IMAGE: UMD MARTIN LIBRARY]

center of the pool. And in 1912 the board enlarged the park by purchasing property along the banks of Miller Creek from Sixth Street all the way upstream to the parkway at Fourteenth Street.

Lincoln Park became the favored picnic location for the Duluth Retail Grocers Association, the Modern Woodmen of America, the United Order of Foresters, the Ancient Order of Hibernians, and the Woman's Christian Temperance Union. Thousands of people attended these gatherings. The Retail Grocers Association picnics regularly drew three thousand or more people for a day filled with sporting events, refreshments, dancing, and musical programs. Following the 1904 grocers picnic, the *News Tribune* reported that "from early in the morning until a late hour of night Lincoln Park was thronged with the retailers and their guests and each was convinced that he had never spent a more enjoyable day."

Of all the gatherings, the annual Swedish-American Midsummer Festival became Lincoln Park's signature event. The first was held on June 23, 1911, when all the Swedish societies of the city joined together to create a celebration similar to the traditional Midsummer Fests they knew in Sweden. The *News Tribune* estimated that—despite the cold, windy weather—nearly 12,000 people attended the "greatest gathering of Swedish Americans ever held in Duluth and one of the largest of any kind."

The festivities began with a parade that moved along Superior Street from Second Avenue East to Lincoln Park. Both the Marine Band and the Third Regiment Band provided music as members of the Order of Vasa and the Linnea Society marched between automobiles carrying the festival chairman, dignitaries including Mayor Marcus Cullum, and the "Midsummer bride."

As paraders arrived for the festival they found that the "park and park buildings were bright with flags and bunting and brilliant with thousands of Japanese lanterns and colored electric lights at night, the Edison Electric Company installing the lights without charge. They were strung along the drives in profusion and outlined all of the buildings, even covering the tall Midsummer pole."

A MODEL SAILBOAT CRUISES THE SMALL, MAN-MADE LAKE IN LINCOLN PARK, 1906. THE LAKE NO LONGER EXISTS.

[IMAGE: UMD MARTIN LIBRARY]

PARK POLICE OF THE ZENITH CITY

When Duluth's Board of Park Commissioners met on March 26, 1890—roughly a year after it was created—President William K. Rogers explained there was a "necessity for police supervision in the several parks and along the connecting driveway to prevent the deposit of offal and garbage and injury to trees and undergrowth." Board members agreed and approved the following resolution: "Resolved: that the President of the Board is hereby authorized to request of the proper city authorities the appointment of two policemen to patrol...public grounds...to the strict enforcement of the police regulations of the City therein. Payment for services to be made by the Board."

Five days later the *Duluth News Tribune* reported that Joseph Plaunt and David Vaugh had been "sworn as special policemen...to do duty on the boulevard through the summer season." The article noted that the men were already park board employees and would serve "without pay from the city." Vaugh was assigned to Lincoln Park, and the board provided him with a modest house to live in. Besides maintenance work on the boulevard ("cleaning gutters, raking and leveling and other wise keeping it in good condition for driving") the park police "looked out for any violation of the ordinances of the board."

In 1896 the board hired two men to serve as combination gardeners/park policemen in Cascade and Portland Squares from May 1 to November 1 of each year, "one for day and one for night duty in either park." The report predicted that Lester and Lincoln Parks, which had one park policeman each, would require additional employees as "it was found necessary to have those same men remain on duty in their capacities of policemen until midnight much of the time." Vaugh's career as a park policeman ended with his tragic death in April 1896; he died six weeks after being violently beaten over the head in Duluth's West End. The case was never solved. Later that year park policeman Charles Johnson arrested two men for fighting in Lincoln Park.

Duluth's common council forced extra duty on the park police in 1902, when an ordinance called for them to act as pound masters. Similar to an animal control officer today, a pound master was responsible for the feeding and care of wayward livestock such as hogs, cattle, horses, and geese placed in the town pound, but he did not control dogs or cats. The ordinance called for park police to perform the added duties "without extra compensation from the city."

That same year the board's annual report lamented of the park police that "The greatest single item of expense in this connection [maintenance] is for the caretakers...whose duties are combined in those of policemen as well as workmen, positions hard to fill...with any great degree of satisfaction to either the Board or public at large." Three years later the city employed a total of fourteen park policemen; by 1910 that number was reduced to eleven: two at Fairmount Park, Lincoln Park, Cascade Square, and Portland Square and one each at Lester Park and the five squares in Lakeside.

The park police mostly dealt with improper conduct and property damage. Such was the case in 1905, when a park policeman arrested a teamster who had allowed his horse to chew the bark off two shade trees. In July 1912, four young men were arrested in Lincoln Park after they hired single-horse livery rigs and raced "through a section of the park reserved for foot passengers" while singing and shouting. Ten days later park police arrested a man for "using bad language within Lincoln Park." Apparently the man had been sleeping in the park and, when awoken by park police, "became angered that his nap should have been disturbed and wanted to fight." In 1921 park police stayed on duty through Christmas in order to "curb vandalism and the theft of evergreen trees." Earlier that year Park Superintendent Henry Cleveland commented after a park policeman interrupted a couple kissing in one of the city's parks. "There is no city ordinance against kissing in Duluth parks," Cleveland said. "There is one, however, against disorderly conduct. We have not instructed our park police to prohibit kissing in the park."

Park policeman John Mullen was accused of negligence in 1922 when a ten-year-old boy drowned at the Indian Point Tourist Camp in Fairmount Park. Cleveland exonerated Mullen, saying that the park policeman could not swim because of an injured limb and "did all in his power to save the boy." Besides, Cleveland explained, the beach had been closed due to pollution, and the board had posted "six signs forbidding swimming"—but boys kept tearing them down. Mullen's job was to supervise the tourist camp, not act as a lifeguard.

When F. Rodney Paine replaced Cleveland as Park Superintendent in 1926, he eliminated the use of the term "park police"; thereafter the men who maintained and policed Duluth's parks were called "caretakers." In 1928 Duluth employed twelve caretakers for its busiest parks: Carl Johnson (Lincoln Park), John Bradley (Lester Park), Ole Anderson (Fairmount Park), George Cauchy (Chester Park, upper), Ernest Wolf (Chester Park, lower), J. Walling (Portland Square), Charles Onraet (Magney Park), John Hate (Kitchi Gammi Park), Paul Lusua (Lake Shore Park), and Arvid Koskinen and C. E. Read (both at Fond du Lac Park). During the 1930s and '40s, the city's larger parks had full-time caretakers while the caretakers at smaller parks worked half time. Caretakers are not mentioned in annual reports after 1949.

For the first five years of the festival, the celebration began on the evening of Midsummer Day with a dance at the privately owned dance hall located adjacent to Lincoln Park. But after fire destroyed the dance hall in 1916, organizers were forced to find a new location for the opening dance, which eventually disappeared completely from the program.

The Swedish-American Midsummer Festival took place annually at Lincoln Park until at least 1949 and usually drew 10,000 to 20,000 people. Speakers at the festival regularly included Duluth's mayor, Minnesota's governor, congressional representatives, and prominent Swedish-American leaders from throughout the Midwest.

The 1918 festival, in addition to celebrating midsummer, also marked the end of World War I. Duluth mayor Clarence Magney's opening speech offered an optimistic view of the future when he said, "We have gathered to celebrate the signing of the greatest document ever signed by man. I feel that today is the beginning of a new era. There is a possibility that all wars will be avoided in the future by some peaceful means."

For nearly a decade, it seemed as if Magney's optimism would hold true. In 1926 the city extended Lincoln Park Drive from Sixth to Tenth Streets (by 1936 Lincoln Park Drive connected with Skyline Parkway). The following year saw the construction of the Lincoln Park Bridge, which carries Tenth Street over Miller Creek. The project was driven by the West End Hillside Improvement Club, which made sure the bridge, built of concrete but faced with rustic stone, could carry streetcar tracks to help increase mobility—and local property values. A bronze plaque commemorated the club's efforts, along with Mayor Snively and the Duluth City Council. Unfortunately, two years after the bridge was completed the United States sank into the Great Depression, followed by World War II.

The 1927 Lincoln Park Bridge, photographed in 1929. (Photo by F. R. Paine.)

[IMAGE: UMD MARTIN LIBRARY]

During the Depression, Mayor Sam Snively and Park Superintendent F. Rodney Paine took advantage of government funding to put unemployed men to work on projects in all the city's parks. Duluth's City Works Administration hired jobless Duluthians to build a toboggan run and ski jump in Lincoln Park in 1931, though the popularity of these winter activities was short-lived in the West End park. Lincoln Park's stone pavilion was built in 1934 with funds and labor from two of the earliest government relief programs—the Emergency Relief Administration (ERA) and the Civil Works Administration (CWA). Reportedly two dozen of the CWA laborers gave three days' work without pay to get the Lincoln Park pavilion ready for the annual Midsummer Festival.

Following the end of World War II, Lincoln Park suffered the same neglect that afflicted all of the city's parks—a result of the 1956 change in Duluth's government combined with a slowing economy. The *News Tribune* reported in 2014 that "after years of deterioration of the pavilion and other parts of Lincoln Park, a neighborhood group initiated repair and restoration work in the park in the late 1990s and early 2000s." That work included a $130,000 restoration of the pavilion in 2002, which earned the project a 2003 award from the Duluth Preservation Alliance. The Lincoln Park Bridge underwent a major rehabilitation in 2006 to 2007. The 2012 flood damaged the bridge and the pavilion, and in July 2014, vandals torched the pavilion, causing another $75,000 in damages.

Yet Lincoln Park's future looks bright. In 2015 the City of Duluth invited residents to participate in meetings about proposed renovations to the park, which qualified for the Grand Avenue Parks Fund, part of the St. Louis River Corridor Initiative. Plans, approved in February 2016, include repairing existing park infrastructure to reduce maintenance; upgrading park destination areas to improve safety and meet ADA accessibility requirements; creating amenities to better serve the needs of children, adult, and senior park user groups; and improved access to the Duluth Traverse and Superior Hiking Trail systems.

Lincoln Park's ski jump, 1933. (Photo by F. R. Paine.)
[Image: UMD Martin Library]

4. Chester Park

'A Primeval Forest in the Heart of the City'

When first established in 1889, Chester Park, created along with Lincoln Park to form the bookends of the boulevard, extended along both sides of Chester Creek between East Fourth Street and today's Skyline Parkway. The area above the parkway, called Upper Chester, was added to the park in 1920. Together these parcels of land tell a greater story of Duluth's history. One was the site of an early Duluth cemetery while the other was once home to the highest ski jump in the world.

The land along the lower reaches of Chester Creek was settled very early in Duluth's history by Charles Chester, who, in September 1857, purchased a large parcel of land along the creek that bears his name. Little is known of Chester during his time in Duluth outside of one or two brief references, including one from pioneer Sidney Luce, whose memoir of those days mentions "Charles Chester and reputed wife." It is thought that Chester left Duluth by 1860 in the wake of the Financial Panic of 1857 and moved to California to look for gold. The census data from 1870 and 1900 show him living in Oakland. If this is the same Charles Chester that Luce wrote of, he was born in Illinois in 1829 and had an actual wife (presumably his second), Carrie, who he married in 1896. According to census records Chester was a widower by 1910 and died in Oakland on December 29, 1913. While we know very little about Charles Chester, for over one hundred years his name has remained firmly attached to the park and creek.

Perhaps the park should instead have been named "Ray Park" in honor of another early Duluth settler, James D. Ray. He first came to the Head of the Lakes in 1855 and stayed to become a highly respected Duluth businessman willing to invest his money and energy in the successful development of the city. In response to a community need, in 1879 Ray laid out a cemetery on land he owned on the west side of Chester Creek above East Fourth Street. He named it Forest Hill Cemetery and planned to eventually enlarge it to thirty-five acres and landscape it with trees and shrubs. He built a receiving vault in 1883, but it quickly proved to be too small. A larger vault was

DULUTH'S FIRST FOREST HILL CEMETERY

As early as 1849, small pioneer cemeteries could be found scattered throughout the area that is now Duluth. By 1870, the year Duluth first became a city, demand surfaced for a truly large cemetery within city limits. In October 1872 the Duluth Cemetery Association organized to find an appropriate site, electing James D. Ray (pictured) as its president. Ray first came to Duluth from Ashtabula, Ohio, in 1855, but left after the Panic of 1857. He returned to Duluth just before the end of the Civil War and began buying up property, much of it abandoned by his fellow 1850s pioneers. He subsequently made a fortune in real estate, accumulating extensive property in Duluth and the Mesabi Iron Range area.

The cemetery association considered several locations and finally chose a spot in November 1872, as the *Duluth Minnesotian* reported: "The tract is a beautifully located one, lying on a gentle rise; covered principally with maple trees; and the small stream which passes Decker's brewery runs though its entire breadth. It is approached by Piedmont Avenue [today's Mesaba Avenue], which intersects the Rice Lake Road." Essentially, today the site would be centered at about the top of Thirteenth Street where Mesaba Avenue becomes Rice Lake Road. Most of the stream—Brewery Creek—has long since been forced underground.

Apparently the Panic of 1873 put a halt to cemetery development, as there are no records of anyone buried in this location. When Forest Hill Cemetery did open—in October 1879—the property was described as running from East Fourth Street up to East Seventh Street between Twelfth and Fourteenth Avenues East. Chester Creek, not Brewery Creek, meandered through the property. This site also contained part of the claim of Chester Creek's namesake, Charles Chester, who like Ray left Duluth before 1860. But Chester never returned, and Ray purchased his property.

The date of the first interment in Forest Hill is unknown, but by the early 1880s notices of burials there appeared in Duluth newspapers, which throughout the 1880s wrote of bodies that had been buried in earlier cemeteries along Minnesota Point being moved by relatives to the new, well-maintained cemetery. In 1883 the association built a receiving vault to hold caskets until burial, but by 1885 it became inadequate in size. That year Ray hired architects Charles McMillan and Edward Stebbins to design a large stone receiving vault for the cemetery. The *Lake Superior Review and Weekly Tribune* described the elaborate structure: "The vault will have a frontage of twenty-five feet and a depth of about thirty.... The material used in its construction will be heavy blocks of Fond du Lac brownstone and Duluth granite.... The entrance will be flanked on each side by pillars of polished granite and surmounted by a stone arch. The doors will be of polished granite, enormously heavy, and an effectual bar to all intrusion. Over the entrance, carved in the stones of the arch, will be the date, 1885, and the words 'Forest Hill Cemetery.' The roof will be of arched brickwork and covered with iron." The *Duluth Weekly Tribune* predicted the vault could hold sixty caskets waiting for burial.

At the same time the new vault was being built, Ray enlarged the cemetery to thirty-five acres by acquiring a city block from Fourteenth to Fifteenth Avenues East between Fourth and Fifth Streets. Despite these actions, by 1887 Forest Hill was crowded almost to capacity with new burials and those moved from other cemeteries. The *Duluth Daily News* also

expressed the opinion of many: the cemetery should not be in a residential neighborhood. In fact, it said, the site of the original Forest Hill "is a very fit place for a park."

In June 1888 the Forest Hill Cemetery Association—which replaced the original cemetery organization—announced it had chosen a new cemetery site along Woodland Avenue that was then far away from Duluth's residential neighborhoods. By May 1890 the new Forest Hill Cemetery was accepting transfers from its original location. Ray remained heavily involved. During May and June 1890, Duluth newspapers carried daily announcements from Ray stating he would meet with relatives or friends of those buried in the old cemetery to make arrangements to move bodies to other cemeteries, usually the new Forest Hill. In October 1890 a judicial order vacated the old Forest Hill Cemetery "preparatory to platting."

The 1885 vault was used during the relocation process. In August 1892 the vault was described by the *News Tribune* as being in "rather bad shape." All caskets were reported moved by the end of 1892—but some were missed. In 1912 while excavating for a basement at Thirteenth Avenue East and Fifth Street, workers unearthed three bodies. They were reburied in the new Forest Hill Cemetery. Apparently the old vault was moved to Forest Hill about this time—at least temporarily. In 1907 the *Duluth News Tribune* announced that ground had been broken in Forest Hill for a new vault and chapel. Eight years earlier the *News Tribune* had reported that the Woodland Cemetery Association was planning extensive improvements to its site on Woodland Avenue north of Calvary Road. The facility was established in 1895 by Temple Emanuel as a Jewish cemetery. By 1910, the 1885 Forest Hill vault had been relocated to the Temple Emanuel cemetery (shown below ca. 2014). It remains there today, although in disrepair. The words "Forest Hill" have also been removed. Today the site of the original Forest Hill Cemetery contains both a residential neighborhood and the southernmost portion of Chester Park.

built in 1885, but by then the neighborhood surrounding the cemetery was growing rapidly. Duluth was booming, and by 1887 public sentiment favored William K. Rogers's plan for establishing a park along both sides of Chester Creek. To create the park system Rogers envisioned, the park board needed to purchase land from individual owners.

Ray was willing to give up a portion of his cemetery—the land he owned between Fourth and Seventh Streets from Fourteenth Avenue westward—which included one of the most scenic waterfalls on Chester Creek. This meant moving the cemetery, and in 1890 Ray began the process of disinterring bodies and relocating them to a new Forest Hill Cemetery on Woodland Avenue.

By September 1891 the park board had acquired most of the land needed for the park; it controlled about 125 acres from Fifth Street to the parkway between Thirteenth Avenue East and Fifteenth Avenue East. Negotiations for the land that fronted on Fourth Street dragged on for many years, and squatters frequently took over the area that the park board wanted for the entrance to the park. It wasn't until 1908 that negotiations were finally completed for purchasing the last of the property required for the main entrance to Chester Park.

The board gave no explanation of why it officially named this public greenspace Garfield Park in 1894, but, as explained in the Lincoln Park chapter, it was likely in honor of President James Garfield, who had been assassinated in 1881. Whatever the reason, Duluthians who lived near the park did not like the name. In 1902 a group of local residents successfully petitioned the park board to change the name to Chester Park, and the board never again tried to alter it.

Chester Park could be reached from downtown Duluth in twelve minutes by streetcar. The board chose to leave the area relatively

POSTCARD OF THE BRIDGE CARRYING TERRACE PARKWAY OVER CHESTER CREEK AT GARFIELD PARK, MADE BY DULUTH LITHOGRAPHERS CHRISTIE & COLLIER IN 1894.
[IMAGE: DULUTH PUBLIC LIBRARY]

POSTCARD OF THE FALLS AND CAULDRON OF THE GLENN WITHIN GARFIELD PARK MADE BY DULUTH LITHOGRAPHERS CHRISTIE & COLLIER IN 1894.
[IMAGE: DULUTH PUBLIC LIBRARY]

CHRISTIE & COLLIER DULUTH.

POSTCARD OF THE FALLS ALONG
CHESTER CREEK BELOW NINTH
STREET MADE BY LITHOGRAPHERS
CHRISTIE & COLLIER IN 1894
WHEN CHESTER PARK WAS
KNOWN AS GARFIELD PARK.

[IMAGE: DULUTH PUBLIC LIBRARY]

undeveloped, leading the *Duluth News Tribune* to describe the park as a "Primeval Forest in the Heart of the City." In 1902, park employees finally constructed stairways into the park from Fifth Street on the east and Sixth Street on the west, connecting to a footpath along the creek and two footbridges to provide access to both sides of the gorge. A few years later the board provided funding for the construction of a pavilion (with drinking water), which was located on the east side of the creek, deep within the park about half way between the upper

and lower footbridges, near today's Ninth Street Bridge. With the addition of the footpath and pavilion, the park became a favorite spot for summer picnics and strolls along the creek.

When the playground movement gained momentum in Duluth around 1911, the park board installed some simple equipment in Chester Park at the corner of Fifth Street and Fifteenth Avenue East. In 1915 this playground was one of three locations selected for a summer experiment that provided supervised daily recreational activities for children. The experiment was overwhelmingly successful, and the city promptly hired organizer John Batchelor as a public recreation director. Today the site is known as the Lower Chester Park recreational area and includes several ice rinks and a clubhouse. (See chapter 15, "Playgrounds and Sports Facilities" for more about Duluth's playgrounds.)

In a foreshadowing of future problems, a torrential rainstorm on July 21, 1909, resulted in damage to many city parks, including Chester, where a disastrous landslide covered the parkway on the west side of the Chester Creek Bridge. According to the *News Tribune*, "a surface an acre in extent moved bodily and was carried a distance of 400 feet. Thousands of tons of earth were in the moving mass. ... The slide filled the creek and started up the opposite hill with such force that even there it snapped and carried before it trees a foot in diameter. It swept away over half of the roadway of the boulevard for a distance of 100 feet just west of the Chester Creek bridge and left a perpendicular declivity there, 40 feet high. ...Where great trees stood, the hillside is swept clean." It took the park board several years to repair the storm damage.

Chester Bowl / Upper Chester

In 1919 Duluth mayor Clarence Magney proposed expanding Chester Park by acquiring land above the parkway, the area now referred to as Chester Bowl or Upper Chester. But even before it officially became part of the park, many people used the Chester Bowl area for recreation, especially ski jumping.

The Duluth Ski Club moved from its first home in the Hunters Park neighborhood when it purchased property and built a ski jump in Chester Bowl in December 1906, naming the jump "Chester Creek Hill." The *News Tribune* pointed out that the new site "is much nearer town than the Woodland hill [so] it will be much easier of access for those who have but a short time once a week to spend on the runners." The club also favored the Chester Creek site because the surrounding hills sheltered it from wind and the northern exposure protected it from the rays of the afternoon sun.

THE CAULDRON AT THE BASE OF THE WATERFALL ON CHESTER CREEK BELOW ROGERS BOULEVARD WITHIN CHESTER PARK, CA. 1905.
[IMAGE: DULUTH PUBLIC LIBRARY] ▶

The Ski Club paid $5,000 for the Chester Creek land, purchasing it from an out-of-town owner. Club members went to work immediately to clear brush and build a wooden scaffold for ski jumping. They also cleared a number of paths down the slopes where, according to the *News Tribune,* "the novice can disport himself merrily with jumps of from two to ten feet" and prepared toboggan slides with "bumps over which the women and children can shoot the chutes and gain some of the exhilarating effects which belong primarily to the ski rider."

On New Year's Day 1907, the *News Tribune* reported that more than five hundred Duluthians enjoyed the new facilities at Chester Bowl. A small tournament was held, but only two members of the club used a temporary jump. Novice jumpers, the newspaper said, furnished "plenty of amusement for the spectators." The permanent jump was finished January 6. More scaffolding was soon added to make the jump higher in order to break distance records—the *News Tribune* claimed the Duluth jump was the largest in the world.

Ches'er Creek Glen, Duluth, Minn.

WALK, CHESTER PARK, DULUTH, MINN.

LITHOGRAPHIC POSTCARDS
SHOWING PATHWAYS ALONG
CHESTER CREEK WITHIN
CHESTER PARK, CA. 1905.

[IMAGE: ZENITH CITY PRESS]

The hill officially opened with a tournament on January 6, 1907, and the most successful skiers of the day landed jumps of seventy-five to eighty feet. For the next nine years, the Duluth Ski Club dominated the sport in the United States, and Chester Creek Hill became the center of American ski jumping.

The club hosted the Fourth Annual National Ski Tournament of America in February 1908. The best ski jumpers from across the country poured into Duluth, along with thousands of spectators. The tournament began on Tuesday afternoon, February 11, with Flaaten's Third Regiment Band leading the contestants in a march from downtown Duluth to Chester Creek Hill. The band remained at the hill throughout the afternoon, playing music to entertain the crowd. Another parade took place in the evening with contestants carrying torches as they walked in a procession along Superior Street from Lake Avenue to Eighth Avenue West.

The next day sleighs carried spectators from the streetcar on Ninth Street up to Chester Bowl for the tournament's main events. Despite warm weather and soft snow conditions, Duluth's John Evenson set the new American record jump of 116 feet. Evenson's teammate Ole Feiring jumped even farther—134 feet—but he fell on his landing, disqualifying the attempt. The festivities ended with a huge banquet at the St. Louis Hotel, which over three hundred people attended. Mayor Marcus Cullum pronounced the tournament a great success and the city of Duluth the best in the world.

In addition to record-setting jumps, many firsts took place at Chester Creek Hill. The *News Tribune* reported that at the club's local tournament in January 1908, skier John Rude "turned a complete somersault on skis...the first time that this trick has ever been accomplished in public at the head of the lakes." And a few years later the ski club advertised that "the first moving pictures of ski jumping ever made in America will be taken...by Lyman H. Howe."

In April 1908 the massive scaffold collapsed following a wind storm; club members rebuilt it by December. In May 1916 another wind storm destroyed the slide, the tower, and the grandstand. The ski club had already faced a financial shortfall every winter trying to keep up with necessary repairs to the structures and this loss,

THE DULUTH SKI CLUB

Ski jumping in Duluth can trace its history back to January 1, 1905, when the *Duluth News Tribune* called on Duluthians to organize a ski club to participate in the "Norwegian sport" of skiing. Nordic skiing and ski jumping as sports were fairly new concepts, and the newspaper felt compelled to describe a ski. "The ski is the Norseman's shoe," the newspaper explained, "differing from the American Indian's footgear [snowshoes] in having its bearing surface of solid wood and not a webbed frame."

Forty-two Duluthians answered the call at Duluth's St. Louis Hotel on November 21, 1905, organizing as the Duluth Ski Club. Its founders consisted almost exclusively of Norwegian immigrants. John Mangseth was named the club's first captain and I. A. Iverson its first president. The club's bylaws stated that "any white man or woman of good standing over twelve years of age may become a member of the club" and that "no liquor can be served or sold at any of the functions of the club." An early proposal to limit membership to those of Scandinavian descent was dropped "as a policy which could work to no good end."

For its first ski hill, the club chose a spot in Hunters Park behind Washburn School on St. Andrews Street. Dubbed Duluth Hill, the site promised an approach of three hundred feet with a minimum jump of one hundred feet. Mangseth and four others tested the hill on December 18, 1905, with the captain jumping seventy-five feet. The Ski Club held its first event there on January 7, 1906, and a crowd of three hundred onlookers saw at least one jumper soar ninety-six feet. Later that month the Duluth Ski Club captured several awards at the first annual ski tournament on White River Hill in Ashland, Wisconsin, with assistant captain Olaf Larson tying for first place and Mangseth coming in third. Two other Duluthians finished in the top ten.

The Duluth Ski Club continued to dominate that year. At the National Ski Tournament on Brasswire Hill in Ishpeming, Michigan, in February, Duluth's Ole Feiring took the $100 first prize and Mangseth came in second. Later that winter on the Aurora Club's hill in Red Wing, Minnesota, Duluth's Gustave Bye jumped 106 feet, a new American record.

The following season the club abandoned its Hunters Park hill when it purchased land adjacent to Chester Creek above the parkway and built a ski jump called Chester Creek Hill, which unofficially opened on Christmas

Day 1906. The new hill's first tournament was held on January 20, 1907, with Feiring jumping 112 feet, shattering Bye's record before a crowd of 3,500. Feiring's new American record was still twenty-seven feet shorter than Norway's best. On their new home hill, the Duluth men took first through fourth place. Feiring's record was short-lived. Four days later in Red Wing, Aurora Club member Ole Mangseth—John Mangseth's brother—jumped 114 feet. Despite this setback, Feiring went on to dominate tournaments for the rest of the season, with several first-place finishes.

A February tournament at Chester Creek Hill drew an estimated crowd of 5,000. The following year, after building a warming house for spectators and a club house for members, the Duluth Ski Club hosted the Fourth Annual National Ski Tournament of America. By nine in the morning on the first day more than 9,000 spectators had surrounded the hill. Feiring, who was greeted by "deafening applause," fell twice, putting him out of the running. Duluth's John Evenson came through for the Zenith City, setting a new national record at 116 feet. Four days later, during a special extension of the tournament, John Mangseth broke Evanson's record when he jumped 117 feet. Later that same month in a tournament in Ishpeming, Evenson landed a 132-foot jump, closing in on the world record. Duluth had become the center of ski jumping in the United States.

Still, the Duluth Ski Club had no monopoly on ski jumping in Duluth. The West End Ski Club organized in 1907 with boys from the Mork Athletic Club and Hill Toppers Club coming

Ames-Huntley Co., Duluth   No. 704

Ski Jumping. Record for America, 112 feet, made by Ole Fiering, at Duluth, Minn., 1907.

SKI JUMPING. DULUTH, MINN.

109   GIANT SKI SLIDE, CHESTER PARK BOWL, DULUTH, MINN.

SKI JUMPING IN NORTHERN MINNESOTA

POSTCARD
IMAGES:
ZENITH
CITY
PRESS

together to host tournaments on a hill adjacent to Piedmont Avenue. That same year the West Duluth Ski Club organized, jumping from a hill located along today's Skyline Parkway between Fifty-ninth and Sixtieth Avenues West. (In 1931 the city built a ski jump in Lincoln Park, mostly utilized by the Zenith Ski Club.)

National focus remained on the Chester hill and the Duluth Ski Club. In February 1908 the club hosted the Fourth Annual National Ski Tournament of America at the Chester Creek Hill. That April the slide and its scaffolding came tumbling to the ground after a wind storm. It was rebuilt, and at eighty-one feet tall the new jump stood twenty-five feet higher than its predecessor.

The Duluth Ski Club continued to play a large role in the National Ski Association for the next nine years, hosting the national tournament again in 1915. By then Duluth skiers had ceased to dominate the winner's platform. When the club raised the jump to ninety feet before the tournament, it appealed in local newspapers for new members—their dues were needed to finance the construction.

In the fall of 1915, the club was in desperate need of money. The following May the entire jump came down in another wind storm, "tossed a hundred feet into the woods and shattered to bits," the *News Tribune* reported. The grandstand tipped over; the slide approach was blown halfway down the hill. The club folded shortly thereafter. In 1918 the city began negotiations to purchase the Chester Creek Hill.

After two promising years of unorganized jumping at the Miller Creek hills—including a tournament each year—former members and new enthusiasts were encouraged to reorganize in 1922. The following year the Duluthians donned the club's green-and-white uniforms for the first time, sending eight skiers to the national tournament in Minneapolis.

Over the years, several Olympic ski jumpers trained at Chester Park as members of the Duluth Ski Club, including Adrian Watt, Greg Swor, and Jim J. Denney. During trials for the 1968 Olympics, Watt landed a jump of 337 feet, setting a record at Pine Mountain in Iron Mountain, Michigan. He competed in the 1968 Olympics and the following year won the U.S. Championship. A member of the U.S. Ski Team from 1970 to 1975, Swor was U.S. junior champion in 1970 and U.S. Champion in 1972. Denny captured the U.S. ski jumping championship in 1976 and 1980 and the 1978 World Cup. He was inducted into the American Ski Jumping Hall of Fame in 2008. Chester Bowl saw its last ski jumping competition in 2005, and the Duluth Ski Club has not been active since then. (It technically still exists as a legal entity called Duluth Nordic Ski Club, Inc., owned by former club member George Hovland.) In August 2014 workers pulled down what remained of Chester Park's historic ski jumps.

THE 1926 BIG CHESTER ALL-STEEL
SKI JUMP, PHOTOGRAPHED IN 1929.
(PHOTO BY F. R. PAINE.)

[IMAGE: UMD MARTIN LIBRARY]

estimated at $1,000 or more, proved to be the final blow for the club. The ski slide was not rebuilt, and the club abandoned Chester Creek Hill—at least for the time being.

The City Takes Control

Chester Park—and indeed all of Duluth's parks—received a boost in 1917 with the election of Clarence Magney as mayor. During his first year in office Magney recommended that the city purchase Chester Bowl as part of a sixty-acre tract of woodland between Skyline Parkway and Kenwood Avenue that would become known as Upper Chester Park. The purchase was finally completed in June 1920, for a price of $37,000. Park Superintendent Henry Cleveland announced plans to rebuild the ski slide and make needed repairs to the toboggan slides as soon as funds became available. He predicted that this new section of Chester Park would be "one of the prettiest and most popular parks in the city some day," a prophecy that has certainly come true.

But before the city had a chance to improve the winter sports facilities, the Chester Bowl area became a summer campsite. After Henry Ford made automobiles affordable to a wider portion of the population in the early 1900s, car ownership exploded, and people across the nation took to the road to tour the country. In 1921 Mayor Snively and Park Superintendent Cleveland formed a plan to cater to

this new group of tourists—known as "autoists." They worked with the Theodore Roosevelt International Highway Association to create three auto tourist camps in Duluth: at Indian Point on the St. Louis River, Brighton Beach on the shore of Lake Superior, and the newly acquired Upper Chester Park.

Cleveland converted the Duluth Ski Club's old building at Chester Bowl into a shelter for tourists, established tent sites, and installed toilet facilities, electric lights, and public telephones so that the autoists would have "all the conveniences of a camp near the city." While the Indian Point and Brighton Beach camps survived for many years, the tourist camp at Chester Park lasted only two years.

Meanwhile, the Duluth Ski Club became active again. Although it had lost its valuable location at Chester Bowl when the city purchased the property, its members voted to rebuild at Chester during a meeting in November 1923. In order to operate their organization on park property, the club made a gesture: it purchased additional land at the top of Chester Parkway and donated it to the city, which then allowed the club to build the new slide that Cleveland had promised. In 1924 the club erected Duluth's largest ski slide to date. Nicknamed Big Chester, the wooden slide was approximately 65 feet or 20 meters high. Two years later a steel-girded slide, reportedly the "largest steel slide in the world," was built at Chester. (While local and national

AN UNIDENTIFIED BOY PREPARES TO DIVE INTO THE ARTIFICIAL POND CREATED BY DAMMING CHESTER CREEK NEAR THE FIELDHOUSE, 1929. (PHOTO BY F. R. PAINE.)

[IMAGE: UMD MARTIN LIBRARY]

newspapers failed to mention the slide's height or length, club historian Ben Rasmussen wrote in 1955 that it was originally 125 feet or 38 meters high.) The club immediately began referring to the new steel jump as Big Chester. The 1924 wooden jump, renamed Little Chester, was thereafter used by the Chester Park Boys Ski Club.

The Ski Club continued to work in cooperation with the city to maintain Chester Park—at least the upper portion, including Chester Bowl and the ski hills. In 1927 the club worked with the park department to build toboggan slides and a new fieldhouse at Chester Bowl. A skating pond was created by damming a portion of the creek below the ski jumps. According to Park Superintendent Paine,

upstream from the ski jumps the creek was shifted farther to the west to make room for full-sized football and baseball athletic fields. Tennis courts were added in 1928. Paine's annual report referred to the effort as "the vision of the Duluth Ski Club and the Duluth Outdoor Club...to make Upper Chester Park a center for outdoor activities the year around."

Designed by Chalmers Agnew, the fieldhouse included a kitchen and lunch counter, a meeting room, dressing rooms for skiers, and living quarters for a caretaker. A separate building provided storage for seventy-five toboggans. According to the *News Tribune*, two toboggan slides started from "just south of the Kenwood car line." The

CHESTER PARK'S 1927 TOBOGGAN SLIDE PHOTOGRAPHED IN 1929, LIKELY BY F. R. PAINE.
[IMAGE: DULUTH PUBLIC LIBRARY]

slides crossed Chester Creek and carried riders six hundred and seven hundred feet, finishing on the athletic field. A third slide traveled eight hundred feet "along the west side of the ravine ending up at the old ski jump and just west of the skating pond." This third slide, the newspaper reported, was "for those who are looking for thrills." Street lights made the skating pond and toboggan slides accessible after dark. Tobogganing cost ten cents a day per person, and checking shoes while skating was also a dime. Toboggans could be rented for twenty-five cents an hour.

Just two years after these improvements were completed, the nation entered the Great Depression. Many employees of the park department lost their jobs following severe budget cuts, and workers from national programs, including the Works Progress Administration and the Civilian Conservation Corps, completed most of the maintenance projects at Chester Bowl during the Depression.

Post-Depression Chester Park

Big Chester was modified in the 1940s after a sixty-meter jump was built at Fond du Lac Park; its rear tower was removed and a new jumping platform was installed at its base. While this reduced the steel structure's height, it actually increased the slide to a fifty-five-meter jump. In 1971 Little Chester was converted to a thirty-five-meter

steel slide. The new jump completed a project begun in 1969 that included the addition of an alpine ski hill and a tow rope. A natural practice slope was also modified into a twenty-meter jump called Rabbit Ears. By the mid 1970s, Chester Bowl boasted five ski jumps: Big Chester (fifty-five meters), Little Chester (thirty-five meters), and training jumps Rabbit Ears (twenty meters), Bunny Ears (ten meters), and Copper Peak-a-Boo (five meters).

In 1977 Chester Park's playing field hosted Duluth's first high school soccer tournament. In winter the athletic field has often been flooded to create a speed-skating practice rink. The fence surrounding the tennis courts still stands, though the courts have not been maintained for decades.

The 1927 fieldhouse was replaced in 1974 with a ski chalet. Two years later the city hired Thom Storm to manage the Chester Bowl Ski Program; he and his family lived in the chalet's caretaker's apartment for seventeen years. A ski lift that had served the beginner's hill at the Spirit Mountain Recreation Area was moved to Chester Bowl in 1985 to replace the tow rope. In 2008 the city announced it was unable to continue funding the program through the Parks and Recreation Department. Storm retired at that time, then became the executive director of the Chester Bowl Improvement Club, a group of volunteers who now operate the ski hill. In 2015 he retired for good, handing the reins to David Schaeffer. The chalet that Storm and his family lived in was renamed the Thom Storm Chalet in 2015, and in February 2016 Schaeffer announced plans to add a third floor to the facility.

In 1979 the park was expanded when George Hovland dedicated seven acres of his own property west of the ski jumps as an extension of the park. The land became part of the park's cross-country trail system, which was appropriate: Hovland has been a long-time

promoter of cross-country skiing in Duluth (he represented the United States in the 1952 Winter Olympics) and the proprietor of the city's Snowflake Nordic Ski Center.

The 1980s saw the advent of two events that still take place in Chester Park today. In the summer a stage in Upper Chester hosts Music in the Park, a free Tuesday-evening concert series. Autumn finds thousands of Duluthians flocking to the park for the Chester Bowl Fall Festival, featuring live music, food, crafts, locally grown fresh produce, vendors, and information booths. The event raises money for the Chester Bowl Improvement Club.

In 1992 Hovland tried to take back the property he donated in 1979, which he planned to turn into a housing development. Hovland's neighbors—including legendary Duluth Ski Club member Jim A. Denney and his son and Olympic ski jumper Jim J. Denney—and the Chester Park Improvement Club fought for twenty years to stop the development. A state district court judge ruled against Hovland. The portion of land Hovland retained west of the park has indeed become a housing development, although as of 2016 only a few homes had been built at the location.

The flood of 2012 ravaged the land along the banks of Chester Creek, and portions of the clay banks in Lower Chester Park collapsed. A stone retaining wall just east of the creek below Chester Parkway near Kent Street collapsed; most of its boulders rolled into the creek bed. The flood also destroyed a bridge over the creek in Chester Bowl and one of the 1928 dams, which allowed the pond to drain. Because Chester Creek is a designated trout stream, there are no plans to reconstruct the pond. Within days after the flood, hundreds of Duluthians young and old descended on the park, armed with shovels, hatchets, bow saws, and chain saws. They worked with city crews to remove debris from the stream and put the park back together.

A FOOTBALL GAME UNDERWAY ON THE ATHLETIC FIELD IN CHESTER PARK, 1931. (PHOTO BY F. R. PAINE.)
[IMAGE: UMD MARTIN LIBRARY]

recognizing Proctor's years of volunteer service, thanking him, and naming the main trail that loops around the creek below Skyline Parkway the Dan Proctor Trail in his honor.

Chester Park's Ski Jumps Come Down

Enthusiasm for ski jumping had declined dramatically by the 1990s with the advent of many other forms of extreme sports that attracted the same thrill seekers that ski jumping once did. Efforts have been made to revitalize the ski jumping program, but plans proved too expensive. Chester Bowl hosted its last ski jumping competition in 2005 on Little Chester. The Duluth Ski Club has been inactive since then.

In 2007 the Duluth Parks and Recreation Department announced it was considering removing the historic Chester Park ski jumps and surrounding facilities—the city had long viewed the jumps as a potential liability. Many fans of the ski jumps showed up to a meeting of the city's Parks and Recreation Commission. Jim A. and Jim J. Denney proposed a plan allowing the former Duluth Ski Club members and others to try to save the jumps. The commission passed it unanimously, but no plan ever materialized.

In the fall of 2011, citing vandalism and safety issues, Duluth's Facilities Management Division removed the lower portions of Big Chester and Little Chester along with adjacent scoring booths and what was left of the Rabbit Ears, Bunny Ears, and Copper Peak-a-Boo training jumps. Duluth Parks and Recreation manager Kathy Bergen explained to *Zenith City Online* that facilities management personnel did not contact the parks commission in reference to its decision before the demolition took place.

On August 18, 2014, Little Chester was torn down. Workers pulled down what remained of the 1926 Big Chester ski jump two days later. While the landmarks symbolized Duluth's epic contributions to American ski jumping, for many years they had become a popular and dangerous spot for underage drinking among high school and college students who often climbed the sides of the jump.

In 2012 the city formed a committee to create a memorial to the history of ski jumping at Chester Park, part of the park commission's "mini master plan" for the park. Finalized in November 2014, the six-phase plan—projected to cost between $3.4 and $5.1 million—is designed to improve the park's trails, buildings, bridges, and other amenities, including a $1 million expansion and renovation of the Thom Storm Chalet.

Among those gathered was Dan Proctor, who lives adjacent to the park near Skyline Parkway. For more than two decades, Proctor has walked the trails along Chester Creek with his dogs (including, over the years, Zoot and Otis and Honey and Waldo and Ralph), a shovel, a saw, and other hand tools. Particularly after heavy rains, Proctor maintains the trails, digging draining trenches and moving dirt to keep the paths dry and safe while his pets greet passersby. Proctor—a baker by trade, an environmentalist by practice—was once employed by the park department to work in Chester Park, but after his job was eliminated in 1991 he continued to improve his beloved park. In 2012 Duluth's city council passed a resolution

5. Lester Park

'An Enchanted Land of Fairy-Like Beauty'

Long before Duluth began developing its park system, the Lester River was a popular destination for fishing, picnicking, and summer outings. In the early 1880s, even before the streetcar line made it easily accessible, picnickers and fishermen arrived at the river by boat, carriage, or bicycle. Anglers took advantage of every good fishing hole, while picnickers headed to the rocky shore of Lake Superior or the shady grove of birch trees surrounding the picturesque waterfalls about three-quarters of a mile upstream from the river's mouth. More adventurous visitors could follow a foot path along the river which took them into the forest where, as the *Duluth News Tribune* described, "every step of the way is through an enchanted land of fairy-like beauty."

According to local tradition, the Ojibwe called the river *Busabika-zibi*, "river where water flows through a worn place in the rocks." The name "Lester" likely came from an early settler—most of Duluth's creeks are named for settlers who arrived at the Head of the Lakes in the 1850s. In 1901, Baltimore resident George V. Leicester wrote to

the short-lived Duluth Historical Society (1898 to 1902) that he was preparing a paper for the organization explaining that he was the river's namesake. The *News Tribune* reported that Leicester claimed the river was named for him (*Lester* is the British pronunciation of Leicester) after he lived for one winter in a cabin on its banks prior to ratification of the 1854 Treaty of LaPointe, which opened the northern shores of Lake Superior to settlement. The fact that Leicester, born in 1837, was just seventeen years old in 1854 certainly lends some doubt to his claims. According to records, Mr. Leicester died in Maryland in 1902 at the age of 65; his place of birth is not recorded.

In 1871 Hugh McCulloch, a business associate of Philadelphia financier Jay Cooke and the U.S. treasury secretary from 1865 to 1869, purchased a large parcel of land between today's Fortieth and Fifty-fourth Avenues East from the lakeshore to today's Colorado Avenue (originally Summit Street) from lumberman John D. Howard. (Prior to Howard, the property belonged to Francis Dermay, a Michigan militiaman who received the land as bounty for his service in the

LITHOGRAPHIC POSTCARD, CA. 1900, OF LESTER PARK'S ICONIC RUSTIC BRIDGE OVER THE LESTER RIVER.

[IMAGE: ZENITH CITY PRESS]

War of 1812.) McCulloch was then living in England, where he and Cooke established the banking firm of Jay Cooke, McCulloch & Co. From his London office, he platted his Minnesota township and, obviously inspired by his newly adopted town, named its streets and public squares for English noblemen and landmarks as well as prominent members of Cooke's banks, including himself. He called his township New London.

New London's first residents were General George B. and Mary Sargent, who built a home at Fortieth Avenue East and London Avenue (today's London Road). Sargent, Cooke's agent in Duluth, purchased all of New London from McCulloch following the Financial Panic of 1873 (caused by the failure of Cooke's bank) which paralyzed development for the next ten years. George Sargent died in 1875 while on business in Germany.

Following George Sargent's death, New London became the property of his widow, Mary. In 1886 the Sargent's son William and other investors formed the Lakeside Land Company, which purchased New London from Mary Sargent and began buying property between Fifty-fourth and Seventy-fifth Avenues East. Because the Lester River ran through the center of this new development, they named it Lester Park. The company built streets and sewers, added water and electricity to the area, and in 1892 built a streetcar line that ran from Twenty-second Avenue East all the way to the Lester River. Prior to that, visitors and residents alike could utilize the Duluth & Iron Range Railroad for transportation.

The Lester River was already a favorite location for summer activities. As early as 1884 Thomas Buckley leased two hundred acres along the river with the goal of establishing a summer resort. Buckley constructed a sixteen-by-twenty-six-foot building near the mouth of the river and created a carriage road from there to the falls. He intended to capitalize on the most popular activities by selling fishing tackle along with food and beverages for picnickers. Newspaper ads announced that the steamship *Mary Martini* would make excursions from Duluth to the Lester River, charging a fare of fifty cents for a round trip, and invited picnickers to visit the summer resort at Lester Falls Park, where "all kinds of temperance refreshments" were available.

In 1889 Lakeside and Lester Park were incorporated together as the Village of Lakeside, which at that time was separated from Duluth by many blocks of undeveloped land. According to the *News Tribune*, the streetcar ride to the river was as scenic as the destination itself: "For the simple pleasure of the view as seen from the car window the one taking this six mile ride is well repaid. The bright green woods, the wild flowers, the fields of freshly mown hay and yellowing grain, the trim, new cottages, and the pure, sweet air—they are the

GEORGE SARGENT, WHO PURCHASED THE TOWNSHIP OF NEW LONDON FROM HUGH MCCULLOCH. SARGENT'S SON WILLIAM AND OTHERS LATER TURNED NEW LONDON INTO DULUTH'S LAKESIDE NEIGHBORHOOD.

[IMAGE: DULUTH PUBLIC LIBRARY]

FROM 1892 TO 1934 THE LESTER PARK LINE OF THE DULUTH STREET RAILWAY COMPANY, ALSO KNOWN AS THE LAKESIDE LINE, PROVIDED STREETCAR SERVICE BETWEEN TWENTY-SECOND AVENUE EAST AND SIXTY-FIRST AVENUE EAST. (PHOTO BY HUGH MCKENZIE, DATE UNKNOWN.)

[IMAGE: ZENITH CITY PRESS]

elixir of life to the nostrils of [the] tired man or woman from the hot, palpitating city!"

Sargent's intention to create a park along the river was well known; in May 1886 the *Duluth Weekly Tribune* reported that brush fires threatened to destroy the birch grove "which Lakeside Land Company intends to be the central attraction of their future park." Fortunately, Sargent and a group of men fought back the flames and saved the birch grove.

By 1890 the park appeared in *Roe's Real Estate Atlas* as "Stearns Park," named in honor of Judge Ozora P. Stearns, president of the Lakeside Land Company. In addition to a small triangle of land between the two branches of the river extending from Superior Street to Tioga Street, the twenty-acre park included a narrow strip of land along both sides of Amity Creek (at that time called the West Branch of the Lester River) upstream to just above the waterfall and swimming hole known today as "the Deeps."

A carriage path, Occidental Boulevard, paralleled the west side of Amity Creek; another path, Oriental Boulevard, paralleled the east side of the creek (today Oriental Boulevard is part of the park's cross-country ski trail system). The park also included a strip of land along the east side of the river from Superior Street to Lake Superior. Several years earlier the Lakeside Land Company had donated land on the west side of the river for the U.S. Fish Hatchery. In 1891 state legislation turned the Village of Lakeside into the City of Lakeside in anticipation of the inevitable annexation of the community by Duluth. After a lively fight among local politicians, compromises were reached and the annexation of Lakeside went into effect on January 1, 1893. Following annexation, Lakeside and Lester Park became neighborhoods of the greater city, and the Lakeside Land Company donated Stearns Park and five public squares in Lakeside to Duluth's expanding park system. (See chapter 1, "Nineteenth-Century Squares," for more information about the squares.)

AN UNIDENTIFIED WOMAN DRIVES HER CARRIAGE ALONG EITHER ORIENTAL OR OCCIDENTAL BOULEVARD WITHIN LESTER PARK, CA. 1900.

[IMAGE: UMD MARTIN LIBRARY]

LESTER PARK'S RUSTIC BRIDGE (1898–1931)

A major rainstorm in July 1897 destroyed most of the bridges spanning the Lester River and caused at least $50,000 damage throughout the city. The *Duluth News Tribune* reported that "the damage at Lester River was quite large. Debris swept against and carried out the lower bridge. A smaller bridge that spanned the river above [Superior Street]...went out and swept down the torrent that filled the rocky gorge through which the river runs."

Later that year Duluth's park board commissioned John Busha to build a new bridge within Lester Park. A native of Green Bay, Wisconsin, Busha was born to an Ojibwe mother and a French-Canadian father in 1847. Busha served in the Civil War with the 12th Wisconsin Infantry, the "Marching Twelfth," which in 1864 joined General William Tecumseh Sherman on his notorious March to the Sea. According to Ojibwe historian Christine Carlson, in 1864 Busha returned to Green Bay and married Rosalie Aino, also of French-Canadian descent, and together they had seven children. Little is recorded about Busha's life in the 1870s and 1880s. In 1893 he moved his family to Duluth and later found employment as Lester Park's first park policeman. Along with Frank Hodges, Busha is thought to have been an early proprietor of Lester Park Pavilion/ Harmonie Hall, which included a confectionary. Busha's two oldest sons, Abraham and George, worked in the confectionary.

In the winter of 1897 to 1898 Busha, along with Abraham and George, set to work felling some of Lester Park's cedar trees and using teams of horses to haul them to a site along the river in preparation for building the bridge. Then the Bushas started putting the unpeeled logs together until they spanned the river. Finally, Busha adorned the masterwork by carving Ojibwe embroidery designs into the wood. According to Abraham Busha, their efforts earned the three men a total of $345.68—less than $10,000 today, and the materials cost nothing.

The Lester Park Rustic Bridge became a popular tourist stop, with picnic tables on the bottom deck and lounging on the upper promenade. The lower deck even featured large square viewing holes (surrounded by rails) that allowed picnickers to look down on the Lester's roiling brown water rushing past on its way to Lake Superior. Each summer ladies' groups from local churches rented space in the lower level and sold refreshments. In 1899 noted American photographer William Henry Jackson visited Duluth, photographing landmarks for the Detroit Publishing Company. The photo he took of the Lester Park Rustic Bridge (below) was made into a color lithographic postcard in 1902. It was the first of many: During the golden age of lithographic postcards, approximately 1900 to 1939, the rustic bridge over the Lester River was Duluth's second-most-popular postcard subject, second only to Duluth's aerial bridge. (See page 77 for an example.)

Unfortunately, nature took its toll on the wooden bridge, and the upper deck had to be removed in 1916 due to safety concerns. In 1931 the lower deck met the same fate. When the bridge came down, only Abe "Candy" Busha survived as one of its original builders. While he had learned his trade at Lester Park's Harmonie Hall, the second-eldest Busha son had earned his nickname as the confectioner of the Oatka Pavilion on Minnesota Point, which was destroyed by fire in 1909. The Oatka fire, like the 1913 conflagration that destroyed the Lester Park Pavilion, was reportedly started by an unattended cigar or cigarette. Candy Busha later worked as a janitor at Duluth's City Hall.

—— IMAGE: **LIBRARY OF CONGRESS** ——

'You Are Invited'

While Duluth's park board welcomed the gift of Stearns Park, it wasn't financially prepared for the addition as it had overextended its budget working to acquire land and make improvements to the parkway, Chester Park, and Lincoln Park. Nevertheless, in its annual report for 1894 the board graciously wrote that "the people of Duluth are indebted to the generosity of the Lakeside Land Co. for the gift of this magnificent tract of land for park purposes." The board renamed the greenspace "Lester River Park," but it was soon referred to as simply Lester Park.

Located at the point where the eastern and western branches of the river come together, the small triangle of land appeared to be an island that could be reached only by crossing one of the numerous rustic bridges. According to the park board, "this island is the picnic grounds and the park board [is] beautifying and at the same time striving to retain its wild features." Large birch and pine trees shaded the picnic grounds that the board had "furnished with long pine tables, rustic chairs and benches, good paths, and a convenient pump."

The area's popularity among picnickers continued to increase after it became an official city park. By 1900 the streetcar from downtown Duluth to Lester Park ran every twenty minutes during the day and more frequently in the early evening. The *News Tribune* described idyllic outings: "Every bright, pleasant morning during the week, picnic parties go from town and spend the day at Lester Park.... They have an abundant and tempting lunch, wraps, hammocks or a swing, and a bit of sewing for the older women. The girls generally tuck away a novel among the sandwiches for private delectation along in the afternoon after the excitement of arrival and lunch is over."

Lester Park also became a favorite place for dances, which were held within one or another of the many pavilions. It is difficult to pin down the exact number and location of pavilions and concession

A RUSTIC FOOT BRIDGE OVER THE LESTER RIVER WITHIN LESTER PARK IN 1908. (PHOTO BY THE DETROIT PUBLISHING COMPANY.)
[IMAGE: LIBRARY OF CONGRESS]

stands that existed in and around Lester Park at the beginning of the twentieth century, but the most famous was the Lester River Rustic Bridge, which spanned the river in the heart of the park from 1898 to 1931 (see page 80).

The Forest House pavilion, located on the island and operated by Fred Pinkham, sold lemonade and ice cream and also served as a dance hall. In September 1896 a fire destroyed the Forest House, and the loss was estimated at $1,000, which included a new piano. Pinkham promptly rebuilt the pavilion, and dances continued. But he soon became the focus of the neighbors' wrath as rumors spread that he was selling beer. Citizens of Lakeside strongly favored temperance—its 1893 annexation agreement with Duluth prohibited the sale and manufacture of intoxicating liquor within Lakeside and

Lester Park. In 1898 Pinkham was arrested and charged with selling liquor without a license. The charges were later dismissed on lack of evidence, but that was the end of the Forest House.

The privately owned Lester Park Pavilion/Harmonie Hall (also spelled Harmony Hall) was located just outside the park, on the east side of what is now the Lester River Road. Newspapers regularly carried brief advertisements for public dances: "A social dance will be given this evening at Lester Park Pavilion. LaBrosse's orchestra. You are invited." Individuals also rented the hall for private dance parties, with full reports in the society page, as in August 1897, when "an informal hop was given on Friday night at Harmonie Hall...by Frank Williamson and to the favored ones proved charming beyond words."

The dance hall was lost (at least temporarily) when in March 1904 "with a deafening crash that could be heard for blocks, that portion of the Lester Park Pavilion devoted to a dancing hall caved in...as a result of the enormous weight of snow upon the roof." This was the same year that the dance hall adjacent to Lincoln Park burned down and neighbors begged the park board to purchase the land so the hall would not be rebuilt. Throughout the country crusades were underway to vilify dance halls as evil places where innocent young people were exposed to unsavory adults who served them intoxicating drinks. As a result of the problems in Lincoln Park, in February 1905 the city council passed an ordinance prohibiting dance halls within five hundred feet of any city park. But the Lester Park Pavilion must have had a good reputation, because in March 1905 the council gave permission for Mr. L. A. Gunderson to build a new pavilion at Lester Park for "dances and entertainment" as long as it did not violate any ordinances.

Gunderson leased the facility to J. F. Condon until February 1913 when a fire in the early morning hours, probably started by a discarded cigarette, completely destroyed the Lester Park Pavilion. In response to repeated requests from the public, Mr. Gunderson rebuilt the pavilion, and Harmonie Hall reopened in July 1914. Advertisements once again announced, "Dance tonight. LaBrosse's orchestra will play. You are invited."

In December 1915 the Duluth Elks Club announced they had received approval from city officials to create a municipal zoo in one of the city's parks. Club members had been negotiating with city officials for many weeks, pressing especially hard in November. On December 6 the city commissioners adopted resolutions to establish the zoo and heard the first reading of an ordinance that would

LITHOGRAPHIC POSTCARD OF AMITY CREEK WITHIN LESTER PARK, CA. 1905.

[IMAGE: LIBRARY OF CONGRESS]

LITHOGRAPHIC POSTCARD OF THE LESTER RIVER WITHIN LESTER PARK, MADE BY THE DETROIT PUBLISHING COMPANY IN 1906.

[IMAGE: UMD MARTIN LIBRARY]

With no animals, the zoo didn't open until the following year, and its first residents consisted of "a couple of deer and two red foxes" donated by a trapper. By mid-May 1916 a goose and a porcupine were added. In June the Lester Park Improvement Club objected to the zoo, saying the animals might cause a nuisance. The zoo did not reopen in 1917 When Duluth finally did get a zoo, it was at Fairmount Park in 1923; its first resident was a deer, penned within the fencing intended for the zoo at Lester Park.

Pushing Boundaries

The Lester River area outside the boundaries of the park continued to be as popular as the park itself. Public access to the upper reaches of Amity Creek expanded after 1900 when real estate investor/dairy farmer Samuel Snively financed the construction of a scenic road that started at the junction of Oriental and Occidental Boulevards and fol-

appropriate the necessary money. A donation of wire fencing by the Pittsburgh Steel Company and fence posts from the Alger-Smith Lumber company helped convince officials the zoo wouldn't be too much of a burden on city coffers.

Newspapers reported the likely spot would be Fairmount Park, but after Mayor William Prince and Commissioner J. A. Farrell accompanied a committee of Elks members on an inspection tour of possible locations, they chose Lester Park. The first two tenants of the zoo were to be, of course, elks—two of them, donated by the game warden of the state of Washington. Unfortunately, the warden gave them to Sioux City, Iowa, before Duluth officials agreed to allow the zoo.

lowed the creek up the hill for about two and a half miles to his farm. He opened his road for public use, but the numerous wooden bridges deteriorated quickly, leaving the road unsafe for traffic. The park board took over responsibility for the road in 1909 and, with the help of Snively, rebuilt the road including beautiful and substantial stone arch bridges. The new road—today called Seven Bridges Road—reopened in July 1912, linking Lester Park to the parkway that already spanned the length of the city. (See chapter 2, "Skyline Parkway," for more about Seven Bridges Road.)

The park board members also recognized they needed to acquire additional land in order to expand Lester Park. In 1907 they began negotiations with Thomas Cole, president of the Oliver Mining Company, who owned four hundred acres surrounding the East Branch of the Lester River. Cole planned to build a summer home for his family on a ten-acre parcel near the mouth of the river, and he generously offered to sell to the park board any other portion of the land that they wanted. He agreed to accept city bonds in payment and was willing to hold the land without interest until the board had the necessary funds. Unfortunately, when Cole attempted to get a clear title to the property he discovered that he would have to bring twenty-eight separate actions against young men who had built hunting shacks on the land. He apparently decided the legal complications were too burdensome, and by 1910 he sold the land to "outside parties" for $200,000.

The park board continued negotiations with the new owners and eventually purchased twenty-three acres from the Edgewater Land Company and seven acres from a private individual, all situated between the east and west branches of the river, thus expanding the triangle of land that formed the core of Lester Park.

In 1915 the Duluth Real Estate Board acquired the portion of Cole's holdings located north of the city park along the East Branch of the Lester River. They named the area "Pinehurst on the Lester" and divided the land into thirty-eight large tracts ranging from 100- to 150-feet frontage and 150 to 300 feet deep. The realtors planned to sell the lots and use the money to construct a real estate exchange building in downtown Duluth. They built a concrete bridge that connected their property to the Lester River Road and constructed a boulevard through the forest, which they intended to donate to the city as part of the parkway system.

A number of summer homes were built at Pinehurst on the Lester, but the historic forest fire in October 1918 swept through the area, burning trees in the park and destroying the Pinehurst cabins. According to the *News Tribune* "Lester Park, save for its southwest corner and the fringe along Superior Street, is ashes, stumps, and half-burned standing timber. Sites of cabins are indistinguishable from the general ruin." Pinehurst on the Lester never recovered. Two lots that abutted the north boundary of the park were purchased by the

THE LESTER RIVER WITHIN LESTER PARK, FROZEN OVER DURING THE WINTER, CA. 1900.
[IMAGE: UMD MARTIN LIBRARY]

LESTER PARK GOLF COURSE

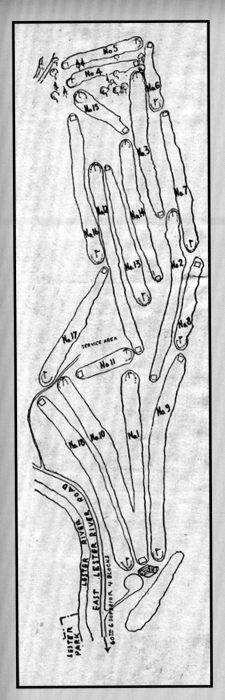

Supported by a citizen committee, Duluth's park department built the city's first municipal golf course at Enger Park. When the nine-hole course opened in 1927, the project was so successful that the department could immediately afford to construct a second nine, and by 1929 the entire investment had been paid back.

In 1930, unemployment caused by the Great Depression and the success of the course at Enger Park gave rise to the idea of a second municipal course in Duluth. Park Superintendent F. Rodney Paine favored the idea, but the city did not have the funds to begin work. He estimated the cost for the course at $45,000, with another $12,000 for a clubhouse; including other features, the total estimated cost came to $76,000. While the idea seemed very feasible, there was no source for the initial capital.

Paine's affluent friends soon provided the needed cash to underwrite construction of the course's first nine holes. Robert

Congdon (as well as the estate of his late father, Chester Congdon), Congdon's brother-in-law Harry C. Dudley, grain trader Ward Ames, George H. Spencer, Julia (Mrs. A. M.) Marshall, Louise (Mrs. A. L.) Ordean, and others—including Paine's father, Frederic W. Paine—formed the City Land Company and pooled $25,000 for the course's creation. It was a selfless act. None of the investors owned any of the land involved, and nearly all of them were members of Northland or Ridgeview Country Clubs—they already had a place to play golf, but saw the greater community need for more public links. The funding required no down payment by the city, and the first payment wasn't due until 1933; no annual payments would exceed $6,000, and the debt would be paid off in five years.

The first thing Paine did for Lester Park Golf Course (LPGC) was to put Andy Anderson in charge of both Enger Park and the new links. Anderson, who had worked on the 1920 expansion of Northland Country Club, drew the course's layout by hand (pictured, left). Construction began on October 24, 1930, when seventy-five unemployed men set to work clearing trees, brush, and boulders from the land. Duluth's City Works Administration (CWA) operated much like the Works Progress Administration and Civilian Conservation Corps that the Roosevelt administration would later establish—providing jobs to those without work while improving the community along the way. A pool of over $16,000 had been established just for work on the city's parks. The workers cleared nine fairways at Lester before December—by hand. The following October the course's front nine was ready for play.

While it was a bit late in the year for golf, the City Land Company presented the Lester Park Golf Course to the City of Duluth on October 2, 1931. Company president L. G. Castle formally turned the course over to Mayor Sam Snively, who hit the official first

drive. The event—pictured below in a photo taken by F. R. Paine)—was marked by a nine-hole match between four of Duluth's most prominent golfers: Northland club champ Bobby Campbell and Ridgeview club champ Ray Belisle against G. R. Ward and Runcie Martin, whom the newspapers called "public links golf stars." The competition ended in a tie.

The first nine holes opened to the public on May 27, 1932, with the same four men participating in the first test match round. The second nine holes of the course were developed that year, financed with $10,000 from a $500,000 bond established in 1926. In May 1933 further improvements were made. More unemployed men were put to work by Duluth's CWA (pictured on the previous page in a photo taken by F. R. Paine). They constructed a rain shelter that resembles a Japanese pagoda, a refreshment stand, a caddy shack, and a tool house and garage built with salvaged lumber. (The rain shelter and refreshment stand—now a rain shelter itself—still remain, but the caddy shack has been reduced to ruins and the tool house has been altered dramatically.)

Lester Park Golf Course was formally dedicated June 11, 1933. Mayor Snively hosted the dedication, making a speech and again driving the first ball. By then, the clubhouse—which cost $15,000—was already complete. The structure was designed by A. R. Melander, a native Duluthian who also designed several Duluth churches and St. Mary's, St. Luke's, and Miller Memorial hospitals.

Since the day the course was dedicated, it has sponsored formal and informal leagues, including a men's league, a women's league, a senior's league, the Lakeview Club, the Sunrise Club, and the Red Caps (another group of seniors), among others. The course has also hosted youth programs and countless tournaments, including charity scrambles and the annual Lakeview Medal, which is still played today. Andy Anderson retired in 1964, replaced by ten-year LPGC veteran Buck Wiley. He stepped down just three years later, turning the reins over to Jim Anderson, Andy's son, who at that point had twenty-two years of

experience on the course—he started there in 1945 while still in high school. Jim managed until his retirement in 1983, marking the end of fifty-seven years of Anderson men maintaining Duluth's municipal golf courses. Andy passed away in 1981, Jim in 2005.

Over the years the course has seen few capital improvements, a testament to its original construction, which included the most sophisticated watering system in the region. During the 1980s Duluth mayor John Fedo changed that. Encouraged by the expansion of I-35 through Duluth and improvements to the Duluth Entertainment and Convention Center, Fedo and other city leaders felt Duluth was poised to become a convention center—and that the rest of the city needed to help attract those conventions. Since the popularity of golf was on the rise nationally, one improvement idea involved adding nine holes to both the Lester Park and Enger Park courses, expanding each to twenty-seven holes. The total costs came to over $4.1 million.

A 1998 *Golf Digest* poll rated Duluth as the "best city in America for public golf." Essentially, the magazine called Duluth "the best urban center in America when it comes to offering excellent and affordable public golf." Despite overwhelming popularity, by 2004 both golf courses were losing money. According to the *Duluth News Tribune*, part of this loss was because the city still owed over $1.3 million on the loan for the 1990 expansion, which was not expected to be paid off until 2007. Mayor Herb Bergson's administration reexamined the way the courses were operated, considered selling them, and even tried to entice developers to build housing alongside the courses. In 2007 Duluth's chief administrative officer concluded that "privatizing golf courses is not a financially viable option." The housing development idea was dropped as well.

In 2014 Duluth mayor Don Ness proposed selling Lester Park Golf Course to private developers to create housing. Following much public outcry Ness shelved the idea. As of 2016 Duluth's municipal golf courses were operated by a private company.

city in 1921 and added to Lester Park. The other abandoned lots, along with the boulevard and concrete bridge, became unofficial park land.

Ten years later the park boundaries expanded once more. The City Land Company financed construction of a golf course on land east of the park and turned the completed course over to the city in October 1931. Sam Snively, who by this time had been Duluth's mayor for a decade, hit the drive that started play in the first match on the new Lester Park Golf Course. That same year the famous rustic bridge met its end. The upper deck had been removed in 1916 due to safety concerns; the rest of the bridge was removed in 1931 for the same reason.

Post-Depression Lester Park

Since that time Lester Park has remained one of Duluth's most popular parks. As they have for decades, young people gather at the Deeps, a large pool formed by erosion just upstream from where Amity Creek joins the Lester River. Here they take part in a very dangerous activity—cliff diving into the pool, thought to be forty feet deep in some spots. Accidents are frequent and occasionally tragic. In August 2011 a thirteen-year-old boy drowned when he was swept downstream by the strong current after diving into the Deeps. One hundred people participated in a five-day search for his body, which was found in Lake Superior.

On a much happier note, since 1998 Lester Park has hosted the Lester River Rendezvous, which celebrates Duluth's connection to the historic fur trade. In the winter the park is a mecca for cross-country skiers, and in the summer it is a hiker's and cyclist's paradise. Since 2009 the Cyclists of Gitchee Gumee Shores (COGGS) has built and maintained bike trails within the park; the organization has done similar work in other parks as it develops the Duluth Traverse, a multiuse, single-track trail intended to stretch the entire length of the city, from Fond du Lac to Lester Park.

A RUSTIC FOOT BRIDGE OVER THE LESTER RIVER WITHIN LESTER PARK, 1928. (PHOTO BY F. R. PAINE.)

[IMAGE: UMD MARTIN LIBRARY]

6. Fairmount Park

'A Breathing Spot for West Duluth'

The Duluth Board of Park Commissioners spent thousands of dollars in the 1890s purchasing land and developing Lincoln Park in the West End and Chester Park in the eastern part of the heavily populated city center. Further east, Lester Park and five small squares were donated to the park system when Duluth annexed Lakeside. West Duluth, however, had no park. In April 1898, the *Duluth News Tribune* reported, "There is a growing sentiment in West Duluth in favor of having a park. For years it is said that West Duluth has been looking for a breathing spot and playground such as is enjoyed in nearly every other part of the city, but so far has failed."

The issue erupted publicly when the park board began work on a retaining wall in Lincoln Park. The cost of the improvement triggered protests from West Duluth citizens, and their frustration made it into the newspapers: "Lincoln Park of the West End has been constantly improved, it is claimed," the *News Tribune* reported, "while all requests for West Duluth's proposed park are met with a deaf ear." The park

board responded defensively: "You never offered us any land, and other parts of the city have donated...large tracts for park purposes."

The dispute succeeded in pushing the development of a West Duluth park to the top of the board's priority list, and its members began searching for a suitable site. By December 1900 the board had identified four areas, and a group of West Duluthians met to consider the options. The group settled on a forty-acre tract along Kingsbury Creek near Seventy-second Avenue West, which was available for $4,000. The park board accepted the group's recommendation and purchased the land in March 1901.

Kingsbury Creek's name came from pioneer William Wallace Kingsbury, a Pennsylvania native, who had established a homestead along its banks in the 1850s. Kingsbury represented northeastern Minnesota as a member of the Territorial House of Representatives in 1857 and served as a delegate to the state Constitutional Convention. That same year the Democrat was elected to congress. By 1865 he was back in Pennsylvania; he died in Florida in 1892.

LITHOGRAPHIC POSTCARD, CA. 1910, OF A FOOT BRIDGE SPANNING THE ROCKY BANKS OF KINGSBURY CREEK WITHIN FAIRMOUNT PARK.

[IMAGE: ZENITH CITY PRESS]

citywide controversy about the evils of dance halls, the board had to assure worried neighbors that the pavilion was only intended as a picnic shelter.

When the street railway company finally extended the streetcar line all the way to the park in early 1905, Fairmount became a favorite summer picnic site for groups ranging from Sunday school classes to the Sons of Norway.

Many labor unions also held their annual picnics at Fairmount Park, and in 1906 the Duluth Trades Assembly formed the "Union Labor Park Pavilion Association" so union members could build their own facilities. Using money donated by members of the various unions, the association purchased sixteen lots adjacent to Fairmount Park and went to work building a pavilion and sports fields. The association hired an extra crew of workers to get the pavilion completed in time for the 1906 Labor Day picnic, which featured tightrope walker Henry DeRouch and a balloon ascension by aeronaut Professor R. Thompson. According to the *News Tribune*, at least three thousand union members marched in the Labor Day parade and ten to fifteen thousand people visited the park grounds.

In 1909 the Duluth, Winnipeg & Pacific Railroad submitted a plan to construct a new line into Duluth. The proposed route of the track cut through the northern portion of Fairmount. Despite protests

The board promptly started work on the new park, which was christened Fairmount Park in response to a request submitted by the Fairmount School Alumni Association. Almost immediately newspapers and even the park board members began misspelling the name as "Fairmont," an error others have perpetuated to this day. The *News Tribune* reported, "The new park...will not need as much work as the others about the city owing to its splendid natural advantages. ...A little stream tumbles through a rocky chasm included in the park, and when the rains come the purling brooklet is suddenly transformed into a torrent, its water deep, treacherous, foaming, and to lovers of the harsh and wild in nature is then one of the most inspiring sights in this region." Park employees built paths and installed benches, and—although the streetcar extended only as far as Fortieth Avenue West—Fairmount Park rapidly became popular for family outings and picnics. In June 1903 an official entrance was constructed for the park and work started on a pavilion. Because of the ongoing

SCENE IN FAIRMONT PARK, DULUTH, MINN.   91852

from citizens, the proposal was approved by city leaders. As part of the agreement, the park board required the railroad to donate a ten-acre parcel of land adjacent to Fairmount Park in exchange for the land lost to the right-of-way, expanding the park to nearly fifty acres. The wild beauty of Fairmount was diminished somewhat by construction of the railroad, but in spite of the intrusion the park's popularity continued to grow.

Indian Point Bathing Beach

Duluth's park system in 1911 included seven major parks totaling nearly 250 acres, but none provided a swimming beach or public access to the St. Louis River. Members of the West Duluth Commercial Club began agitating for the park board to remedy this by expanding Fairmount Park along Kingsbury Creek all the way to the river. The board agreed to the idea, but making it a reality was more difficult than expected.

At the board's prompting, in late 1911 the city council approved the issuance of park bonds to raise money to purchase the land along both sides of Kingsbury Creek. In early 1912 the city began condemnation proceedings on forty acres, extending from Sixty-third to Seventieth Avenues West and including a piece of land along the river known as Indian Point, nearly half of which was underwater at the

time. Real estate appraisers valued the land at roughly $26,000. Property owners representing ten acres agreed to sell, but owners of the other thirty acres were not satisfied. They wanted $2,000 per acre, arguing that the land had potential for future docks and manufacturing plants. They refused to sell and appealed to the district court. The case was settled in January 1914 when Judge Josiah D. Ensign ruled that the appraised value was fair. Still unsatisfied, the landowners appealed to the Minnesota Supreme Court. By this time World War I had erupted in Europe, creating what the newspaper described as "financial quietude" and a drop in land prices. Recognizing defeat, the landowners abandoned their appeal and finally agreed to sell. The city succeeded in purchasing the additional forty acres for Fairmount Park in early 1915.

While the land transaction was tied up in court, in 1913 Duluthians approved a new city charter that eliminated the park board. Development of Indian Point became the responsibility of Park Superintendent Henry Cleveland and newly elected Mayor William Prince, who also served as Commissioner of Public Affairs in charge of the city's park system. Cleveland and Prince decided to create the city's first municipal bathing beach at the mouth of Kingsbury Creek. In anticipation of the 1915 swimming season, the seventy-one-year-old Cleveland announced that the facility would provide separate areas

SUBMISSIONS TO DULUTH PARK SUPERINTENDENT HENRY CLEVELAND'S 1915 CONTEST FOR AN APPROPRIATE SWIMMING SUIT FOR WOMEN AT THE INDIAN POINT BATHING BEACH WITHIN FAIRMOUNT PARK, INCLUDING THE WINNER, THE "STATUESQUE," RIGHT.

[IMAGE: ZENITH CITY PRESS]

INDIAN POINT TOURIST CAMP

By the time the Indian Point bathing beach opened in 1915, the introduction of affordable automobiles was changing the lifestyle of Americans. As families discovered the adventure of travel, the new pastime of "auto tourism" became a booming business. "Tents of Auto Campers Bloom on U.S. Highways," proclaimed the *Duluth News Tribune* in May 1922. "All along the highways, east or west, wherever the wind blows, are seen the more or less white tents of the auto campers.... What was a continent has become a state; what was a state has become a village. Distance has been obliterated; the east and the west have been hyphenated by the indomitable spirit of gypsying, which springs eternal in the human breast."

For many in Duluth, this was hardly news. The executives at Duluth Tent & Awning—who in 1911 purchased Duluth pioneer Camille Poirier's patent for the "Duluth pack," a canvas canoe portage pack—had already noted the trend, and in 1918 the company had begun manufacturing the "auto pack," which clamped on an automobile's running board to hold extra gear.

When Sam Snively became mayor in 1921, he announced his vision to "make Duluth second to no city on the American continent." Improving the existing parks was the heart of what became known as Snively's "City Beautiful" plan. He proclaimed that "beautiful parks, broad scenic highways, and modern tourist camp sites are the strongest advertisements a city can have. It is my hope that Duluth's parks and beauty spots will make it universally known." Snively promised to establish tourist camps and extend the boulevard system to link together the parks.

Hot summer days brought as many as seven hundred Duluthians to the bathing beach at the mouth of Kingsbury Creek. Many families set up tents in the shady grove on Indian Point and spent much of the summer camping along the river. Recognizing that tourists would also enjoy camping at Indian Point, Mayor Snively and Superintendent Cleveland chose it as the site for one of the city's first tourist camps. (The other two camps were at Chester Bowl and Brighton Beach.) Cleveland made only a few improvements before opening Indian Point to the autoists in 1922. The camp (shown above in a detail from a postcard, date unknown)

included a rustic shelter, running water, fireplaces, tables, and benches. And, as the *News Tribune* boasted, "A distinctive feature of this camp site is its bathing beach on upper St. Louis bay where autoists, dusty from the day's travel, may indulge in a refreshing dip."

Unfortunately, just as the tourist camp opened, the city closed the bathing beach because the water had become contaminated by sewage flowing into Kingsbury Creek. Cleveland announced that "bathing has been prohibited in the waters off Indian Point because of pollution and the waters there are no longer officially conducted by the city as a municipal bathing beach." City leaders discussed diverting the sewage to eliminate the pollution, but the beach never reopened.

Despite the loss of the bathing beach, the Indian Point Tourist Camp succeeded, although it never became quite as popular as the Brighton Beach camp; the tourist camp at Chester Bowl only operated for two years. In 1926 F. Rodney Paine, who replaced Cleveland as park superintendent, reported receipts of $842.50 from Indian Point and $2,402.00 from Brighton Beach. He speculated that tourists preferred Brighton Beach because "most of the people coming from southern and western states seem to want to see Lake Superior and to camp near it." Paine also reported numerous problems at Indian Point that made it less appealing: there were no showers, the toilets were in "very dilapidated condition" because the buildings had been heaved by frost, and the only entrance required crossing two dangerous railroad tracks and a decaying bridge that had been condemned. Paine asked city commissioners for funds to make improvements, but they did not respond. In the summer of 1929, Indian Point recorded only 1,693 visitors, while 4,553 people had stayed at the Brighton Beach Tourist Camp.

The onset of the Great Depression forced budget and staff cuts to all city departments. Paine reported that "during the year [1930], it has been found necessary to give relief to the unemployed, both by private and public funds. The park department was fortunate in having work that could be done by common labor." Paine's focus shifted toward minimizing maintenance costs and maximizing any revenue the park system could generate. He believed that investments in the tourist camps would pay off, so in 1930 his work crew built a new toilet building and two cabins at the Indian Point Tourist Camp. Six more cabins were built by 1934. Throughout the Depression the city's tourist camps were profitable. From 1933 through 1935, Paine reported a net annual income of about $250 from the Indian Point Tourist Camp, about $4,200 in today's dollars.

Business slowed during World War II. The Park Department reported in 1943 that, "The two tourist camps...due to the lack of tourists, showed a small profit but nothing compared to previous years." Nevertheless, from 1952 through 1955 Indian Point brought in a net income of about $450 each year, and the park department rightfully claimed that "the tourist camp project...is the only activity which has been self-sustaining and from which the taxpayer has enjoyed a profit."

Renovation projects in 1965 and 1970 brought additional improvements, and the cabins were removed. Today Indian Point Campground, now managed by a private company, still welcomes travelers. The budget for the St. Louis River Corridor Initiative, announced by the city in March 2015, included $1.5 million to "renew and update Indian Point Campground." A master plan for the improvements will be prepared in 2016, and work will start in 2017.

—— IMAGE: HERB DILLON ——

for men and women. As he explained to the *News Tribune*, "The bathing beach will be so divided that families, young women, young men, and juniors will have the use of their portions of the beach, safe, untrammeled and care free."

Cleveland also banished "form-fitting" bathing suits, but was willing to consider public opinion on what type of suit would be acceptable. He told the *News Tribune*, "Personally, I think all bathing suits must have skirts, but let's hear from the people." Despite his conservative viewpoint, he had a great sense of humor, and in March 1915 he announced a contest to design the best "appropriate" bathing costume for women. He offered a prize of five dollars for the winner. The guidelines were to "send in just the kind of costume you think would look the 'nicest' and still 'get by.' But don't make your drawing too bold." For the next two weeks, sketches of bathing suit designs filled the newspaper.

To evaluate the fifty entries, Cleveland put together a judging committee of nine women who represented all sections of the city, from Lakeside to Fond du Lac. According to the *News Tribune*, Cleveland met with the judges at Southwick's Soda Fountain and "over steaming chocolate, salads, and other dainties to be provided at the

THIS HUMOROUS SUBMISSION TO THE CITY'S 1915 BATHING SUIT CONTEST, WHICH APPEARED IN THE *DULUTH NEWS TRIBUNE*, SUGGESTS THAT THE OUTSIDE TEMPERATURE IN DULUTH IS RARELY WARM ENOUGH TO ENJOY A SWIM.

[IMAGE: ZENITH CITY PRESS]

CHILDREN FROM THE ST. JAMES ORPHANAGE ENJOY LUNCH AT FAIRMOUNT PARK IN AUGUST 1932. MAYOR SAM SNIVELY PAID FOR THE OUTING, AND MANY OTHERS LIKE IT, DURING HIS FIFTEEN YEARS AS MAYOR.

[IMAGE: M. RYAN COLLECTION]

captain's expense" the designs were turned over to the committee for a decision. On April 8 the women met at the home of the committee chair, Miss Jean Poirier, to make their selection. They chose as the winner a "statuesque" design from Mrs. M. P. St. Pierre. The committee reported to the *News Tribune* that the swimsuit "was the most practical and artistic design, commensurate with modesty, of all costumes submitted." Cleveland planned to have several hundred of the bathing costumes made in Duluth by local knitting mills for renting to bathers who did not have their own.

To prepare for the official July 4 opening of the beach, Pulaski Street was surfaced with gravel to provide access for horse teams and automobiles. Cleveland installed two dozen metal dressing booths (twelve for women and twelve for men) and a thirty-foot tent pavilion for lounging and refreshments. Roland B. Reed, a former swimming instructor at the YMCA, was hired as the "natatorial supervisor" for forty dollars per month to provide free swimming lessons for children and adults.

In the first week an average of sixty bathers used the beach each day. Although "proper clothing" was required, within two weeks the newspaper reported the shocking news that "some aquatic enthusiasts entered the surf in their underwear." And a few bold women immediately ignored the official bathing costume and donned men's bathing suits, which at the time covered the entire torso. Although swimming without a suit was not tolerated, the women's rebellion aroused sympathy. City Commissioner Bernard Silberstein offered his opinion to the newspaper that "as long as they wear stockings and keep them pulled up nice they don't have to wear the women's kind."

By August 1915 the Indian Point Bathing Beach was one of the most popular spots in town, not just for swimming but for picnicking and camping as well. An average of two hundred people used the beach every day, and the *News Tribune* reported that "scores of families are taking advantage of the ideal camping facilities at Indian Point to pass the summer in the open. Dozens of tents are pitched in the grove, and picnic parties as well are held near the beach every day."

KINGSBURY CREEK FLOWING THROUGH FAIRMOUNT PARK IN 1927. (PHOTO BY F. R. PAINE.)

[IMAGE: UMD MARTIN LIBRARY]

A Zoo is Born

About the same time the city purchased the land for Fairmount Park, other cities throughout the country were creating "zoological gardens" to house wild and exotic animals. Duluth's leaders—always in competition with Chicago—usually followed the latest trends, but surprisingly, Duluth did not have a municipal zoo until 1923.

Several small, privately maintained animal parks existed in Duluth as early as 1905. In the eastern end of town, Mr. L. A. Gunderson, proprietor of the Lester Park Pavilion, briefly kept several bears and deer that had been captured nearby. And on Minnesota Point, Oatka Beach once boasted a collection of bears, timber wolves, deer, and porcupines.

But despite frequent requests from the public, there was no municipal zoo. Even the *News Tribune* called for a city zoo in a September 1905 editorial that declared: "A Duluth Zoo need not be expensive or very elaborate.... To begin with, there should be a deer park of twenty acres.... A heavy wire fence eight feet high would enclose it.... The care would be simply a matter of throwing in hay and salt." The author of the editorial clearly did not understand the reality of caring for wild animals.

In May 1910 Frank Heimick, who owned land near the French River, offered to give the city two friendly moose that lived in his woods. However, Park Superintendent Henry Cleveland adamantly opposed the idea. He candidly told the *News Tribune*, "Duluth doesn't need a zoo anyway. We can go out in the country here...and find all the natural zoo we need and that is better than the best in any park.... Every time a man has a bear or a moose on his hands, he wants to sell it to the city to start a zoo, little realizing the expense and trouble its acceptance would entail." Heimick instead gave the moose to Chicago's Lincoln Park Zoo.

Despite Cleveland's opposition, the movement gained momentum in 1915 when members of the Elks Club, with the support of Public Works commissioner J. A. Farrell, convinced the rest of the city commissioners to accept two elks from the state of Washington.

Fuzzy Wuzzy, the first polar bear at the Duluth Zoo within Fairmount Park, 1927.

[IMAGE: UMD MARTIN LIBRARY]

BERT ONSGARD

As the oft-told story goes, in 1923 West Duluth businessman and avid sportsman Bert Onsgard encountered an orphaned white-tailed deer fawn at a northern Minnesota logging camp while on a fishing trip. He took the tiny deer, which he named Billy, back to his West Duluth Printery at 5312 Ramsey Street. Onsgard was an active member of the community and belonged to several business clubs. His sporting interests included memberships in the Izaak Walton League, the West Duluth Sportsmen's Club, and the West Duluth Gun Club. His passions merged when Billy inspired him to open a menagerie.

With permission from city commissioners, Onsgard led a campaign to organize a zoo, staging several programs to raise money and purchase equipment. The park department set aside ten acres within Fairmount Park, and Billy became the facility's first official resident, housed in a pen made of donated fencing originally intended for a zoo in Lester Park.

In 1926 Onsgard—the zoo's unofficial curator—was elected to Duluth's Hall of Fame. One of the early zoo's stranger policies under Onsgard called for not feeding carnivorous animals on the Christian sabbath, as they "should fast on Sundays." Zoo researcher Matthew Waterhouse views this as Onsgard's humor on display. With little money, food shortages during the zoo's early years were common, according to Waterhouse, so Onsgard "scoured the countryside for sick cattle or horses for the lions and tigers. He went to grocery stores for expired produce to feed the elephant and the monkeys. He heavily encouraged zoo visitors to feed the animals."

Despite his lack of training in zoology, the zoo grew steadily under Onsgard. His children told Waterhouse they remember that he "insisted the zoo should be something that all children and families can enjoy regardless of class, money, or race." In 1927 city officials named him Duluth's "most civic-hearted man." Park Superintendent F. Rodney Paine reported that "the largest development of the year has been at the Duluth Zoo, the popularity of which has been conclusively proved by the large crowds which are there on every pleasant day. Through the untiring efforts of Mr. Onsgard, animals have been added to the Zoo rapidly and it has been difficult to furnish accommodations rapidly enough." Onsgard owned some of those animals.

When Mayor Snively lost his reelection bid in 1937, Paine and Onsgard both lost their jobs under new mayor Rudy Berghult. Berghult thought Snively had given Onsgard too much free rein and suspected the city was paying for the food and shelter of Onsgard's animals—Onsgard kept no records of acquisitions. When Edward Hatch became mayor in 1941, new park superintendent John V. Hoene rehired Onsgard. In 1944 new mayor George W. Johnson promptly dismissed Onsgard because, he said, the zoo was in "very bad shape." Onsgard demanded a retraction, blaming the city council for lack of funding for proper maintenance. According to Waterhouse, the Onsgard family believes that Johnson's dismissal of Onsgard came from the fact that both men were professional printers, and therefore business rivals.

By then Onsgard had opened the Arrowhead Amusement Park, located across Grand Avenue from the zoo. The facility featured a merry-go-round, tilt-a-whirl, and other rides. Onsgard often transported the rides—and some animals—to fairs and other events throughout the region. A stroke forced him into retirement. Onsgard died on July 8, 1971, in Scottsdale, Arizona. In 1993 the zoo opened the multi-purpose Onsgard Room in its main building in his honor.

Although supporters first suggested Fairmount Park as the best site for the zoo, city officials settled on Lester Park. But Duluth was too late—the elk were given to Sioux City, Iowa, instead of Duluth.

Then in 1923, West Duluth businessman Bert Onsgard approached city leaders with a new plan for a zoo at Fairmount Park, and commissioners gave him the go-ahead. Because the zoo was located in a city park, responsibility for its maintenance fell to the park department, but Onsgard provided the early leadership to make it a success. In 1927 Park Superintendent F. Rodney Paine turned all animal care responsibilities over to Onsgard. That year the zoo acquired a cassowary and a pair of lions with money raised by Duluth school children. Black bears that had been trapped after wandering into town were soon added to the collection.

BERT ONSGARD HOLDING CHIMPANZEES TOM AND JERRY AT THE DULUTH ZOO WITHIN FAIRMOUNT PARK, 1927.

1930s Zoo Expansion

By 1928 the facility held about two hundred animals and birds. The zoo grew steadily under Onsgard. Over the years regional animals like bear, wolf, moose, elk, and deer were joined by exotics including hyenas, monkeys, and an elephant. The zoo's main building was constructed in 1929. The one-story facility was designed to house a variety of animals, and a second floor was added later as the zoo's population grew. Artists from the Minnesota Art Project painted murals representing flora and fauna on the building's walls. The *News Tribune* reported that the zoo contained "eleven varieties of deer including the yellow, white and black fallow deer; mountain lions, African lions, pumas; polar, black, Russian and brown bear; fox,

raccoons, bobcats, skunks, badger, coyotes; jackals; cranes, pheasants, swans, ducks, pelicans, storks, ostriches, eagles, doves, parrots, canaries; monkeys, seals and mountain goats."

The number of visitors increased steadily, with approximately half a million people enjoying the zoo in 1934. As the number of animals grew, the city struggled to add buildings to house them. During the 1930s workers from a variety of federal programs—including the Emergency Relief Administration (ERA), Civil Works Administration (CWA), and Works Progress Administration (WPA)—constructed bear dens, wolf runs, an elephant house, and a monkey island. Federal relief funds in 1934 and 1935 provided more major improvements, not only to the zoo, but also to Fairmount Park itself. Workers

THE DULUTH ZOO AT FAIRMOUNT PARK, 1939. (PHOTO BY L. PERRY GALLAGHER JR.)

[IMAGE: UMD MARTIN LIBRARY]

ARNE EDGAR NYBAK CREATED THIS MURAL WITHIN THE MAIN ZOO BUILDING IN THE 1930S FOR THE MINNESOTA ART PROJECT.

[IMAGE: UMD MARTIN LIBRARY]

from the ERA constructed paths throughout the park, five bluestone bridges over Kingsbury Creek, a bluestone pavilion for picnickers (with a fully equipped kitchen), and terraces in the natural bowl area for summer band concerts.

The zoo grew to seventeen acres and its population included several very popular characters. Bessie the Asian elephant, known for her frequent escapes, was two years old when she arrived in 1929 and was the only elephant ever housed at the Duluth Zoo. In July 1941 she pushed over a portion of the fencing surrounding her enclosure and "roamed about the west end of the city for several hours." She traveled over a mile before Onsgard retrieved her. Longtime Duluth newspaper columnist Jim Heffernan remembered Bessie in 2015: "She was billed as 'the dancing elephant' for reasons I can understand...there was Bessie, shackled in her wing, rocking constantly back and forth as though she was nervous about something." Bessie lived at the zoo until she passed away in 1974. Heffernan recalls that her corpse was "laid to rest in the Rice Lake landfill with the wretched refuse of decades of the city's garbage. An ignominious ending for a lonely elephant."

Valerie the Asiatic black bear came to the zoo in 1946 after a rather remarkable life—for a bear. While serving in Asia in 1942, Lieutenant Edward R. Ashton purchased a captured cub and made the young bear the "copilot" of his cargo plane. Ashton and Valerie flew

164 missions over the "Hump"—what Allied pilots called the eastern end of the Himalayan Mountains—before the bear became a mascot for U.S. War Bonds. She eventually became too large to fly and was sold to Duluth's zoo, where her love for Coca-Cola and beer made her a favorite until her death in 1966.

Tragedy struck the zoo on November 11, 1950, when a tame deer named Bambi was killed. Newspapers reported the deer had "won the hearts of hundreds of Duluth youngsters by licking their hands through the fence when they gave her food." Some time after midnight, two young men approached Bambi, lured her near them with food, then slit her throat. City officials were furious and established a reward for the capture of the perpetrators as well as a citywide committee to solve what Johnson called "our zoo problem." Bambi was the fifth zoo animal to die in just a few months: an elk, a white deer, and two aoudads (also called Barbary sheep) died of poisoning. And it wasn't the first time an animal had been killed—in the 1930s a sloth bear was beaten to death by an elderly man wielding a cane, and several other animals were killed by trespassers over the years.

The Arrowhead Zoological Society Takes Over

The zoo continued to expand over the years, leaving few traces of the original Fairmount Park. For nearly thirty-five years Duluth's mayor appointed the zoo's management, which changed with almost every new administration. After Duluth changed its form of government in 1956, that system no longer worked. This prompted the creation of the nonprofit Arrowhead Zoological Society (AZS) in 1959 to help the city operate, maintain, develop, and raise funds for the zoo. The city maintained ownership of the buildings and property and hired the zoo director, maintenance workers, and zookeepers. The zoological society hired and managed staff to operate and market the zoo as an attraction. During that time the animal population continued to grow, with the addition of a giant tortoise, chimpanzees, kangaroos, and large cats, including a jaguar and a cougar.

In the 1960s the zoo played host to its most popular tenant, an Indian mongoose named Mr. Magoo. A merchant seaman had smuggled Mr. Magoo into the United States in 1959, but a federal ban on mongoose appeared to be a death sentence for Magoo. Duluthians were

BESSIE THE ELEPHANT, CA. 1929, SHORTLY AFTER SHE ARRIVED AT THE DULUTH ZOO WITHIN FAIRMOUNT PARK.

[IMAGE: UMD MARTIN LIBRARY]

THORNTON'S KIDDIELAND

In 1939 Robert and Mabel Thornton (pictured, right) moved to Duluth from Des Moines, Iowa, and opened Thornton's Kiddieland adjacent to the zoo at Seventy-second Avenue West and Grand Avenue. It catered to children "toddler stage up to twelve years old" and for seven years its sole attraction was a miniature train.

According to Robbie Bailey, the Thornton's daughter, Robert's father Elmer O. Thornton built eleven steam-powered miniature locomotives, and his son Robert owned two of them. One operated at Kiddieland, and the other was used for the Austin and Owatonna county fairs and the Minnesota State Fair. Running Kiddieland wasn't Robert's only job. He also worked as an engineer for the Duluth, Missabe & Iron Range Railroad from 1942 until his death.

Thornton began expanding Kiddieland in 1947, first with a car ride and then a boat ride, a Chair-O-Plane ride (pictured, below), a Ferris wheel, and a "Little Dipper." In 1964 the facility acquired the merry-go-round from the recently closed Minnesota Point Amusement Park. That year the *Duluth Herald* noted the facility's twenty-fifth anniversary. At the time, the paper reported, Sunday was the busiest day for Kiddieland, but Monday—free day at the zoo—was a close second. About half of its customers were tourists, and elderly residents of St. Louis County's Cook and Arlington homes also "enjoyed the train ride" along with the children.

The Thorntons were big supporters of the Duluth Zoo. In 1958 Mabel Thornton helped organize an event to raise money to help the zoo purchase a hippopotamus and donated the day's Kiddieland receipts to the cause. They also helped the zoo purchase black panthers in 1964. After Robert Thornton's death in 1965, Mabel sold the facility to Jerry Mitchell, who later turned it over to Jeff Vollma. Over the years the facility added a moonwalk, a roller coaster, and a large slide that children slid down on wool blankets. The miniature train was removed.

In September 1975 Duluth's Park and Recreation Advisory Board recommended that the City Council close Kiddieland because "the amusement center detracts from the main thrust of the zoo." The council sent the recommendation back to the board, but, even so, Kiddieland would be gone soon enough.

On June 3, 1977, between one and two hundred "young people" gathered at the zoo's parking lot next to Kiddieland. The spot had become a popular place to party. A twenty-two-year-old man entered Kiddieland (some say he jumped a fence, others said the fence was in disrepair and easily circumvented) and climbed to the top of the big slide using the structure's girders—the stairs were not accessible because they had been blocked to prevent unauthorized use of the slide. The man did not know that a chain had been stretched across the base of the slide, also intended to keep trespassers off. When he slid down the man's throat hit the chain, sending his head backward against the slide, causing fatal injuries. In 1981 the victim's widow brought a successful lawsuit against Vollma, although the victim was also determined to be partially responsible for the accident. As a result, Vollma closed the amusement park.

Adjacent to Kiddieland, Gerry and Sophie Little ran the Zoo Snack Shop, a concession stand that sold candy, ice cream, hot dogs, popcorn, and other treats. Ron House, a grandson of the Littles, recalls that the zoo's elephant, Bessie, was known for her wandering and welcomed his grandfather at the stand on several mornings. Another of the Little's grandchildren, Harvey "Bud" Simonson, ran the concession stand after Gerry entered a nursing home. Simonson purchased the business following his grandfather's death in 1979. The Zoo Snack Shop closed along with Kiddieland.

— IMAGE: T. KASPER COLLECTION —

— IMAGE: ROBERT RODRIGUEZ —

outraged, and their anger spread across the country and up the chain of government. During his last months in office, President John F. Kennedy signed a presidential pardon written by the secretary of the interior, and Magoo was spared. He lived at the zoo until 1968, when he died of natural causes. While Mr. Magoo was at the height of his popularity in 1964, Faru—the first black rhinoceros born in captivity—became a resident. Five years later a Volkswagen bus dropped off Nemo, an African lion famous for siring cubs two years after he had a vasectomy.

Basil Norton became the zoo's director in 1967 and served until retiring in 1994. He is credited for modernizing the zoo, implementing educational programs, and operating some very successful breeding programs, particularly with big cats, hoofed animals, and primates. During Norton's tenure fifty-seven South China tigers—considered extinct in the wild since 1996—were born at the zoo. Following his death in 2015 Norton's daughter Amy told newspapers that Norton "hoped to inspire people at the zoo so that they would be dedicated to conserving animals in the wild." During his tenure the city added a wing to the main building, funded by a donation of $250,000 from Richard Griggs, a philanthropist who enjoyed big-game hunting. Griggs had many of his kills stuffed as trophies, which he wanted to show off at the zoo. Despite some backlash from those who, as Heffernan explained, "believed zoos were for displaying live animals and not dead ones," the wing was built. Today the facility, named the Griggs Learning Center, contains very few of Griggs's trophies and helps to promote Norton's ideology.

Norton was followed as zoo director—changed to chief executive officer in 2006—by Michael J. Janis (1995–2005), Ryan Gulker (2006–2007), Sam Maida (2009–2013), and Dr. Dawn Mackety (2013–2016). Julene Boe served as interim CEO during vacancies, and Corey Leet will take over the position in 2017.

The Lake Superior Zoo became an accredited member of the Association of Zoos and Aquariums (AZA) in 1985 and two years later began modernizing the facility. With $4 million from the state and $3 million from the city, zoo officials began initiating a three-part plan that included more naturalistic facilities for its residents. The name was changed to the Lake Superior Zoo, and the Arrowhead Zoological Society became the Lake Superior Zoological Society (LSZS). The second stage of the plan moved forward in the 1990s and included renovating the zoo's old main building, turning animal cages into offices, a restaurant, and a gift shop. The third stage was delayed after Governor Arne Carlson vetoed funding in 1996.

THE DULUTH ZOO'S MOST FAMOUS RESIDENT, MR. MAGOO THE MONGOOSE, HELD BY BOB WAHLSTERN, WHO WORKED WITH ZOO DIRECTOR BASIL NORTON TO BRIDGE THE GAP BETWEEN THE ARROWHEAD ZOOLOGICAL SOCIETY AND ZOO WORKERS EMPLOYED BY THE CITY OF DULUTH. FORMER ZOO VETERINARIAN TOM DOUGHERTY DESCRIBED NORTON AND WAHLSTREN'S WORK AT THE ZOO AS A "TRUE PARTNERSHIP" THAT PUT AN END TO "YEARS OF POLITICAL AND LEGAL SPATS BETWEEN THE CITY AND THE ZOOLOGICAL SOCIETY OVER THE LEADERSHIP."

[IMAGE: ERIN WALSBURG]

In 2006 the zoo lost its AZA accreditation after failing to make improvements called for in 2001. Two years later, zoo officials unveiled a master plan for a $40 million refurbishment. In 2009 the Duluth city council voted 6–3 in favor of transferring all of the zoo's operations to the LSZS. According to the *News Tribune*, the vote came after Mayor Don Ness gave the council just two options: "Vote to turn over all management of the zoo to the Lake Superior Zoological Society or the city will have to close the zoo." Under the LSZS, the Lake Superior Zoo regained its accreditation in 2011.

ZOO WORKERS TRY TO GET THE ATTENTION OF A SEA LION PERCHED ALONGSIDE KINGSBURY CREEK AS IT FLOWS THROUGH THE DULUTH ZOO WITHIN FAIRMOUNT PARK, 1930. ORIGINAL ZOO DIRECTOR BERT ONSGARD HAD THE CREEK REROUTED AND LINED WITH CONCRETE TO CREATE SEASONAL ISLAND HABITATS FOR SEA LIONS, SEALS, MONKEYS, WATERFOWL, AND OTHER SPECIES. THE CREEK'S MANIPULATION LIKELY INCREASED DAMAGE CAUSED TO THE ZOO DURING SEVERAL FLOODS, INCLUDING THE FLOOD OF 2012.

[IMAGE: UMD MARTIN LIBRARY]

And then came the flood of June 20, 2012, which devastated many areas in the city. Kingsbury Creek became a torrent, sweeping though the zoo and damaging buildings and grounds. Fourteen animals and birds died, including sheep, goats, a donkey, a turkey vulture, a raven, and a snowy owl. The popular Polar Shores exhibit was hit particularly hard. A polar bear named Berlin floated out of her exhibit; while she stayed near her home she nonetheless had to be tranquilized. Feisty the harbor seal was found in the middle of Grand Avenue. Berlin, Fiesty, and Vivian—another harbor seal—and several other exotic animals were later moved to other zoos.

The flood also delayed the renovation of the park's 1933 bluestone pavilion, built by the Works Progress Administration, until August 2013. According to the *News Tribune*, the formerly open-air facility was converted into "a three-season event and education center for hosting the zoo's educational programming and special events." The $520,000 effort earned an award from the Duluth Preservation Alliance in 2015, and the pavilion is now a WPA historic site.

In April 2015 the LSZS reported that during the previous year the Lake Superior Zoo welcomed 87,112 visitors. Later that month the Ness administration proposed several different restructuring plans for the zoo; ideas included scaling back the facility's size, reducing the number of exhibits, and eliminating the animals altogether. After initial public backlash, the city and LSZS came together to create a "consensus concept for the future of the Lake Superior Zoo."

Writing in March 2015, Duluth City Council President Zack Filipovich described the plan: "The footprint of the zoo will be reduced to about ten acres, all on the east side of Kingsbury Creek.... Educational opportunities will be enhanced with a new grizzly bear exhibit, an amphitheater for educational programs featuring live animals, and an exciting Forest Discovery Zone area that will mix education, play and up-close animal experiences.... The west side of Kingsbury Creek will be converted into a signature public park—Fairmont Park [sic]—with planned picnic areas, trails connecting the hillside and the riverfront, and a sledding hill for our exciting Duluth winters."

The Duluth City Council unanimously approved the plan on March 13, 2016, yet ongoing struggles to achieve accreditation and sufficient funding leave the zoo's future in question.

7. Leif Erikson Park

A Park Along Lake Superior's Shore

Perhaps due to its location along the shore of Lake Superior and because the Duluth Lakewalk passes through its heart, Leif Erikson is one of Duluth's most-visited parks. It has also undergone more changes—including name changes—than any other park in the Zenith City. Various plans for its development in the early 1900s included expanding the park by creating new land along the lakeshore as far as the Duluth Ship Canal. While these plans never came to fruition, at least not as part of the park, today they are reflected in the recent developments of the Lakewalk and Lake Place Park.

The Birth of Cullum Park

Early in 1905, a small triangle of land at the convergence of East Superior Street and London Road became the spark that ignited a community effort to create a new park on the shore of Lake Superior. The triangular sliver, roughly between Ninth and Tenth Avenues East, had already been divided into sixteen fifty-foot-wide lots, several of which were occupied by houses. In addition, the city's board of public works was getting ready to install a large granite fountain at the westernmost point of the triangle, which extended west of Ninth Avenue. As the *Duluth News Tribune* explained, the new fountain would "take the place of the cheap iron affair placed in the locality by the city several years ago." Donated by Clara Stone Blood of St. Paul, the fountain was a monument to the memory of her father, pioneer George C. Stone, who arrived in the city in 1869 to work as the cashier of Duluth's first bank.

Despite these obstacles, John Millen, vice president of the Alger-Smith Lumber Company and managing director of the Alger-Sullivan Lumber Company, offered to donate to the city one undeveloped lot in the middle of the triangular plot. Millen asked only that the city acquire the remainder of the area and dedicate it as a park.

The *News Tribune* reported that the proposition met with "instant and popular approval." The newspaper promised to donate $1,000 toward purchase of the additional lots and recommended the project to

LITHOGRAPHIC POSTCARD, CA. 1930, OF THE REPLICA VIKING VESSEL *LEIF ERIKSON* ON DISPLAY WITHIN LEIF ERIKSON PARK, FORMERLY LAKE SHORE PARK, AND ORIGINALLY CULLUM PARK.

[IMAGE: ZENITH CITY PRESS]

the Duluth Board of Park Commissioners "in the hope that this greatly desired feature of Duluth's landscape shall be quickly added."

Park board Vice President Bernard Silberstein responded by saying, "The site would certainly make a handsome park. It was intended originally for such a purpose, but through accident houses were built there." Board President Luther Mendenhall agreed, but he called on the citizens of Duluth to find the money. "The park board has no funds to make a purchase of this land at present, but I would think that it ought to be easy to raise the required amount among the neighboring property owners."

The triangle of land was soon forgotten, however, after real estate investor Louis Loeb, who lived nearby at 1123 East Superior Street, suggested that the project be enlarged to include the lakeshore below London Road. The Northern Pacific Railroad (NP), owner of the lakeshore property, offered to sell the land from Eighth to Thirteenth Avenues East for $20,000, half of its market value. The park board agreed to provide half the purchase price if Duluth citizens would come up with the rest.

Duluth's newly elected mayor, Dr. Marcus B. Cullum, announced his support with the comment that "any movement toward the extension of the park system is good. It is to be regretted that the park fund is so small.... The project would have to be carried out by public subscription since the park fund is not sufficient to keep the present parks in the proper order. It is a great pity that more of the lake shore property was not reserved when it was not so expensive."

Other than contributing $10,000, the park board did very little to help acquire the land. Instead, Mayor Cullum took the lead. In May 1905 he called together property owners and interested citizens to discuss ways to raise money for the project, which at that point was referred to by a variety of names including East End Park, Lakeside Park, Lake Front Park, and Lake Shore Park.

MARCUS B. CULLUM, NAMESAKE OF CULLUM PARK, THE ORIGINAL NAME OF LEIF ERIKSON PARK.

[IMAGE: DULUTH PUBLIC LIBRARY]

DETAIL OF A SANBORN INSURANCE MAP OF DULUTH, 1909. THE SHADED AREA INDICATES THE SITE JOHN MILLEN PROPOSED FOR A PARK; THE STAR INDICATES THE ORIGINAL LOCATION OF THE STONE MEMORIAL FOUNTAIN, NOW A FEATURE OF LEIF ERIKSON PARK'S ROSE GARDEN.

[IMAGE: ZENITH CITY PRESS]

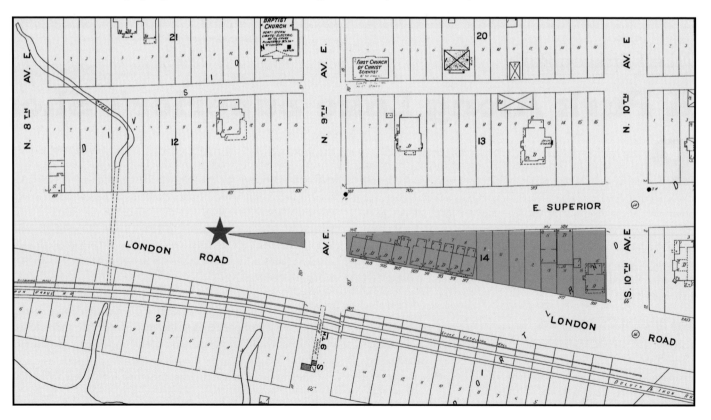

Money came in slowly despite frequent pleas in the newspapers. One editorial published in The *News Tribune* on May 21, 1905, came from local businessman Charles Schiller, who wrote, "The funds at the disposal of the board are insufficient to do much in the way of acquiring new properties and it is therefore up to the public spirited citizens to come to the front and show their loyalty to their city by loosening their purse strings."

A year later nearly $5,000 had been collected, leaving the city $5,000 short. Mayor Cullum continued to lead the fundraising drive. "In response to repeated admonitions from numerous residents of the East End," the *News Tribune* reported, "and from his own deep conviction of the desirability of the park, he is now trying to bring the matter to a successful conclusion."

By August 1906 time was running out on the city's option to buy the land, and the mayor made a final strong push by sending out urgent appeals to many of the prominent property owners in Duluth's East End. The *News Tribune* editorial staff also continued to encourage the public: "Duluth has not today a foot of lake front park.... It will be exceedingly short-sighted and false economy if this park is not secured, and if this opportunity passes, the day will come when every citizen of Duluth will bitterly regret it."

The mayor's efforts finally succeeded. On September 30 he announced that Watson S. Moore, First Ward alderman and part owner of the Spencer-Moore Grain Company, "has assured the people of Duluth that the ten acres...have been practically secured by the city and will be converted into a park."

In June 1907 the city took ownership of the land below London Road from Eighth Avenue East to Thirteenth Avenue East. Although the park board never officially named the new greenspace, it became known as Cullum Park in recognition of the mayor's key role in acquiring the land.

Cullum Park becomes Lake Shore Park

Almost as soon as Duluthians unofficially named their new park for Mayor Cullum, local entrepreneurs decided that the park should be expanded into a much larger facility and named Lake Shore Park.

A GROUP OF BOYS SKIPPING STONES ALONG THE LAKE SUPERIOR SHORE NEAR LAKE SHORE PARK, TODAY'S LEIF ERIKSON PARK, IN 1911.

[IMAGE: DULUTH PUBLIC LIBRARY]

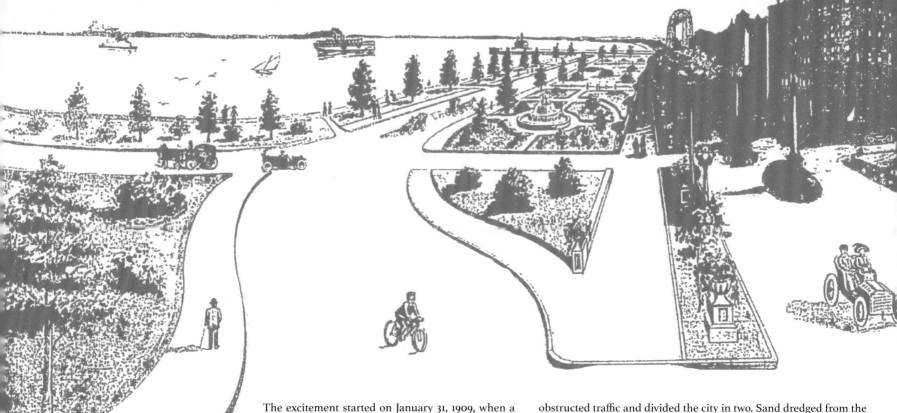

THIS SKETCH FOR A PROPOSED
WESTERN EXPANSION OF CULLUM
PARK ALONG WHAT IS KNOWN
TODAY AS THE CANAL PARK
BUSINESS DISTRICT, WHICH
APPEARED IN THE *DULUTH NEWS
TRIBUNE* JANUARY 31, 1909,
MIGHT REMIND READERS OF
DULUTH'S LAKEWALK, FIRST
DEVELOPED IN THE 1980S.

[IMAGE: ZENITH CITY PRESS]

The excitement started on January 31, 1909, when a grand new plan for Duluth's lakefront filled the front page of the *News Tribune*. Inspired by Chicago's example, which since the late 1800s had been adding fill to its lakefront to create parkland, the newspaper proposed that the City of Duluth acquire the rest of the Lake Superior shoreline from Cullum Park's western border at Eighth Avenue East all the way to the ship canal, build a breakwater about five hundred feet out from the shore, and fill in the lake between the wall and the existing shore.

As the newspaper explained, "The plan would be to have the government fix a harbor line where one does not now exist, to construct a concrete sea wall to mark the outer limits of the park and driveway and by a filling-in process to make solid ground where now there is water, then to go ahead with the beautification of the grounds with walks and driveways, with trees and shrubbery, fountains and flowerbeds and all things that go to make up an ideal public park."

Proponents of the plan suggested that the breakwater could be constructed from boulders blasted from Point of Rocks, which engineers were working to eliminate because the massive rock outcrop

obstructed traffic and divided the city in two. Sand dredged from the harbor could be used as fill. The result would be forty-five acres of new land that could be turned into a beautiful park.

Not only would the project create an attractive park on the lakefront, it would also clean up the St. Croix District—the eastern portion of today's Canal Park Business District—which at that time served in part as the city's red light district, filled with boarding houses, saloons, and "houses of ill fame," more commonly known as brothels.

A few days later the *News Tribune* reported that the proposal had "created much interest and is being endorsed on every hand by Duluth people." G. W. Preston, advertising manager of the *News Tribune*, received credit as the original creator of the Lake Shore Park idea. A group of local businessmen led by Albert Comstock, vice president of Marshall-Wells Hardware, offered support.

All agreed that the plan would be costly, but they believed the investment worthwhile. They also argued that the land should be purchased right away, before it became even more expensive. On February 23, 1910, the *News Tribune* speculated, "If it is done now it will cost, on the estimate, $120,000. If done in the future, no one knows what the cost will be, but in ten years it would probably be ten times as great. It is true that the city has not now any money to invest in this way. But that does not mean that the movement must stop and wait."

But wait it did. Despite the proclamations of widespread support, nothing happened. Over the next few years the proposal—with creative variations—reappeared periodically in the newspaper. Not all the ideas were good ones. When Dr. John McCuen took office as Duluth's new mayor in March 1912, his first message to the citizens of Duluth included an unfortunate choice of words: "The city could make use of the lake shore as a public dumping ground for the disposal of excess material and in the course of time as the amount of material deposited increases, the city would acquire a park...at practically no cost."

Others suggested building a "sewage purifying plant" in the filled area. Park Superintendent Henry Cleveland, always ready with big plans, envisioned a public swimming pool with water warmed by a steam-heating plant that would also supply a public laundry, where poor people could find hot and cold water and facilities for doing the family washing.

Encouraged by Mayor McCuen's support, in the spring of 1912 the park board began negotiations with representatives of the NP, which controlled the rights to most of the lakefront property. In November the men reached a tentative agreement that would hand over the shoreline to the city provided the breakwater was built within three years. The newly created land was to be used for park purposes only, except for nine acres that would be deeded to the railroad. Park Commissioner F. A. Patrick strongly supported this arrangement, which, as a result, became known as the Patrick Plan.

Unrealized Dreams

Although Cullum Park became known as Lake Shore Park, the project faded quietly away following the introduction of a new city charter in April 1913 that eliminated the park board and removed all elected officials from office. William I. Prince, first mayor under the new charter, also served as the Commissioner of Public Affairs, which gave him responsibility for the parks. While he did not pursue the grand vision

TWO LITHOGRAPHIC POSTCARDS, CA. 1900 TO 1915, OF THE LAKE SUPERIOR SHORE AT NINTH AVENUE EAST (TOP) WITHIN LAKE SHORE PARK AND AT "LOOKOUT POINT" WHICH APPEARS TO BE A ROCKY OUTCROPPING EAST OF THE PARK.

[IMAGE: ZENITH CITY PRESS]

North Shore, 9th Ave. East, Duluth, Minn.

LEIF ERIKSON PARK'S ROSE GARDEN

Outside of the *Leif Erikson* boat itself, Leif Erikson Park is best known for its Rose Garden, first planted by F. Rodney Paine in 1930. In his annual report Paine wrote that "the beds in upper Leif Erikson Park which had previously been planted every spring to annual bedding plants were planted this year to hybrid tea and hybrid perpetual roses. Some of these plants were furnished from the municipal nursery and the balance were furnished by the Duluth Garden Flower Society. It is the intention of this group to be responsible for these rose beds in that they will replace any plants that may die from time to time." Over the years the garden fell into neglect, was resurrected by volunteers, then removed for highway development and finally reinstalled and improved. One of the most popular features of Duluth's entire park system, today the Rose Garden features a marble gazebo with a wrought-iron dome, stone benches, and two monuments: a fountain in memory of a Duluth pioneer and a statue of the park's namesake.

One of the garden's most prominent features is the Stone Memorial Fountain, built to commemorate Duluth pioneer George C. Stone. In 1869 Stone and George Sargent came to Duluth as agents of Jay Cooke and set up Duluth's first bank. Stone was credited for actually running the business and was described as "a peculiar-looking man... [who] was not very well dressed, talked smoothly, seemed to have had considerable experience of the world, and transacted all the business." When Duluth became a city in 1870, he was appointed as its first treasurer and helped found the first Duluth Chamber of Commerce; he also promoted iron mining on the Vermilion Range and later helped the Merritt family open the Mesabi Iron Range.

The fountain, designed by St. Paul architect Thomas Holyoke and financed by Stone's daughter, Clara Stone Blood, was erected in October 1905 on a small triangular plot between Ninth and Tenth Avenues East at the junction of Superior Street and London Road (pictured, below left). Made of granite quarried at Ortonville, Minnesota, the fountain included a bronze electric lantern for illumination. It was used to water horses and even had access for dogs to get a drink, but when Duluth's ice delivery men started using its water to rinse debris from ice, the public protested. In 1927 it was moved (pictured, below, in a photo by F. R. Paine) to the eastern edge of Lake Shore Park, adjacent to the Duluth Curling Club, perhaps because it was no longer needed on the street since automobiles had replaced horse-drawn carriages.

The western edge of the Rose Garden is marked by another monument, a bronze statue of Leif Erikson, which was erected in 1956 and contributed to the city by the now-defunct

PHOTO: ZENITH CITY PRESS

PHOTO: UMD MARTIN LIBRARY

Norwegian American League of Duluth, a conglomerate of a dozen church and civic organizations with strong ties to Norway. Individuals also donated by subscription. The statue depicts Erikson holding a ship's rudder in his right hand while his left hand appears to be shielding his eyes, though it has been suggested that his hand is "positioned to hold a solar navigator." A crucifix hangs from a chain around his neck, referencing his conversion to Christianity. The polished-granite base on which the statue stands includes the legend LEIF ERIKSON DISCOVERER OF AMERICA 1000 A.D. City Council proceedings following the statue's installation state that "part of the land upon which now stands the Leif Erikson Statue, the land formerly known as Lake Shore Park, be now named, and shall thereafter be known as Leif Erikson Park." Apparently in 1956 no city officials were aware that the park had already been christened Leif Erikson Park in a grand ceremony held in 1929.

The statue (shown at left in a postcard made ca. 1956 from a photograph by L. Perry Gallagher, Jr.) was sculpted by Norwegian immigrant John Karl Daniels, and it wasn't Daniels's first depiction of Erikson. In 1949 his thirteen-foot-tall bronze statue of the Norseman was installed next to Minnesota's state capitol building; its plaque also reads LEIF ERIKSON DISCOVERER OF AMERICA 1000 A.D That statue—dedicated on October 9, 1949, aka Leif Erikson Day in Minnesota—was sponsored by the Minnesota Leif Erikson Monument Association and paid for by popular subscription. The monument association was organized in 1931, the same year a statue of Christopher Columbus was raised on the capitol grounds. At the time, there was a rivalry between Norwegians and Italians over which man first "discovered" America.

Daniels's depictions of Erikson in Duluth and St. Paul are noted for the wings sprouting from the explorer's helmet, making him look like a mythological Greek or Roman god rather than an actual Norse adventurer. History experts agree that no Viking ever wore a helmet adorned with wings or horns or any other animal parts; that idea is a product of twentieth-century imagination, reinforced by popular culture. Statues of Erikson stand in eight U.S. cities and in Iceland, Greenland, and Norway. Only those sculpted by Daniels show the Norse explorer wearing a winged helmet.

In 1967 a new rose garden bloomed at Leif Erikson Park when Ronald Thomas and Ausma Klintz formed the Duluth Rose Society and created what was then the second-largest rose garden in Minnesota. With $5,000 in donations, Klintz designed a garden 620 feet long, stretching from the Erikson statue to the Curling Club parking lot. She called her design European for its use of concentric circles (others called it English) and placed the Stone fountain at the center of the largest circular bed. The society planted more than two thousand bushes of over seventy varieties of roses.

For two decades volunteers maintained the garden, which is now managed by the city with a lot of help from the Lake Superior Rose Society. Klintz, a Latvian immigrant who came to Duluth in 1921, later planted and tended eight hundred rose bushes near the Lake Superior Zoo. When she passed in 2007, Duluth city gardener Tom Kasper told the *Duluth News Tribune* "She's one of the biggest advocates the city of Duluth has ever had for gardening."

In the late 1980s Leif Erikson Park's Rose Garden was temporarily removed during the expansion of Interstate 35 through eastern Duluth, then rebuilt in 1994 using a design reflective of Klintz's original layout. Today the English-style garden contains more than three thousand rose bushes of at least one hundred varieties as well as more than twelve thousand other plantings.

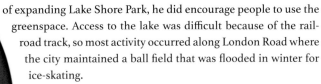

of expanding Lake Shore Park, he did encourage people to use the greenspace. Access to the lake was difficult because of the railroad track, so most activity occurred along London Road where the city maintained a ball field that was flooded in winter for ice-skating.

With the help of Park Superintendent Henry Cleveland, in October 1913 Mayor Prince hosted a citywide Halloween celebration at Lake Shore Park. Jack-o'-lanterns, apples, games, speeches, and costumed children filled the park late into the evening. A huge bonfire chased away goblins while the Grand Army of the Republic fife-and-drum corps provided music. The *News Tribune* reported, "The boom of the drum and the shrill notes of the fifes were kept up as incessantly as human musicians can play and were heard above the din of the clamoring youngsters."

Because the celebration was such a success, the mayor planned an even bigger event for 1914. According to the *News Tribune*, the Third Regiment band led a parade in which "hundreds of children and a few grownups, many of them masked and in costumes, marched to an accompanying din produced by tin pans, copper boilers and squawkers." Two bonfires and dozens of carbon lamps were lighted when the parade-goers arrived at the park. The highlight of the evening came when youngsters scrambled for nuts that leaked from a hole in the one-hundred-pound bag of peanuts carried by Police Sergeant Aldrich Youngberg as he ran through the park.

Every year thousands of Duluthians flocked to the Halloween celebration, which the mayor and park superintendent continued to sponsor through the 1920s. The only year without a Halloween party was 1918; because of the influenza epidemic, the event was cancelled to prevent the spread of sickness. The annual Halloween party was one of the few large community activities at Lake Shore Park in the first decade of its existence.

In 1921 Cleveland planned the biggest Halloween celebration the city had yet seen. He put out a call for volunteers to play in a "barnyard and kitchen band" that would lead the parade. He wanted "49 dish pan players, 49 frying pan artists, 49 pie tin specialists, 49 cow bell ringers, 49 sleigh bell jinglers, 49 horn blowers, 49 baby rattlers, 49 tin can soloists, and 49 Chinese whistlers." The noisy procession started at the Duluth Armory and continued down Jefferson Street to Fourteenth Avenue East, then to London Road, and west to Lake Shore Park for the biggest bonfire ever. (The article did not explain the significance of the number "49.")

While citizens happily used the park for picnics and ballgames, city leaders continued to propose a variety of big plans for the site. In 1912 the Duluth Curling Club, which boasted several indoor curling and hockey rinks, was built along the park's eastern border. The following year the park nearly became the site of Duluth's new armory. The existing Third Regiment Armory, located at First Street and Second Avenue East, had been built in 1896 to house two companies. By 1913, three companies of infantry, two divisions of the naval militia, and the Third Regiment band all used the building. Recognizing that it was time for a larger space, the city administration hoped to take advantage of the state's offer of financial aid up to $15,000 for constructing armories.

A committee of officers from the Third Regiment known as the Military Lunch Club led the search for a location. In May the *News Tribune* began promoting the eastern end of Lake Shore Park as the site for the new armory. "The park includes 14 acres, which is more than sufficient for a splendid parade ground. The drills would afford amusement and instruction to tens of thousands," the paper suggested. "It

TOP: Mayor William Prince who, along with Park Superintendent Henry Cleveland, hosted city-wide Halloween celebrations at Lake Shore Park beginning in 1913. [IMAGE: DULUTH PUBLIC LIBRARY]

BOTTOM: The Halloween parties at Lake Shore Park were designed to cut down on pranks, which, if this *Duluth News Tribune* cartoon from 1913 is any indication, included placing wagons upon church roofs. [IMAGE: ZENITH CITY PRESS]

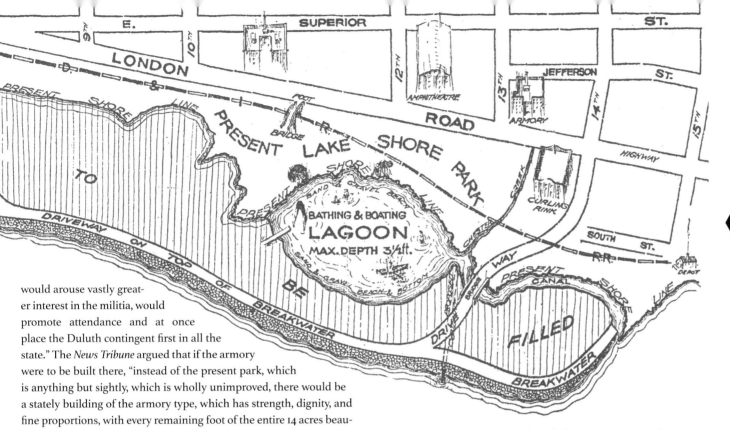

would arouse vastly greater interest in the militia, would promote attendance and at once place the Duluth contingent first in all the state." The *News Tribune* argued that if the armory were to be built there, "instead of the present park, which is anything but sightly, which is wholly unimproved, there would be a stately building of the armory type, which has strength, dignity, and fine proportions, with every remaining foot of the entire 14 acres beautified and made useful."

The decision of whether to build an armory in the park fell to the five commissioners who made up the city council. They knew consent would be needed from NP, which had sold the land on condition that it would be used only for park purposes. However, the commissioners didn't realize that they would also need the approval of Duluth citizens. In September, businessmen Frederic W. Paine and Victor Stearns appeared before the commissioners to register their opposition to the proposal. Both knew what they were talking about: Paine had been a park commissioner from 1889 to 1891, and Lester Park had originally been named Stearns Park in honor of Victor Stearns's father. Both men had donated money to purchase the land for Lake Shore Park, and Stearns told the council, "The residents who contributed to buy the park are opposed to giving away part of it.... This is the only park on the lake front, and we don't want to see it given away. I appeal against the proposed deed on the ground of ordinary honesty."

As a result of their protests, Mayor Prince announced that he would contact the other seventy-five to one hundred people who had given money. Unfortunately, although the mayor exhausted every resource to get the names of the contributors, no records were found. The need to contact donors became unnecessary by October. Attorneys advised the mayor that the council did not have the legal authority to give away property belonging to the city, and the proposal was abandoned. Instead, the commissioners decided to purchase land for the new armory; they settled on a site directly across London Road from the park, at the northeast corner of Thirteenth Avenue East. The Duluth National Guard Armory was built there in 1915, and Lake Shore Park remained intact.

The following year Park Superintendent Henry Cleveland once again proposed a large municipal center for Lake Shore Park, including an auditorium, public gymnasium, and bathhouse. According to Cleveland, "when not in use as a convention place, the building could be utilized as a public gymnasium with complete equipment and qualified instructors in charge.... The building would have a roof garden, affording a magnificent lake view." The commissioners ignored his proposal.

Lake Shore Park becomes Leif Erikson Park

Despite the persistent but unrealized dream of building a breakwa-ter and creating new land to expand Lake Shore Park, two unrelated events in 1926 finally determined the direction of the park's develop-ment: Mayor Sam Snively chose F. Rodney Paine to replace the re-tiring Henry Cleveland as Duluth's new park superintendent, and a replica Viking vessel set sail from a small Norwegian village, eventu-ally heading for Duluth.

One of the first projects Paine took on was Lake Shore Park. He soon reported, "That portion of the park lying next to London Road which has been a dumping ground for years was leveled off, top-dressed and seeded.... The area was designed to accommodate large crowds and is to remain practically unobstructed."

Snively and Paine offered a new variation on the park's expan-sion. They proposed a breakwater that would extend five hundred feet into the lake from the back of the Duluth Curling Club and run southwest approximately parallel with the shore for about 1,500 feet to a point opposite Eighth Avenue East. A road would be built on top of the breakwater, and the enclosed area would be filled to create more parkland. As in earlier proposals, boulders from Point of Rocks would be used to build the breakwater. Although city engineers did their best to blast away Point of Rocks, they eventually abandoned that project as too costly, eliminating the rock source for the break-water and once again putting the expansion project on hold. Outside of relocating the Stone memorial fountain from the junction of Supe-rior Street and London Road to within Lake Shore Park, the fourteen-acre public space remained relatively undeveloped.

Paine's plan for Lake Shore Park changed, however, when the *Leif Erikson* sailed into the Duluth harbor in June 1927. Captain Ger-hard Folgero and his crew had sailed the vessel—which was outfitted to resemble a Viking ship—from Hemnesberget, Norway, to Boston and on to Duluth. As the ship entered the Duluth harbor, thousands of cheering people lined the canal. After docking, the crew members paraded through the city and were congratulated by the mayor and other local dignitaries. Following the festivities, Congressman Wil-liam Carss suggested Duluthians raise funds to purchase the ship and move it to Lake Shore Park. West End furniture dealer—and

Norwegian immigrant—Bert Enger then stepped forward and offered to purchase the vessel and donate it to the city using funds from his furniture business. Enger's requirements included that the boat be permanently placed at Lake Shore Park as a monument to Norwegian history in America, and, at Carss's suggestion, that the park be renamed after the Norse explorer and boat's namesake.

The city accepted Enger's gift and temporarily placed the vessel in storage at the Duluth Boat Club until a permanent location could be selected. In his annual report of 1927, F. Rodney Paine reflected, "The presentation to the city of the Lief Ericson [sic] boat necessitated the making of a new general plan of development as one of the requirements accompanying the gift was that it be placed in this park."

As part of this new plan, park department employees constructed an outdoor amphitheater for band concerts and pageants with a stage designed by Abraham Holstead and William Sullivan. Paine described the building as "attractive and unique in design... of native stone and slate construction. The stage is backed by a wall and flanked with a tower on either side. Under the stage are dressing rooms, store rooms and toilets." The amphitheater was completed in 1928 for a cost of nearly $22,000. It promptly became a popular spot for community gatherings.

Paine's staff also began planting trees and large flower beds (mostly annuals) in the area between London Road and the railroad tracks. In 1928 the Veterans of Foreign Wars presented a memorial flag pole to the city for installation at Leif Erikson Park, and the Duluth Peony Society donated fifty named peonies to be planted around the base of the pole.

By September 1929, the *Leif Erikson* had been moved to Lake Shore Park, which was officially dedicated as Leif Erikson Park on September 8. Unfortunately, because of rain the dedication ceremony had to take place inside the nearby armory. Four hundred people gathered to listen to grand orations by Mayor Sam Snively, Judge Clarence Magney, and other dignitaries from across the state, including Enger himself. Magney gave the key address, praising those of Norse blood and declaring that Duluth needed more parks, especially along the North Shore. Snively's speech echoed Magney's. For the next few decades the *Leif Erikson* was considered Duluth's second-largest tourist attraction, just behind the Aerial Lift Bridge.

THE 1927 AMPHITHEATER, PHOTOGRAPHED IN 1928. THE FACILITY WAS BUILT AS THE PARK WAS RENOVATED IN ANTICIPATION OF ITS NEW ROLE AS THE HOME OF THE *LEIF ERIKSON* REPLICA VIKING BOAT. (PHOTO BY F. R. PAINE.)
[IMAGE: UMD MARTIN LIBRARY]

THE *LEIF ERIKSON* REPLICA VIKING VESSEL

Leif Erikson Park takes its name from the *Leif Erikson*, a replica Norse vessel that traveled from Norway to Duluth under the guidance of Captain Gerhard Folgero (1886 to 1950). According to *Leif Erikson* researcher Randy Ellestad, Folgero grew up in Sandnessjøen, Norway, and like other Norwegian children, listened to the Icelandic sagas. He was particularly taken by Leif Erikson's tale: how, around the year AD 1000, the Norse sailor traveled from his birthplace in Greenland to his ancestral home of Norway, converted to Christianity, then got lost on his way back to Greenland and ended up in what he called Vinland on the eastern coast of North America. To many, including Folgero, that meant that Leif Erikson had "discovered" America nearly five centuries before Columbus set sail from Spain.

Cynics said the journey would have been impossible for the type of vessel Erikson likely used—an open boat with one sail. Even as a boy, Ellestad writes, Folgero became determined "to build and sail an open boat over the course taken by Leif Erikson, his hero, thus proving to the skeptics that it could be done and that the sagas spoke the truth." At age fourteen Folgero went to sea; by 1910 the twenty-four-year-old seaman was a full captain. Fifteen years later he had enough experience—and money—to make his dream come true.

Folgero hired a shipbuilder in the remote Norwegian village of Korgen. Johan Peterson—along with his son Knute, grandson Christian Overlier, and others—constructed the vessel in a barn on the family farm using traditional techniques. Folgero claimed the boat was "a true type of the vessel that Leif Erikson used in the discovery of America in 997." Historian Pat

Labadie agrees—almost. According to Labadie, the *Leif Erikson* is a forty-two-foot wooden "fembøring" craft "patterned after the traditional Norwegian working craft that served coastal shippers and fisherfolk for centuries [and was] used by medieval Norse adventurers and explorers." Labadie called the ship a "1920s small craft with some influence of the Viking tradition" but noted that it "can't be construed as a replica of a historic vessel." So the *Leif Erikson* is not a precise replica of a Viking craft, but rather a representation of the same class and style of boat likely used by Leif Erikson himself.

When the boat was complete it was adorned to look like a Viking ship. Norwegian architect Gerhard Lilletvedt designed the boat as well as the head and tail pieces that resemble a dragon, which were hand carved by Adreas Nilsskog. Round wooden "shields" bearing Viking devices were fastened along the boat's sides. The vessel was then loaded onto wooden supports and pulled over the snow by horses to the town of Elsfjord, where it was put into a fjord and then towed to Hemnesberget to be fitted with a sail before heading to Bergen for the official start of the journey.

On May 22, 1926, Folgero and his crew—John Johnson, Thomas Stavanes (often misidentified as Osvald Gabrielson), Kristian Anderson, and the captain's dog—set sail from Bergen to retrace Erikson's voyage from Norway to Iceland to the coast of Labrador and on to "Vinland." At the time many mistakenly believed that Vinland was actually modern Massachusetts, so Boston became Folgero's ultimate destination. (Erikson's Vinland was more likely the Canadian province of Newfoundland.)

It wasn't easy. The crew faced hurricane-like winds, icebergs, and weeks of fog. But they made it to Labrador and on to Boston, covering 6,700 miles in fifty days. There Folgero met with disappointment: a deal to sell the replica vessel to a community on the East Coast fell through, and he was counting on the money to finance his next adventure. So he accepted an offer to sail to Philadelphia to represent Norway at the Sesquicentennial Exposition and then another offer from H. H. Borgen, president of Duluth's Nordlandslaget Society, to come to the Zenith City to participate in the organization's state convention. By the time Folgero and his crew arrived in Duluth on June 23, 1927, they had covered roughly 10,000 miles.

Five miles from the Duluth harbor the U.S. Naval reserve training ship USS *Paducah* met the *Leif Erikson* with an orchestra on board playing the Norwegian anthem. Closer to port, more vessels joined the convoy and thousands of people lined the Duluth Ship Canal in welcome and "roared" as Folgero and his crew navigated the channel. After landing, the crew paraded through the city to the courthouse, where Mayor Snively and Congressman William Carss praised the Norsemen's courage and enterprise. Folgero reported in his diary, "We had made it to our destination. It was an event for us, our country, and Duluth." During their stay, the Norsemen were the toast of Duluth.

The next day the *Duluth News Tribune* announced Carss's suggestion that Duluthians raise funds to purchase the ship and move it to Lake Shore Park, then rename the park Erikson Park. The city council considered contributing $1,200 toward purchase of the boat if the remainder could be raised by public subscription. Instead, Bert Enger offered to donate the entire amount, $5,000, from the coffers of Enger & Olson, the West End furniture dealership he operated with the recently deceased Emil Olson. The city council agreed to the terms of Enger's offer: that Lake Shore Park be officially renamed Leif Erikson Park and that the boat be permanently installed at the park, protected from the elements, and open to public inspection.

The boat was docked at the Duluth Boat Club until the park department could prepare a home for it. In the meantime, the *Leif Erikson* participated in a flotilla of vessels celebrating the opening of the Duluth-Superior Arrowhead Bridge. After receiving the payment for his boat, Folgero asked to borrow the vessel for one last voyage: the *Leif Erikson* and her crew had been invited to Chicago to participate in the dedication of Leif Ericcson Drive. They left in August and returned in October. Folgero then went back to Norway and began work on another replica Viking vessel named for Norwegian polar explorer Roald Amundson. In 1929 to 1930 Folgero used this boat to retrace Columbus's journey from Spain to the New World.

The *Leif Erikson* sat in storage at the Duluth Boat Club for two years, waiting for a permanent home at Lake Shore Park. Finally, in the fall of 1929, the boat was moved to the park, and on September 8 dignitaries gathered at the Duluth Armory for a ceremony to officially change the name to Leif Erikson Park. An evening banquet at the Spalding Hotel honored Bert Enger for donating the boat to the City of Duluth.

During its first few decades in the park, the *Leif Erikson* was a favorite tourist attraction, second only to Duluth's Aerial Lift Bridge in popularity. But neglect and vandalism took their toll, and to protect the vessel it was placed within a cage of chain-link fencing and, later, a modest wood-and-chicken wire enclosure. In 1984 the boat was in such poor condition that the *News Tribune* suggested that it should be given a proper Viking funeral: towed out onto Lake Superior and set aflame. In 1984 Neill Atkins and Will Borg (a grandson of Emil and Marie Olson) established Save Our Ship (S.O.S.) to renovate, preserve, and protect the vessel. Over the years the group struggled to find the funds to properly protect the boat. It took over a decade to raise money for a major renovation project, completed in 1996. The boat was then moored in a more elegant berth within the park. Because of vandals, it was covered in shrink wrap as it continued to wait for a proper home.

In the late 1990s S.O.S. considered moving the *Leif Erikson* to the Great Lakes Aquarium. The idea couldn't have sat well with Borg, as he was once quoted as saying, "Leif Erikson Park without a ship is like Canal Park without a lift bridge." In 2012 a group of developers suggested moving

LEIF ERIKSON CREW

PHOTO BY VANG STUDIO

the boat to a proposed retail development west of Bayfront Park. Those plans changed, but the boat was moved to the site for safe storage and has been there since June 2013. In March 2015, S.O.S. announced plans to break ground on a shelter to be built within the park near the intersection of Superior Street and London Road, but the project was delayed. The *Leif Erikson* is expected to be back within its namesake park and in its new home some time in 2017. Fittingly, the planned new home for the *Leif Erikson* will be erected on a triangular piece of land at the southwest corner of Superior Street and London Road, essentially the same plot of land John Millen suggested in 1905 become Duluth's first park along Lake Superior's shore.

IMAGES: T. KASPER COLLECTION

After World War II

A bronze statue of Leif Erikson was added to the park in 1956, donated by members of Duluth's Norwegian community. In more recent times, for several decades Leif Erikson Park was the home of the Duluth International Folk Festival and the Lake Superior Shakespeare Festival. Since 2006 Trent Edgerton's Twin Ports Outdoor Movies has presented Movies in the Park, free family-friendly movies projected on a twenty- by forty-foot inflatable screen set up in front of the stage on Friday evenings throughout the summer.

Nearly two decades before the arrival of the *Leif Erikson* and F. Rodney Paine, the *News Tribune* had proposed a grand plan for expanding fourteen-acre Lake Shore Park by filling along the shoreline. The newspaper described the vision in idyllic terms, writing, "It needs little imagination to picture the completed pleasure ground, with its driveways and walks, its playgrounds, lawns, flower beds, shrubbery and ornamental trees, its fountains and lights, its artistically designed pavilions and colonnades. The mind's eye can easily see the thousands who will throng there on summer evenings to enjoy the breezes, watch the ships come and go, meet their friends and mingle with the crowds."

Although that plan was not implemented, much of this vision became reality when the development of I-35 through central Duluth resulted in the creation of the Lakewalk, Lake Place Park, and the expansion of the rose garden, providing everyone with the opportunity to enjoy the Lake Superior shoreline. The *Leif Erikson* vessel suffered from neglect and vandalism over the years, and in 2013 it was temporarily put into storage. As we write this in 2016, the borders of the park are about to change once again, as a small triangle of land at the southwest intersection of London Road and Superior Street is slated to become the home of the *Leif Erikson* replica vessel and an enclosure to protect it from the elements and vandalism. Appropriately enough, that triangle is part of the original parcel of land that John Millen 110 years earlier had suggested become a city park—an idea that evolved into today's Leif Erikson Park.

THE *LEIF ERIKSON* REPLICA VIKING BOAT WITHIN LEIF ERIKSON PARK, 1940. (PHOTO BY L. PERRY GALLAGHER JR.)
[IMAGE: UMD MARTIN LIBRARY]

8. Congdon and Kitchi Gammi Parks

Inspired by an Iron Ore Attorney

Duluth's Chester Congdon is best known as the man who built Glensheen, the elegant Jacobean manor house and estate perched along the shore of Lake Superior at 3300 London Road. Congdon, an attorney by trade, made his fortune after becoming chief counsel for the Oliver Mining Company in 1892. When the company was bought out by J. P. Morgan in his effort to create U. S. Steel, Congdon became one of the wealthiest men in Minnesota. The lifelong Republican was an admirer of Teddy Roosevelt—particularly Roosevelt's efforts to expand the national park system. Using his newfound wealth, Congdon created a Duluth city park and laid the groundwork for an international highway along Lake Superior's North Shore.

Congdon Park: A 'Most Picturesque Sylvan District'

In 1905 Chester Congdon began construction of his magnificent Duluth home. Congdon's estate included twenty-two acres of wooded land along Tischer Creek, extending from the shore of Lake Superior up to Greysolon Road. Much of the land had been settled in the 1850s by Swiss immigrants Urs and Elizabeth Tischer, whose name became attached to the stream. The Tischers owned land from the mouth of the creek up the hill through most of what is now Congdon Park. They farmed some of the land, and at the waterfront, Tischer's landing was considered one of the best on the lake.

As part of the grand plan for his estate, Congdon approached the Duluth Board of Park Commissioners with the idea of creating a public park along Tischer Creek from the border of Glensheen upstream to Vermilion Road. Congdon's East Duluth Land Company already owned much of this land. Congdon offered to donate land and cover the cost of purchasing additional property for the park. The park board's help was needed to acquire the remaining land through condemnation.

Congdon's offer was based on more than simple aesthetics. Tischer Creek served as a sewer for houses in the Woodland area, and its water was badly contaminated. The *Duluth News Tribune* referred

LITHOGRAPHIC POSTCARD, CA. 1910, OF A RUSTIC BRIDGE DESIGNED BY MORELL & NICHOLS SPANNING TISCHER CREEK WITHIN CONGDON PARK.

[IMAGE: ZENITH CITY PRESS]

CHESTER ADGATE CONGDON

Perhaps best known as the man who built Duluth's historic Glensheen estate, Chester A. Congdon also contributed generously to the development of Duluth's park system with the creation of Congdon Park and Congdon Boulevard. Moreover, Glensheen's construction introduced Minnesota to Anthony U. Morell and Arthur R. Nichols, who would go on to become the state's foremost landscape architects.

Congdon was born in Rochester, New York, in 1853. In 1871 he enrolled at Syracuse University where he met San Francisco–native Clara Hesperia Bannister—like him, the child of a Methodist minister—and together they graduated in 1875. Clara took a job teaching in a women's college in Ontario; Chester studied law and was accepted to the New York bar. After a brief, financially frustrating stint as a school principal in Chippewa Falls, Wisconsin, he was off to St. Paul, Minnesota, to practice law.

There he took a job as assistant to William Billson, the U.S. district attorney for the State of Minnesota. A year later Billson left his post to move to Duluth to begin a private practice. Congdon, meanwhile, married Clara in Syracuse and brought his bride west to St. Paul. There they started a family while Chester made the transition to private practice. His work often brought him to Duluth, where he visited with Billson. In 1892 he accepted Billson's offer of a partnership and moved his growing family to the Zenith City.

Chester found early success in Duluth. Henry Oliver of Pittsburgh's Oliver Steel—the second-largest steel maker in America—hired Congdon to oversee his ore purchases in Minnesota. Together they created the Oliver Mining Company, which would become the largest iron ore producer on Minnesota's Mesabi Iron Range. Working for Oliver, Congdon expanded and defended the company's Minnesota interests. He also purchased stock in the company. In 1901 J. P. Morgan bought out John D. Rockefeller, Andrew Carnegie, Oliver Mining, and others to form United States Steel. In six short years the value of Congdon's stock rose 555 percent; almost overnight Congdon had become one of the wealthiest men in Minnesota. He then partnered with Oliver and others investing in ore property on the Western Mesabi and diversified by opening copper mines in Arizona and building an irrigation canal in Washington's Yakima Valley, where he developed fruit orchards. In Duluth he served as an executive with the American Exchange National Bank of Duluth, the Marshall-Wells Company, the Gowan-Lenning-Brown Company, and other enterprises.

Construction of Glensheen began in 1905 and took four years to complete. While the estate was being built, Congdon became interested in politics. He served as the Republican representative from Minnesota's Fifty-first Congressional District from 1909 to 1913. In November 1916, just days after Democrat Woodrow Wilson won the presidential election, Chester Congdon died of a pulmonary embolism in St. Paul.

His obituary read in part, "Not because he was a rich man but because he was a good man with sound instincts and large capacities for service and with an ever increasing will to give his energy and means to wholesome public enterprises the loss of Chester A. Congdon is a great blow to the community, to the state and to the nation."

—— PHOTO: GLENSHEEN HISTORIC ESTATE | SKETCH: ZENITH CITY PRESS ——

to the stream as "the open sewer known as Tischer's Creek." Congdon wanted to use water from the creek for the extensive gardens he planned to establish at Glensheen, and his offer to create a park was contingent on the city taking action to redirect sewage into a holding tank.

The park board officially accepted Congdon's offer in August 1905. By the end of 1907, the board had completed the acquisition of about thirty acres of undeveloped land along Tischer Creek at a cost of $5,125.71. On March 2, 1908, board members passed the following resolution: "Resolved, that this Board, for, and on behalf of the city, hereby extends a hearty vote of thanks to Mr. C. A. Congdon for the very generous donation of the Tischer's Creek park grounds; a very desirable acquisition to the city's holding in that particular, and be it further resolved that the said grounds be, and the same hereby are, named and designated 'Congdon Park'."

Congdon's generosity continued when in May 1909 he offered the services of landscape architect Charles W. Leavitt of New York to prepare a plan for Congdon Park. Leavitt, who had designed the landscaping at Glensheen, proposed improvements to the park that included a roadway at the top of the slope on both sides of the creek valley, footpaths close to the creek, and a bridle path in between. The initial plan showed the most elaborate improvements in the area between Greysolon Road and Superior Street, where Leavitt proposed a botanical garden and a "Swiss chalet which could be used for shelter, for basket lunches, and a place for mothers and nurses to sit while they watch the children play." As with Glensheen, Leavitt's plans would be carried out by his associate, Anthony U. Morell.

Unfortunately, Park Superintendent Henry Helm had already begun work on a road through the park, located close to the creek. A brief firestorm broke out as a number of unhappy citizens appeared before the park board in June to complain that Helm's road was destroying the park's natural beauty and to urge the board to follow Leavitt's design. Board members assured the concerned citizens that they intended to follow the landscape architect's plans, and the storm subsided. Realistically, the board did not have money to carry out all the improvements anyway and had to rely on Congdon to pay for the work of the landscape architects.

One reason for the citizens' concern may have been that in early 1909 a syndicate of local men—including F. A. Patrick (a member of the park board), Alexander Hartman, Albert M. Marshall, and C. E. Van Bergen—had purchased a sixty-six-acre tract of land extending from Superior Street to St. Marie Street on both sides of Tischer Creek at a cost of $66,000. The developers planned to make this the "finest residence section in the city." They intended to put the property on the market "only in large blocks such as are in demand for fine residences with spacious grounds." By then landscape architects Anthony Morell and Arthur R. Nichols had created a partnership and set up a practice in Minneapolis. The investment group hired Morell & Nichols to lay out fifty-four new building sites surrounding Congdon Park, each large enough to permit for ample drives and the preservation of groves in their natural state.

The plan also required that all deeds contain the proviso that only "magnificent homes" would be constructed. Absolutely no flats, double houses, or apartments of any kind were permitted in the new district. According to the *News Tribune*, Congdon Park had already been "transformed through the efforts of the park board into the most picturesque sylvan district within the city limits," and the new homes would take advantage of this lovely park setting.

Despite the elaborate landscape plan prepared for Congdon Park, the board made few changes. By 1911 they had completed on the west side of the park a twenty-foot roadway, an eight-foot bridle path, and a footpath at the edge of the stream that included stairs, rustic bridges, and stepping stones. No additional developments were made.

Over the years, sections of the footpath disappeared as the creek washed away the loose soil, but the bridle path and roadway remained intact. The park fell into disrepair after Duluth's change in government in 1956. In 1972 the Junior League of Duluth, working with the Department of Parks and Recreation, restored the nature trail with the help of local Boy Scouts and students from the University of Minnesota Duluth. The flood of June 2012 damaged parts of the footpath and nearly wiped out the roadway between Fourth Street and Vermilion Road. Despite the damage, thanks to the natural beauty of Tischer Creek, Congdon Park remains one of the loveliest stream parks in Duluth's park system.

A PHOTOGRAPH, LIKELY MADE BY F. R. PAINE, SHOWING ONE OF THE STONE STAIRWAYS WITHIN CONGDON PARK, CA. 1929.
[IMAGE: T. KASPER COLLECTION]

MORELL & NICHOLS, MINNESOTA'S PREMIER LANDSCAPE ARCHITECTS

When Chester and Clara Congdon hired renowned landscape architect Charles W. Leavitt, Jr. to design the grounds of Glensheen, Leavitt sent two of his best men to make sure his plans were followed to the letter: Anthony U. Morell and Arthur R. Nichols (pictured). While in Duluth the pair made significant connections, and by the time they had finished their work at Glensheen in 1908 they decided to permanently settle in Minnesota, where they created the state's foremost landscape architecture firm.

Anthony U. Morell was born Anthony Urbanski in 1875 in France, where he received his education. In 1902 he immigrated to the United States to take a job with Leavitt's firm in New York City. At the same time he adopted his mother's maiden name, Morell. While working for Leavitt he became acquainted with Arthur Richardson Nichols, a native of Springfield, Massachusetts. Nichols became the first person to earn a degree through the Massachusetts Institute of Technology's landscape architecture program in 1902. He joined Leavitt's firm that same year and cut his teeth working on Monument Valley Park in Colorado Springs; Long Beach on Long Island, New York; and John D. Rockefeller's estate in Pocantico Hills, New York.

According to biographer Gregory Kopischke, Morell was once described as "an artistic, creative, theoretical designer with high ideals, a hot temper, and little patience." Nichols, on the other hand, was "a good designer, mild-mannered, and a skilled promoter who inspired people and who saw an important synergy between civil engineering and landscape architecture." Despite their different styles, the pair obviously respected one another and worked together well. In 1909 the pair, recognizing Minnesota as an untapped market for their skills, formed a partnership and opened an office in Minneapolis.

Kopischke notes that Morell & Nichols became "one of the first and most productive landscape architecture firms in the state. The partnership blended Morell's European training and Nichols's eastern background with both men's appreciation of Minnesota and its regional character. The firm's broad-ranging design services included master and site plans of residential subdivisions, city and state parks, country clubs, cemeteries, hospitals and sanatoriums, schools, colleges, universities, seminaries, hotel and resort grounds, private grounds and estates, state capitol grounds, historic parks, Works Progress Administration sites,

— IMAGE: U OF MINNESOTA MORRIS —

and state highways." This included 1918 plans for "civic improvements" of the entire town of Stillwater, Minnesota. While most of their work was done in Minnesota and other Midwestern states, they executed projects throughout the United States and Canada.

In Duluth, Morell & Nichols worked on Congdon Park and drew plans for Central Park, Lester Park, Washington Square, Portman Square, the stone bridges of Seven Bridges Road, the Lester River Bridge, and Congdon Boulevard. Unfortunately Duluth's park board was eliminated in 1913 and many plans, including those for Central Park and Lester Park, were never implemented. They also designed the layout of Duluth's Morgan Park, a model company town built by U. S. Steel, as well as the Crescent View Park subdivision of Duluth's Congdon neighborhood. The firm also designed the grounds of Duluth's H. B. Fryberger (now lost) and A. M. Chisholm estates. They have been credited with designing the Morley Heights neighborhood, and Nichols acted as a consultant with C.H Smith on the layout of Duluth's Civic Center. Much of their non-park-related work is thought to have been done by Nichols alone. In 1911 Morell & Nichols published a small book titled simply *Landscape Architecture*. It includes drawings of many of their Duluth projects, even those thought to be Nichols's private commissions.

Both men were active outside of the firm. Morell consulted with the Minneapolis City Planning Department and served as the Minneapolis Planning Commission's secretary. Nichols acted as a consultant to the Minnesota State Board of Control, designing sites for state institutions such as hospitals and prisons. One of his most successful designs was for Duluth's Nopeming Sanatorium. For more than forty years Nichols acted as the University of Minnesota's consulting planner, designing grounds on campuses throughout the state.

After Morell's death in 1924, Nichols retained the firm's name and continued to practice. His work includes the Minnesota State Capitol approach, Carlton College in Northfield, the University of Minnesota's Northrop Mall, Cambridge State Hospital, Willmar State Hospital, and St. Paul's St. Catherine University. Eleven of the projects the firm is credited for designing on behalf of Minnesota's highway department—most executed by Nichols, who served as the department's consultant from 1932 to 1940—are listed on the National Register of Historic Places, including Duluth's Lester River Bridge. Kopischke writes that Nichols believed there was a "need to integrate aesthetic design with utilitarian highway engineering objectives to maintain the natural beauty and scenic quality of the land and, therefore, to enhance the driving experience."

During his career Nichols also became a noted designer of cemeteries, including Minneapolis's Sunset Memorial Park and the northeast section of Lakewood Cemetery. As Kopischke points out, he built an impressive résumé along the way: Member, fellow, and vice president of the American Society of Landscape Architects; honorary associate in the Minnesota Chapter of the American Institute of Architects; life member of the Engineers Club of Minneapolis; and member of the American Society of Planning Officials. In the early 1920s he helped establish Iowa State University's landscape architecture program, and in 1933 he became Minnesota's first registered landscape architect.

In 1950 Arthur R. Nichols retired. Three years later he was convinced to return to work to consult for the Minnesota State Parks Department, preparing "master plans and site studies for virtually every new or existing state park" until his final retirement in the early 1960s. He died in Rochester, Minnesota, on January 23, 1970.

London Road and Congdon Boulevard

Chester and Clara Congdon were living in St. Paul, Minnesota, in the 1880s—the time when neighboring Minneapolis was developing its extensive parkway system that linked together parks, lakes, residential neighborhoods, and the river.

In 1889 Duluth's new Board of Park Commissioners—likely inspired by the Minneapolis parkways as well as board president William K. Rogers's experience with rival Chicago's park system—set out to build its own parkway system. The board members planned a boulevard across the hillside that would be connected by stream corridor parks to a boulevard along the shore of Lake Superior. In their 1894 annual report, park board members wrote, "London road is the Lake Shore boulevard and continues on to the Lester River.... This drive is in full view of the lake where one can enjoy the cool and refreshing lake breeze, and also enjoy the wild scenery of rocks and woods. This boulevard is to Duluth what the Lake Shore Drive is to Chicago."

London Road had been built around 1871 to connect Duluth with the newly platted township of New London (now Lakeside). When, in August 1872, editors of the *Duluth Minnesotian* went on an inspection tour of the new development, they traveled to New London on what they called London Avenue. According to the newspaper, "the expense of building the road between the city and London has thus far been borne by the city, the town of Duluth, Mr. Tischer, and Messrs. Norton & Wisdom—only one property owner, Mr. Mitchell, of Lexington, Ky., having refused to contribute to that object.... As the town of Duluth and the county have each been taxed to the utmost limit for road purposes, the property owners along the road, except Mr. Mitchell, have determined to complete the road in front of their premises in the same manner as that portion in the city limits." The newspaper also reported that the road had already become "quite a fashionable drive-way."

By the 1890s, London Road was paved with macadam, a type of road surface made up of even-sized broken rock that was compacted

Congdon Boulevard near Kitchi Gammi Park, 1929. (Photo by F. R. Paine.)

[IMAGE: UMD MARTIN LIBRARY]

The mouth of the Lester River photographed some time between 1888 and 1926, before there was a bridge over the river along London Road. The building at right is the 1888 U.S. Fish Hatchery; the street at left is Lester River Road. Prior to 1924 there was no road east of the river along the same path as London Road.

[IMAGE: DULUTH PUBLIC LIBRARY]

and held together with tar. Bicycles were all the rage, as they had become available and affordable for middle-class families, and London Road was a popular place for "wheeling," the term used for the new sport of bicycle racing. In 1892, the same year Chester Congdon moved his family to Duluth, the local cycle club held its first annual Duluth-to-Lester Park race on London Road.

When Chester and his wife, Clara, chose the site for their home, London Road was still mostly forested between Twenty-first and Fortieth Avenues East. He was likely already forming plans to extend this scenic road north to Canada, but he did not share his vision publicly. According to Glensheen Director Daniel Hartman, around the time he began construction of the estate, Congdon also started purchasing land along Lake Superior's North Shore, from Duluth's Tenth Avenue East to the county line just outside of Two Harbors.

Congdon knew he would not be able to purchase all the land needed for the road on his own, and he recognized that the City of Duluth did not have the power to condemn land outside the city limits. While serving as a state legislator between 1909 and 1913, he introduced a bill allowing "cities of the first class" (Minneapolis, St. Paul, and Duluth) to annex land outside of city limits for transportation reasons. Passage of this bill was an important step

in making it possible for Congdon to realize his vision for a scenic North Shore road.

By 1913 he had succeeded in purchasing about one-third of the land he needed to build the road from Duluth to Two Harbors. He went public with his plan when he asked the city to condemn the parcels he had been unable to buy outright. He offered to cover the cost of acquiring the land and constructing the road, which he called the Lake Superior International Highway.

The plan, as described by the *News Tribune* in May 1913, included a bridge across the Lester River near the U.S. Fish Hatchery (at that time the only bridge was on Superior Street). Beyond the Lester River, the roadway would be one hundred feet wide and divided into five sections: two for automobiles, one for other vehicles, and two paths for pedestrians—one on each side of the road. And "at Stony Point, 17 miles from Duluth, the boulevard will take a turn from the lake shore and circle around a 165-acre tract, which will be converted into a park." The newspaper predicted that "Stony Point will undoubtedly become the mecca for all tourist parties coming to the head of the lakes."

The city began condemnation proceedings on fifty-three tracts of land for what was informally called the North Shore Boulevard, and in May 1915 city commissioners officially accepted Congdon's gift and agreed to abide by its conditions that the boulevard property would never be converted to any other purpose. As the *News Tribune* explained: "Mr. Congdon has paid all engineering expenses in connection with the boulevard sight [sic], and has borne the cost of award through condemnation by the city. Mayor Prince announced that this amounted in round numbers to $40,000. The right-of-way includes rights in the lake along the scenic stretch."

Unfortunately, Congdon died unexpectedly in November 1916, leaving city leaders without the assurance of financial backing, and construction was postponed. According to his family, shortly before his death Congdon had written a letter in which he stated that improvement of the lakeshore road should be taken up "when the appropriate time shall arrive." A little over three years after Chester's death, in March 1920, Clara felt that the time had arrived. Speaking on behalf of the estate, she offered to pay up to $125,000 for half the cost of the five-mile portion of the road that was within city limits—provided the entire boulevard was improved and paved.

After the St. Louis County Board of Commissioners agreed to build the road from the city limits to the Lake County line, construction moved forward, with the cost shared equally by the Congdon family, the county, and the city. Morell & Nichols were hired to design the parkway's landscaping. Construction of the concrete-paved road from the Lester River to the Knife River, already called Congdon Boulevard, took place between 1923 and 1925.

During this same period Minnesota politicians were developing State Highway 1, which would span the state from the Iowa border south of Albert Lea to the Canadian border at Pigeon River. Congdon Boulevard became a link in this new state highway—as well as a link to the city's parkway system—and in the 1920s state tourism actually referred to the road by the name Congdon gave it: the Lake Superior International Highway. While the full measure of Congdon's investment in this highway has never been detailed, in 1933 Park Superintendent F. Rodney Paine outlined his calculations of Chester Congdon's gift:

> Mr. Chester A. Congdon...made a gift to the City of inestimable value—probably the greatest park asset Duluth has next to the Rogers Boulevard [Skyline Parkway]. Mr. Congdon authorized the city to acquire, and he paid for, the right of way for what is now Highway No. 1, from Lester Park to the Lake County line. In this was included the land between the road and the lake wherever the distance was less than about four hundred feet. This preserved two hundred thirty acres and 8.8 miles of lake frontage forever for the enjoyment of the people of Duluth, of the State, and of the country.

The bridge over the Lester River was built between 1924 and 1925 on land acquired from the U.S. Fish Hatchery. As with the boulevard, the Congdon family, the county, and the city shared the construction costs. Morell & Nichols were hired to design the bridge; they received help from Duluth city engineers William H. Cruikshank and John Wilson as well as the Minneapolis architectural firm of Tyrie & Chapman. The bridge was built by Duluth contractor C. R. McLean, whose firm constructed the road through Jay Cooke State Park the following year. In January 1926 the *Duluth News-Tribune* called the bridge a "Work of Art" and went on to describe it:

> The bridge is constructed of reinforced concrete faced with native stone carefully selected both as to color and texture. The trimmings are of granite from Rockville, Minn. The lanterns and lantern supports are of special design to

LESTER RIVER BRIDGE, HIGHWAY No. 1, DULUTH, MINN.   107536

harmonize with the delicate yet substantial lines of the bridge. The lanterns are painted to conform with the granite trimmings, while the glass was specially rolled and burned to give the diffusion of light and shade desired, Mr. Nichols of Morell and Nichols giving much of his personal attention to this small but important detail.

The dedication ceremony for both Highway 1 and Congdon Boulevard—each recently completed—took place on the bridge simultaneously in September 1925. Organized by the Duluth Automobile Club, the event kicked off with a parade from central Duluth to the bridge with the U.S. Naval Reserve Band leading the way. Mayor Sam Snively gave a speech, as did his predecessor Judge C. R. Magney, and County Commissioner W. H. Tischer, whose family had once owned the land that became Congdon Park and the Glensheen estate. The Congdon family was represented by Edward Congdon, Chester and Clara's second-oldest son.

The Lester River Bridge was placed on the National Register of Historic Places in 2002. According to the International Concrete Repair Institute, in 2011 the bridge was "selected as one of twenty-four Minnesota bridges to receive a higher level of maintenance and

LITHOGRAPHIC POSTCARD, CA. 1926, OF THE LESTER RIVER BRIDGE FEATURING LANTERNS DESIGNED BY ARTHUR NICHOLS.

[IMAGE: ZENITH CITY PRESS]

Brighton Beach at Kitchi Gammi Park, 1929. (Photo by F. R. Paine.)

[IMAGE: UMD MARTIN LIBRARY]

preservation due to its historical significance." In 2013 it underwent a major rehabilitation as its integrity had been undermined by decades of exposure to deicing chemicals, which had corroded the bridge's steel reinforcement. Contractor PCI Roads of St. Michael, Minnesota, completed all repairs "to replicate the original historic appearance of the bridge"—right down to the ornamental lanterns Arthur Nichols had designed so carefully.

Kitchi Gammi Park: Built for Automobile 'Gypsies'

As automobiles became widely available in the 1920s summer vacations turned into road trips, creating a new style of tourism. When Sam Snively had become Duluth's mayor in 1921, he recognized the potential to attract the new "auto tourists" to town. Snively, along with Duluth's Commercial Club, Auto Club, and the Theodore

Roosevelt International Highway Association, supported the local Lions Club's campaign to develop tourist campsites in the city. In an interview with the *News Tribune*, Snively said, "Relying upon the persuasiveness of our natural attractions to draw the tourist to our city, we sit and watch the tourists come and watch the tourists go, without taking thought of their comfortable entertainment while they dwell within our gates."

Snively knew that when Congdon Boulevard was completed, public access to the lake would be crucial for the auto tourists. The city already owned some shoreline property between Lester River and the Lakewood Pump House at Eighty-first Avenue East. The land had been purchased in 1896 when the pump house was built to supply Duluth with clean drinking water that would help prevent typhoid epidemics. In 1921 Snively convinced city commissioners to purchase additional land east of Lester River where he wanted to develop a tourist camp. After visiting the site, he told the *News Tribune*, "The preservation of our lake frontage means much in bringing tourists to Duluth, as it is primarily the lake they come for." In September 1921 the city commissioners agreed to pay $46,200 for a sixty-nine-acre parcel of lakeshore that was known as Brighton Beach.

In 1922 Snively and Park Superintendent Henry Cleveland created the city's first tourist camps at Brighton Beach, Indian Point, and Chester Bowl. The timing was perfect for taking advantage of the boom in auto tourism. In August 1922 the *News Tribune* reported "Northern Minnesota's 'Playground of a Nation', that pine-scented park-and-land of ten thousand lakes...is drawing heavily on the vastly increased automobile 'gypsies' this summer. At times the arterial highways present almost a parade-like appearance as cars of high and low estates, each carrying the inevitable camping outfit, some elaborate and others confined to a lean-to and anti-rain hope, proceed on their journey."

The Brighton Beach Tourist Camp was hugely successful. The original camp provided tent sites, water, and toilet facilities. By the time F. Rodney Paine replaced Cleveland as park superintendent in 1926, the new Lester River Bridge connected London Road directly to Congdon Boulevard, providing an easy route for tourists to reach the campground. Paine added eight cabins at the Brighton Beach Tourist Camp and unofficially began calling the entire lakeshore area Kitchi Gammi Park, although he did not explain why he chose this name.

While there are no records of how the park was named, it may be in recognition of some of the wealthy Duluthians who donated

WORKERS PLANTING TREES IN KITCHI GAMMI PARK, 1929. (PHOTO BY F. R. PAINE.)

[IMAGE: UMD MARTIN LIBRARY]

BRIGHTON BEACH TOURIST CAMP - DULUTH - MINN.— 7/00

money and land to Duluth's parks and who also belonged to Duluth's exclusive Kitchi Gammi Club, founded in part by Paine's father, Frederic W. Paine, the secretary of Duluth's first park board. These men included Luther Mendenhall and Major John Upham (both members of Duluth's first park board), Chester Congdon and his sons (including Edward, once the club's president), Guilford Hartley, William Sargent, and even C. R. McLean (builder of the Lester River Bridge), and others, including Paine himself.

In 1927 the tourist camp hosted over four thousand cars; the price was fifty cents per night per car. Paine added four more cabins in 1930, five in 1931, and three in 1934. By this time the nation was deep into the Great Depression, so work on city parks was limited by budget constraints. The tourist camps at Brighton Beach and Indian Point provided a bright spot in an otherwise dark time by bringing in a profit every year. The Brighton Beach Tourist Camp operated into the late 1950s. By the 1960s the camp was gone, and the land became the site for the National Water Quality Laboratory, which today is the Environmental Protection Agency's Mid-Continent Ecology Division.

Thanks to the foresight of Chester Congdon, Sam Snively, and many other Duluthians, public access to Lake Superior has been preserved along this scenic segment of the shoreline. Although the tourist camp is gone, Brighton Beach at Kitchi Gammi Park and the scenic Congdon Boulevard remain some of the city's most popular public areas.

TOP: TENTS AND A PAVILION AT THE BRIGHTON BEACH TOURIST CAMP WITHIN KITCHI GAMMI PARK, DATE UNKNOWN.
[IMAGE: DULUTH PUBLIC LIBRARY]

BOTTOM: A POSTCARD OF CABINS AT THE BRIGHTON BEACH TOURIST CAMP WITHIN KITCHI GAMMI PARK, DATE UNKNOWN.
[IMAGE: T. KASPER COLLECTION]

9. Enger Park

A Gift from a Furniture Salesman

Located atop one of the highest points in Duluth, Enger Park was envisioned long before it received the name it bears today. Thirty acres of this rocky hillside below Skyline Parkway, which the Duluth Board of Park Commissioners named Central Park, was set aside as one of the city's first parks. As early as 1890, members of the park board planned to expand Central Park by acquiring additional land at the top of the hill, but they never had enough money. Finally, in 1920, a generous donation from a West End furniture dealer allowed the city to begin developing it into what eventually became the most popular tourist stop along Skyline Parkway.

Duluth's Undeveloped Central Park

Duluth's Central Park bears no similarity to the more famous Central Park in New York City, which covers over eight hundred acres in the midst of one of the country's largest urban areas. Most of New York's Central Park is manicured and landscaped with ponds, trails, fountains, sports fields, and monuments. Duluth's Central Park includes about thirty acres of the some of the wildest and steepest land in the heart of the city—and no landscaping. Located on the rocky hillside below Enger Park, it covers a nine-block area between Fourteenth and Seventeenth Avenues West from First Street up to Fourth Street.

The original owners of the land dedicated it as a park in 1870 when they platted the area for development. The *Polk Directory* of 1884 to 1885 referred to it simply as a "public park." In 1889 it became the responsibility of the newly created Duluth Board of Park Commissioners. Although not formally named until 1894 when park board members christened it Central Park, the area was recognized early on as an important location for a larger park. In 1887, inspired by William K. Rogers, city engineers drew up a plan for a coordinated

LITHOGRAPHIC POSTCARD, CA. 1939, OF ENGER MEMORIAL TOWER WITHIN ENGER PARK.
[IMAGE: ZENITH CITY PRESS]

HENRY "GRAMP" CLEVELAND: SUPERINTENDENT OF PARKS, 1909 TO 1925

The Duluth Board of Park Commissioners hired sixty-five-year-old Henry Cleveland as the city's second park superintendent in October 1909. Retaining his position as park superintendent when responsibility for the parks shifted from the park board to the mayor in 1913, Cleveland provided the continuity needed to keep the park system on track. As the growth of recreation and the availability of automobiles changed the way people used the parks, he was involved in many new and innovative projects, including creation of the city's first bathing beach, playgrounds, and tourist camps.

Cleveland was born in Connecticut in 1844 and enlisted in the Union Army while he was still a teenager, serving during the Civil War (while he was called "Captain Cleveland," that title may have been honorary, as research has yet to reveal his war record). After the war he settled in New York and worked as a landscape gardener alongside the country's most famous park designer, Frederick Law Olmsted. Cleveland left New York in 1900 and moved to Duluth, a place he chose for the northern climate. He later told the *Duluth News Tribune*, "When I first heard of Duluth, years ago, I heard of the excellent summer weather.... My informants told me of the wonderful air and water of this country.... Duluth summers are delightful."

After arriving in Duluth, Cleveland continued his work as a landscape gardener and was unanimously selected as Henry Helm's successor as park superintendent in October 1909. Cheerful, creative, and practical—and occasionally a bit old-fashioned—Cleveland quickly became a beloved local personality.

Shortly after taking on his new job, the *News Tribune* reported that Cleveland "has been unusually successful in winning the children to his way of thinking and in keeping good order and discipline at the outing places. In laying out the ball parks on the playgrounds and parks of the city, Mr. Cleveland has consulted with the boys as to the location and has explained to them that the city gives them such grounds to be used with judgment and that they themselves are in charge and must maintain order and look out for the weaker boys." He also gave boys permission to swim in the streams of the parks, but only if they wore bathing suits. "No one has worked more persistently for the things the boys and girls want. ...[The children] have come to know him by the familiar title of 'Gramp' Cleveland."

Henry and his wife Julia lived on the east side of Chester Creek just below Eighth Street. They fed the birds every winter, in their yard as well as in Chester and Lincoln parks. "Captain Cleveland makes his home in a very pretty little bungalow, familiar to thousands, at the edge of Chester Park," the *News Tribune* reported. "Birds have come to recognize this institution as a place where they are always welcome.... In addition to this winter feeding ground, Captain Cleveland maintains a veritable municipality of bird homes, which invariably reaches capacity in the summer." Cleveland paid the bills for maintaining all the feeding stations, which he referred to as "lunch counters." In the winter of 1920, because deep snow covered the birds' usual food sources, he enlisted school children to help feed the birds and encouraged them to keep track of the species they identified. By the end of that season he had distributed two hundred pounds of bird feed.

Cleveland regularly offered creative proposals for a municipal swimming pool, usually as part of a larger convention-center complex. He first suggested building a pool at Lake Shore Park (today's Leif Erikson Park), then at Lafayette Square on Park Point, and then in the area that later became Enger Park. These dreams were never realized, but in 1915 he did succeed in opening the city's first bathing beach at Indian Point on the St. Louis River (see page 91).

In 1917, as war in Europe began to impact the world economy, Americans were encouraged to grow more of their own food in backyard "victory gardens" as a way to save money and reduce pressure on the public food supply. Cleveland helped to create the city's first community garden program when he spearheaded a project to make land available for family vegetable gardens. He opened a thirty-acre parcel of city-owned land in the West End, located below the parkway between Piedmont Avenue and Coffee Creek. The land was divided into 150 plots, each approximately 25 feet square. These free garden plots were available for use by people who did not have garden space adjacent to their homes.

By the 1920s automobiles were becoming a necessity rather than a novelty throughout the country, but Cleveland wasn't interested in driving one. He responded to a query from the *News Tribune* by stating, "I have no desire to go driving about the city, forced to keep my eye on the road in front of me and taking chances on running down someone or causing an accident.... [A]s for driving an automobile of my own, and being compelled to drive it and take care of it myself, I don't want one." But he did recognize the importance of the changes brought about by the automobile, and in 1921 he and Mayor Sam Snively—who also refused to drive a car—established municipal camping sites as a way to attract the new "auto tourists."

Henry Cleveland was also an inventor. A 1921 headline in the *News Tribune* proclaimed "Cleveland Invents Road Signal to Cut Hazards of Traffic." When warning signals were needed at a dangerous corner, he objected to the $12 cost of purchasing them and invented his own, manufactured for about $3 each. His signals were made up of round iron pans resembling searchlights mounted on red painted poles. Inside sat a reflector covered by red glass. When the sun shone on the reflectors, they glittered "like balls of fire." At night, the light from automobile headlights created a flare that could be seen for more than a block.

Duluth citizens regularly lobbied the park board to provide band concerts in the city parks. Cleveland supported the idea, but he estimated that $1,200 would be needed for twenty-four summer concerts at Lincoln, Fairmount, and Lester parks. Because the park department had a limited budget, he suggested using "phonograph concerts" as a cheaper alternative. In 1921

he implemented this idea and installed phonographs and amplifiers in parks so music could be available without a live band. The first phonograph concert was held on a Sunday afternoon in June at the Lincoln Park pavilion.

City employees benefitted from Cleveland's fondness for leaving gifts on the desks of coworkers, including jack-o'-lanterns at Halloween, miniature turkeys at Thanksgiving and Christmas, and Easter eggs in tiny baskets. He also masterminded Duluth's annual Halloween party. He and Mayor Prince cooked up the idea in 1913, and Cleveland carried on the tradition until he retired. He always claimed that the Halloween celebrations did not cost the city any money because all materials were paid for by private individuals (including Cleveland himself) and voluntary contributions. He once told the *News Tribune,* "The only expense I can remember having been connected with the celebrations was the appropriation from the city of a penny box of matches, used to start the big bonfire. All the material used in the bonfires has been collected in the parks during the summer cleanups and saved expressly for Halloween."

The eighty-one-year-old Cleveland retired as park superintendent at the end of 1925. He died less than two years later from kidney disease. At his funeral, W. S. McCormick, commissioner of finance, described Captain Cleveland as "one of the kindliest men I have ever known." His obituary provided a fitting tribute: "His unselfish career with the park department had won him one of the widest circles of friends enjoyed by any Duluthian."

Henry Cleveland was buried in Forest Hill Cemetery. In keeping with his sense of humor, creativity, and love of the natural world, the Cleveland family plot is marked by one of the most unique headstones in the entire cemetery: a large boulder mounted on a simple slab bearing the family name (pictured above).

— IMAGE: ZENITH CITY PRESS —

system of parks that would be connected by a scenic parkway across the hillside. On December 6, 1887, the *Lake Superior Review & Weekly Tribune* reported, "A communication from the board of works regarding the proposed park system was laid before the council, and was accompanied by a finely executed map, which had been hung on the wall. The communication was full of high falutin words." The plan included a proposed one-hundred-acre "Zenith Park" covering the hilltop above Central Park, including the high rocky knob that is today occupied by Enger Tower. ("Zenith Park" was also the name of an amusement park that operated on Whiteside Island, aka Clough Island, in the St. Louis River during the 1890s.)

When the park board laid out the route of the parkway from Chester Creek to Miller Creek in the 1890s, they split the road into two branches that looped around the base of the rocky knob above Central Park, which was known as Grand View Mountain. Excavation and the damming of Buckingham Creek created two small bodies of water northeast of the landmark. Called Twin Ponds today, they were originally named Twin Lakes or Gem Lakes and were intended to be a spot for those on tallyho excursions to stop for a picnic lunch; the parkway crossed over the creek between the two lakes.

The city did not own the land inside the loop around Grand View Mountain; nevertheless, board members considered it to be part of the parkway. They could not officially designate the area as Zenith Park until the city gained ownership of the land, but they intended to make that happen eventually, as was clearly stated in the board's annual report for 1911: "The bare rock that heaves itself in the center of this park area has never been acquired by the city. It is not likely to be taken for any other use and when eventually it becomes part of the park system in legal fact, it needs only the making of paths over the peak and the cultivation of such trees as formerly grew there, to make it the most romantic city park in the world unrivaled for wonders of far spreading view."

At about the same time, in response to requests from the West End Hillside Club, the park board engaged the Minneapolis landscape architects Anthony Morell and Arthur Nichols to help decide how to "improve" Central Park. The men were already well known in Duluth, working on behalf of New York landscape engineer Charles W. Leavitt on the grounds of Chester and Clara Congdon's Glensheen estate and Congdon Park along Tischer Creek.

At the time Morell and Nichols began plans for Central Park, First and Third Streets already extended across the hillside, but

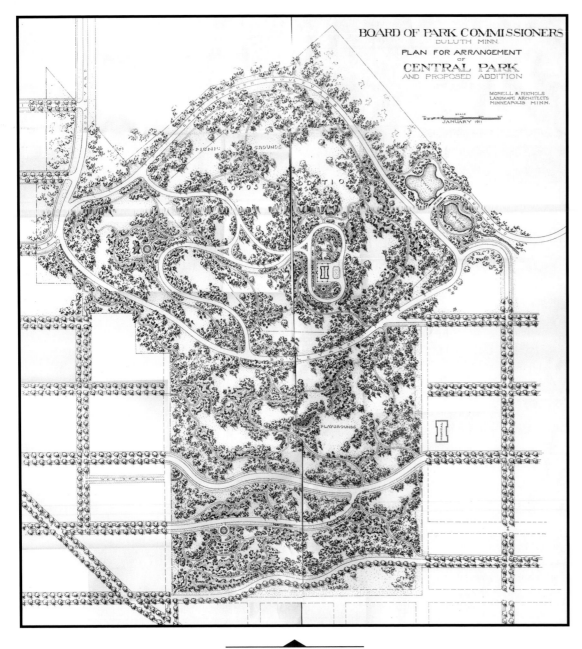

MORELL & NICHOLS'S 1911 PLANS FOR DULUTH'S CENTRAL PARK, DIGITALLY STITCHED TOGETHER FROM A WORN AND TORN ORIGINAL BLUEPRINT.

[IMAGE: T. KASPER COLLECTION]

most of the steep rocky land remained untouched. The Minneapolis firm's landscape plan for "Central Park and Proposed Addition," dated January 1911, included a connecting road from Second Street to Third Street, walking paths, a playground just below Fourth Street, picnic grounds, and a building on "Grand View Knob" within the proposed Zenith Park. Unfortunately, the board was short of money and could not implement the plan. When the new city charter eliminated the park board in 1913, responsibility for the park system shifted to the new mayor, and he did not consider development of Central Park to be a priority.

Following the end of World War I, Park Superintendent and Civil War veteran Henry Cleveland proposed an elaborate plan to create a "castle" that would serve as a memorial to Duluthians who fought in the Civil War, the Spanish-American War, and World War I. The *Duluth News Tribune* reported that the memorial was to be built on the rocky knob above Central Park, which Cleveland called Grand Mountain.

He envisioned a building that would include a huge auditorium with room for three thousand people; a first-class café for visitors; rooms that would hold copper tablets engraved with the name of everyone who served in the wars; a camera obscura that would reflect a miniature, but magnified, reproduction of any bit of scenery that its lens was trained on; a parapet with a periscope; a flag staff at the top of the roof that would be "the same distance from the level of the lake as the lake is from the level of the sea" (about six hundred feet); and a sun dial on the tower. The grounds would be filled with pergolas, walks, vines, fountains, flower beds, and statuary. Cleveland's proposal also included a municipal golf course and a large bathing pool.

Cleveland estimated the project would cost a minimum of $100,000. His plan was undoubtedly too extravagant and costly for the park department's budget. The memorial castle never materialized.

A Furniture Salesman Shares His Fortune

Less than a year later, in January 1920, the *News Tribune* announced that an anonymous donor had pledged $50,000 to purchase Grand Mountain and the surrounding land. In his letter to the city, the donor requested that "a sufficient amount of land be acquired so as to accommodate municipal golf links, baseball diamonds, tennis courts, swimming pool, toboggan slides, and other summer and winter sports and recreational establishments."

Mayor Clarence Magney was reluctant to accept the money without knowing the name of the donor; nevertheless, he asked the city council to begin condemnation proceedings on Grand Mountain and five forty-acre parcels located north of Twin Lakes. Although he did not expect the city to purchase all the parcels, Magney wanted the council to have the option to choose the best that could be obtained with the $50,000 gift. He informally called the area Twin Lakes Park.

Soon after the land purchase was completed in early 1921, Duluth businessman Bert Enger surprised everyone by admitting that he was the anonymous donor. A quiet man, he had emigrated from Norway in 1877 at age thirteen, and in 1903 he and partner Emil Olson had started a successful furniture store in Duluth's West End. As the *News Tribune* reported, "While Mr. Enger has always been known as a public-spirited man and has ever been ready to be enlisted as a supporter of any worthy cause, his stride into the too-seldom entered field of philanthropy is bound to cause general admiration."

The council promptly named the area Enger Park, proclaiming, "The city of Duluth through its council assembled, hereby expresses gratitude of its people, his fellow citizens, for this, his most generous and meritorious act."

Enger's donation had made it possible for the city to acquire the land, and other Duluthians soon became involved in helping to develop the area. Throughout the city, organizations and individuals supported the idea of creating a municipal golf course. In July 1922 one woman told the *News Tribune*, "Golf has particular appeal to women. It is not an expensive game, and women take to it readily. It is not by any manner or means an old man's game, as some think.... I am much in favor of the idea of a municipal links not only for the men, but for the exceptional opportunities which it will offer the women."

Golf course supporters were led by J. B. Clinton, a well-known businessman, sportsman, and Exalted Ruler of the Duluth Elks. He sent a letter to local Elks lodges and civic organizations that stated,

HAGBERT "BERT" J. ENGER

Born March 24, 1864, in Hamar, Norway, Hagbert "Bert" J. Enger came to America in 1877 along with his maternal grandparents (his mother stayed in Norway; his father is thought to have abandoned the family). The thirteen-year-old immigrant found work on a farm in Eau Claire, Wisconsin. Later jobs took him to Wisconsin sawmills, Dakota wheat fields, and the iron mines of northeastern Minnesota and Michigan's Upper Peninsula.

He later settled in Pine City, Minnesota, where he purchased half interest in a general store. According to Enger family historian Jim Insbell, the store "was a bad experience for several years due to old and shopworn merchandise. He eventually was able to pay off all debts, and he and his partner split the store, with Hagbert taking the hardware and furniture part of the business." Enger then hired Emil Olson, a native of Minnesota's Chippewa County, to work in the store while Enger made sales calls to farmers. Recognizing that the market was too small for the business to survive, Enger and Olson—now partners—decided to try their luck in Duluth.

In 1903, with less than $500 worth of furniture as stock, the pair moved to Duluth and set up shop in the West End as Enger & Olson. Within a year they had moved to 2012 West Superior Street, right between two larger furniture stores. Surrounded by competition, their business thrived. Two years later they had to rent additional space. Three years later they needed more space, so they built a warehouse at 1872 West Michigan Street which stands today and still bears the name "Enger & Olson Inc."

Insbell writes that the business prospered because "they were complementary to one another. [Enger] was cautious and conservative, and Olson was enthusiastic and impulsive. Enger was slow of speech, deliberate, and retiring. Olson was quick in speech and action, and enjoyed being in the public eye. In essence, the two men formed a perfect partnership, and they used an intermediary (a friend) very effectively when unable to agree on something. Both were extremely honest, intelligent and loyal." Olson died in 1926.

Enger never married. He lived with his uncle Bernt and aunt Pauline Enger and their daughter Cornelia in an apartment on the store's third floor. In 1928 he was installed as the fifth member of the Duluth Hall of Fame. On April 5, 1931, Enger suffered a stroke while in Hawaii and died three days later. Insbell claims Enger's remains are interred within Enger Memorial Tower, but that has never been verified. A plaque located inside the tower reads:

Enger Observation Tower

To the memory of Bert J. Enger, 1864–1931, Native of Norway, Citizen of Duluth.

From Common Laborer to Merchant Prince, he demonstrated in his own life that America is a land of opportunity for the immigrant, and that her civilization is enriched by his citizenship.

In his life time, by a very generous gift, he enabled the City of Duluth to acquire and develop the land adjacent to this tower as a park and golf course for the enjoyment of future generations, and at his death bequeathed two-thirds of his estate to the people of Duluth.

Hereabout, in his life time, he spent leisure hours in admiration of the panorama of Duluth and its environs which you now may see from this tower.

In recognition of his devotion and generosity, the people of Duluth elected him to their Hall of Fame and will always cherish his memory.

Dedicated June 15, 1939, by Olav, Crown Prince of Norway.

—— IMAGE: UMD MARTIN LIBRARY ——

ENGER PARK MUNICIPAL GOLF COURSE. DULUTH, MINN.   746-30

ENGER GOLF COURSE FROM ENGER MEMORIAL, DULUTH, MINNESOTA.

"May I ask that you submit this suggestion to your organization with the thought that if it be deemed best one of your members be selected to act on a committee in conjunction with one of our members to devise ways and means by which this health giving game may be available to all of Duluth's residents and visitors." The Duluth Chamber of Commerce established a Municipal Golf Committee, and Clinton organized an outing for the committee to visit the Enger Park site, which they agreed was most suitable for a golf course. They estimated the cost to develop the course at $1,000.

Boosted by the efforts of the citizen committee, construction began in 1926. That summer Park Superintendent F. Rodney Paine announced that Arnold "Andy" Anderson, an employee at Northland Country Club, had been hired as the new course's head greenskeeper.

The clubhouse, designed by Abraham Holstead and William J. Sullivan, was completed on June 1, 1927, a month before the grand opening. The park department reported that the building "was decorated and furnished under the direction of Mrs. Torrey Ford." Bert Enger contributed additional funds for the clubhouse, and "Mr. W. J. Olcott very generously supplemented the small amount that the Park Department was able to spend by donating a considerable part of the furniture and decorations." The *News Tribune* later described the building as "modern in every respect and includes lounging rooms, dressing units and shower baths."

Olcott also designed and built the caddie house using lumber donated by Charles Woodruff and hardware donated by the Kelley-Duluth Company. An old garage purchased from Minnesota Power and Light Company was moved to Enger Park to be used as a tool house. The nine-hole municipal golf course was ready by the end of June 1927. Course manager Roger Borgeson told the *News Tribune* that the initial course was 3,184 yards long. The longest hole, number four, was 505 yards long; the shortest, number five, was a 171-yard par three. As often happens in Duluth, the opening was delayed by weather. The Park

TOP: Lithographic postcard, ca. 1927, of Enger Park Golf Course's clubhouse.

[IMAGE: ZENITH CITY PRESS]

BOTTOM: A postcard showing Enger Park Golf Course photographed from Enger Memorial Tower, ca. 1940.

[IMAGE: T. KASPER COLLECTION]

Department reported that "the spring was wet and rather cold and it was not found possible to open the course before the 2nd of July."

Enger was scheduled to drive the first ball at 2 P.M. on Saturday, July 2. The Naval Reserve band played and speeches were made by Tom Hastings, president of Minnesota's State Association of Public Golf Courses, and Judge Clarence Magney—who actually drove the first ball, stating that Enger was "too modest." Mayor Sam Snively was supposed to officially accept the course on the city's behalf, but he could not attend and Commissioner W. S. McCormick stepped in as the mayor's replacement. Every civic group in town had been invited, and the festivities included various golfing competitions including driving and low medal score for both men and women, with trophies and other prizes donated by Bagley & Co. Jewelers, Kelley-Duluth Hardware and Sporting Goods, Silberstein & Bondy (retailers), Big Duluth (retailers), and M. Cook and Son (clothiers).

The golf course was an immediate success, and by September it had generated enough money for the city to begin planning a second nine holes. Two years later, despite the Great Depression, the Enger Park golf course had earned back the city's investment, and the park department initiated plans to build a golf course at Lester Park. The Enger Park course was in fine shape except for one thing: the exotic bent grass used on its greens was not hearty enough to withstand Duluth's cold winters. While struggling with this issue, Andy Anderson noticed a patch of grass growing along a nearby creek. On closer examination he discovered it to be a native bent grass, and he immediately began developing the strain for use on the golf courses. He called it "Enger bent" and used it on the new greens at Lester Park. At Enger Park the original greens were torn up and reseeded with Enger bent. Several other courses in the area began using it on the greens as well, including the short-lived Lakewood Golf Club east of Lester Park.

Both of Duluth's municipal golf courses were expanded in the 1980s, with nine holes added to each. Paying back the investment

THE INITIAL SKETCH BY ARCHITECTS MELANDER AND LIGHTER FOR AN OBSERVATION TOWER ATOP GRAND MOUNTAIN, MADE POSSIBLE BY THE ESTATE OF BERT ENGER.

[IMAGE: DULUTH PUBLIC LIBRARY]

MELANDER AND LIGHTER
ARCHITECTS

MELANDER and LIGHTER
ARCHITECTS

severely compromised the finances of both courses. Since the 1990s a variety of plans have come forward for their management, including hiring private companies to operate the courses, allowing developers to build homes adjacent to the courses, and even selling all or portions of the courses to housing developers. As of 2016 all fifty-four holes of the municipal courses remain open to play under the management of a national company.

Enger Memorial Tower

When lifelong bachelor Bert Enger died in 1931 at the age of sixty-eight, he left two-thirds of his estate to the City of Duluth for development of Enger Park's Grand Mountain area. He specified that the development should include a lookout tower surrounded by beautified grounds and footpaths to accommodate tourists.

In 1933 a citizen committee selected the highest point of the park as the location for the tower, and the following year the park was re-dedicated as Enger Park. A stone comfort station was built in 1935; picnic tables, water, sewer, and electricity were added a year later. In 1937 workers from the National Youth Administration—a branch of the Works Progress Administration that focused on providing work and education for Americans between the ages of sixteen and twenty-five—built rock benches, stone pathways and steps, campfire sites, and outdoor ovens.

Construction of the tower began in late 1937, based on a design by architect A. R. Melander. Melander's initial design was fairly elaborate, a six-story square tower with a four-gabled roof and an elaborate entrance. A second design was similar to the tower that was built, although several stories shorter. The final design was for an octagonal tower five stories high made of native stone gathered on site. Unglazed window openings look out in every direction. At its peak—531 feet above sea level—workers installed a green light that could be seen for miles.

By 1939 the $30,000 tower was complete, paid for with funds provided by the Enger estate. Crown Prince Olav of Norway and his

MELANDER & LIGHTER'S SECOND SKETCH FOR THE PROPOSED TOWER, A CLOSER MATCH TO THE FINAL DESIGN, BUT A FEW STORIES SHORT.
[IMAGE: DULUTH PUBLIC LIBRARY]

wife Princess Martha traveled to Duluth in June to dedicate the tower to the memory of Bert Enger. A crowd of five thousand gathered to hear speeches by the Norwegian royals and other dignitaries, including Judge Clarence Magney.

The headlines stated that the royals "captivate[ed] Duluthians by Informality." The prince wore a simple black suit; the princess a black lace dress she described as "everyday." He smoked casually, and when reporters pressed him on his fishing skills—a Norwegian point of pride—he admitted, "I am really not passionate about it." He was more of a yachtsman. Martha was a typical young mother, spending a great deal of her travel time buying toys and souvenirs for her children.

The prince expressed pride in the ways that Norwegian immigrants had influenced Duluth and indeed all of America: "[Enger] is a truly Norwegian name. As the princess and I have traveled about your country, we have been greatly pleased to note the recognition that has been accorded American men and women of Norwegian birth and Norwegian ancestry."

Over the years vandalism and neglect took their toll on the tower. As early as the 1940s, papers reported vandals shooting out the beacon lights, forcing fund drives to purchase replacement bulbs. In the 1960s, vandals dropped heavy rocks from the top of the tower, and

the city had to temporarily block access to the observation platforms. In 1978, someone shot out the beacon with a .22 rifle. In 1989, vandals created a bonfire of burning tires on top of the tower.

In 2010 to 2011 the City of Duluth gave the park and tower a $400,000 renovation in anticipation of a visit by King Harald V and Queen Sonja of Norway. A $100,000 grant from Duluth's Rotary Club 25 paid for new lighting. According to the Enger Park Restoration Project, the tower renovation included "repairs such as tuck pointing, plaster, concrete patching, electrical and lighting repair, weatherization, roof repair and increased accessibility." Thanks to Rotary 25, new LED lights replaced the old beacon and other LED lights were aimed at the building itself, so that the entire tower could be lit in a variety of colors to recognize a variety of events—for example, on April 21, 2016, Enger Tower was bathed in purple light to honor the unexpected passing of Minnesota music legend Prince. Other renovations were made to the park, including the addition of a new gazebo large enough to accommodate one hundred people and new trails designed to be accessible to people of all ages and abilities. The old pavilion and restrooms were updated and the parking lot expanded.

Norway's royal couple visited Duluth on October 17, 2011, to rededicate Enger Tower to the memory of Bert Enger. Minnesota

MEMBERS OF DULUTH SOCIETY GATHER IN THE BALLROOM OF THE HOTEL DULUTH ON JUNE 17, 1939, IN HONOR OF NORWAY'S CROWN PRINCE OLAV AND PRINCESS MARTHA, WHO WERE VISITING DULUTH TO DEDICATE ENGER MEMORIAL TOWER. (PHOTO BY L. PERRY GALLAGHER JR.)

[IMAGE: UMD MARTIN LIBRARY]

Public Radio reported that Harald told the crowd of over five hundred Duluthians that it was "very moving" for him to follow in his father's footsteps. The king added, "Standing here, I can easily see why so many Norwegian immigrants decided to settle here in this area, by the splendid shores of Lake Superior. They must have missed Norway and those they left behind, but I'm sure they found comfort in this peaceful and beautiful landscape. Thanks to recent extensive restoration work, Enger Tower will continue to be a symbol of the hard work and dedication of the Norwegian immigrants, and their stories will continue to be told to future generations of Americans."

The American-Japanese Peace Bell

Enger Park's most recent addition is the Japanese Peace Bell Garden, installed in 2010. The garden surrounds the Peace Bell, which is a replica of a cherished Buddhist temple bell in Ohara, Japan. At the end of World War II, American sailors on the USS *Duluth* brought the original bell home with them as a war souvenir. They had found it in a Japanese shipyard, waiting to be melted down as part of the war effort. The crew of the *Duluth* gave it to the City of Duluth upon their return to the United States. In 1954 a visiting professor from Japan traced the bell's origins back to Ohara. Duluth mayor George D. Johnson, acting on a request from Japan, returned the bell. Grateful Ohara citizens renamed it the American-Japanese Peace Bell. In 1990 Duluth and Ohara became sister cities at the suggestion of Mayor Yoshihito Saito. As a gift, the citizens of Ohara had a replica bell fabricated and sent to Duluth, arranging the construction of a bell tower to house it as well. The bell and tower were placed in Enger Park, oriented so that persons who ring the bell are facing Ohara. In 2005 Ohara merged with the city of Isumi. The Japanese garden surrounding the bell was dedicated in April 2010, with past and present mayors of Duluth and Isumi City (aka Ohara-Isumi), city councilors, and representatives of both cities' Sister City committees on hand for the celebration. Barbara Auerbach, daughter of the late Mayor Johnson, spoke of her father's gesture in 1954, stating that he considered returning the bell "an act of common decency between people of goodwill."

AN AERIAL PHOTOGRAPH, CA. 1958, SHOWING ENGER TOWER AS IT OVERLOOKS DULUTH, THE HARBOR, AND LAKE SUPERIOR. (PHOTO BY L. PERRY GALLAGHER JR.)
[IMAGE: UMD MARTIN LIBRARY]

10. Chambers Grove and Historical Parks

Small Riverside Parks with a Huge History

Two small parks, Historical and Chambers Grove, sit within a stone's throw of one another along the St. Louis River in the neighborhood of Fond du Lac, which is the oldest settlement at the western end of Lake Superior and the oldest established community in the city of Duluth. The roots of Historical Park lie in the first half of the nineteenth century, before the area was even part of the United States, while those of Chambers Grove Park are firmly planted in the Zenith City's boom-and-bust growth spurts from just before its establishment in 1870 to its relative stabilization by 1910. Linked first by location, their stories became entangled by the creation of a Depression-era attraction built by the Civilian Conservation Corps.

Historical Park: Duluth's First European Settlement

Historical Park has the unique distinction of being one of Duluth's newest parks, but with the oldest history of any of Duluth's public spaces. The tiny park—a single lot near the intersection of 133rd Avenue West and Second Street—was officially created in 2006 when Daughters of Liberty and Greysolon du Lhut chapters of the Daughters of the American Revolution (DAR) transferred ownership of the lot to the city. However, the space had been long been considered a park, and prior to 2007 its name honored America's first multimillionaire.

The history of the Fond du Lac area predates the arrival of Europeans. According to the Fond du Lac Band of Lake Superior Chippewa, and confirmed by archaeologists, ancestors of the present day Ojibwe (Chippewa) have resided in the Great Lakes area since AD 800. The Ojibwe came from the east, migrating along the Great Lakes to the western end of Lake Superior and pushing the Dakota tribes further west. By the 1670s they had established a village on an island on the St. Louis River at a place they called *Wayekwaagichigamiing* or "End of great body of water."

When French fur traders and missionaries arrived here in the seventeenth century, they named the entire region Fond du Lac or "Bottom of the Lake," which the English mistranslated as "Head of

the Lakes," a term used to describe all of western Lake Superior until well after the cities of Superior and Duluth were established. The French also called *Wayekwaagichigamiing* Fond du Lac.

The Ojibwe became trading partners with the French, but ongoing conflicts between the Dakota and Ojibwe interfered with the fur trade. Duluth's namesake, Daniel Greysolon Sieur du Lhut, canoed to Fond du Lac from Montreal in 1679, intending to bring peace to the region and hoping to find a passage to the Pacific Ocean. On September 15, 1679, du Lhut gathered representatives of Ojibwe, Dakota, Cree, and Assiniboin peoples at Fond du Lac, encouraging them to hunt, feast, and intermarry. Within three years the Ojibwe and Dakota were conducting trade as far as 150 miles from Fond du Lac, but the peace was short lived, and by 1736 the conflicts erupted again.

Along with the Ojibwe, independent agents licensed by France known as *coureur des bois* ("wood runners") also trapped fur-bearing animals. Those who traveled by canoe became known as *voyageurs*. These independent agents later went to work for England's Hudson's Bay Company and the private North West Company. In the 1780s the North West Company controlled the western Lake Superior region and established Fort St. Louis at the mouth of the St. Louis River in what is now Superior, Wisconsin; the post became the region's center of trade.

The fur trade changed dramatically after America achieved independence. In 1809 German immigrant John Jacob Astor formed the American Fur Company and set up a trading post at Fond du Lac adjacent to an Ojibwe village. Astor, considered to be America's first multimillionaire, was a German-born businessman and investor who

JOHN JACOB ASTOR, SHOWN HERE IN AN 1825 PORTRAIT BY JOHN WESLEY JARVIS, BUILT A POST FOR HIS AMERICAN FUR COMPANY AT FOND DU LAC ON THE SITE OF TODAY'S HISTORICAL PARK IN 1817.

[IMAGE: PUBLIC DOMAIN]

JAMES OTTO LEWIS PAINTED THIS DEPICTION OF THE AMERICAN FUR COMPANY POST IN 1826 WHEN HE VISITED THE POST WITH COLONEL THOMAS MCKENNEY TO DOCUMENT THE 1826 TREATY OF FOND DU LAC.

[IMAGE: PUBLIC DOMAIN]

made his fortune in fur trading, selling real estate, and smuggling opium. While the Ojibwe preferred to trade with the French and British, the War of 1812 put an end to that, when, in the wake of the war, the U.S. Congress barred foreigners from trading in American territory. And so in 1816 Astor took over the North West Company's interests in western Lake Superior and a year later built a new, larger trading post at Fond du Lac, managed by William Morrison. (A map of historic Fond du Lac appears on page 150.)

Astor's facility eventually included a two-story trading facility, a granary, an ice house, a stable, a dormitory for traders, and the post commander's house. The complex faced the St. Louis River near today's 133rd Avenue West and included a cedar-post stockade that protected vegetable gardens and a graveyard. An Ojibwe village with a population of roughly 150 occupied Nekuk ("Otter") Island directly across from the post. They kept vegetable gardens on nearby Amik ("Beaver") Island.

The fur post became a center of trade and a natural spot for gatherings. In 1826 Michigan territorial governor William Cass (namesake of Minnesota's Cass County) and Colonel Thomas L. McKenney, the head of the newly formed United States Indian Department, travelled to Fond du Lac. They gathered native leaders from throughout the region at Astor's fur post to ratify the Treaty of Fond du Lac, designed to grant the U.S. rights to minerals exploration and mining within Ojibwe lands located in the region.

Astor's charter to operate the post expired in 1833, leaving trader Ramsay Crooks in charge of the operation. A year later a Methodist mission was established just north and east of the fur post. Unfortunately for Crooks, the 1830s saw a decline in the popularity of fur in Europe, and the post turned to commercial fishing on Lake Superior to bolster its profits. The fisheries saw bountiful harvests but had few customers, and there was no rail line—let alone refrigeration—that would allow Crooks to bring the catch to a larger market. A financial panic in 1837 essentially put an end to the fur trade by the early 1840s. The American Fur Company failed in 1842. The Missouri Fur Company then operated the post until 1847, the same year the Second Treaty of Fond du Lac was signed, ceding Ojibwe land west of the Mississippi to the U.S. Two years after that the mission closed as well. (See chapter 11, "Fond du Lac Park, for more about the cemetery and mission.)

In 1854, representatives of the United States government and the Lake Superior Ojibwe signed the Treaty of La Pointe, which ceded Ojibwe lands in northeastern Minnesota to the U.S., opening the area for settlement. It also created the Fond du Lac

Ruins, Hudson Bay Trading Post, Fond du Lac, Minn. 1797

Reservation, 100,000 acres of land twenty miles west of Fond du Lac, and the Ojibwe population declined. In 1856 settlers of European descent, including Francis Roussain, established Fond du Lac Township and platted streets and building lots on the fur post site. Roussain had worked at the post and had built a home along the river adjacent to the stockade along today's 133rd Avenue West. He and his fellow incorporators platted streets over the stockade's footprint and homes were built on portions of the fur post site. The last of the fur post buildings fell into ruin and were reportedly destroyed around 1900, although there is evidence that some buildings may have stood until 1917.

By 1922 there was very little left of the property that once housed the fur post, less than one city lot. That year Duluth's Daughters of the American Revolution affiliates collectively purchased the property and placed a historical marker at the site. Although not officially part of Duluth's park system, Duluthians who were aware of the site referred to it as Astor Park and, occasionally, Heritage Park. The DAR donated the land to the city in 2006, and the next year the Duluth City Council passed a resolution officially accepting the gift and designating the land as a "passive park" named "Historical Park."

The change in the park's name was deliberate—DAR representatives wanted to be more respectful of other aspects of the site's

LITHOGRAPHIC POSTCARD, CA. 1905, OF THE RUINS OF THE AMERICAN FUR POST, BUILT IN 1817; THE CARD MISIDENTIFIES THE RUINS AS THOSE OF THE "HUDSON BAY TRADING POST" AND MISTAKENLY SUGGESTS THE POST WAS BUILT IN 1797.
[IMAGE:ZENITH CITY PRESS.]

Lundberg & Stone, Duluth

No. 703

Old Fond du Lac Indian Trading Post on St. Louis River, Duluth, Minn.

history, particularly the native peoples who lived there. In 2010 another city council resolution made the park a Duluth landmark property. The resolution called the park "John J. Astor Park aka Historical Park" and newspaper articles referred to the park as "John Jacob Astor Park." As of this writing the city is again considering changing the park's name to again include Astor's name.

Chambers Grove: "A Good Place to Go"

Fond du Lac became a township in 1856 and joined the City of Duluth in 1870. Decades after the fur post and mission closed, Fond du Lac once again bustled with activity. "Tomorrow a party of young people will go up to Fond du Lac for a picnic," the *Duluth Weekly Tribune* announced in 1884. "It is a good place to go." Those picnickers were likely headed to Chambers Grove, where tall maple and elm trees created a delightful shady spot on the banks of the St. Louis River several hundred yards west of the Astor fur post site

Michael and Emily Chambers purchased the land that bears their name in 1869, when Fond du Lac was a small but lively township. Chambers was an auctioneer, originally from County Cork, Ireland. He lived in St. Paul before he and his wife, Emily, a French-speaking Canadian, moved to Fond du Lac.

Their property in Fond du Lac, previously a farm owned by Rueben Carlton, namesake of Minnesota's Carlton County, included extensive outcrops of sandstone along the St. Louis River. Chambers leased that portion of the land to various brownstone quarrymen intermittently from 1870 until his death in 1895. The stone from Chambers Quarry was used to construct many buildings in Duluth, few of which remain.

Michael and Emily Chambers began building a new home near the river in 1870 and finished it in 1872. The two-story mansion, faced with chocolate-brown sandstone from their own quarry, included more than twenty rooms with deep stone walls and tall, narrow arched windows. The house stood on high ground overlooking the St. Louis River and attracted sightseers who traveled to Fond du Lac for a view of the mansion. The Chamberses often entertained in the house's large second-floor drawing room, which featured a grand piano (Emily was an accomplished pianist). They covered the floors with Brussels carpeting, which they protected with burlap for dances. Newspaper reports indicate the house may have operated as a hotel in the mid-1870s.

In addition to the brownstone quarry and mansion, Michael and Emily Chambers's property included a plum orchard and, as the *Duluth News Tribune* described, "a grove of old maples, between which is no underbrush, but whose interlacing foliage casts its dark shadows on a smooth carpet of short, thick grass; a high hill on one side, and the broad, still river on the other."

Local newspapers noted the popularity of picnic outings to Fond du Lac as early as 1871, when the *Duluth Minnesotian* reported that Duluth's Germania Society planned to travel up the river on the steamer *Kasota* for a Fourth of July picnic. By 1882 Michael Chambers had opened his maple grove along the river as a public picnic ground; he even provided a platform for dancing and swings for youngsters. Chambers Grove became a favorite site for clan gatherings, church and school groups, labor unions, and service organizations.

While Emily Chambers was quite refined—she was educated in a Quebec convent—Michael Chambers could be difficult to deal with. Historian William Coventry describes Chambers's career as "punctuated by friction with partners, unstable financial situations, and

PICNICKERS GATHERED IN FRONT OF THE RUINS OF THE MICHAEL AND EMILY CHAMBERS HOUSE IN CHAMBERS GROVE, CA. 1900.

[IMAGE: H. DILLON COLLECTION]

THE BROWNSTONE QUARRIES OF FOND DU LAC

Although Chambers Quarry bore his name, Michael Chambers wasn't much of a quarryman, just a transplanted auctioneer who bought a farm along a river whose banks were lined with brownstone—naturally formed sandstone found in various shades of red and brown. The western Lake Superior region was rich in the material, and from 1868 to 1910 fifteen quarries operated along the St. Louis River near Fond du Lac, on the Apostle Islands, and various sites along Wisconsin's Lake Superior shoreline. Chambers, who bought the property in 1869, had good timing: the rise of Richardsonian Romanesque architecture made brownstone a popular building material, and the Lake Superior & Mississippi Railroad came through Fond du Lac the next year. Its tracks were adjacent to the quarry, making transportation of the heavy stone feasible.

Like everything else in the region, the fledgling brownstone industry came screeching to a halt with the financial crisis of 1873. Chambers posted an ad offering to sell his quarry but received no response. Four years later he threatened to tear down his home rather than pay property taxes, and he briefly disappeared in 1879 (his creditors assumed he had skipped town, but he returned claiming an attack of neuralgia had left him partially demented and that he had traveled to Nova Scotia and California before he "came to"). Martin Boyle took charge of the operation in Chambers's absence, and the site became known as the Fond du Lac Quarry. Other than leasing his property, Chambers was essentially out of the brownstone business after 1879. He died in 1895.

Duluth buildings constructed with Fond du Lac brownstone included the 1883 Grand Opera House, perhaps the most opulent edifice ever erected in the Zenith City. In the late 1880s Duluth built a new fire house, a new city hall, and a new police headquarters and jail, all designed by renowned Romanesque architect Oliver Traphagen and trimmed with Fond du Lac brownstone. Along with apartments built in 1891 at 216 East Fourth Street, they stand as Duluth's only remaining examples of brownstone from Chambers Quarry.

Ingalls Quarry, located on the Wisconsin side of the St. Louis River less than a mile upstream from Fond du Lac, was opened by lumberman Edmund Ingalls. He first came to the region in 1861 to establish a sawmill and logging operation. In 1869 Ingalls purchased Durfee's Farm, a sixty-three-acre plot less than a mile up river from Fond du Lac. A year later the site was known as Ingalls Quarry and featured a bluff fifty feet high and four hundred feet wide. It would become the region's most productive quarry, but not under Ingalls's watch. Described by one historian as an intelligent businessman but one who "did not regard an obligation or his word as of any value," Ingalls left Duluth after the Panic of 1873 and in 1879 leased the quarry to Nils Nelson. By 1885 Ingalls had returned to the Zenith City and traded his property to another lumberman, Andreas M. Miller, who turned quarry management over to John H. Crowley. Ingalls remained active in Duluth business until his death in 1895. Stone from the Ingalls/Crowley Quarry faced at least a dozen Romanesque buildings and homes constructed in Duluth during the 1880s and 1890s, but only two remain standing today: the Hunter Block at 31 West Superior Street and the Wirth Block at 13 West Superior Street. The only other known location of Ingalls/Crowley brownstone is in the boathouse at Glensheen, the historic Congdon estate.

Charles Adolph Krause, another Fond du Lac quarryman, moved to the township as a child and stayed his entire life, serving as the community's postmaster in the 1870s. Krause learned the brownstone business by quarrying along Mission Creek north of the ruins of the American Fur Company post where Nehemiah Hulett had first established a quarry in 1872. Krause and Martin Boyle leased the quarry together in 1882, but their relationship has been described by historians as "turbulent." It seems Boyle was the more tempestuous of the two, and in 1883 he—like Chambers five years earlier—was accused by the local press of skipping town on his creditors. A headline in the *Duluth Tribune* asked, "Where is Martin Boyle?"

Later that year the press lauded the news that Krause would take over sole operation of the quarry, describing him as "a substantial and reliable man." The Krause Quarry quickly gained a reputation as producing the area's best stone, and the quarry operated steadily until the industry's demise, with most of the brownstone shipped for use outside the region. Much of it found its way to New York, Chicago, Philadelphia, and Boston. Krause and his wife lived out their lives as celebrated citizens of Fond du Lac, where he died in 1937. By then, Duluth's age of brownstone was long over. Brownstone had fallen out of fashion as a building material just after the turn of the century, and by 1910 all of Lake Superior's brownstone quarries had ceased production.

IMAGE: UMD MARTIN LIBRARY

scuffles with the law." Over the years he accused a fellow pioneer of a "murderous assault," attempted to sue another for defamation of character, and was himself accused of selling liquor to an Ojibwe; each case was dismissed. In October 1882 the *News Tribune* reported that quarryman Martin Boyle confronted Chambers on a train. Boyle grabbed him "by the beard and...drew a revolver and threatened to shoot him." Other passengers intervened "before much harm was done."

In May 1891 it was Alphonse Guerard's turn to assault Chambers, this time over a property dispute. That July an arson fire gutted the Chamberses' mansion; Guerard was the prime suspect. Months later Guerard's home was also destroyed by an arson fire. No legal action was taken in either case. The mansion was never rebuilt. Michael Chambers died in 1895, but the remains of the house were not removed. Promoters made colored postcards of the ruins of the Chamberses' house, claiming it was the "Old Fond du Lac Indian Trading Post on the St. Louis River, Duluth, Minn." The picnickers kept coming, and exploring the ruins became part of the grove's allure until they were cleared away in 1912.

Some picnickers arrived by the Lake Superior & Mississippi Railroad, but most took the river route. As early as the 1880s, steamships that already made daily runs to Fond du Lac began to offer "pic-nic cruises." Following Michael Chambers's death in 1895, Emily leased (and later sold) the eastern portion of the picnic grove to the Clow & Nicholson Transportation Company, which operated a number of the excursion boats. Newspaper advertisements announced that Chambers Grove at Fond du Lac was not a public park, but was under lease to Clow & Nicholson, and was free only to the patrons of their boat line. Other visitors had to pay to use the picnic grounds. The area became so popular that a hotel operated on Nekuk Island, also called Peterson Island, from 1895 to about 1915.

In 1907 Duluth Alderman William E. McEwen, who owned a summer cottage at Fond du Lac, proposed the idea of purchasing the Chamberses' property for a city park. He described the land as "containing 120 acres of rolling ground, dotted with handsome shade trees, lying along the windings of the St. Louis river, removed from the chill of the lake breezes, and away from the hum...of the city, it would make the most ideal park in the northern part of the state." But the park board had little money and decided to focus instead on maintenance of existing parks.

Judge William A. Cant also encouraged the city to create a public park in Fond du Lac. In August 1913, Judge Cant told the *News*

Tribune that "Duluth has an opportunity at this time to acquire a public playground that she sorely needs. Watch the people who come on every excursion boat, with no place to go, picnicking on private property in many instances, and then one sees what a need there is for the city to own a place for the people at the end of this boat trip— the most popular of the sightseeing trips out from Duluth." However, just a few months earlier, the new 1913 city charter had eliminated

THIS CARTOON, CA. 1905, BY THE *DULUTH NEWS TRIBUNE*'S R. D. HANDY, DEPICTS SCENES IN AND NEAR CHAMBERS GROVE.

[IMAGES: DULUTH PUBLIC LIBRARY]

Duluth's park board and handed responsibility for the park system to the mayor. Although Mayor William Prince appreciated parks, he had more pressing problems to resolve.

An ad in the *Duluth Herald* in June 1915 announced that Clow & Nicholson had purchased enough water frontage at Fond du Lac west of the fur post site to establish its own dock and terminal. The company built the Fond du Lac Inn, a large pavilion with "plenty of floor space for dancing, big roomy porches for lounging, big cheery fireplace..., outdoor tables, seats, swings,...row boats, bathing beach, etc." The outside of the building was painted a cheerful yellow and white. In 1919 construction was begun on a bridge over the St. Louis River, which separated the Clow & Nicholson property from Chambers Grove.

Duluthians also journeyed to Chambers Grove via trains running along the original LS&M line between Fond du Lac and West Duluth at Seventy-first Avenue West, which in 1905 became known as the Northern Pacific Railway's Fond du Lac Branch. In order to turn around and return to Duluth, engines—including gasoline-powered models from 1909 to 1910 and 1923 to 1925—used a turntable adjacent to passenger and freight depots built at 133rd Avenue West in 1895. (Fond du Lac's first depot, built in 1870 at 122nd Avenue West, was moved to 13308 West Third Street in 1896 and operated as the Olde Depot Inn restaurant from 1929 to 1985; it is a private residence today.) Streetcar service to New Duluth and the increased availability of automobiles ended train service to Fond du Lac in 1925.

City commissioners finally took steps to acquire Chambers Grove in 1920 by initiating condemnation proceedings. However, Mayor Clarence Magney delayed the action because Emily Chambers still lived on the site, and he feared that taking away her home would shorten her life. Condemnation proceedings were started again in 1922 when Mayor Sam Snively and Park Superintendent F. Rodney Paine recognized the importance of the area for connecting Duluth's parkway system to Jay Cooke State Park. The city finally purchased 577 acres from Emily Chambers in 1923. She died three years later at the home of her niece in Morgan Park. Ten acres of the Chambers property between the quarry and Highway 23, including the grove and former home site, were designated as Chambers Grove Park.

The park saw its first major improvements in the 1930s, even though budget cuts during the Great Depression reduced city park staff to a bare minimum. Using labor provided by Duluth's City Work Administration, the park department in 1933 built a log fieldhouse (also referred to as a pavilion) at Chambers Grove. The rustic log building, constructed almost entirely of material from within the park, included a large auditorium, a piano, a fireplace, and a fully outfitted kitchen.

Two years later, Chambers Grove became home to a reconstruction of the nineteenth-century fur trading post. During the 1930s the Minnesota Historical Society sponsored a series of pageants throughout the state, and the topic of the 1935 pageant was to be the early

A CROWD GATHERED ON THE FRONT PORCH OF THE FOND DU LAC INN, DATE UNKNOWN.

[IMAGE: H. DILLON COLLECTION]

ST. LOUIS RIVER EXCURSION BOATS

In the late 1880s, steamships that made the twice-daily run delivering mail and goods (and commuters) to Fond du Lac began to offer "pic-nic cruises" and the excursion trade was born. A variety of excursion boats transported people from a dock at the foot of Duluth's Fifth Avenue West to Fond du Lac. A round-trip steamer ticket cost fifty cents. The trip could take an hour and a half or more, with stops along the way at Garfield Avenue, Superior, West Duluth, and Gary. Boats docked at the end of 133rd Avenue West in Fond du Lac at the site of the American Fur Post ruins, and picnickers headed off on foot to find a comfortable spot for lunch—often following the river upstream to Chambers Grove.

Excursion boat rides to Fond du Lac and back became even more popular in the early 1900s, and over the years vessels including the *Henrietta*, *Plow Boy*, *Chicora*, *Columbia*, and *Newsboy* steamed regularly up and down the St. Louis River. The photo below shows passengers on the steamer *Dell Queen* as she rests on the St. Louis River near the Oliver Bridge, just down river from Fond du Lac

Duluth's Clow & Nicholson Transportation Company—which owned and operated many of the excursion boats, including the *Newsboy*, first leased Chambers Grove following Michael Chambers's death in 1895. In 1919 the company, which by then had opened the Fond du Lac Inn at the site, purchased the sidewheeler *A. Wehle Jr.* and brought her to Duluth for the Fond du Lac route. Company owner David Clow, who was also president of Duluth's Rotary Club, renamed her *Rotarian*. She ran to Fond du Lac twice a day, charging sixty cents for a round trip. The *Rotarian* also ran a special "Around the Horn" route through the Duluth Ship Canal and into Lake Superior, south along Minnesota Point to the Superior Entry, through the entry, and north along Minnesota Point back to its berth. The ride, also called the Moonlight Trip, cost thirty-five cents.

STEAMER "MONTAUK" CRUISING ON DULUTH-SUPERIOR HARBOR

Despite a capacity of six hundred passengers, the *Rotarian* proved so popular that Clow & Nicholson purchased the paddlewheeler *Montauk* in 1923 to keep up with demand. The *Montauk* (pictured above) had begun life in 1891 as the flagship of the Montauk Steamboat Company before serving the same capacity for the Long Island Railroad. Originally a sidewheeler, the 175-foot boat featured three decks, and her opulent state rooms were finished in mahogany and cherry. The *Montauk* first worked as an ocean-going vessel, taking passengers up and down the East Coast of the United States until 1902, when she was sold to a Canadian company and renamed the *King Edward* and later the *Forest City*. A newspaper report from 1944 claims she arrived in Duluth in 1918, once again christened as *Montauk*, and served Superior, Wisconsin, as a hospital ship during the flu epidemic. Another sale brought her to Chicago, where new owners converted her to an excursion boat. The new *Montauk*, propelled by a one-cylinder engine, could reach speeds of eighteen knots (about twenty-one miles per hour) and carry over 1,000 passengers running between Chicago's municipal dock and Jackson Park.

Clow purchased the vessel in 1923, and she began the Fond du Lac route the next year. The *Rotarian* was sold in 1927, leaving the *Montauk* as the last of the Fond du Lac steamers. By 1930 the *Rotarian* was tied up in Chicago and used as a floating restaurant and dance hall; she sank at her moorings that year. Piloted by Captain Burdette J. Roberts, the *Montauk* ran the Duluth-to-Fond du Lac route until 1939. By then a one-way trip to Fond du Lac cost seventy-five cents; Around the Horn cost fifty cents. She lay docked at Fond du Lac until 1944 when the Lyons Construction Company purchased her. By that November she was in Whitehall, Michigan, where her new owners stripped off her cabins and converted her into a barge. There are no records of the *Montauk* past 1947.

"discovery" of the headwaters of the Mississippi River in 1832, and the final three episodes showed life at the Fond du Lac post and Indian camp life as portrayed by members of Chippewa tribes still residing in the area.

The replica stockade's popularity was short lived, and it fell into a state of neglect; flooding caused further damage. Writing in 2014, longtime *News Tribune* and *Herald* columnist Jim Heffernan remembered that when he was a child in the 1940s and early 1950s, the facility was primarily used "as a urinal" by men and boys. By the 1960s it had been abandoned for many years. According to park department records the stockade was demolished in 1967. The fieldhouse/pavilion was condemned in 1968 and razed in 1969. The park department constructed a new pavilion in 1973.

By that time fire had destroyed the Fond du Lac Inn, the last remnant of the days when the excursion boats of Clow & Nicholson

fur trading days. Fond du Lac was the obvious location for a performance. Nothing was left of the original trading post, so city leaders decided to build a replica as the setting for the historical pageant.

Park Superintendent Paine indicated in his notes that the committee chose not to build the trading post in the original location because by this time the property was privately owned and surrounded by modern buildings. Instead, organizers decided on a site about five hundred feet upstream, within Chambers Grove Park, where the St. Louis River and a wooded island provided an appropriate backdrop. According to Paine, "the Post is typical of the Trading Posts of about 1816.... It does not pretend to be a replica of the Fond du Lac Post, but all of its features are substantiated by existing records for the posts in this territory."

A crowd of fifteen thousand people gathered in Chambers Grove to hear Minnesota governor Floyd B. Olson dedicate the facility on August 4, 1935. The previous day twenty thousand Duluthians had lined Superior Street for eighteen blocks to witness a parade, led by oxcarts, depicting the early history of the Head of the Lakes. The four-day event included performances of a seven-episode pageant depicting Fond du Lac's early history. The first three episodes of the pageant dealt with the activities of explorer John Baptiste Cadotte and his voyageurs in 1792, episode four highlighted Henry Schoolcraft's

carried crowds to Chambers Grove. That era had come to an end with the steamer *Montauk*'s last cruise in 1939. The Clow & Nicholson pavilion served as a roller skating rink beginning in 1956 and was abandoned some time before it burned in 1962. Today the property the pavilion sat on is a privately owned campground and boat landing. In 2008 the Highway 23 bridge was renamed Biauswah Bridge to honor Native American military veterans. The name comes from two legendary Sandy Lake Ojibwe chiefs, father and son; the younger Chief Biauswah married a Fond du Lac woman.

After the Flood: Changes Afoot in Chambers Grove

The 2012 flood that devastated much of Duluth hit Fond du Lac particularly hard, as the surging waters of Mission Creek and the St. Louis River overflowed their banks. Roads were destroyed, and several families lost their homes. A sheet metal wall that had separated Chambers Grove Park from the river was compromised, and currents undercut the shoreline, causing serious erosion. In September 2015 funds from the Great Lakes Restoration Initiative paid for the

installation of three rock weirs in the river adjacent to the park. The J-shaped formations steer fast-flowing water away from the banks to the middle of the river; a side benefit is that the weirs create good spawning habitat for sturgeon. Changes were also made to the slope of the park land, providing better access to the river.

Chambers Grove currently serves as the western access point for the Upper and Lower Cathedral mountain bike trails of the Duluth Traverse, which extends across the length of the city. In summer 2016 the city's Property and Facilities Management Division began work on the Chambers Park Improvement Project; plans include construction of a new monument sign, handicapped-accessible bathrooms, expanded parking and playground space, LED lighting, a boardwalk through the site of the former Chambers Quarry, and a series of signs interpreting the entire community's rich heritage.

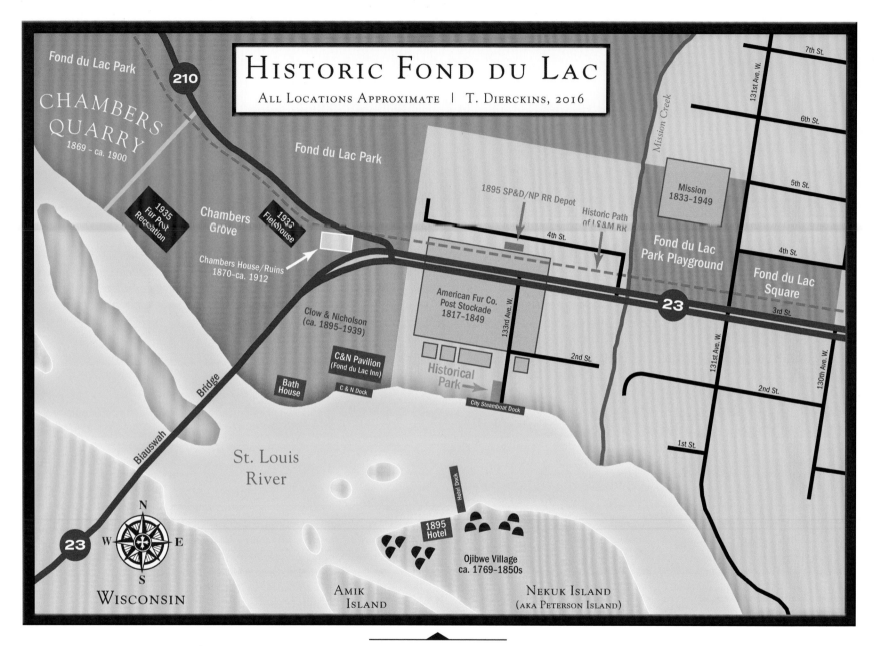

HISTORIC FOND DU LAC

ALL LOCATIONS APPROXIMATE | T. DIERCKINS, 2016

Fond du Lac Park

210

CHAMBERS QUARRY
1869 – ca. 1900

Mission Creek

Fond du Lac Park

1895 SP&D/NP RR Depot

Mission
1833–1949

131st Ave. W.

7th St.

6th St.

5th St.

1935
Fur Post
Recreation

Chambers
Grove

1933
Fieldhouse

Historic Path
of LS&M RR

4th St.

Fond du Lac
Park Playground

4th St.

Chambers House/Ruins
1870–ca. 1912

Clow & Nicholson
(ca. 1895–1939)

American Fur Co.
Post Stockade
1817–1849

133rd Ave. W.

Fond du Lac
Square

23

3rd St.

131st Ave. W.

C&N Pavilion
(Fond du Lac Inn)

Bath
House

C & N Dock

2nd St.

130th Ave. W.

Historical
Park

2nd St.

City Steamboat Dock

Bridge

1st St.

Biauswah

St. Louis
River

Hotel Dock

1895
Hotel

23

N
W   E
S

Ojibwe Village
ca. 1769–1850s

WISCONSIN

AMIK
ISLAND

NEKUK ISLAND
(AKA PETERSON ISLAND)

AS THE EXACT LOCATIONS OF MANY OF THE SITES SHOWN ABOVE WERE NEVER RECORDED, THE MAP IS BASED ON WRITTEN AND
ORAL DESCRIPTIONS FROM A VARIETY OF SOURCES, PHOTOGRAPHS MADE BETWEEN 1870 AND 1938, AND A 2015 ARCHAEOLOGICAL
SURVEY OF THE AREA. THE FORMER CLOW & NICHOLSON PROPERTY IS NOW THE PRIVATELY OPERATED FOND DU LAC CAMPGROUND.

[MAP: ZENITH CITY PRESS]

11. Fond du Lac Park

A Summer Nursery and a Winter Playground

Today the name Fond du Lac Park is associated with a small recreation area adjacent to Mission Creek on the north side of Highway 23 in Duluth's Fond du Lac neighborhood. But in 1923 Mayor Sam Snively gave this name to one of Duluth's largest greenspaces after the city purchased over five hundred acres of Emily Chambers's land along Mission Creek. In 2012 Snively's Fond du Lac Park became part of the larger F. Rodney Paine Forest Preserve. Accessible only by a few trails today, in the late 1920s this huge forest park became a key link in Duluth's parkway system and served as a winter playground for Duluthians during the Depression and World War II. In addition, for over three decades the area was home to an arboretum and a municipal nursery that provided trees for the city's boulevards and flowers for the entire park system. But, just like nearby Chambers Grove and Historical Parks, the story of the land that makes up Fond du Lac Park reaches even deeper into the past.

Mission Creek and Fond du Lac Square

Mission Creek flows through the heart of Fond du Lac. The creek's name came from the first Christian mission in the area, which was located along its eastern bank. Europeans arrived in the Fond du Lac area in 1817 when the American Fur Company built a trading post along the St. Louis River at what is now 133rd Avenue West.

In 1833 the American Board of Missions sent twenty-four-year old Reverend Edmund F. Ely to Fond du Lac to convert the native Ojibwe people to Christianity. Ely built his mission directly north and east of the trading post—above State Highway 23 between Mission Creek and 131st Avenue West on today's maps. There he set to work creating an Ojibwe language dictionary and taught English grammar and arithmetic to the native and mixed-race children who lived nearby. (See map on facing page.)

LITHOGRAPHIC POSTCARD, CA. 1905, OF TOURISTS ENJOYING A CALM ROW ON THE ST. LOUIS RIVER ADJACENT TO DULUTH'S FOND DU LAC NEIGHBORHOOD.

[IMAGE: ZENITH CITY PRESS]

The missionary witnessed two significant firsts at the Head of the Lakes. September 10, 1834, saw the first Protestant wedding in the region, the union of Ely's colleague Reverend William T. Boutwell and Hester Crooks. Crooks was the daughter of Ramsay Crooks, who had taken control of the American Fur Company when Astor's charter expired in 1833. Two years later, on May 29, 1836, Ely's wife Catharine gave birth to Mary Wright Ely, thought to be the first child of entirely European descent born in what is now Duluth.

The board of missions transferred Ely to Lake Pokegama in 1839. A number of ministers followed him at the Fond du Lac mission, but they all faced the same frustrations: the fur post had its own lay priest, clerk Pierre Cotte, and most of the native population either had no interest in Christianity or had already been converted to Catholicism by the French. The mission closed in 1849, but it is remembered today because the creek still bears its name.

Six years after the mission closed, a handful of pioneers established Fond du Lac Township. They included Reuben Carlton (namesake of Carlton County), Alexander Paul, George Morrison, Joshua B. Culver (Duluth's first mayor), and Francis Roussain, who had lived in the area since the days of the fur trade. When they platted the township's streets in 1856, they set aside one block of public greenspace known as Fond du Lac Square, located not far from the site of the old mission, between today's West Third Street (State Highway 23) and West Fourth Street from 130th to 131st Avenues West.

The small park remained undeveloped, and when Jay Cooke's Lake Superior & Mississippi Railroad was built along the St. Louis River in 1870, the tracks were laid right through Fond du Lac Square. Then, in the 1930s, the state of Minnesota took additional land from

REVEREND EDMUND F. ELY RAN THE FOND DU LAC MISSION FROM 1833 TO 1839.

[IMAGES: DULUTH PUBLIC LIBRARY]

THE ROUSSAIN CEMETERY, ALSO KNOWN AS THE FOND DU LAC INDIAN CEMETERY, WITHIN FOND DU LAC PARK, 1927. (PHOTO BY F. R. PAINE.)

[IMAGE: UMD MARTIN LIBRARY]

the square for Highway 23. Because little was left of the greenspace, the City of Duluth dedicated a two-block rectangle of land west of the square (between 131st to 132nd Avenues West from West Third Street north to West Fifth Street) for a small recreation area where, according to park department records, tennis courts were built in 1929 with funds donated by the Fond du Lac group of the Garden Flower Society. An athletic field and basketball court were added later, and the area was christened Fond du Lac Park.

The railroad tracks also cut through a graveyard that had been established north of the fur post. The cemetery is thought to have had two distinct sections: one for the bodies of European Christians and Ojibwe who had converted to Christianity, the other for Ojibwe who practiced the traditional Medewiwin faith (some accounts claim there were three sections: one for Europeans, one for Ojibwe Christians, and the third for Medewiwin Ojibwe). The cemetery contained the remains of Francis Roussain's family and other relatives of Fond du Lac settlers as well as members of the Ojibwe community who still called the area home.

Roussain owned property roughly a mile northwest of the fur post site, and he offered the use of this land for a new cemetery. As the railroad was being built, the bodies from the trading post graveyards were disinterred and reburied at the new site, known as both the Roussain Cemetery and the Fond du Lac Indian Cemetery. The last burial took place in 1926, when Mary Wan-Ne-Gow Roussain—Francis Roussain's daughter-in-law—was interred there. (In 1937 workers constructing Highway 23 through the original cemetery site unearthed the remains of four people, one still wrapped in "birch bark and an old Indian blanket.")

The Roussain cemetery is located on the far western edge of the F. Rodney Paine Forest Preserve adjacent to Jay Cooke State Park; it was maintained through the 1950s by the Duluth Park Department. It has since become the property of the Fond du Lac Band of Lake Superior Chippewa, which has allowed the cemetery to grow over so it is less tempting to vandals.

MISSION CREEK FLOWING THROUGH FOND DU LAC PARK, 1927. (PHOTO BY F. R. PAINE.)

[IMAGE: UMD MARTIN LIBRARY]

Fond du Lac Park and Mission Creek Boulevard

In the early 1900s, automobiles began changing the face of the land, as people could travel more easily and connections became a high priority. Minnesota officials recognized the need to develop links between the state's major cities by connecting existing road segments and paving the entire system. As an editorial in the *Duluth News Tribune* explained in February 1909, "A highway beginning somewhere and with a definite ending...would be the best possible example of the value of a permanent trunk highway as compared to the present system of a few miles good and a few more bad and without any definite character or purpose."

Encouraged by the affordability of automobiles, by the 1920s middle-class families with recently acquired cars enthusiastically embraced the new pastime of auto tourism, in turn creating demand for more and better roads that would connect them to all parts of the country. The Minnesota highway department had decided that Trunk Highway 1 would be the first road to span the state from south to north—from the Iowa state line through the Twin Cities to Duluth and along the North Shore to the Canadian border.

At the same time, Duluth leaders recognized the importance of connecting the city to the new Jay Cooke State Park near Carlton and Highway 1. While the trunk highway was under construction, Snively and former Duluth mayor Judge Clarence Magney, together with Jay Cooke State Park Superintendent F. Rodney Paine, worked on creating a link between the new highway and the North Shore of Lake Superior—a link that would carry tourists across the length of Duluth. The State of Minnesota had connected the village of Thomson to the state park entrance in 1916, but the road did not continue all the way to Fond du Lac. After visiting the state park, tourists heading north from the Twin Cities had to backtrack to Highway 1 to continue their journey to Duluth. Snively, Magney, and Paine envisioned an alternate route—a scenic parkway that tourists could follow from Jay Cooke Park, along the St. Louis River, and across the Duluth hillside to the North Shore.

TWO MEN ON HORSEBACK TRAVEL ALONG A BRIDLE PATH IN FOND DU LAC PARK, 1931. (PHOTO BY F. R. PAINE.)

[IMAGE: UMD MARTIN LIBRARY]

JAY COOKE STATE PARK

Jay Cooke State Park, located about ten miles southwest of Duluth on the St. Louis River, includes 8,938 acres of forested land. The park spans both sides of the river from the western edge of Fond du Lac to the town of Carlton, Minnesota. The focal point of the park is the river, which flows over the ancient bedrock exposing stunning rock formations created by eons of seismic activity and erosion.

The park takes its name from Philadelphia financier Jay Cooke, whose investments helped spur the development of Duluth in the 1860s. Cooke's largest investment was financing construction of the Northern Pacific Railroad, which promoters planned to build from Carlton, Minnesota, west to the Pacific Ocean. While visiting the area to see where the railroad would start, Cooke recognized that the surging waters of the St. Louis River's rapids above Fond du Lac (also called the "dalles") could produce electricity to power nearby towns. Cooke purchased thousands of acres along the river but did not live long enough to see his vision realized. His land was purchased in 1902 by a group of investors including C. C. Cokefair. They formed the Great Northern Power Company, built a dam near the town of Thomson, and began generating electricity in 1906.

In 1915 the company, by this time the St. Louis River Water Power Company, donated to the state 2,350 acres of surplus land along the river. The Minnesota State Legislature passed a bill in the 1915 session creating Jay Cooke State Park and authorizing $15,000 to purchase an additional 4,000 acres. Duluthian F. Rodney Paine was hired as the park's first manager; in 1926 he became superintendent of Duluth's park system.

Jay Cooke State Park is best known for its swinging bridge (shown above in a lithographic postcard ca. 1925), first constructed in 1924 by the U.S. Forest Service. The swinging bridge spans a particularly rocky and narrow portion of the river. The bridge's pylons are made of local stone, and steel cables support the two-hundred-foot span of wood and steel; it is one

of just two suspension bridges in all of Minnesota's state park system. In 1933 the Civilian Conservation Corps (CCC) set up camp in the park while workers constructed picnic sites and completed projects to prevent soil erosion. The following year the CCC rebuilt the park's famous bridge. The camp closed in 1935 and reopened in 1939, the year the CCC built the park's River Inn, one of the largest buildings in the state park system and known today as the Oldenburg Interpretive Center. Like the bridge, the inn and its accompanying water tower, latrine, and other structures are all made of logs and stone in the Rustic Style tradition.

In 1945 the state purchased another large piece of land for the park and has since added even more property to the site. Five years later floodwater damaged the deck of the swinging bridge; it took three years to replace the bridge with a new span whose deck rested seven-and-a-half feet higher than that of the previous bridge. The flood of June 2012, largest on record in the park, again destroyed most of the swinging bridge and caused major damage in many areas of the park. A reconstruction of the bridge, designed to replicate the 1934 span, was completed in November 2013.

As of 2016 the original 2,350 acres of Jay Cooke State Park have grown to nearly 9,000. More than 300,000 people visit Jay Cooke State Park every year, enjoying fifty miles of hiking trails, thirty-two acres of Nordic ski trails, ten miles of snowshoe trails, and more than eighty campsites—and its iconic bridge once again swings over the St. Louis River.

Jay Cooke became the namesake of a Duluth park in 1922 when a statue of Cooke (pictured at right in a detail of a 1922 photograph by Hugh McKenzie) designed by Henry Shrady was placed within an existing triangle at the convergence of Superior Street and London Road. When the triangle was eliminated with the expansion of Interstate 35 through Duluth, Jay Cooke Plaza was created atop a highway tunnel, and the statue now rests there. Learn more about Jay Cooke Triangle on page 230 and Jay Cooke Plaza on page 223.

To create this connection, Snively began purchasing forested land near Fond du Lac. He planned to build the linking road through the area, which he called Fond du Lac Park. He shared his vision with the *News Tribune* in June 1925: "God gave us most wonderful natural scenic advantages and it is to these we must look to bring into our city the ever-increasing thousands who are to fill our hotels, buy from our merchants and leave with us some of the money that is now going to other cities that have been far-sighted enough to capitalize their natural resources."

City engineers built the parkway along Mission Creek in the summer of 1926. Similar to the Seven Bridges Road at the eastern end of the city, the road included five stone bridges across the creek. Snively also planned to build a branch road into the village of Fond du Lac to satisfy the local community club. After receiving an estimate of $20,000 to build the branch road, Snively decided to avoid the time-consuming red-tape of finding funds in the city budget. He convinced ten citizens to contribute fifty dollars each for clearing the right-of-way. Four other citizens contributed $700 for grading the roadway. He appealed to the county commissioners and received $5,000 for two bridges.

Snively even spent time personally helping to build the branch road. According to the *Duluth Herald*, "to urge the road builders on, Mayor Snively frequently went to Mission Creek, clad in working clothes, seized a pick or shovel and worked side by side the whole day long with the road laborers, doing his share of the work and urging them on to greater efforts." Thanks to the untiring efforts of Mayor Snively, the Mission Creek Boulevard—including the branch road—was completed and dedicated on November 5, 1927. Several hundred motorists drove the new road to attend the opening ceremony, where residents of Fond du Lac served as hosts and provided refreshments. Judge Magney gave a short speech to celebrate the occasion.

The life of Mission Creek Boulevard was brief—just thirty years. The road frequently washed out when the creek spilled over its banks. In 1958 floodwater took more of the parkway than the city was willing to repair, so the road was closed and the bridges left to deteriorate.

MISSION CREEK BOULEVARD UNDER CONSTRUCTION IN 1927. (PHOTO BY F. R. PAINE.)
[IMAGE: UMD MARTIN LIBRARY]

Duluth's Municipal Nursery

As work on the Mission Creek road got underway, Snively turned his attention to developing a municipal tree nursery. Since 1889 the park board, and later the park department, had been responsible for planting trees and flowers in the city's boulevards and greenspaces. Mayor Snively thought it would be more economical for the city to grow plants instead of buying them from commercial nurseries, so in 1926 he approved the purchase of approximately thirty-six acres of the "old Windom farm" for a cost of $7,500. Located adjacent to Fond du Lac Park at the end of 131st Avenue West, the farm was worked in the early 1900s by Judge William Windom, a friend and colleague of Guilford Hartley, whose Allandale Farm later became Hartley Park. Windom had specialized in raising Guernsey dairy cows and Rhode Island Red chickens on his Fond du Lac acreage. The site offered deep, rich soil, a good water supply, and protection from the cold winds.

NURSERY CARETAKER DAVID NUMMI SHOWS AN UNIDENTIFIED WOMAN A GROVE OF YOUNG TREES, 1929. (PHOTO BY F. R. PAINE.)
[IMAGE: UMD MARTIN LIBRARY]

F. RODNEY PAINE, A MAN OF FAR-REACHING VISION

On the first day of 1926, thirty-seven-year-old F. Rodney Paine (pictured left ca. 1918 and right in 1930) stepped into the role of superintendent of the Duluth Park Department. An appreciation for parks had surrounded Paine since his youth. He was born in Duluth on June 17, 1889, the year the city's first Board of Park Commissioners was created. His father, Frederic William (F. W.) Paine, was a charter member of that park board. His mother, Emilie, was the sister of William Sargent, a developer of Lakeside who in 1893 donated to Duluth the greenspace we know today as Lester Park. Rodney Paine seemed destined to become Duluth's most visionary and influential park superintendent.

After graduating from Princeton, Paine went on to Yale University, where he earned a master of forestry degree in 1914. He worked with the U.S. Forest Service in Montana and Idaho until 1916, when he accepted the job of managing Minnesota's newly created Jay Cooke State Park. He took a leave of absence during World War I to serve with the 109th Division of the U.S. Army Corps of Engineers. Following his discharge in 1919, he returned to Duluth and his work at the state park. During the early 1920s he cooperated closely with Duluth mayors Clarence Magney and Sam Snively to create Mission Creek Boulevard, which would link the state park to Duluth's Skyline Parkway.

At the end of 1925, eighty-one-year-old Henry Cleveland announced his retirement after sixteen years as Duluth's park superintendent. Mayor Snively promptly appointed Paine as Cleveland's replacement, announcing that he "has the advantage which youth and vigor gives to a man and a love for the work which he now enters upon for the city."

Paine brought to the park department a talent for planning, organization, and record-keeping. When he took over, the park department equipment consisted of one team of horses and two discarded army trucks and there were no office records or development plans more recent than 1912, the last year the park board existed. Full-time caretakers maintained the larger parks, but the smaller parks did not receive the same level of attention. Paine immediately started working to modernize the department.

To improve the efficiency of the maintenance work, Paine added new equipment and created what he called the Flying Squad—a small crew of men using a light truck to travel from park to park, focusing especially on the smaller parks that did not have caretakers. He also developed a system for keeping detailed records—including photographs—of the work done on each park.

(A collection of Paine's photos owned by the Duluth Public Library, many of which appear in this book, is held in the University of Minnesota Duluth Kathryn A. Martin Library Archives and Special Collections.) By 1928 the park department, including office staff, numbered at least thirty people.

Paine spoke often of the importance of planning intelligently for the future of the park system. Part of his vision included a major shift in the department's mission, toward developing more recreational and revenue-producing activities. During his administration, Paine oversaw development of the golf courses at Enger and Lester Parks, construction of cabins at the

Brighton Beach and Indian Point Tourist Camps, creation of the city nursery in Fond du Lac Park and the outdoor stage at Leif Erikson Park, acquisition of the Longview Tennis Courts, and extension of the parkway from fifteen miles to over forty-six miles. He also initiated

development of the Minnesota Point Recreation Area, Ordean Field, Wheeler Field, and the winter sports centers at Chester Bowl and Fond du Lac.

In October 1929, just three and a half years after Paine took over the park department, the stock market crash dragged the country into the Great Depression. Although the department had never been funded to the extent needed to carry out all the park board's plans, the Depression made things much worse. Paine did what he could to cut costs and keep the park system afloat, but he spent the remainder of his term as park superintendent dealing with massive cuts to the department budget and loss of staff. When reporting on the accomplishments of 1929, Paine wrote that "funds are not now provided for the printing of an annual report of the park department and only a few mimeograph copies can be gotten out. The following report is therefore made as an administrative record and in the form most convenient as such rather than a popular one." This was the case for the remainder of his time as superintendent.

Paine's annual report for 1933 reveals the painful struggles Duluthians faced during the Depression. Every man who worked for the park department "not only took a cut of sixteen and two-thirds percent of his wages but took an additional layoff of at least one month. A large number of the men did not make more than six month's wages and were forced to go to the Poor Commission for relief. Some of these were men who have been on the city payroll for twenty years and have served the public faithfully."

To keep the park department functioning, Paine took advantage of local and federal programs to bring in relief workers. He reported that "for a large part of the year this department had about two hundred men working from three to six days at a time, getting no cash for their work but receiving relief orders in accordance with their needs and the amount of work which they had done. In order to carry on this work and cover the cost of supervision, tools, street car fares and other incidental expenses, the city council appropriated money from the Unemployment Bond Issue. ...The fact that the men did not get any cash, the short period of time which they worked, and the character and physical condition of the men all tended to cut down the efficiency of the actual work. Nevertheless, it was very satisfactory on the whole and it was a fine thing for the morale of those who wished to do something for the help they were receiving."

Despite these challenges, by modernizing the park department, increasing receipts, and taking advantage of relief labor, Paine managed to maintain and operate the parks at a cost below that of previous years. In 1932 the *Duluth News Tribune* described Paine as "[t]he tall, slender gentleman...in the inner sanctum of the city park department, usually wearing boots and knickers.... Not an office man, he enjoys going from park to park and from project to project, personally supervising the work."

When Mayor Snively lost his reelection bid in spring 1937, newly elected mayor Rudy Berghult chose to replace Paine as park superintendent. Those who had worked closely with Paine were surprised by this turn of events. Following his exit from the park department, Paine received a supportive letter from renowned Minneapolis landscape architect Arthur Nichols, who along with Anthony Morell had executed the landscaping of Chester Congdon's Glensheen estate and designed Congdon Park, the bridges of Seven Bridges Road, the Lester River Bridge, and plans for several other Duluth park projects. Nichols wrote to Paine, "I want to take this opportunity of expressing my personal appreciation of the splendid service you have rendered to the city, and the constructive program that you have achieved during your administration. The City cannot fully realize the full measure of comprehensive work that has resulted from your far reaching vision and broad planning for the future."

After leaving the park department, Paine (pictured above in 1968 enjoying a picnic with a beloved companion in Jay Cooke State Park) plunged into various business pursuits, primarily real estate and investment firms. He served as president of the Nantucket Company and the Niles Land Company and as a director and vice president of the Northwestern State Bank. He also served on the St. Louis County Welfare Board from 1940 to 1961.

Paine, his wife Anna, and their four children lived in the Congdon neighborhood. During World War II the family spent summers in a log cabin at the small farm that his father had established near Hawk Ridge. According to Paine's daughter, Anne Paine Williams, a caretaker managed the garden, sheep, cows, turkeys, pigs, and chickens. During the summer the children helped out by milking cows, weeding the garden, picking vegetables and fruit, and boxing eggs. Paine maintained a large raspberry patch and numerous apple trees. In 1950 he built a permanent home adjacent to the old log cabin and created a new entrance to the farm off Jean Duluth Road known as the Paine Farm Road.

Rodney Paine died on May 8, 1968, at the age of seventy-eight. In recognition of his extraordinary vision and leadership in developing Duluth's park system, in 2012 the Duluth City Council—driven by council President Daniel Hartman, currently director of Glensheen—created a fitting memorial to Paine when they designated two thousand acres of parkland and municipal forest centered on Fond du Lac Park as the F. Rodney Paine Forest Preserve.

—— PHOTOS: UMD MARTIN LIBRARY ——

Park employees renovated the Windom home, and early in 1927 the new caretaker, David Nummi, took up residence on the old farm. Workers repaired the barn and divided it into rooms for offices and storage. They turned the chicken building into a greenhouse to grow annual flowers for park displays. The park department purchased 3,500 deciduous trees of various sizes and varieties, 3,000 evergreen trees, and 9,400 shrubs—a total of 15,900 plants—at a cost of about $8,000. The nursery also included numerous native seedling trees, as well as a variety of perennials and shrubs, for a total of nearly 18,000 plants.

Despite the difficult economic times of the Depression, the city nursery survived into the 1940s. Conditions changed, however, with World War II and the end of the federal relief projects. A shortage of funds and workers resulted in a lack of regular maintenance and the continued deterioration of many park facilities. After the war, the city administration's focus shifted away from creating parks and moved toward providing the public with recreational opportunities. In 1952 the nursery reported a net gain of over $12,000, but just two years later the city ended the tree-planting program and in 1956 reported a net loss of about $2,000 for the nursery. In the spring of 1960, under Mayor Eugene Lambert, the city announced plans to close the municipal tree nursery.

Fond du Lac's Winter Sports Center

F. Rodney Paine, soon after he took over as Duluth's Park Superintendent in 1926, began developing a plan for the forested parkland surrounding the city nursery. He designated the area as a municipal forest and in his 1928 annual report introduced a new vision for the city: "There is no reason why Duluth should not enjoy a reputation as a winter sports city equal to Montreal, Quebec, or other cities where a great many people go for the sole purpose of participating in winter sports activities." Paine planned to develop winter sports opportunities at Fond du Lac and several other parks. Park department staff went to work establishing picnic sites with tables, fireplaces, and benches; they also cleared dead wood throughout Fond du Lac Park to minimize the risk of fire.

NURSERY CARETAKER DAVID NUMMI AND HIS DOG, NAME UNKNOWN, POSE
FOR A PHOTOGRAPH AT THE CITY NURSERY IN 1927. (PHOTO BY F. R. PAINE.)
[IMAGE: UMD MARTIN LIBRARY]

The stock market crash of 1929 brought a temporary halt to all park development. In response to the economic depression, President Herbert Hoover created the Emergency Relief Administration (ERA) in 1932, and Paine promptly took advantage of this government program, bringing in relief workers to resume efforts at Fond du Lac Park. They cleared trees and built a road and log bridge, a toboggan slide, a ski slide, and one mile of trails that could be used for skiing in winter and bridle paths in summer. A log cabin constructed on the west side of Mission Creek served as a warming house. Paine reported that all of the relief work was accomplished using mainly salvaged materials and "the most primitive methods and with practically no equipment." Paine also expanded the park, adding just under 577 acres acquired by condemnation from various owners in May 1934.

In early 1935, Franklin Roosevelt's Works Progress Administration (WPA) replaced the ERA, and Paine continued to utilize workers provided by the federal relief programs. However, his vision of making Duluth a winter sports city was not yet completed when Mayor Snively lost his re-election bid in early 1937—and Paine lost his job.

Duluth's newly elected mayor, Rudy Berghult, replaced Paine with Earl Sherman, and in 1939 the new park superintendent began developing an arboretum adjacent to the municipal nursery. Relief workers planted trees and shrubs and constructed gravel walks, foot trails, rest benches, and a parking lot. The arboretum included a variety of habitats: lily pond, swamp, bog, dry meadow, lowland meadow, dense ravine, oak-maple forest, and pine-spruce forest. According to Sherman's 1940 annual report, "the Arboretum is not large or elaborate, nor has much money been spent in its development, but it

A STYLIZED MAP OF THE
FOND DU LAC WINTER
SPORTS CENTER PUBLISHED
BY THE CITY IN 1941.
[IMAGE: DULUTH PUBLIC LIBRARY]

TRANSLATION
Gitche Manitou - Great Spirit
Moje   ~ Bad
Onnebita   ~ Let Us Rest
Roussain   ~ French Indian Pioneer
Fond du Lac   ~ Head of the Lake
Ely   ~ Missionary-Schoolmaster
Kesheca   ~ Run Fast
Wawashish   ~ Deer
Matchi   ~ Wicked
Mukwa   ~ Bear

**FOND DU LAC PARK
WINTER SPORTS CENTER**
DULUTH PARK DEPARTMENT
COMM. of PUBLIC AFFAIRS · MAYOR E.H. HATCH
SUPERINTENDENT of PARKS · JOHN V. HOENE

LEGEND
1. 60 Meter Ski Jump
2. 3 Toboggan Slides
3. Onnebita Lodge
4. Skating Rink Music
5. Sleigh Rides
6. Ski Joring Horses
7. Dog Team Rides
8. Gitche Manitou Ski Bowl
9. Ely Trail Cross Country
10. Roussain Trail Cross Country
11. Kesheca Trail
12. The Headwall

13. Practice Ski Slopes
14. Wawashish Trail Cross Country
15. Mukwa Trail
16. Moje Down Mt. Trail
17. Matchi Run
18. Big Rock Run

HISTORICAL INTEREST
A. Indian Cemetery
B. Grand Portage
C. Stockade
D. Lookouts and Shelters
E. Tourist Cabin

SCALE 1" = 400'
DRAWN BY

contains so much history, beauty and plant and animal life that in our opinion it ranks highly in comparison with other Arboretums."

Workers later added picnic tables and fireplaces and completed the Onnebita Lodge, a log building that provided rest rooms and served as a retreat from rain storms and mosquitoes. They built a pond by damming up a small cold spring and introduced over one thousand rainbow trout from the French River hatchery. In October the fish were set free in the upper of Twin Ponds, located along the parkway immediately east of Enger Park.

Sherman and his successor, John Hoene, continued to develop winter activities at Fond du Lac Park. In 1940 the park department—with help from the WPA—completed a ski-jumping scaffold and judges' stand and dedicated the Fond du Lac Winter Sports Center during a tournament in February 1941. Hoene described the project in his 1942 annual report: "For several years we have been developing a giant winter sports center within this park. This winter sports area combines ski jumping, recreational skiing, down mountain skiing,

cross-country skiing, ski-joring [with horses, not dogs], tobogganing, skating, and sleigh rides." In the summer the cross-country ski trails could be used as bridle paths. A map produced by the park department in 1941 calls the ski jump hill "Big Ojibwe Mountain." By 1949 the ski hill had been nicknamed the Ojibway Bowl.

The Winter Sports Center also became another home for the Duluth Ski Club, which hosted tournaments at the site while continuing to train at Chester Bowl. The ski jump was first used in a tournament in February 1941, when 5,000 spectators turned out for the facility's dedication and an exhibition by famed Norwegian jumper Torger Tokle, who set the hill's initial record at 203 feet. A year later, Duluth hosted the 1942 National Ski Tournament on the sixty-meter jumping hill at Fond du Lac; over 12,000 spectators viewed the championship. Hoene wrote:

"Of course, for the conducting of the tournament we cannot praise too highly the work of the Duluth Ski Club, the

FIVE THOUSAND SPECTATORS GATHERED AT THE FOND DU LAC WINTER SPORTS CENTER FOR THE FACILITY'S INAUGURAL SKI JUMPING TOURNAMENT IN FEBRUARY 1941.
[IMAGE: DULUTH PUBLIC LIBRARY]

organization which was responsible for the construction of the hill and responsible for the promotion of this tremendous tournament. All of the worries and all of the planning for such a long period of time was fruitfully realized during the weekend of the tournament when the weather turned out to be absolutely perfect and the crowd taxed our capacity to the very limit....We were very pleased to have this crowd gather out there and to hear them exclaim with delight over the completeness of the facilities and the beauty of the area."

During a 1954 competition at Fond du Lac, Duluthian Joe Nowack jumped a record-setting 226 feet. His Ojibway Bowl record was tied in 1960 by Gene Kotlarek, also of Duluth. In 1964 the ski jump was increased to seventy meters.

While the Duluth Ski Club continued to hold annual tournaments at Fond du Lac's Ojibway Bowl, Mission Creek eventually won the erosion contest. Spring floods in 1972 washed away the land around the ski jump, creating a dangerous situation. The jump was removed in 1975 after the club agreed to abandon it due to continuous soil erosion problems on the landing area. The jump site was filled with soil and seeded with grass to prevent further erosion.

Very few remnants of the winter sports center remain, and the park department considers Fond du Lac an undeveloped park. The Superior Hiking Trail passes through the park, along with the Upper and Lower Cathedral mountain bike trails that are part of the newly developed Duluth Traverse.

Fond du Lac Park, along with Carson Park, Napolean B. Merritt Memorial Park, 391 acres of state-owned property, and 1,191 acres of forfeited tax property together make up the 2,246-acre Fond du Lac Forest Park. In 2012 Duluth's city council designated the land within Fond du Lac Forest Park as the F. Rodney Paine Forest Preserve, in honor of Paine's vision and leadership during his eleven years as park superintendent.

12. Hartley Park

From Lettuce Fields to a Learning Center

Guilford Graham Hartley was a man of varied business interests. He invested in just about every growing industry active in northern Minnesota in the late nineteenth and early twentieth centuries, from logging camps to iron mines, real estate to street railways, newspapers to wholesale food and dry goods, vaudeville theatre to shoe manufacturing, and cattle ranching to vegetable farming. In the early 1900s his 780-acre Allandale Farm, then the largest agricultural facility within the Duluth city limits, became famous as the producer of the highest quality head lettuce and celery in the nation. Today Hartley Park—as well as nearby Woodland Park—serves as a reminder of Hartley's influence during Duluth's boom times.

When Guilford Hartley arrived in Duluth in 1885, he already had a strong interest in farming. As the *Duluth News Tribune* later wrote, "He knew instinctively that wealth is in the soil." Hartley believed that northeastern Minnesota had great potential for agriculture, and in January 1890 he spent $15,000 to purchase the first eighty acres of what would become Woodland's Allandale Farm. This parcel was bounded on the north by Anoka Street, on the east by Allendale Avenue, on the south by the extension of Fairmont Street, and on the west by the extension of Rendle Avenue. Woodland Avenue cut through the northeastern corner of the property.

A month later, Hartley and about twenty other real estate investors—many of whom owned land along Woodland Avenue—created the Motor Line Improvement Company. Their goal was to buy and sell real estate and to construct streetcar lines and other means of transportation that would facilitate development of the Woodland area. By November 1890 the company had completed the first Woodland Avenue streetcar line, which split off from the existing East Fourth Street line. After the Woodland line was completed, operation was turned over to the Duluth Street Railway Company.

Hartley planned to use the new streetcar line for shipping produce from his farm, and once the line was in place, he hired laborers to work year-round clearing the land, much of which was wet, mucky,

IMAGE FROM A VINTAGE LITHOGRAPHIC SEED PACKET PRODUCED ABOUT THE SAME TIME GUILFORD HARTLEY'S ALLANDALE FARM WAS PRODUCING LETTUCE. THERE ARE NO LITHOGRAPHIC POSTCARDS OF HARTLEY PARK BECAUSE THE SITE DID NOT BECOME A CITY PARK UNTIL 1941, AND THE COLOR LITHOGRAPHIC POSTCARD ERA ENDED ROUGHLY IN 1939.

[IMAGE: ZENITH CITY PRESS]

GUILFORD G. HARTLEY

Born in the town of Shogomac along the banks of the St. John's River in New Brunswick, Canada, Guilford Graham Hartley moved to Brainerd, Minnesota, in 1871 at the age of eighteen. There he started his own logging business, taking on contracts for cutting and hauling logs. The cattle he used for winter hauling spent the summer breaking the prairie land he owned in what was then Dakota Territory. While in Brainerd he also served as a state representative and branched out into many additional businesses, including general contracting, hardware, and merchandise.

In 1885, two years after they wed, Hartley and his wife Caroline (often called Carrie) came to Duluth following his appointment as registrar of the Duluth land office. He left the job within a year to manage the Duluth Street Railway Company, in which he had invested heavily. Hartley expanded his other business interests as well. He continued to invest in logging and branched out into real estate, wholesale foods and dry goods, shoe manufacturing, and more—Hartley had a hand in nearly every industry in Duluth. He and James J. Hill, Minnesota's "Empire Builder," each owned a major interest in the *Duluth News Tribune*—until Hartley bought out Hill. Along with his friend Chester Congdon and others, Hartley was instrumental in developing the western Mesabi Iron Range; their associate John Greenway developed a process that washed and concentrated the softer ore of the western Mesabi so it could be used to make steel. While undergoing this work Hartley platted the Iron Range towns of Bovey, Cass Lake, Sparta, Grand Rapids, and Nashwauk.

In 1889 the Hartleys built a grand twenty-one-room Romanesque Revival mansion adjacent to Chester Creek at 1305 East Superior Street designed by Oliver Traphagen, Duluth's premier architect from 1886 to 1896. (Conveniently enough, the house stood at what was then the eastern end of the Duluth Street Railway Company's Superior Street line.) The house is thought to have been the first in Duluth to be wired for electricity and its own telephone line. There the Hartleys raised five children. In 1914 their eldest daughter, Jessie, married Chester and Clara Congdon's eldest son, Walter.

Hartley's efforts to sell the produce grown at his Allandale Farm in the Woodland area helped popularize celery throughout the nation. He also owned Island Farm, about eighty miles northwest of Duluth, where he raised prize-winning Guernsey cows. Meanwhile he developed his Dakota Territory property into Hartley Stock Farms of Page, North Dakota—another town platted by Hartley. The ranch raised Aberdeen-Angus hybrid cattle.

Socially, Hartley helped establish the Northland Country Club and built Duluth's 1910 Orpheum Theatre, the city's premier vaudeville house. As a member of the Kitchi Gammi Club, he oversaw the construction of its 1912 headquarters at 831 East Superior Street, designed by renowned Neo-Gothic architect Bertram Goodhue. Hartley also hired Goodhue to design his office building, which stands at 740 East Superior Street, across the street from the Kitchi Gammi Club.

When he died in 1922 at age sixty-eight, Hartley's estate was estimated at $3 million, about $40 million today. A few years earlier, Minnesota governor Jacob Preus said of Hartley, "Since James J. Hill passed away, G. G. Hartley [now] stands as the man of the broadest vision, most indomitable energy and greatest accomplishment of the citizens of Minnesota." The *News Tribune*, which he sold in 1921, remarked, "His love of life was intense, his happiness when surrounded by the members of his family were illimitable, his interest in all the affairs going on about him was of the keenest. His mind was ever conceiving new projects. Planning and accomplishing was his life."

and covered by thick brush. By 1892 workers had cleared fifty acres on the west side of Woodland Avenue. Hartley established a dairy, which was operated from 1894 to 1895 by tenants John and Sarah Berry before James Keough and Daniel Ryan took control. The *News Tribune* referred to the Keough & Ryan Dairy on the Hartley farm as "a body of fine rolling grazing land, traversed by a clear creek fed by springs of the purest water." The dairy barn was located near Tischer Creek, not far from today's Hartley Nature Center.

The farm was well known for its clear spring water. At a time when people in some parts of the city suffered from typhoid fever, those who got their drinking water from the Hartley Springs claimed to be free of sickness. Several springs were located on the farm, including one at the base of the massive rock outcrop on the east side of Woodland Avenue, south of Anoka Street. According to the *News Tribune*, "it would be impossible to find a spring located in any better manner to avoid pollution either by accident or design, and the crystal purity of the water is delightful." This spring was fitted with a pump, and the Keough & Ryan Dairy furnished their customers with several hundred gallons of pure spring water daily.

The rock outcrop was covered by maple trees, which Hartley tapped in the spring to harvest sap to make maple syrup. The *News Tribune* described the bluff as "a veritable maple orchard" and explained that "Mr. Hartley has reserved this...so that no one can ever put up a building or maintain anything that might become a possible source of contamination to the adjacent spring.... In the springtime a quantity of sap is procured from the grown maples and really pure maple syrup is not altogether unknown in Woodland."

In 1897 Hartley cleared more of his eighty acres and began planting lettuce, celery, and potatoes. As the *News Tribune* told the story, "Mr. Hartley had a conviction that mucky, soggy, tree-bound swamp lands ought to be good for head lettuce and celery. So he went to work. He cleared, ditched, drained, and fertilized a piece of muck land and planted it to head lettuce. It grew 30,000 heads to the acre, with two crops a season, making a gross return of about $3,000 an acre on land that was bog the previous season."

By 1909 Hartley had expanded Allandale Farm to over 350 acres. He stocked Tischer Creek with trout and began selling timber as well as vegetables. Bluestone quarried from the area known as Hunter's Hill, on land Hartley purchased from Ronald Hunter, was used in many of the homes and buildings in the neighborhood, including Glen Avon Presbyterian Church and Hunter's Park

Grocery, known to many as the Snow White. To facilitate movement of produce, he built a road through the farm that connected Woodland Avenue to St. Marie Street. In 1911 Hartley added another 320 acres to the farm for a total of more than 650, and according to the *News Tribune*, it was a banner year for Hartley's enterprise. The newspaper reported that "Mr. Hartley had a gross income of more than $9,000 from three acres of lettuce, shipping to Chicago after the Duluth market was supplied, and the quality of his product caused such a sensation among lettuce-growers throughout the middle west that some of the most successful of them, after visiting Duluth, announced their intention of buying farms in the vicinity."

In 1913 he dammed Tischer Creek to create a pond. A farm house went up in 1919, the same year a large root cellar was installed east of the massive outcrop known as Rock Knob. Although Hartley was always actively involved in running the farm, it was a long way from his home along Chester Creek at Thirteenth Avenue East and Superior Street where the family continued to live. Most of the farm work was done by hired laborers, although the family visited the farm frequently. According to Allandale Farm researcher Robert J. Slabodnik, "the Hartley family enjoyed the farm and forest land in their log cabin (called Rabbit Camp) as a place to escape the city." The Hartley's seemingly idyllic way of life, however, would not last forever.

From Farm to Park

Guilford Hartley died in his home in 1922 after being taken suddenly ill while attending a concert at the First Methodist Church. According to his obituary, he had been in poor health for two and a half years following a struggle with influenza. By this time the Hartley children were grown and busy with their own lives.

Within two years of Hartley's death, operations at the farm and dairy had come to a halt. By then refrigerated train cars could ship produce cheaply across the country, and the increased competition along with a steep hike in property taxes meant the end of the Allandale Farm. In 1929 the Hartley family donated to the city a ten-acre tract of the property located on the east side of Woodland Avenue where Hartley had once tapped his maple trees. The family requested that the area be used for a recreational field.

The *News Tribune* editorial board wrote, "The gift of this fine tract by the Hartleys is a generous act.... It will stand as a permanent memorial to its donors, and will be appreciated by Duluth people." The city designated the area Hartley Field, and between 1930 and 1931 the park department oversaw the construction of a football field, baseball diamond, and tennis court at the site.

National Youth Administration Projects in 1940 included the development of a children's play area, landscaping, and the construction of fireplaces, picnic tables, horseshoe courts, a baseball diamond, and sand boxes. Today that ten-acre tract, known as Woodland Park, is the home of Fryberger Arena, the Woodland Community Club, the John Baggs Memorial Field (Duluth Eastern Little League), the Tony Emanuel Memorial Field, three tennis courts, and two outdoor hockey rinks.

The Hartley family rented out the pasture land west of Woodland Avenue until 1931, the same year they stopped paying taxes on the property. In 1939 the State of Minnesota declared the land tax forfeited and took ownership. The St. Louis County Board, which administers tax-forfeit parcels on behalf of the state, classified the Hartley tract as conservation land, meaning it was set aside for forest management and recreation. In 1941, with help from the Duluth Conservation Club, the City of Duluth acquired about 418 acres of the Hartley tract to use as a public park.

The city, however, was short on resources. During the Depression in the 1930s, some work on Duluth's parks continued under the Works Progress Administration, but the municipal budget was cut dramatically. Those cuts continued during World War II and on into the late 1940s, and all city parks suffered from a lack of maintenance. The park department reported that its budget for 1942 was about equal to its 1932 budget, even though the workload had doubled because of new parks and recreation areas added to the system.

Development and Benign Neglect

Volunteers from the community stepped in and helped with the development of Hartley Park. Many projects were proposed; some were realized and some forgotten. The story of Hartley Park became one of benign neglect alternating with ambitious community-driven projects.

"Transformation of Hartley Estate into Retreat Gains Impetus: Wildlife Sanctuary is Pushed," proclaimed a *Duluth Herald* headline on April 6, 1942. This plan included creating rearing ponds for trout, an eight-acre pond with nesting geese and ducks, an upland game bird sanctuary, a thirty-acre municipal forest of pine and spruce, a five-acre Christmas tree farm, and a wildflower sanctuary. The Duluth Conservation Club intended to furnish most of the labor.

By the end of 1942, the park department reported that the conservation club had succeeded in the reforestation of five acres of a grassy area using seedling evergreens from the state forestry department. Club members also improved the fence around the small duck pond, which Guilford Hartley had created in 1913 by damming Tischer Creek. The club brought in mallard ducks that nested and raised several dozen young, some of which flew south in the fall. A few ducks stayed behind; club members sheltered them in a barn over the winter.

Other groups carried out additional projects. Duluth's Parent-Teachers Association, the Duluth Board of Education, and the WPA worked together to organize a school garden project. Twelve acres were planted with vegetables; the produce was canned and used for the hot-lunch program in several Duluth schools.

The next year the conservation club planted pine seedlings, raised more ducks, and released game birds such as pheasant and partridge. A caretaker lived at the park most of the year. He helped prevent vandalism, fed the game birds and ducks, assisted in planting trees, and removed countless rotting fence posts. The Boy Scouts planted several hundred pine and spruce seedlings around the old stone house where they hoped to establish an overnight camping site.

After the United States entered World War II, the Civilian Defense Victory Garden Committee encouraged citizens to plant Victory Gardens. At Hartley Park, the Victory Gardeners plowed up the best gardening area and divided it into 33 x 66 foot plots. Over two hundred gardeners took advantage of these plots and produced many fine crops. By the time the war was over, all of Allandale Farm's buildings had been removed; only the steps to the farmhouse and the root cellar's partially excavated ruins remained.

After the war ended, priorities shifted to recovery, and activity at Hartley Park slowed. Budgets remained tight, and the park

WORKERS LOAD A WAGON WITH BUSHELS OF LETTUCE AT G. G. HARTLEY'S ALLANDALE FARM, CA. 1916.

[IMAGE: UMD MARTIN LIBRARY]

department struggled to catch up on projects that had been put on hold during the war. In 1947 the city welcomed a proposal from the federal government to purchase a twenty-acre tract on the north side of Hartley Park for the site of a multimillion-dollar veteran's hospital. The project never materialized, and the government eventually declared the land to be surplus property and sold it to a private party for $2,304. Houses were later built in the area, permanently eliminating any possibility of returning it to park status.

Although the city did not have the resources to develop Hartley Park, people continued to use the land for a variety of recreational activities. Willard "Buck" Doran, a sportsman and owner of a hardware store in the Woodland neighborhood, personally made sure there were fish in the pond. Starting in the mid-1950s, Doran supervised an annual trout planting program at Hartley. Ben Gustafson, fishing supervisor for the French River Fish Hatchery, acquired the trout from the Lanesboro Fish Hatchery, and Doran enlisted the help of local children to release them. By 1962 the children planted five hundred to one thousand trout every spring.

Trout planting continued for at least fifteen years, providing a fun day for everyone involved. In April 1969, the *Herald* reported that "150 to 200 children are expected to turn out for the annual trout planting program at Hartley Pond.... Children who take part in the program assist conservation officers. In past years they have turned up with every type of container, including coal buckets and even scoop shovels."

Unfortunately, the trout did not always survive, and by the early 1960s the fifty-year-old dam on Tischer Creek began to fail. Doran reported in 1962, "Last winter the trout froze out because the dam

DULUTH'S DERBY DOWNS AT HARTLEY PARK

During the 1960s Hartley Park became home to Duluth's Soap Box Derby track. The derby, a national event that challenged young boys to design and build a motorless race car propelled only by gravity, had originated in Ohio in 1934. The boys, between the ages of eleven and fifteen, were required to build their own cars and could spend no more than ten dollars above the cost of wheels and axles.

Duluth's first All-American Soap Box Derby, described as a "coaster wagon race for boys," took place in July 1947 at Lemon Drop Hill, a portion of London Road between Twenty-sixth and Thirtieth Avenues East where the Lemon Drop restaurant was located. Sponsors included the Junior Chamber of Commerce (Jaycees), the *Duluth News Tribune* and *Duluth Herald*, and local Chevrolet dealers. A crowd of about 10,000 spectators watched Duluth's first race. The winner, fourteen-year-old Don Schafer, was flown to Akron, Ohio, to participate in the All-American Soap Box Derby. Unfortunately, he did not win the national derby.

Increased traffic soon made London Road too busy and dangerous for the race, so in 1961 the Duluth Derby Track Committee (made up of Jaycee members and other interested citizens) raised funds to build a dedicated track. The Jaycees leased land on the north side of Hartley Park, and volunteers built a track 20 feet wide and 960 feet long. They completed the course, known as Duluth's Derby Downs, in time for the race on July 15, 1961. According to a 1967 *News Tribune* article, Duluth's Derby Downs was a rarity—"one of just eleven in the country owned by a local derby."

The high point for the Soap Box Derby in Duluth came in 1963. With a crowd of 1,500 spectators watching intently, twelve-year-old Harold "Bo" Conrad reached a speed of thirty miles an hour to beat a field of thirty-three other boys from the region. His final opponent, Steve Ingle of Hoyt Lakes, Minnesota, finished just a half length behind. It was a tough loss for

Ingle, who had crashed twice already that day. Five other drivers lost control of their vehicles as well, including Duluth's Keith Larivy, who ended up in the hospital with head injuries suffered when he went off the track and into the crowd. Like Schafer sixteen years earlier, Conrad went on to the national championship in Akron. This time, Duluth's hometown champion won the race. The *News Tribune* reported that in Akron 75,000 people watched Conrad—at forty miles per hour—win by just four inches. He returned to Duluth All-American Soap Box Derby Champion and was greeted with a Superior Street parade. Duluth's final Soap Box Derby race took place in 1968. Plans were underway for the 1969 race, but it was cancelled due to lack of interest and organizational problems.

Hartley Park's days as home of the Soap Box Derby have not been forgotten. Derby Downs racer Dale Mell—who represented Duluth in Akron in 1964—donated his car to the Hartley Nature Center, where it is on display today. Dale is shown in the photos winning the final race of the 1964 Duluth derby (left) and talking with his father before the race (above). And the asphalt remains of Duluth's Derby Downs track, now overgrown with vegetation, can still be found near the nature center.

——— IMAGES: HARTLEY NATURE CENTER ———

OUTDOORSMAN AND HARDWARE STORE OWNER WILLARD "BUCK" DORAN, SEEN HERE NEXT TO HARTLEY POND IN 1972, HELPED STOCK THE POND WITH FISH IN THE 1950S AND 1960S. (PHOTO BY CHARLES CURTIS.)

[IMAGE: DULUTH NEWS TRIBUNE]

couldn't hold water and the pond water level got too low." The Woodland Community Club, assisted by an engineering unit of the Duluth Army Reserve, drew up plans to build a new and bigger dam. A committee headed by club member Arvid Gross raised money to pay for a bulldozer and concrete, and Army Reserve engineers helped build the new dam in September 1963. Doran's family recalls that a plaque was installed near the dam, thanking Doran and the Army Reserve for their work to keep the pond alive.

Resurgence: The Hartley Nature Center

By the 1970s Hartley Park had once again fallen into a state of benign neglect. Trails created by dirt bikes and all-terrain vehicles were causing extensive erosion. A massive flood in August 1972 destroyed the dam (and likely took with it the plaque honoring Doran and the Army Reserve). Restoration began a few years later when the city rebuilt the dam, making it bigger and higher, resulting in a larger pond. Izaak Walton League members took an interest in the park, organizing cleanups and tree plantings and lobbying the city to create a management plan for the area. A citizen committee began working to make the park a center for environmental education.

The Hartley Nature Center nonprofit environmental education corporation was established in 1987 and immediately began providing educational opportunities in the park. Next, organizers began raising funds for a building. At the same time the park was expanded by twenty acres when the children of Len Naymark—who had owned the parcel and hoped to develop it into senior housing—donated land at the park's southeastern corner in honor of their father.

Completed in 2003, the nature center features four classrooms, office space, a library/meeting room, bathrooms, an exhibit hall, and green building elements throughout. Partially powered by a grid-tied solar energy system, the structure is used as a teaching tool to illustrate low-impact building techniques and living. In 2015, under the direction of executive director Tom O'Rourke, the center reported that it served 24,000 visitors annually through programs such as field trips, summer camps, nature-based preschool, stewardship internships, ecological data collection, restoration, and more. Hartley Nature Center has a lease with the City of Duluth to co-manage the park and operate and occupy the nature center building until 2052.

The story of Hartley Park is far from finished. In 2016 the city received a $600,000 state Legacy Grant to make improvements to the park and existing trails. According to the *News Tribune*, those plans include "thinning about ten acres of red pine stands, creating wildlife openings in about five acres of the park dominated by aspen, building new multipurpose trails and expanding parking." The work includes better bike trails and the removal of environmentally harmful invasive buckthorn thickets.

Because of its history, Hartley Park remains unique among the city's major parks, most of which were established before significant development had taken place on the land, thus preserving relatively undisturbed forests and streams. In contrast, Hartley Park records a century of changes, from mucky, tree-bound swampland to productive lettuce fields to reforestation projects to today's community-based environmental education center.

13. Minnesota Point

Duluth's Summer Resort

In 1900 the *Duluth News Tribune* poetically described Minnesota Point as "a penciled eyebrow on the face of nature." Since the establishment of Superior, Wisconsin, and the townships that make up modern Duluth, residents of both cities, along with thousands of visitors, have taken advantage of this narrow sandbar as a delightful summer resort—a place to picnic, camp, swim, and play on the Lake Superior shore.

Minnesota Point is the northern portion of the world's longest natural sandbar, which formed over the last several thousand years at the place where Minnesota's St. Louis River and Wisconsin's Nemadji River meet the waters of Lake Superior. As the sand and silt carried by the flowing water was deposited, it built up a narrow barrier that shelters the bay behind it from the wind and waves of Lake Superior. The same natural processes that formed the sandbar also cut it into two sections: Minnesota Point makes up the northern seven miles, Wisconsin Point the southern three miles. When European explorers first came to the area in the 1600s, there was only one opening through the sandbar—the natural gap between the two points, now the location of the Superior entry.

Prior to the increasing westward expansion of the United States, both Minnesota Point and Wisconsin Point served as summer gathering spots for generations of native peoples, a tradition that continued with the Ojibwe in the 1850s. After the 1854 Treaty of LaPointe opened land north and west of Lake Superior to settlement, pioneers moved in quickly. Between 1856 and 1859, they established eleven townships on the Minnesota side of the lake, including several along Minnesota Point. Near the northern end of the point, early settlers platted Duluth Township. Further down the point, Robert Reed and T. A. Markland platted a township that extended from today's Thirteenth Street South to Thirty-ninth Street South. They called the fledgling community Middleton and set aside a parcel of land for an open public space called Lafayette Square. Another open space, Franklin Square, was platted at Middleton's northern border. (See chapter 1, "Nineteenth-Century Squares," for more information.) The federal

LITHOGRAPHIC POSTCARD, CA. 1935, OF BATHERS ENJOYING THE SURF AND BEACH ON THE LAKE SIDE OF MINNESOTA POINT.

[IMAGE: ZENITH CITY PRESS]

DULUTHIANS, INCLUDING MEMBERS
OF THE FIRE DEPARTMENT, GATHERED
ON MINNESOTA POINT, PERHAPS
AT THE CENTENNIAL PICNIC
GROUNDS OR FRANKLIN SQUARE,
TO CELEBRATE DECORATION DAY
IN 1871. (PHOTO BY PAUL B.
GAYLORD.)

[IMAGE: UMD MARTIN LIBRARY]

government owned the remaining land on Minnesota Point south of Middleton; known as the Barrens, this long stretch of sand and pine forest extended to the Superior entry.

Although Minnesota Point had two public squares, most of the summer activity during Duluth's first fifty years centered around Oatka Beach, four blocks of sand on the bay side of the point beginning roughly at today's Fortieth Street South. Oatka is Ojibwe for "an opening"—in this case probably referring to an opening in the forest that covered much of the sandbar. As early as the 1860s, day-trippers from Superior and surrounding Minnesota townships came to the point by rowboat, sailboat, or canoe to spend the day at the public picnic grounds, referred in the *Duluth Minnesotian* as the "Centennial

Picnic Grounds" and likely located at Oatka Beach. Reminiscences shared with the *Minnesotian* by an unnamed "lady friend" in September 1869 called the point "a resort for the citizens of Superior" and described the grounds and activities held there:

A platform for dancing, over which a broad canvas spread its protecting wings, was erected nearly opposite the town [Superior], and swings were suspended from the overhanging trees. At evening parties of ladies and gentlemen visited this shore, crossing the placid waters in boats and canoes, to the music of flutes, violins, and guitars, mingled with the voice of song.

She forgot to mention promotional speeches. It was at an Independence Day picnic on Minnesota Point in 1868 that *Minnesotian* publisher Dr. Thomas Foster first called Duluth the "Zenith City of the unsalted seas."

In March 1870 the townships, including those on the point, combined to form the City of Duluth. The next spring the city completed the first cut of a ship canal through Minnesota Point along Portage Street; the following spring the canal was complete, but it had turned the point south of the canal into an island. The citizens of Middleton lobbied hard for a bridge over the new waterway. A temporary bridge was built for use during the winter, when shipping traffic was halted, But life for those living south of the canal became complicated.

The Financial Panic of 1873 caused great economic hardships in Duluth, and in 1877 the city lost its state charter. Many of the original townships then reverted to independent status, but Middleton and others stayed with Duluth Township to form the new Village of Duluth. In 1881, with no bridge in sight, citizens living south of the canal—the area now collectively called Park Point—had had enough. That March state legislation turned the community of Middleton into the independent Village of Park Point. When Duluth returned to city status in 1887, Park Point refused to rejoin until they had a more convenient way to cross the canal. Duluth promised a bridge, and in 1889 Park Point rejoined Duluth. The bridge, however, wouldn't arrive until 1905.

DULUTH (OR SUPERIOR) PIONEERS ENJOY A GAME OF CROQUET IN A PINE GROVE ON MINNESOTA POINT, CA. 1870. (PHOTO BY PAUL B. GAYLORD.)

[IMAGE: UMD MARTIN LIBRARY]

THE BARRENS OF MINNESOTA POINT

Until the 1930s, the entire segment of Minnesota Point south of today's Forty-sixth Street South was known by locals as the Barrens. Owned by the federal government since 1856, the area wasn't as bleak as its name implies. Although most of the sand dunes were covered by beachgrass and a variety of shrubs, it also contained an extensive stand of tall majestic white and red pine trees.

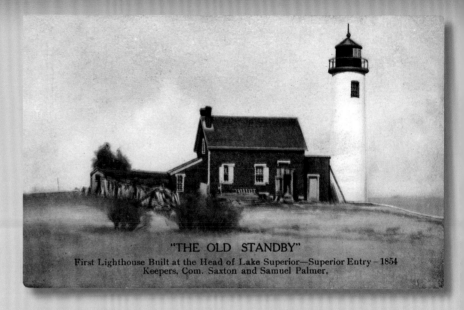

"THE OLD STANDBY"
First Lighthouse Built at the Head of Lake Superior—Superior Entry - 1854
Keepers, Com. Saxton and Samuel Palmer.

The southernmost end of the Barrens was occupied by the St. Louis River Military Reservation, which contained mile marker zero—the point from which all geographic surveys of Lake Superior began. The marker was set in 1823 by Henry W. Bayfield of the British Royal Navy (and namesake of Bayfield, Wisconsin). In 1852 the U.S. government sent surveyor George Stuntz to the Head of the Lakes to survey western Lake Superior. Stuntz, a pioneer of both Duluth and Superior, Wisconsin, augmented his living by trading with the local Ojibwe who summered on the Point. He established a trading post and dock north of mile marker zero on the bay side of the Point.

In 1858 the U.S. government built the Minnesota Point Lighthouse on this portion of the Barrens to serve mariners using the natural Superior entry between Minnesota Point and Wisconsin Point. Legend has it the fifty-foot tall lighthouse was constructed directly over mile marker zero. When thick fog rendered the light useless, original keeper R. H. Barrett blew a warning through a logging camp dinner horn; local residents called it Barrett's Cow.

The lighthouse was rendered all but unnecessary in 1871 when the Duluth Ship Canal was created, allowing vessels headed for Duluth to bypass the Superior entry. Traffic through the entry became so rare that the government closed the lighthouse in 1885. The keeper's house was abandoned in 1895 and torn down soon after. The lighthouse still stands, albeit in ruins.

The photo at left was taken ca. 1900; the postcard above was made about the same time, but from an image captured some time between 1858 and 1885.

Like the rest of the Point, the Barrens was enjoyed in the summer by local Ojibwe, who established at least three cemeteries on the sandbar. One was located near today's Tenth Street South. A second stood near what is now the Sky Harbor Airport; photos from the 1870s show its graves surrounded by a simple fence. It is believed that a few of the earliest white settlers were buried there as well. The third cemetery lay hidden just west of the lighthouse. It was discovered in 1876 when a strong winter storm blew away several feet of sand. In his recollections, Superior pioneer James Bardon (namesake of Duluth's Bardon's Peak) remembered the event, writing that the wind "exposed the bones and crude coffins and birchbark wrappings of skeletons. It also blew many of the skulls and bones across the [frozen] bay.... All sorts of Indian implements and ornaments, including beads, cone-shaped copper ornaments, pipes, flint-lock guns, tomahawks, hatchets, and a few stone implements were uncovered."

The Barrens area is located directly east of Superior, and as early as the 1850s it was just a short ferry ride across the bay to a pleasant summer holiday. Many Superiorites established cottages near Stuntz's trading post in the large pine grove north of the lighthouse. (Exactly how private citizens came to own cottages on federal property has never been explained.) By 1900 Stuntz had abandoned his enterprise, and Minnesota Point residents John H. and Charlotte Peabody took over his dock, operating a ferry service for the wealthy Duluthians and Superiorites with summer homes nearby. The entire enclave of cabins became known as Peabody's Landing. Superior mayor Charles O'Hehir built a cabin at the site called Pine Knot; once four feet from the bay, dredging waste dumped at the landing widened the Point in the 1930s, "moving" the Pine Knot cabin much farther from the water. The Pollock family, who acquired the cabin in 1927, donated it to the City of Duluth in 1999. It was demolished in 2010. (Some believe the original Pine Knot may have been destroyed by fire and replaced at an unknown date.)

The Superior Water, Light & Power Company purchased a segment of the Barrens in 1889. The property (just south of the Sky Harbor airport) contains a pump station built to provide fresh water to the city of Superior from an intake pipe reaching far into Lake Superior. The city of Cloquet, Minnesota, also pumps water from this area. The Walter Stock Pump Station #1 sends Lake Superior water twenty miles to provide Esko, Carlton, and Cloquet with auxiliary reserves of fresh water for industrial use and emergencies.

The federal government built the U.S. Lighthouse Service Depot south and west of the Minnesota Point Lighthouse in 1905 to store buoys and calcium carbide. The carbide was brought to the Duluth Ship Canal's North Pier Lighthouse, South Pier Lighthouse, and Inner Harbor Light. Water dripped onto calcium carbide created acetylene gas, which powered the lights. The U.S. Corps of Engineers did not want to store the raw material for a dangerous gas close to Canal Park and the aerial bridge. So the vessels *Amaranth* and *Marigold* loaded and unloaded calcium carbide and other supplies at the building from 1905 until World War II, when the lights were electrified. Today the ruined building's walls are covered with graffiti, and there is evidence it has been used as a party location for decades.

The same year the buoy depot was constructed saw the great storm of November 1905, also called the *Mataafa* Storm. As the storm raged, Lake Superior's waves crashed along the Point, striking the Barrens south of Oatka Beach particularly hard and opening a channel nearly two hundred feet wide through the sandbar. By mid-December the shifting sand had sealed the breach.

The 1930s saw a dramatic change when the City of Duluth acquired all but the southernmost portion of the Barrens and brought in 150,000 cubic yards of fill to create the Minnesota Point Recreation Area. As World War II erupted and the buoy station became obsolete, the federal government built a seventy-acre seaplane base south of the recreation area's amusement park, again expanding the point with fill. In 1946 the seaplane base became Sky Harbor Airport. By then Duluth had acquired rights from the federal government to occupy the fifty acres of the military reservation at the very southern end of the point for recreational purposes. City officials intended to use it for Boy Scout and Girl Scout groups and planned to convert the former buoy warehouse and dock to a Sea Scout base. That idea never materialized. Instead, the area remains undeveloped except for the Minnesota Point Nature Trail that circles through the property.

As of 2016, the ruins of the lighthouse and buoy station still stand. In 1974 the lighthouse ruins were placed on the National Register of Historic Places, but other than installing a chain-link fence around it, nothing has been done to protect or preserve this first lighthouse at the Head of the Lakes. But that may soon change. In 2015 the Lake Superior Marine Museum Association announced the Save Minnesota Point Lighthouse project, hoping to preserve the iconic landmark.

——— PHOTO: F. R. PAINE, 1936, VIA UMD MARTIN LIBRARY ———

A GROUP OF YOUNG MEN GATHERED OUTSIDE OF THE OATKA PAVILION SOMETIME IN THE MID TO LATE 1890S.
[IMAGE: DULUTH PUBLIC LIBRARY]

THE SARGENT CABIN ON MINNESOTA POINT, CA. 1900.
[IMAGE: DULUTH PUBLIC LIBRARY]

A Summertime Campground

Picnics at Oatka Beach remained popular through Duluth's tough financial times and the boom period that followed. According to Minnesota streetcar historian Aaron Isaacs, the Minnesota Point Street Railway (MPSR) Company started operating a horse-drawn trolley on the Point in 1889 or 1890. Described by the *News Tribune* in 1894 as "old fashioned and slow," the trolley carried passengers three miles from the canal to Oatka Beach. There visitors took advantage of the picnic grounds and swimming beach and enjoyed band concerts and dancing in the Oatka Beach Pavilion.

Newspaper ads announced other special events, such as Signor Levenso, who in July 1890 gave two daily performances of his "startling and wonderful acts, the aerial flight or the slide for life, and tight rope performing 100 feet in mid-air." On Sundays, the clairvoyant Madame Johnson was available to read the past, present, and future.

Picnickers began to prolong their visits by setting up tent camps all along the point, from the canal to the Barrens. Duluthians and

Superiorites alike used the point as a place to relax or recreate for an afternoon or camp for an extended period of time; the more affluent stayed for the entire summer. Near the southern end along the Barrens an enclave of cabins first built in the 1850s for wealthy Superiorites clustered around what later became known as Peabody's Landing.

Few regulations governed the camps, and property ownership was often unclear, as the *News Tribune* reported in June 1898: "In the great majority of cases no inquiry is made as to the owners of the lots on which the camp is pitched, and the owner makes no inquiry as to who camps on his lot.... Some campers own lots, and others have permission to occupy the lots on which they are located.... Others occupy several lots."

Most folks located their camps on the bay side of the point, where the land was lower and sand dunes and pine groves offered protection from strong lake winds. In 1894 the *News Tribune* described the facilities as ranging "from neat little cottages occupied by a dozen or more people down to a 7 x 7 tent tenanted by two small boys." Campers christened their sites with creative names such as Cold Water Camp, Koo-Koo Camp, Old Point Comfort, Cozy Cottage, Frogville, Camp Featherbed, and Sleepy Eye Camp. Judge Ozora P. Stearns, president of the Lakeside Land Company, owned the Lazy Lodge; William Sargent, founder of Lakeside and Lester Park, kept a cabin on the point that had been built by his parents in the early 1870s. A 1903 *News Tribune* story reported that the Sargent cabin

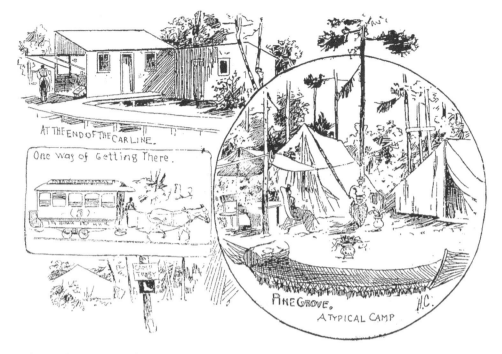

was haunted, as "queer sights and sounds of unearthly seeming have distinguished the old Sargent cottage for this long time."

Once the trolley began providing easier conveyance along the point, entrepreneurs established enclaves called Hay Fever Havens—clusters of cabins inhabited by those who could afford to summer in Duluth to avoid allergens in their own towns (antihistamines were a long way off). Similar facilities sprang up along Lake Superior's North Shore and on Isle Royale, but Duluth was the most accessible of these pollen-free locations. In 1900 Duluth became home to the Hay Fever Club of America.

The MPSR changed hands in 1896 and in 1898, under new owners, became the Interstate Traction Company (ITC), which electrified the car line. The streetcar line was extended four blocks in 1902 after Charles F. Hartman—one of the principle owners of the ITC—purchased the Oatka Beach property and platted the Oatka Beach Addition, which was intended as a new residential section between today's Thirty-ninth Street South and Forty-fourth Street South. The 1.5-acre block between Forty-third and Forty-fourth Streets South was dedicated as Hartman Park.

The Bridge Effect

After fifteen years the city kept its promise to Park Pointers by constructing the 1905 Aerial Transfer Bridge, predecessor to today's Aerial Lift Bridge. The bridge brought major changes to the point. Crossing the canal became easy and efficient, and almost everyone could afford to take a streetcar to the canal, cross on the bridge, and transfer to the Park Point trolley. In anticipation of the bridge, the Duluth Boat Club moved its headquarters to Park Point; once the bridge was built,

its wealthy members could drive to the club. On opening day, April 8, 1905, more than 32,000 people boarded the bridge in one twelve-hour period. Edward J. Filiatrault—Duluth's earliest car dealer—was the first person to drive an automobile south of the canal; he wanted the beach to be turned into a raceway like Florida's Daytona Beach.

Shortly after the bridge opened, the *Duluth Herald* announced that local investors intended to build a grand hotel on the sandbar within the Oatka Beach Addition. The proposed facility, a U-shaped

WHITE CITY AMUSEMENT PARK

In 1906, attempting to take advantage of the popularity of Minnesota Point, members of Duluth's Retail Merchant's Association, Real Estate Exchange, and the Duluth Commercial Club established the Duluth Amusement Company with the goal of building an amusement park in Duluth that would be modeled after Chicago's White City Amusement Park, built in 1905. The Chicago amusement park's name came from its numerous buildings outlined with white lights. The name also recalled Chicago's 1893 World's Columbian Exposition, which took place near the same location.

The Duluth company included park board vice president Bernard Silberstein and eighteen-year-old O. C. Hartman, a principal of the Interstate Traction Company, which owned the streetcar line on Minnesota Point. His father, Charles Hartman, owned the Oatka Beach Addition at the end of the streetcar line where the Oatka Pavilion stood. They planned to build Duluth's White City on Hartman's land; the old pavilion would be retained and, like everything else, it would be painted white.

Designed by St. Paul contractor Thomas H. Ivey, White City opened June 30, 1906. Festivities featured a speech by Duluth mayor Marcus Cullum and music by the Third Regiment Band. The three thousand people who filled the park had their choice of rides such as the Mystic River boat trip, a merry-go-round, a toboggan water slide, and a miniature railroad (pictured below) made by the actual Duluth, South Shore & Atlantic Railway. Visitors also enjoyed acrobatic and vaudeville acts and circus tent performers such as Olga, "the lady who ties herself into all kinds of shapes." In the evening, LaBrosse's Orchestra played dance music in the pavilion while the park glowed with the light of hundreds of electric globes arranged in beautiful designs. No alcohol was served; White City was dry. Adults paid ten cents and each child was charged a nickel.

More attractions were added later, including a Ferris wheel (pictured at right), the Old Mill, an undescribed ride called "Bump the Bumps," and the Fun Factory, where ticket payers

lost themselves wandering on twisted paths and "[ran] up against all kinds of funny and startling adventures." Other attractions included a corral of deer, a Gypsy Village, an automated baseball game, and a roller skating rink. White City was outfitted with sitting rooms (for the ladies), cafés and restaurants, and bathhouses. Plans for the future involved more attractions, including a roller coaster and a $7,500 gasoline-propelled airship to be named *Duluth No. 1*.

Neither was built. Despite reports in the *Duluth News Tribune* that the summer of 1907 found "the White City at the height of patronage and popularity," and "each and every attraction in the park is meeting with merited success," it survived for only two seasons. In May 1908 the Duluth Amusement Company revealed that it was unable to pay debts of over $19,000. Thomas Getz took control of the operation and renamed it Joyland on the Point, but the change didn't help. The park opened for the last time in July 1908.

By the spring of 1909 the amusement park closed for good and its buildings were dismantled and taken away. The grounds, officially named Hartman Park, became popularly known simply as Oatka Park. It once again became a spot for picnics, and the streetcar company continued to sponsor free band concerts. Abe "Candy" Busha ran the pavilion until a suspected arson fire destroyed it in June 1909. That year the Duluth Boat Club relocated one of its facilities to the pavilion site. A portion of White City's band shell was later incorporated into a house, which still stands at 4010 Minnesota Avenue. As of 2016, most of the White City site is occupied by the Duluth Rowing Club and the Franciscan Health Center.

THE DULUTH BOAT CLUB

Eleven Duluth sailing and rowing enthusiasts organized the Duluth Boat Club in July 1886. The next year membership had nearly tripled and the group built a clubhouse on Slip #1 in the Duluth Harbor, located between Sixth and Seventh Avenues West roughly where the stage of Bayfront Festival Park stands today. The facility stood three stories tall and was wrapped with verandas on its second and third stories; a square tower adorned one corner.

By 1895 the Boat Club boasted 193 members who enjoyed access to a fleet of fifteen rowing shells and more than twenty pleasure boats. As the century turned, the club's numbers swelled, and it soon required a larger facility. Knowing the recently approved aerial bridge over the ship canal would allow easy access to Minnesota Point, club officers chose to build their new complex, designed by John J. Wangenstein, on the bay side of the Point at Tenth Street and St. Louis Avenue. (Pictured above in a photograph by Hugh McKenzie made ca. 1911.)

Built in 1903 for $5,000, the new facility boasted a larger boat house, viewing stands, a café, tennis courts, and a dance floor. The two-story central building featured a tower at each corner and, like the original, many verandas for viewing club activities. Five hundred people attended its gala opening. The society columns of Duluth's newspapers called the dance floor "the most exclusive ballroom in the city."

The Duluth Boat Club became Duluth's social center, hosting regattas, water carnivals, and national competitions. By 1912 club membership had swelled to 1,400 members, making it the largest such organization in the United States. Membership had received a boost in 1907 when the Boat Club merged with the Duluth Yacht Club, whose clubhouse stood on the bay side of the Point at Fourteenth Street South. In 1909, club members moved the former Yacht Club facility to Fortieth Street South, the site of the Oatka Beach Pavilion that had burned earlier in the summer. They also operated a clubhouse on Spirit Lake from 1907 to 1917, the year club president Julius Barnes paid $75,000 for an indoor pool or "natatorium" at the main facility.

Barnes hired James Ten Eyck to coach the club's rowing squads. From 1911 to 1923, Duluth rowers dominated their competitors, taking home twenty national championships. The club's "Invincible Four"—Max Rheinberger, Dave Horak, and brothers Doug and Phil Moore—did not suffer a loss between 1913 and 1916, taking home trophies from twenty-two national and international regattas. In 1922 Duluth Boat Club rower Walter Hoover became known as the world's best rower after winning the prestigious Diamond Sculls competition on London's River Thames. On his return to the United States, a flotilla of boats in New York Harbor saluted the Duluthian. In the Zenith City, 65,000 people turned out to greet the returning hero.

Rowing's popularity declined sharply in the 1920s, when many club members' enthusiasm shifted to automobiles. By 1923 Ten Eyck had left; the club folded in 1926. Barnes—then the president of the United States Chamber of Commerce—convinced the city to lease the club, and in 1931 the city handed the Boat Club over to the Park Department for management. To distance the facility from its reputation as a private club, and to provide a more accurate description, Park Superintendent Rodney Paine changed its name to the Duluth Water Sports Center. Activities included swimming, canoeing, archery, volleyball, horseshoes, picnics, card games, and dances twice a week. The sports center sparked a renewed interest in rowing, and the swimming pool was popular, but the facility was not financially successful. It closed in 1933.

The boat house was used to store boats until April 23, 1951, when an early morning fire destroyed the building along with sixteen vessels stored inside. The former Boat Club became the site of the Duluth Yacht Basin and later the Lakehead Boat Basin. The Park Point Marina Inn, which opened in May 2014, currently occupies a portion of the site.

The Boat Club was revived in 1955 as the Duluth Rowing Club. In 1964 gale-force winds destroyed the 1907 Yacht Club/Oatka clubhouse facility. Today the Duluth Rowing Club's boathouse stands in its place.

building four stories high, featured several verandas and a rooftop observatory surrounded by gardens. Inside tourists would find forty guest rooms, refreshment rooms, private dining rooms; outside they would find a bathing pavilion and "ample facilities for boating."

The hotel was never built, but just a year later the White City Amusement Park opened, built on the footprint of the Oatka Beach Addition. Increased traffic to the point motivated the Interstate Traction Company to improve its streetcar line. This in turn prompted a building boom in 1908, which included the summer home of Fitger's

Brewery president Percy Shelley Anneke and his wife Lydia at 4500 Minnesota Avenue, the only permanent home built south of Hartman Park.

By 1909 the amusement park was gone, and a suspected arson fire destroyed the old dance pavilion. The Duluth Boat Club merged with the Duluth Yacht Club and moved the Yacht Club's facility from Fourteenth Street to the pavilion site, where it became known as the boat club's Oatka Branch. Once Oatka Beach became the Boat Club's domain, non-members picnicked at spots further down the point

within the Barrens, which became popular for summertime gatherings of the YMCA, Boy Scouts, and Girl Scouts. Today the pavilion site is home to the Duluth Rowing Club's boathouse, and the Oatka Beach Addition is covered by houses. Much of what was once the bathing beach was expanded with dredge spoils in 1935, and in 1999 the city dedicated it as the Mira M. Southworth Lake Superior Wetlands Preserve.

In 1911 the former Yacht Club site at Fourteenth Street South became a privately owned recreation facility. The new owners of the Duluth White Sox professional baseball team—Jack Desmond, Joe Maitland, and future Duluth mayor Dr. John. A. McCuen—hired the Interstate Dredge and Dock Company to build a 3,500-seat $30,000 ballpark. According to White Sox expert Anthony Bush, "Construction involved creating land by pumping 600,000 yards of sand into the bay [but] by the time the field was ready, the season had already started." That year the Sox played at Athletic Park, as they had since 1903.

The facility became known as Desmond Park and was described as just the thing for "making of young manhood, good morals and healthy muscle in boys." Dewsmnd added a swimming pool in 1912, and the park was used for amateur baseball and football as the "official grounds for the City League of Duluth, the Commercial League, the Elks Club, the Moose Club and the Owls Club." In 1915 Park

Lake Superior
Park Point.

Superintendent Henry Cleveland unsuccessfully lobbied the city to lease the facility as a public swimming beach. The name Desmond Park disappeared from newspapers after 1919. Today the site is home to the United States Army Reserve Center.

Thanks to the bridge, crossing the canal had become so easy that more and more people decided to visit Minnesota Point and become permanent residents of Park Point. By the mid-1920s, as more cottages and campsites gave way to homes, the transfer bridge could not keep up with the demand of those who wanted to cross the canal. In 1930—at the insistence of the Park Point Community Club—the city had the bridge converted into today's Aerial Lift Bridge; Park Point property owners covered a large part of the expense.

The Minnesota Point Recreation Area

Oatka Beach may have been the most popular gathering place on Minnesota Point, but pleasure seekers also made use of the beaches all along the Lake Superior shoreline with little regard to whether the land was privately or publicly owned. In 1919 Henry Cleveland, still pursuing a city-maintained bathing beach on the point, announced plans to construct dressing rooms at Hartman Park, which he described as "the big bathing beach on the lake side of Park Point." Cleveland explained that "bushes heretofore have been used as shields for impromptu dressing rooms." He intended to use lumber salvaged from the U.S. Thrift Stamp Sub Treasury, a temporary

DULUTHIANS ENJOY A
SUMMER'S DAY ON THE BEACH
ALONG THE LAKE SIDE OF
MINNESOTA POINT IN 1930.
[IMAGE: UMD MARTIN LIBRARY]

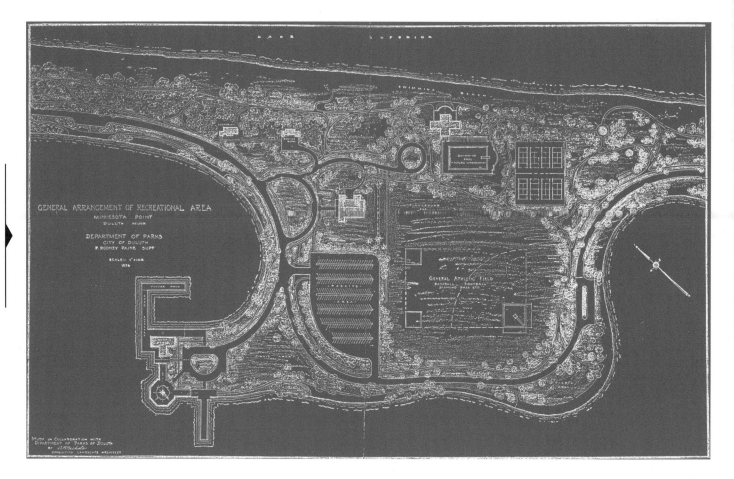

building constructed during World War I that sold stamps to finance the war. "From thrift stamps to bathing beaches!" the *News Tribune* proclaimed. Again the city council rejected his plan.

Dreamers periodically came up with schemes for developing additional facilities on the point, but none were implemented until the mid-1930s after Park Superintendent F. Rodney Paine submitted a proposal to the federal government for $1.5 million worth of improvements to parks throughout the city. Paine's plan included $338,000 to create a recreation center on Minnesota Point along the Barrens south of the Anneke house. City leaders hoped to turn the point into one of the leading recreational and summer resort sites in the state. Representatives of local government and civic clubs, including the Park Point Improvement Association, worked for over a year to gain

approval for the project. In early 1936 the Works Progress Administration (WPA) finally agreed to allocate $200,000 for the recreation area. The city pledged $35,000, and the Minnesota Executive Council contributed $90,000 to purchase the necessary land.

As part of the development, in 1936 the city acquired the rights to the lakeshore between the Duluth Ship Canal and Hartman Park, opening to the public the entire length of the beach from the canal to the Barrens. With the exception of the parcel of land owned by the Superior Water, Light & Power Company, Duluth also acquired the Barrens from Forty-sixth Street South to Peabody's Landing.

Construction of the recreation facility started in spring of 1936, when WPA workers hauled in approximately 150,000 yards of fill to create additional land and bring the entire area above water level.

Development of the recreation area helped to broaden the community's view of the point, which had served for decades as Duluth's summer playground. Speaker of the Minnesota House of Representatives George W. Johnson—later Duluth's mayor—reminded the community that while the term Park Point was commonly used for the entire sandbar, "in view of the fact that the WPA project…is sponsored largely as a state job, it is proper that the location be known as Minnesota Point."

In March 1937 Paine released an architect's sketch, drawn by landscape architect Arthur Nichols, of the proposed facility, which included a dock and a boat launch and, for the future, a swimming pool. That summer workers extended Minnesota Avenue about three-quarters of a mile, laid down six inches of top soil for the athletic fields, and broke ground on the bathhouse. A miniature train was used to carry materials over the sand to the construction site.

Just a month later Rudy Berghult replaced Sam Snively as Duluth's mayor and Earl Sherman took over from Paine as the new superintendent of the park department. Sherman continued to oversee work on Minnesota Point; roads were blacktopped, and workers constructed paths and stone steps, planted trees, built picnic benches, and created a football field and two baseball diamonds.

In April 1938, before the WPA even finished constructing the recreation area facilities, the city council agreed to add an "amusement zone" south of the new athletic field. That June the council set aside over $10,000 to develop the amusement park, expecting that revenues from the rides and parking fees would cover the expenses, which included salaries for a manager, ticket sellers, parking lot attendants, a caretaker, and two merry-go-round attendants. Earlier that month the city had spent $5,300 for a merry-go-round, a 1906 steam-driven Alan Herschel 36-horsepower carousel with hand-carved wooden horses suspended on brass poles. A "flying scooter"—similar to modern Chair-O-Plane rides—was also acquired. The amusement park opened for the first time later that summer with A. H. Muir as its manager. A miniature railway and Ferris wheel were added the following

WORKERS EXTEND MINNESOTA AVENUE ALONG MINNESOTA POINT IN 1937 SO THAT AUTOMOBILES COULD REACH THE MINNESOTA POINT RECREATION AREA, WHICH WAS ALSO UNDER CONSTRUCTION AT THE TIME. (PHOTO BY F. R. PAINE.)

[IMAGE: UMD MARTIN LIBRARY]

MINNESOTA POINT RECREATION
AREA BATHHOUSE, ALSO KNOWN AS
THE BEACH HOUSE, CA. 1940.

[IMAGE: MN HISTORICAL SOCIETY]

year. Private contractors maintained the rides, with the city receiving 25 percent of the gross revenues. Unfortunately, operation of the amusement park in 1938 resulted in a net loss of $221.53.

The bathhouse—the recreation area's focal point—opened in June 1939. Located on a ridge directly above the sandy beach, the building was constructed of heavy cedar timbers in a Nordic design. According to Muir, the bathhouse could accommodate two thousand people at a time. A fee of fifteen cents provided guests with a basket for checking their clothing, a towel, and access to the dressing and bath facilities. Despite the bathhouse, that year's losses were nearly double those of the previous year. The deficit was blamed on cold and rainy weather.

In 1940 the park opened two weeks earlier, on May 25. In an attempt to increase revenue, the park department continued to make improvements, offering weekly band concerts and adding a Dodgem Cars ride. The older rides were fitted with "new and colorful fronts," and the miniature train's railway was tripled in length. These improvements helped increase income by nearly $3,000, but despite the

long summer and new attractions, the amusement park operated at a loss. While the Dodgem ride increased receipts, renting the ride and building a facility to hold it cost over $2,600.

The next year saw the addition of an archery range; a giant checker board; outdoor Ping-Pong tables; and courts for shuffle board, horseshoes, croquet, and quoits. These additions helped make it a popular picnic location for large groups such as the American Legion, Duluth Retail Druggists, and the Hay Fever Club of America. The facility also got a new manager, J. C. Shields. Despite the thousands of people who made use of the recreation area in the 1940s, the facility continued to struggle financially, partly the result of unfavorable weather—either too cold or too rainy. By 1942 the flying scooter and Ferris wheel were removed from the amusement park, leaving just the merry-go-round, Dodgem ride, and miniature railway.

The situation improved in 1943, at least temporarily. The park department completely remodeled one section of the bathhouse and installed a separate entrance, making the large room available for picnics and other activities. Warm weather helped, and, according to the 1943 annual report, "Minnesota Point [Recreation Area] enjoyed the greatest attendance since its establishment." For the next twenty years the park operated between Memorial Day and Labor Day, depending on the weather. A snack bar called Fritz's was added, topped with a large concrete ice cream cone. Later a penny arcade was added, complete with with a photo booth and a record-making booth.

By 1960 the amusement park was under the management of H. C. and Mae Onsgard, both familiar with the amusement park business. It was H. C.'s father Bert who first suggested the idea of a municipal zoo at Fairmount Park in 1923; he later operated the Arrowhead Amusement Park across from the zoo. According to former employee Charlie Willis, the city maintained ownership of the carousel and the Dodgem cars and the Onsgards owned the other rides.

Willis, who earned fifty cents an hour operating the carousel during the summers of 1960 and 1961, remembers that by then the Dodgem cars were well past their prime. Willis wrote that "the bumper cars were in terrible condition and the building was pretty dilapidated. If you bumped the cars, the steering chains would fall off the bottom, and two or three of us would have to tip the cars over on their sides and put on the chains."

In 1964 Duluth mayor George D. Johnson proposed closing the park. He thought the point should remain natural and that the amusement park drew crowds of "black jackets," likely young men with too much time on their hands. Johnson's proposal resulted in a petition to oust the mayor. The park did not reopen, and Johnson kept his job. That year park maintenance foreman Ozmo E. Tahja reported that his crew transferred the carousel to Kiddieland at Fairmount Park. The site of the Minnesota Point Amusement Park has since been redeveloped with baseball diamonds, soccer and rugby pitches, volleyball courts, playground equipment, and picnic amenities.

Minnesota Point Pine Forest Scientific & Natural Area

In the Barrens south of the recreation area, a remnant of Minnesota Point's original sand dunes and pine forest ecosystem has been preserved. Sky Harbor Airport and the Superior Water, Light & Power Company's water intake facility are located within the pine forest, but this section of the point has otherwise remained mostly undeveloped through the years. The last cabin of Peabody's Landing was removed

in 2010. The federal government technically owns the southernmost portion of the point, which contains the ruins of the Minnesota Point Lighthouse and a former buoy depot, but in 1940 the city was granted the right to use the site for public recreation.

Thanks mainly to the efforts of the Park Point Community Club, in the late 1990s the Minnesota Department of Natural Resources (DNR) designated seventeen acres of the pine forest and sand dunes as a State Scientific and Natural Area (SNA) on land donated by Superior Water, Light & Power (with assistance from the Minnesota Land Trust).

According to the DNR, the Minnesota Point Pine Forest SNA is a uniquely significant remnant of the once-vast Great Lakes Pine Forest. The SNA includes a healthy mix of trees of all ages and is home to the only old-growth red and white pine forest found on Lake Superior sand dunes in Minnesota. Core dating carried out by DNR biologists indicated the oldest tree in the SNA began growing in 1798. Other native plant communities on the site include sand beach, beachgrass dune, and juniper dune shrubland. The forest also provides important habitat for a number of rare plants and is used frequently as a rest area for migrating warblers and shorebirds, making this a great area for birdwatching. A hiking trail through the SNA provides access to this unique environment and reminds visitors of what all of Minnesota Point looked like before it became Duluth's favorite summer resort.

FRITZ'S SNACK BAR, PART OF THE MINNESOTA POINT RECREATION AREA'S AMUSEMENT PARK, DATE UNKNOWN.

[IMAGE: TOM MCKAY]

Minnesota Point Today

While the Zenith City has many parks and Park Point is a fully developed residential neighborhood, Minnesota Point still serves as Duluth's "summer resort." The entire length of its lakeside beach remains open to the public and can be accessed at several points, including Lafayette Square and the S-curve at the site of Franklin Square, which is now known as the Franklin Tot Lot. The carnival rides are long gone, but people still swarm to the Minnesota Point Recreation Area in the summer for access to the beach, recreation fields, and the hiking trail through the pine forest.

In the 1890s, when Duluth officials considered industrializing Minnesota Point, the *News Tribune* wrote that "it would be a sacrilege to allow any such profanation of this beautiful spot; it should be kept as a pleasure resort forever and ever." The editorial continued: "There will be great hotels, cottages and pavilions extending from shoulder to finger tips of this mighty arm...and Duluth's fame as a summer resort will be second to none in the world." Today Duluth is indeed well known as a summer destination, and much of that reputation was built on the sandy dunes of Minnesota Point.

14. Undeveloped Parks

'Many Beautiful Breathing Spaces'

Although many of Duluth's well-known parks have complex histories that reflect the changing needs and tastes of each generation, other parks have a much simpler story—one of quietly remaining in their natural state. Today these undeveloped parks make up over six thousand acres within the city's limits. They are found from Fond du Lac to Lester Park, and they became part of the park system through a variety of methods.

Some undeveloped parks were platted along with first townships and later neighborhoods as the city grew, but plans to develop them were never carried out or, in many cases, were never made. Other park land was acquired to create a right-of-way for the city's boulevards, particularly Skyline Parkway—in fact, most of Duluth's undeveloped parks are found adjacent to the twenty-seven-mile-long roadway. And some of the city's undeveloped parks came through private donations; these were often named to memorialize the person who gave the property to the city or someone he or she greatly admired.

Many more acres came from acquiring tax-forfeited properties. During the Great Depression, thousands of acres of land became tax delinquent as owners could not or would not pay their taxes. In 1935, in an attempt to return these acres to private ownership, the Minnesota Legislature provided for forfeiture of these delinquent lands, thereby enabling their resale to others. As a result, in the State of Minnesota, when land owners don't pay their property taxes, the land is forfeited and becomes the property of the state. Tax-forfeited land is managed by the local county board, which classifies each parcel as conservation or non-conservation. "Conservation" parcels remain in public ownership, to be used mainly for forest management. "Non-conservation" parcels are put up for sale at public auction. Duluth, as a "city of the first class" can request that the county board classify parcels within city limits as "conservation" land to be used for public purposes such as parks. Some of Duluth's tax-forfeited conservation lands have been formally acquired by the city and dedicated as parks,

LITHOGRAPHIC POSTCARD, CA. 1910, OF A STREAM FLOWING THROUGH UNDEVELOPED DULUTH PARK PROPERTY.

[IMAGE: ZENITH CITY PRESS]

while other areas have been set aside under the less formal designation of "forest parks."

According to Duluth's 2006 Comprehensive Plan, forest parks "are not official parks, but areas within which tax forfeited lands are managed for a public purpose. Some of them essentially function as and are widely regarded as parks, while others have been developed or partially developed for a variety of purposes." Some of these forest parks include state-owned land as well. In fact, according to the city, "the borders of the forest parks have been mapped, but the borders are not coincident with publicly-owned land parcels. Land within the Forest Park boundaries includes a variety of types of land ownership. Land ownership can be private, public, or owned by a non-profit entity."

The four largest of these preserves are Fond du Lac Forest Park (see chapter 11, "Fond du Lac Park"); Bardon's Peak Forest Park; Oneota Forest Park; and Colbyville, Lakeview, and Lester River Forest Park.

Bardon's Peak Forest Park

The largest of Duluth's forest parks, Bardon's Peak Forest Park encompasses 2,775.5 total acres and includes Magney-Snively Park (once two separate parks), tiny Gasser Park, Spirit Mountain Recreation Area, 21 acres along Knowlton Creek Boulevard, and 986.5 acres of state-owned land.

Gasser Park, just two acres in size, was dedicated in 1911 as part of the plat of Spirit Lake 2nd Division, intended to be a residential neighborhood. The park and nearby street of the same name were christened in honor of Mathew M. Gasser, a German immigrant who started a very successful grocery business in Duluth in 1889. This neighborhood was never developed, and the property is now part of the Spirit Mountain Recreation Area, which includes more than one thousand acres of land set aside by state legislation in 1973, much of it acquired using Land and Water Conservation Fund financing.

Managed by the Spirit Mountain Recreation Area Authority, the area offers alpine ski hills, cross-country ski trails, a campground, an alpine coaster, a zip line, a miniature golf course, and two chalets. Although far from being "undeveloped," Spirit Mountain makes up a large portion of the forest park.

Magney Park

In 1920 Mayor Clarence R. Magney—a strong supporter of the city's park system—initiated a project to create a connecting road between Duluth and Jay Cooke State Park. To find the best route he worked closely with F. Rodney Paine, who at that time served as the manager of the state park. Magney wanted to extend the parkway from its western terminus near Thompson Hill across the hillside to Becks Road and then south along Mission Creek to the St. Louis River. He intended to acquire land around Bardon's Peak to provide a right-of-way for this new segment of the parkway.

Magney did not remain in office long enough to see the western extension of the parkway become a reality. He resigned as mayor on September 15, 1920, to campaign for a position as judge of Minnesota's Eleventh Judicial District (he won). At the time of Magney's departure from office, the *Duluth News Tribune* wrote, "[Magney] was a park fan.... In fact, he is in a large way, the father of our park system.... To him Duluth owes a great debt for many beautiful breathing spaces."

Former Duluth mayor Trevanion Hugo finished out Magney's term as mayor, and seven months later, in April 1921, Sam Snively was elected the city's chief executive. Snively had already contributed a great deal to the development of the city's parks as a private citizen, and as mayor he intended to do even more. Shortly after his election, Snively announced his vision to make Duluth the most beautiful city in the area. "Beautiful parks, broad scenic highways, and modern tourist camp sites are the strongest advertisements a city can have," Snively told the newspapers. "It is my hope that Duluth's parks and beauty spots will make it universally known." An important part of this plan was to extend the parkway both west and east so tourists would be able to drive from Jay Cooke State Park to the Lester River, with connections along the way to all the city's parks.

Snively also recognized the importance of the mature hardwood forest surrounding Bardon's Peak, which had survived the 1918 Cloquet Fire. "A far-sighted person can see that forested areas of northern Minnesota are fast dwindling," Snively said, "and that in not more than 10 years a stand of timber of this size will be almost a novelty."

CLARENCE R. MAGNEY

Clarence Reinhold Magney was born in 1883 in Trenton, Wisconsin, the son of Swedish immigrants. His father, Jonas Magnuson, had shortened the family name after arriving in America in 1858. Jonas was the first student to enroll at Gustavus Adolphus College in St. Peter, Minnesota, and after graduation he became a Lutheran pastor. Clarence was the first of six children born to Jonas and his wife Hilda. The family lived in various communities in the St. Croix Valley area near Stillwater, Minnesota.

Magney attended his father's alma mater, graduating in 1903. He then made his way to Boston, graduating Harvard Law School in 1908. After passing the Minnesota bar he joined the Duluth law firm of Jenswold & Jenswold, whose principal partner, John Jenswold, served as a member of Duluth's Board of Park Commissioners from 1907 to 1913. Magney married Lillian Lundgren in 1911, and over the next ten years they had three children.

Duluthians elected Magney as their mayor in 1917 when he was just thirty-four years old. During his very eventful administration the United States entered the war in Europe, the Spanish influenza epidemic reached Duluth, the 1918 Cloquet Fire killed nearly five hundred people, and three young black men were lynched by a mob of Duluthians. Historians wrote that while in office, Magney "gave a vigorous administration of municipal affairs throughout the critical period of the war, and showed every qualification for heading the government of one of the best cities in the northwest." He also expanded Duluth's park system, acquiring the land that became Magney, Memorial, Upper Chester, and Enger Parks, a total of 1,433 acres—the most park acreage acquired during any period of Duluth's growth. He also contributed to the establishment of Jay Cooke State Park.

Despite his success, Magney did not complete his term in office, resigning as mayor on September 15, 1920, to run for district court judge. He won the election less than two months after he left city hall, and he remained a district judge until 1943 when he began his tenure as an associate justice of the Minnesota Supreme Court. He retired January 11, 1953—his seventieth birthday—and was immediately appointed a Commissioner of the Supreme Court, a title he held until his death on May 14, 1962.

His former associate Edwin Kenny recalled that Magney "had deep sympathy for the unfortunate and a kindly understanding of the failings of his fellow man.... He was a deeply religious man and had an innate and inflexible standard of what is right and what is wrong. At the same time he had a profound respect for law and the necessity of upholding it in order that there might be stability in the rules by which we live." But Magney wasn't all business, as Kenny explained: "[Magney] had a good sense of humor and enjoyed a good joke, even if it was on himself, and many a time the corridor in the Court House rang with his hearty laughter."

As a judge, Magney maintained his love of the outdoors. He was particularly enamored with Lake Superior's North Shore—he had a home at the mouth of the Caribou River—and was instrumental in acquiring lakeshore property for parks, often purchasing the land himself and giving it to the state.

In retirement Magney continued this "hobby" of acquiring park land. His work resulted in the establishment of a dozen state parks along the North Shore, which in 1962 made up twenty thousand acres or one-sixth of the state's entire park system. He also helped establish Grand Portage National Monument in the 1950s. In 1958 the Minnesota Junior Chamber of Commerce named Magney among the top one hundred living Minnesotans. In 1963 land along the Brule River north of Grand Marais was named Judge C. R. Magney State Park in his honor.

———— IMAGE: DULUTH PUBLIC LIBRARY ————

Snively wasted no time in carrying on the work that Magney had started. In May 1921 he completed the purchase of 330 acres surrounding Bardon's Peak for $37,000. Snively named the new area Magney Park in recognition of his mayoral predecessor's contributions to the Duluth park system and announced that few changes would be made to the land. "The source of the proposed boulevard extension is now a mere footpath through the densely wooded beauty spot," the mayor pointed out. "I should like to see this wood land left in its natural state with the only mark of improvement being a hard surfaced highway through it." In 1925 Snively opened Bardon's Peak Boulevard to traffic.

Snively Park

Located east of Magney Park, Snively Park was created in 1926 when George W. Martin and his wife Olive donated to the city a twenty-one-acre parcel of land along Stewart Creek. They requested that it be named in honor of Mayor Snively for the work he had already done to expand and improve the city parks. By this time Snively had hired F. Rodney Paine as Duluth's park superintendent. In his first annual report Paine described Snively Park as "beautifully and heavily wooded with almost all species of native trees and shrubs and affords a wonderful panoramic view of the St. Louis River." He decided to develop a rest point along the parkway that would feature a memorial to Mayor Snively.

The memorial was completed in 1927 on the east side of the Stewart Creek Bridge, and Paine described the site in his annual report as consisting of "a flag-stoned area into which is set a small reflecting pool backed by a rough dry wall of native stone over which cascades a small stream of water into the pool. A drinking fountain of purified spring water is set into the wall and the whole development is dominated by a larger boulder upon which a bronze tablet is to be placed. To the rear, the area has been brushed out and picnic tables, benches, and fire places installed. The Park has proven very popular for small picnic parties."

THE STEWART CREEK BRIDGE WITHIN SNIVELY PARK, 1927. (PHOTO BY F. R. PAINE.)

[IMAGE: UMD MARTIN LIBRARY]

Magney-Snively Park

While Paine did not intend to make any significant changes to Magney or Snively parks, memories of the devastating fire that had swept through parts of Duluth in 1918 still lingered, and even though the forest on the western hillside had not burned, Paine remained conscious of the ongoing threat. So in 1927 he set out to reduce the potential of forest fires in the area. "Fire protection is...particularly important in this park," he wrote. "The land from two hundred to five hundred feet back on either side of the road was cleaned of dead and down material during the past winter. Over one hundred cords of wood were obtained from this work, part of which was sold and part used as firewood for Tourist Camps, Tool Houses, Golf House, etc. Cleaning has been started along the boundary lines so as to form fire breaks where any fires from the outside may be stopped."

The city soon gained ownership of an additional two hundred acres of forested land on the city's western hillside when Thomas A. Merritt donated five forty-acre tracts north and west of Magney Park as a memorial for his uncles Leonidas, Alfred, Cassius Clay, Jerome, and Andrus Merritt, who played key roles in developing the Mesabi Iron Range and the city of Duluth. (In 1925 Merritt also donated a forty-acre parcel in honor of his father Napolean B. Merritt, located farther to the south at 128th Avenue West near the base of Ely's Peak.)

AN UNIDENTIFIED MAN, POSSIBLY GEORGE W. MARTIN, STANDS AT THE MEMORIAL TO SAM SNIVELY WITHIN SNIVELY PARK, 1927. (PHOTO BY F. R. PAINE.)

[IMAGE: UMD MARTIN LIBRARY]

THE MERRITTS OF ONEOTA

Between 1913 and 1925, eight Duluth parks were established and named in honor of members of the Lewis and Hepzibah Merritt (pictured, left) family, true pioneers of the Zenith City. Family patriarch Lewis Howell Merritt (1809 to 1880) and his son Napolean arrived in Superior, Wisconsin, on July 3, 1855, having travelled from the family home in Ashtabula, Ohio. The Merritts were jacks-of-all-trades, and they had journeyed to Superior after they were hired to build a sawmill on Connor's Point for Superior pioneer Newell S. Ryder. Their eyes soon strayed to the Minnesota side of St. Louis Bay, which had been opened to settlement following the 1854 Treaty of La Pointe. Lewis quickly made a claim near today's Forty-second Avenue West, adjacent to land previously claimed by Reverend Edmund Ely and Henry Wheeler—both, like the Merritts, dedicated Methodists. The Merritts started calling the area Oneota, a word taken from a local Ojibwe legend meaning "the rock from which the people sprang." The rest of the Wheeler, Ely, and Merritt families arrived in 1856. Over the years Lewis and Hepzibah Merritt (1812 to 1906) raised eight children, all boys: Jerome (1832 to 1878), Napolean B. (1834 to 1924), Lucien F. (1835 to 1900), Leonidas (1844 to 1926), Alfred (1847 to 1926), Lewis J. (1848 to 1929), Cassius Clay (1851 to 1894), and Andrus R. (1854 to 1937).

At Oneota the three families built the first school—which until 1871 doubled as a church—using lumber from the Wheeler mill. In 1869 the Merritts again used lumber they milled themselves to build the *Chaska*, a seventy-two-foot-long, forty-nine-ton schooner—the first ship built at the Head of the Lakes. Three years earlier Lewis Merritt had travelled to Lake Vermilion along with many others to seek the truth behind rumors of vast deposits of gold. Like most, he found no gold, but when he returned he told his sons that the region would one day be covered with iron mines worth "more than all the gold in California."

Not all of the Merritts remained in Duluth; by 1870 Lewis, Hepzibah. Napolean, Jerome, Lewis J., and Andrus had moved to Missouri; Lucien had gone to Ohio to become a minister and on to Pennsylvania to practice his trade. By 1880 Lewis H. and Jerome had died, and Hepzibah and Andrus returned to Duluth. Leonidas, Alfred, and Cassius never left the Zenith City. They worked as lumbermen, shipbuilders, sailors, timber cruisers, and mineral explorers.

In 1889 Leonidas, Alfred (pictured, left), and Cassius finally heeded their father's prediction and went looking for iron ore west of the Vermilion Range. In 1890 an expedition of six men led by Alfred Merritt discovered large deposits of soft hematite containing 65 percent iron. The Merritts named the range Mesabi, Ojibwe for *Giant Mountain* or *Grandmother of Them All*. They named their first mine Mountain Iron. Those Merritts involved in the iron mining enterprise have been called Duluth's "Seven Iron Men" by biographers, but in reality the Merritts who engaged in iron mining totaled just five: Leonidas, Alfred, Cassius, and two of their nephews, Jerome's son Wilbur and Lucien's son John. Other family members, including Lewis J. and his son Hulett, also invested but did not participate in the operations.

Creating infrastructure for their iron mining operation—including building the Duluth, Missabe & Northern Railway and its ore docks in West Duluth—proved expensive. The first load of iron ore was shipped to Allouez Bay in Superior in October 1892. It took until 1893 to deliver the first load of ore to the new Duluth docks, not far from where Lewis H. Merritt had helped establish Oneota thirty-five years earlier. But by then John D. Rockefeller had become the controlling investor in the Merritt's enterprises. When the Financial Panic of 1893 shook the nation's economy, Rockefeller called in his debts, and by February 1894 he essentially took control of everything the Merritts had built.

The fallout left the family reeling. Cassius died in April 1894; Leonidas blamed his death on Rockefeller's actions. Lewis J. and his son Hulett, who had actually profited from Rockefeller's hostile takeover to become the black sheep of the family, moved to California. (Hulett would later become the largest individual stockholder in U. S. Steel and, it was often claimed, the richest man in California.)

On behalf of the family, Alfred Merritt successfully sued Rockefeller for fraud. Rockefeller appealed; unable to afford the expense of a second trial, the Merritts were forced into a disappointing settlement. Alfred, Andrus, and Leonidas then launched their next venture, the American Exploration Co., which established and sold mineral rights to silver and copper mines in Mexico, Canada, and the western United States. Meanwhile Lucien, now a Methodist minister, had returned to Duluth in 1887. The Merritt family had helped build a wooden Methodist church in Oneota near Forty-sixth Avenue West and Superior Street in 1871, and by 1890 Lucien became its pastor. With the promise of a fortune in iron ore, a new brick-and-sandstone Romanesque church was built on the same site in 1892. Lucien served as its minister until 1895, returning to Ohio where he died in 1900. Following his death the church was renamed the L. F. Merritt Memorial Methodist Episcopal Church in his honor. (The building later became Asbury United Methodist Church and was razed in 1992; the new Asbury United at 6682 Grand Avenue contains one of the 1892 church's stained-glass windows.)

Leonidas, pictured on previous page reenacting the brothers' 1889 search for ore in 1917, remained civic minded, serving on Duluth's park board from 1911 to 1913 (see page 9 for more about Leonidas Merritt). Thomas Merritt (pictured, below), son of Napolean Merritt (pictured, above) honored Leonidas along with four other Merritt brothers (Alfred, Cassius, Jerome, and Andrus) by donating forty acres of land in the name of each to be dedicated as Duluth parks; these parcels are now part of Magney-Snively Park.

Three Duluth parks still honor the Merritts: Merritt Park at 4017 West Seventh Street, established in 1913 as Merritt Playground; Napolean B. Merritt Memorial Park at 128th Avenue West, established in 1925 on land also donated by his son Thomas; and Reverend L. F. Merritt Memorial Park at 46th Avenue West and Superior Street, established in 1924 adjacent to the church named in his honor.

Other Duluth landmarks bear the Merritt name. In 1911 pioneer Jerome Merritt—considered by many as the first teacher in what is now Duluth—was honored when a new elementary school at 510 North 40th Avenue West was named for him. In 1993 the building was converted to apartments. West Duluth's Merritt Creek is also named for the family, following the tradition of naming local creeks after pioneers who homesteaded near them. The creek runs from north of Brewer Park roughly adjacent to Haines Road before entering the Denfeld neighborhood west of the Wheeler Athletic Complex and Wade Stadium before emptying into the bay near Thirty-fifth Avenue West.

Maintenance work at Magney, Snively, and the Merritt memorial parks focused on building trails that also served as fire breaks. One trail traversed the hillside out to what Paine described as the "promontory at Ely's Peak from which a wonderful panoramic view of the surrounding country is obtained." City workers cleared a few picnic areas and built a portable warming shack on a large rock outcrop located above the parkway at the Bardon's Peak overlook. This high point, locally known as Rock Mountain, was owned by the Universal Cement Company, a subsidiary of the United States Steel Corporation, until 1937. That year—after Snively lost the mayoral election, ending his tenure as Duluth's longest-serving mayor—the company donated the land to the city "as a perpetual memorial to the memory of Samuel F. Snively in recognition of his services devoted to the establishment and development of a comprehensive system of parks, park driveways and boulevards within the limits of the city."

Paine was also conscious of the need for the park system to generate money to help cover maintenance costs. In 1928 he suggested designating these western parks as a municipal forest that would be managed "on a forestry basis" to ensure a future stand of timber. He also recommended purchasing additional forested land in the area. He planned to sell some of the more valuable timber and use the profits to maintain and improve other city parks. Paine's plan was modeled on the revenue-generating municipal forests that were common in many towns in Europe and the northeastern United States. The *News Tribune* supported the idea and reported that "the city forest...will preserve the natural wild land, forest, and stream for the people to enjoy, form a sanctuary for game and birds, provide beautiful walks and drives and eliminate fire hazards, as well as provide employment during dull periods of the year."

Over the next few decades the city acquired at least sixty additional acres of forest surrounding Snively Park, but despite its designation as a municipal forest, little timber cutting took place. Magney and Snively Parks were nearly forgotten until the early 1970s when the Spirit Mountain Recreation Area (SMRA) was created. As part of this development, the city acquired a number of tax-forfeit land parcels between Snively Park and Bardon's Peak. In the legislation that created the SMRA Authority, this land was designated as a "western peripheral area," with uses restricted to recreational trails and public roadways. Acquisition of the additional parcels made it possible to consolidate all the publicly-owned land along the western end of Skyline Parkway and rename it Magney-Snively Park.

THE VIEW OF THE ST. LOUIS
RIVER FROM BARDON'S PEAK
WITHIN MAGNEY PARK, 1927.
(PHOTO BY F. R. PAINE.)
[IMAGE: UMD MARTIN LIBRARY]

The twenty-first century brought a renewed interest in this unique expanse of hardwood forest. In 2002 the City of Duluth created the Duluth Natural Areas Program, stating that "The city council finds that the city of Duluth is the owner of a substantial number of tracts of real estate, both inside and outside the city, some of which are of special or unique ecological or environmental significance to the community, which properties should be considered for conservation designation in order to protect those values."

Because of its significant native-plant communities and unique geological landforms, the city council designated approximately 1,800 acres of the Magney-Snively area as Duluth's first Natural Area in 2006. According to its nomination document, Magney-Snively Park is unusual because it has the largest known tract of sugar maple–basswood forest in Northeastern Minnesota. "It is a complex landscape," the nomination reads, "with a matrix of sugar maple–basswood forest containing smaller patches of black ash or alder swamps, rock outcrops, and rock outcrop woodlands." In addition, "as a large forested tract along a well-known migration route, Magney-Snively provides important stopover and nesting habitat for migratory songbirds and raptors." The city's primary goals for designating the forest as a Natural Area include "maintaining the ecological integrity of the native plant communities of the Magney-Snively area and protecting the area's special species and geologic landforms." In 2012 the park and surrounding undeveloped greenspaces were designated as the Magney-Snively Forest Preserve.

Magney-Snively Park now includes nearly ten miles of city hiking/ski trails and four miles of the Superior Hiking Trail. The 1927 memorial to Sam Snively was rehabilitated by the City of Duluth in 2013. The Bardon's Peak overlook provides spectacular views of the St. Louis River valley and Lake Superior, making the stretch of parkway adjacent to Magney-Snively especially popular in the fall when the hardwood forest is ablaze in shades of red, orange, and yellow.

As the *News Tribune* wrote in 1921, "Neither fire nor the lumberman can be permitted to wreck [sic] havoc on this only remaining forest section on the west. It must belong to the city and be protected by the city." As of 2016 the people of Duluth have fulfilled this mandate by preserving this unique area that honors the two men who did so much to create Duluth's park system.

Oneota Forest Park

Oneota Forest Park surrounds a portion of Skyline Parkway between Highland Street and Haines Road and includes Oneota Park, Ericson Place, Bellevue Park, and Brewer Park. Over 90 percent of the 1,123 acres are on state property.

Bellevue Park, just three acres of land purchased in 1889 for the future expansion of Duluth's boulevard system, rests on either side of Skyline Parkway and within the larger Brewer Park, which includes more than forty acres of undeveloped land above and below Skyline Parkway between Keene and Merritt Creeks. This property was donated by Duluth Crushed Stone in 1926 and named in honor of the company's owner, Frank A. Brewer, who also owned the Duncan & Brewer Sawmill and sat on the Duluth School Board. The land was originally part of the company's quarry, located south of what is now park land.

As part of its St. Louis River Corridor Initiative, in 2015 the city announced a plan to dedicate as a park thirty acres of land, including the twenty remaining acres of the quarry as well as ten acres owned by adjacent Oneota Cemetery. The abandoned property—between Forty-sixth and Fifty-ninth Avenues West below Skyline Parkway and known informally as Casket Quarry—includes a one-hundred-foot-high rock face that has been popular with rock and ice climbers for decades. In April 2016 the Parks and Recreation Commission approved a plan for the space. The three-phase plan is expected to take ten years to implement at a cost of $638,500. As of January 2016, the new park has been informally called Quarry Park, but a final decision on its name has not been made.

West of the historic quarry, Oneota Park is a narrow slice of land—wedged between a loop of Skyline Parkway once called Oneota Loop Boulevard—that runs along both sides of Keene Creek from Highland Street to the convergence of the parkway and St. Louis River Road; its lower portion runs along the western border of Oneota Cemetery.

Tiny Ericson Place is simply a half acre of land sitting among many other acres of undeveloped property east of the remaining quarry property and above the historic railroad tracks that lead to Duluth's ore docks. A 1937 park department report indicates that the property was donated, but the benefactor's identity was not disclosed and there were many people of Swedish descent named Ericson (or Erickson, Erikson, Ericcson, etc.) living in Duluth at the time.

Colbyville, Lakeview, and Lester River Forest Park

Stretching from the Woodland neighborhood to Lester Park, the 1,417 acres of Colbyville, Lakeview, and Lester River Forest Park includes Downer Park, Hawk Ridge Nature Reserve, Amity Park, and Janette Pollay Park.

Downer Park's 17 acres are located north of the Forest Hill Cemetery in the eastern portion of Duluth's Woodland neighborhood. The property was donated in 1918 by Boston real estate mogul and legislator Charles A. Downer, namesake of Vermont's Downer State Forest. While Downer belonged to Duluth's Kitchi Gammi Club, he never lived in the Zenith City. Amity Creek runs through the park, and what may be the original path of the Vermilion Trail, built in the 1860s during a short-lived gold rush, can still be seen along its banks.

As early as 1951, members of the Duluth Bird Club had gathered along the highest part of eastern Skyline Parkway at an area known today as Hawk Ridge, roughly midway between Seven Bridges Road and Glenwood Street, for a few days each September to watch the annual migration of hawks. By 1972 the club had become the Duluth Audubon Society and the bird watching activities stretched from August to November. That year, with financial support from the Minnesota Chapter of the Nature Conservancy, the group gave the City of Duluth the funding to purchase 115 acres above Skyline Parkway west of Seven Bridges Road as a nature reserve. The following year St. Louis County conveyed 250 adjoining acres to the city to add to the preserve. Today the property is managed by the Hawk Ridge Bird Observatory, a nonprofit organization, and each fall thousands of birders from across the United States and forty other nations gather to watch the hawks migrate.

East of Hawk Ridge, Amity Park was created when Sam Snively and his friends built Seven Bridges Road (originally called Snively Boulevard) between 1901 and 1910. Snively acquired land along the road on either side of Amity Creek, also known as the west branch of the Lester River. When the road was donated to the city, the property, over 150 acres, came along with it. There is no mention of this park until 1928, when superintendent F. Rodney Paine referred to it as Snively Boulevard Park. Paine began calling the area Amity Park in 1930. The

LUMBERMAN FRANK A. BREWER, OWNER OF THE DUNCAN & BREWER LUMBER COMPANY AND DULUTH CRUSHED STONE. THE LAND ONCE OWNED BY DULUTH CRUSHED STONE, MUCH OF IT DONATED BY BREWER, NOW MAKES UP BREWER AND QUARRY PARKS.

[IMAGE:DULUTH PUBLIC LIBRARY]

THE GIRL SCOUTS AT JANETTE POLLAY PARK

In April 1921 Sam Snively became mayor of Duluth. Snively realized that, following the Fire of 1918, the scorched remnants of the forest at Janette Pollay Park no longer provided the "exquisite specimen of nature's handiwork" that had made the area special. He offered to let local Girl Scouts of America troops use Pollay Park. The scouts were delighted by this offer, and in exchange for use of the land, the girls agreed to protect the park, clean up the underbrush, and aid in "general beautification."

As a mayoral candidate, Snively had promised to restore some of the citizen boards that were eliminated by the 1913 city charter. Soon after taking office he created a nonsalaried park board, made up of citizens representing all sections of the city. Snively's new board had no real power. Its role was to advise the mayor on "all matters pertaining to parks, driveways, and other projects tending to beautify the city." Snively appointed eleven people to his advisory park board. Mina Merrill Prindle (pictured, above), donor of the Janette Pollay Park land, became a member of Snively's advisory board, along with Mrs. W. J. Olcott, Mrs. C. R. Keyes, and Mrs. John Millen. These women were soon called on to offer suggestions for the Girl Scouts' beautification program.

The scouts adopted Janette Pollay Park as their hiking base and made plans to construct a shelter for overnight stays. In recognition of their good stewardship, in September 1925 Mina Prindle gave the Girl Scouts ownership of fifteen acres of land in the middle of the park. As she had before, Mrs. Prindle made this donation in memory of her mother, Janette Pollay, and requested that the Girl Scout camp be known by that name. The scouts built their rustic cabin on a high bank overlooking Amity Creek. They opened the building for public inspection on August 21, 1926, and the next day officially dedicated it as the Janette Pollay Cabin. A portrait of Janette Pollay in her lavender silk wedding dress was hung in the cabin's main room. In 1929 local Girl Scouts helped plant over 4,500 trees within the park to help replace those lost in the 1918 Cloquet Fire.

The cabin, now called the Janette Pollay Cabin and Outdoor Program Center, still serves area Girl Scouts today. The building itself is used for meetings, crafts, games, and overnight stays—it can sleep up to twenty-four campers. More amenities surround the cabin, including a large fire pit, a picnic shelter with rustic fireplace, a playing field, and six campsites.

PORTRAIT: UMD MARTIN LIBRARY | PHOTO: ZENITH CITY PRESS

park includes the Lester-Amity Winter Sports Chalet, built in 1960 as a warming house for an adjacent hockey rink.

Janette Pollay Park

Mention Janette Pollay Park and most Duluthians think of the Girl Scout camp located along the north branch of Amity Creek near the intersection of Jean Duluth and Martin Roads. What they don't realize is that the surrounding land is a sixty-acre city park of the same name. Created in 1914, this was Duluth's first park located above Skyline Parkway, or "up over the hill," outside the densely populated urban area and beyond the end of the streetcar line.

In January 1914 Mina Merrill Prindle, wife of local real estate magnate William Prindle, donated this forested land to the City of Duluth. She wanted it to be used as a public park named in honor of her mother, Janette Pollay. Although the park is often described in newspaper stories as 70 or more acres, the city's record of Mrs. Prindle's donation describes 58.43 acres in two oddly shaped parcels along Amity Creek, separated by a smaller piece of land that was not included (available records do not explain why she split the land this way). Two more acres were added to the north side of Janette Pollay Park in 1916—a gift from the Park View Farms Company.

Referred to in 1914 as one of the largest and most beautiful of the city's parks, Janette Pollay Park was reportedly covered by virgin forest. Adjacent landowner Sam Snively, in an August 1915 *News Tribune* story, called it "an exquisite specimen of nature's handiwork. Through it, in circuitous manner, courses the northern branch of Amity Creek, bounded on its outer curves, by high and graceful ridges, and enfolding by its inner curves beautiful plats of more even and level timbered land."

This was a time when Duluth business leaders were working hard to promote local agricultural development as a way to bring down the cost of food. The Duluth Commercial Club had convinced the University of Minnesota to establish a demonstration/experimental farm in Duluth; it was completed in 1913, across the road from Janette Pollay Park. Homecroft developments of one to two acres, such as Greysolon Farms and Exeter Farms, filled suburban areas surrounding the city. Snively, President of the Duluth Land and Improvement Company, operated a four-hundred-acre dairy farm south of Janette Pollay Park.

Mina and William Prindle owned a beautiful mansion on Greysolon Road in eastern Duluth. Mina was actively involved in the real estate business along with her husband. He was President of

W. M. Prindle & Company, which dealt in real estate of all types, from high-class properties to Homecroft developments. In December 1909 they formed a new business, the Nisswa Company, with Mina M. Prindle as secretary, her brother Eugene A. Merrill as vice president, and William M. Prindle as president and treasurer. The incorporation papers described the purpose of the company as "to buy, own, mortgage, sell, convey, and deal in real estate." Mina Prindle's name appeared frequently on real estate transactions involving both farmland and city lots through the 1920s.

Mayor William Prince graciously accepted Mina Prindle's land donation and announced his plan to connect Janette Pollay Park to the eastern end of the city's boulevard system. The park department started building a winding, scenic gravel drive through the park in 1915. It began at Jean Duluth Road, meandered through Janette Pollay Park, crossing the stream numerous times, then followed the creek through Samuel Snively's farm and connected with the main parkway at the junction of the north and south branches of Amity Creek.

On the last day of September 1917, Mayor Clarence Magney formally opened the new road linking Janette Pollay Park to the city's parkway system, and Sam Snively spoke poetically about the beauty of the drive, calling it "a scene entirely sylvan, but which leads again to and along the river which it crosses to rise and overlook the waters

of the great Lake Superior, and hides again in the forest along the higher slopes of the ridges, overlooking the valley and the winding river."

Just a year later the massive 1918 Cloquet Fire swept through this area, causing major damage. The conflagration completely wiped out many of the small Homecroft farms and left only one building standing on Snively's property. After touring the devastation, Mayor Clarence Magney reported that "every one of the seven bridges in Janette Pollay Park has been destroyed.... I doubt if there are more than 15 trees in the entire seventy acres that are alive."

The forest could not be replaced, but within six months Park Superintendent Henry Cleveland announced his plan to repair the road and build new bridges "of rustic design...constructed of boulders and native rock, most of the material being found in the immediate vicinity." He celebrated the completion of the first replacement bridge in October 1919, just one year after the fire. The *News Tribune* reported that construction of the remaining bridges would begin the following year, after the new park budget was prepared. However, this little-used area at the edge of town apparently did not make it into the city's 1920 budget; no additional bridges were built in Janette Pollay Park, and the roadway gradually disappeared as the burned-over area began to recover.

THE RUINS OF THE HOMECROFT SCHOOL, PHOTOGRAPHED SHORTLY AFTER IT WAS DESTROYED BY THE 1918 CLOQUET FIRE. (PHOTO BY HUGH MCKENZIE.)

[IMAGE: UMD MARTIN LIBRARY]

THIS DIAGRAM OF JANETTE POLLAY PARK APPEARED IN THE *DULUTH NEWS TRIBUNE* IN AUGUST, 1915.

[IMAGE: ZENITH CITY PRESS]

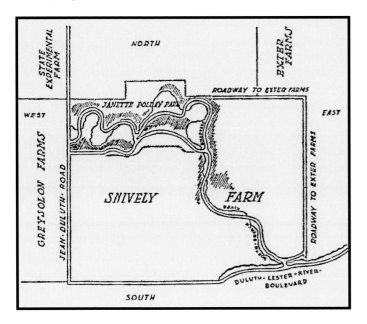

DULUTH: THE HOMECROFT CITY

In the late 1890s the booming city of Duluth was a major transportation center where railroads and ships loaded the region's natural resources of iron ore and timber for distribution across the country. But few farms existed in the area, and food of any sort commanded a premium price. Without automobiles, city dwellers lived close to their work and depended on streetcars for transportation. Houses were built close together with little open space, leaving families without a place to grow their own food. The availability of jobs drew many middle class families to Duluth, but the cost of living was unacceptably high, mainly due to the expense of bringing in food.

Duluth entrepreneur Guilford Hartley operated one of the few successful farms in the city. Located on Woodland Avenue, his 780-acre Allandale Farm produced celery and lettuce that he shipped throughout the country. Around 1900, land developers Charles Craig and John Williams (pictured, left), partners in the Jean Du Luth Company, established the area's largest agricultural operation. Their Jean Duluth Stock Farm covered over 4,000 acres along the Lester River on the East Duluth and Lester River Road (which became the Jean Duluth Farm Road and eventually the Jean Duluth Road).

Other prominent Duluth businessmen, including future mayor Sam Snively, set up smaller farms in the Woodland/Colbyville area. Millionaires Chester Congdon and John Sebenius included vegetable gardens, orchards, and dairy cows on their grand estates along the Lake Superior shore. But the plight of the ordinary citizen did not change significantly. Economic recession and a near collapse of the financial system in late 1907 drove the cost of living even higher.

To help solve this problem, members of Duluth's Commercial Club focused their efforts on increasing agricultural production in northern Minnesota. They hired expert A. B. Hostetter to work as superintendent of agriculture. Hostetter soon realized that in this area large farms were possible only for men of wealth. As he told the *Duluth News Tribune*, "This is no place for the 160-acre farm. The task of clearing is too great, too slow, and expensive for the poor man; it is the lumberman's job, not the farmer's. Here you must have the dairyman and the gardener, the small farm, and enough of the land must be cleared for him to let him make a living cropping the soil from the first year."

In response to Hostetter's advice, the Commercial Club formed the Greysolon Farms Company and purchased two full sections of land near the intersection of Jean Duluth and Martin Roads. They planned to clear the land before selling it, making it possible for the new owners to start planting immediately.

To promote agricultural education, they lobbied state legislators to establish a demonstration farm in the Duluth area. In March 1911 the legislature appropriated $65,000 for the University of Minnesota to acquire a site of at least 200 acres with good soil that would be accessible to farmers throughout northeastern Minnesota. University regents considered eleven sites, including one within the Greysolon Farms development. They chose the Greysolon Farms land, believing that the Commercial Club would soon succeed in obtaining an extension to the streetcar line that would make the site accessible to city dwellers. The Northeast Demonstration Farm and Experimental Station, built in 1913, quickly became an important center for agricultural education and experimentation.

At the national level, the 1907 recession stimulated a back-to-the-land movement. The National Homecrofting Association encouraged industrial workers to acquire an acre of land and save money by growing their own food. Executive Director George H. Maxwell of Chicago coined the word *homecroft* from the Scottish word *croft*, which referred to a small homestead that supported a single family with a mixture of cash crops and subsistence farming.

Homecrofters were not expected to earn their livelihood from the land. Rather, homecrofting meant supplementing the family income by raising vegetables and poultry using whatever ground was available, whether it was a nearby vacant lot or a five-acre farm in the outskirts. As the national homecrofting movement gained strength, the Duluth Commercial Club began promoting this idea of self-sufficiency by encouraging backyard gardens and the creation of "garden suburbs" where middle class families could live and garden on a one- or two-acre parcel.

Homecroft Park on Calvary Road was one of Duluth's first garden suburbs. Located about three-quarters of a mile from the end of the Woodland streetcar line, one-acre lots were offered for sale by W. M Prindle & Co. beginning in 1909. (Company president William Prindle, pictured above, was the husband of Mina Prindle, the benefactor of Janette Pollay Park.)

The prices ranged from $200 to $275; terms were $1.00 down and $1.50 to $2.00 per week until paid for, no interest, and no payments when sick—as shown in the advertisement at right from the May 5, 1910 *Duluth News Tribune*. By early 1910 enough families had moved into Homecroft Park to justify construction of the Homecroft School.

The Alliance Real Estate Corporation created Exeter Farms, one of the largest suburbs of one-acre tracts, located just north of Lester Park along Maxwell Road. Until automobiles became widely available, the residents of Exeter Farms hiked up the hill to their homes from the end of the streetcar line on Superior Street.

George Maxwell visited Duluth in early 1911. He was so impressed that he christened Duluth "the Homecroft City" and moved the headquarters of the National Homecrofting Association here. Maxwell devoted the entire September issue of his magazine *The Talisman* to the homecroft movement in Duluth. He made famous "the Duluth Idea." Maxwell suggested homecrofters "keep house by the year"; essentially, garden for the year around: go to the garden in summer, go to the larder in winter, let sunshine and soil supply fruits, berries, and vegetables for all home needs from the home gardens, and educate the children in the public schools to live this way.

Life changed in 1914 when World War I erupted. Food production dropped dramatically in Europe, as agricultural workers entered military service and the conflict devastated farmland. To help the war effort, Americans were encouraged to conserve food so more could be shipped abroad to the Allies. In 1917 the government urged citizens to use all available lands for growing food, and homecroft gardens were transformed into war gardens.

Then in October 1918, the massive forest fire that wiped out the city of Cloquet swept through the outskirts of Duluth, burning through Janette Pollay Park, Sam Snively's farm, and many of the garden suburbs. Numerous homes at Exeter Farms and Homecroft Park were destroyed, along with the Homecroft School.

The war, the fire, and the growing availability of automobiles, refrigeration, and the corner grocery store all contributed to the demise of the homecrofting movement. By 1919 George Maxwell shifted most of his energy to his other favorite topic—irrigation. He moved on to Arizona where he spent the remainder of his career working for the National Irrigation Association.

Although few Duluthians remember the name of George Maxwell or the meaning of the term "homecroft," ghosts of this back-to-the-land movement of the early 1900s can still be seen in and around the city. And everyone who maintains a backyard garden, raises a flock of urban chickens, or sells produce at the Farmers' Market is carrying on the rich agricultural legacy of Duluth's homecroft movement.

F. Rodney Paine replaced Henry Cleveland as superintendent of the city's parks at the beginning of 1926. It wasn't until 1928 that Paine mentioned Janette Pollay Park in his annual report, writing that "the dead standing trees resulting from the 1918 fire had never been entirely cleaned out and during 1928 the rest of this material was cut down and burned up so that the park now is comparatively safe from fires." And in 1929 Paine reported that "through the generosity of Mrs. W. M. Prindle who furnished the plants, a forest plantation of 2,000 Norway Pine, 2,000 Black Hills spruce and 500 Colorado blue spruce" was established. Local Girls Scouts helped to plant the trees. This is the last recorded improvement at Janette Pollay Park.

Mina Prindle's donation came with numerous conditions. She requested that the property would "forever be known as Janette Pollay Park" and that it would forever be available "for the use and enjoyment of all the inhabitants of the city." She also wanted the land to be preserved in its "natural condition." In keeping with Prindle's wishes, the park today remains undeveloped and open to the public, although there is no sign identifying it. The land is wild—there are no trails, just thick northern Minnesota second-growth forest that challenges the casual hiker. Amity Creek meanders freely through the area, eroding the steep banks and building gravel bars in the low spots. Other than the road that leads to the Girl Scout camp, there is little evidence of the winding scenic drive that Mayor Clarence Magney and Sam Snively celebrated in 1917. Several stone piles that once supported bridges, a rusty culvert in an eroded stream channel, and a hint of the level roadbed that traversed what Snively described as "high and graceful ridges" are all that remain of the city's attempt to provide access to the park.

In 1979 the city attempted to purchase 205 acres between Amity Park, Hawk Ridge, and Janette Pollay Park—once the site of the Springhill Dairy—to both connect trails within the parks and help preserve the banks of Amity Creek. The property owner had decided against developing it into a housing community and hoped the city would purchase and preserve it. He asked $131,000, and state and federal funding was found to cover 75 percent of the cost. Both the city's parks and recreation department and the Duluth Audubon Society supported the idea, as the property had essentially been used as a park for decades. City councilors including future mayor John Fedo voted 6–3 against a resolution to make the purchase. The *News Tribune* reported that the councilors against the purchase said, "The city already had enough park land."

Smaller Forest Parks

Duluth's smaller forest parks—Memorial, Hartley Tract, Minnesota Point, Kenwood, and Moose Hill—are scattered throughout the city. Many more parcels of property dedicated as park land have never been developed (information on other undeveloped Duluth parks can be found in the appendix).

Bayview Forest Park, 353 acres located south of Bay View Elementary School, includes 275.5 acres of state land. Central Park Forest Park, 31.55 acres of land on the steep hillside between Fourteenth and Seventeenth Avenues West, is one of the city's early platted parks that was never developed (for more information see chapter 9, "Enger Park").

Memorial Forest Park is a 163-acre parcel of land located above Wheeler Athletic Complex roughly centered on the east branch of Merritt Creek between Haines Road and Hutchinson Road.

The 975 acres of the Hartley Tract Forest Park includes all of Hartley Field, Como Park, and 406.5 acres of state-owned land (for more information see chapter 12, "Hartley Park").

Minnesota Point Forest Park contains 146 acres, including all of the Minnesota Point Pine Forest Scientific and Natural Area and the Barrens (for more information see chapter 13, "Minnesota Point").

Kenwood Forest Park's ten acres — almost entirely tax-forfeited property—lie immediately west of the College of St. Scholastica.

Moose Hill Forest Park is the same as Moose Hill Park, an undeveloped eighty-acre rectangle of land east of the Lester River Road and north of Highway 61. Moose Hill is not the same as the Moose Mountain Scientific and Natural Area, 177 acres of hardwood forest owned by the Minnesota Department of Natural Resources found east of the Lester River Road 3.5 miles north of Superior Street.

THE SUPERIOR WATER, LIGHT & POWER COMPANY'S PUMPHOUSE WORKS ON MINNESOTA POINT, 1936. TODAY THE FACILITY IS WITHIN THE MINNESOTA POINT PINE FOREST SCIENTIFIC AND NATURAL AREA. (PHOTO BY F. R. PAINE.)
[IMAGE: UMD MARTIN LIBRARY]

15. Playgrounds and Sports Facilities

'Play is the Business of Boys and Girls'

The role of urban parks started to change nationally by the early 1900s as more people recognized that children in cities needed safe places to play—someplace other than empty lots or busy streets. Reformers began to advocate for the creation of playgrounds for the children, not just because the streets were dangerous, but also because they believed that unsupervised play encouraged juvenile crime. As the movement gained momentum, supporters formed the Playground Association of America in 1906, a citizen organization with the goal of building playgrounds for the benefit of children.

Duluth was receptive to the idea; in fact, letters advocating for the creation of playgrounds began to appear in the local newspapers as early as 1904. The park board set aside a few areas for children to play in the parks, but it provided no playground equipment and no supervision.

Things began to change in April 1908, when Mayor Roland Haven invited Leo Hanmer, field secretary of the playground association, to visit Duluth. Hanmer shared his message that cities should build playgrounds for the benefit of the children. He explained:

"Play life in the great cities has been considerably changed because of the progress which has been made in commercialism and industry. The children years ago had many corner lots to play on, and the streets were not as crowded with people and vehicles as they are today. The cities have been increasing in population, buildings have been erected upon once vacant lots, and with the increase of business the streets have filled with teams. The conditions have become such that the children have been crowded into small quarters, and it is here that juvenile crime starts. Moreover, these conditions are detrimental to the health of children. Play is the business of boys and girls…. In their play they develop physically, intellectually, and morally, and the importance of this development must be realized by the people of our cities."

LITHOGRAPHIC POSTCARD, CA. 1905, OF THE WHEELER RACE TRACK (FOREGROUND, RIGHT) AND ATHLETIC PARK (CENTER).

[IMAGE: ZENITH CITY PRESS]

Duluth's Chapter of the Playground Association of America

Following Hanmer's visit, a group of Duluthians, including members of the park board, formed a chapter of the Playground Association of America with Mayor Haven serving as president. Other officers included Lucien Barnes, Mrs. H. C. Marshall, Mrs. W. S. Woodbridge, John Miller, and park board members Bernard Silberstein and Bishop James McGolrick. Everyone interested in playgrounds could join the association for a minimum fee of $1 per year.

Schools were the logical place to establish playgrounds, but members of Duluth's association eyed the city parks as well. Luther Mendenhall, president of the park board, assured them that the board would do everything in its power to aid the playground association. He reported that some locations within the parks had already been set aside for children, but that "the park board has always looked forward to an organization of this kind as the children had no instructors or supervisors to look after them."

Association members decided to raise enough money to establish at least one playground before the end of the year and hire two men as supervisors—one for the small boys and girls and the other for older children. They began their fundraising campaign in June with the goal of $1,000, but the money did not pour in as readily as they had hoped. It seemed that not everyone embraced the idea of playgrounds. A *Duluth News Tribune* editorial from June 29, 1908, bemoaned the lack of interest shown by the people of Duluth: "The men and the women have their parks, their clubs, their links and their socials and other places of amusements, but what have the children? The vacant lots are rapidly being filled up and many of those still unimproved are forbidden to the children by the owners, who want no trespassing."

Despite the lukewarm support, the park board announced that swings and sand piles for children would be installed at Portland Square. Unfortunately, the surrounding neighbors complained that the children were too noisy, and the board removed the playground equipment after only three days. The *News Tribune* described the scene vividly: "Little ones in scores watched in mute astonishment their little merry-go-round pole come down, their swings fall before the hands of the workmen, and all the apparatus which had been a joy to them carted away on a truck. Half a dozen little girls sat on the curbing and wept." The failure of this first experiment led playground advocates to realize that, to be successful, playgrounds would require adult supervision.

Duluth's First Supervised Playground

Duluth's playground association did not let the Portland Square fiasco stop them; members pushed the park board to allow the organization to install playground equipment at Lincoln Park. As a result of their persistence, the board agreed, but only as an experiment and only if the children were supervised. On July 17, 1908, the first public playground established by the Duluth Playground Association was opened at Lincoln Park, and the children loved it. Two supervisors—one man and one woman—kept the youngsters under control. The playground closed for the season in September, but Mayor Haven considered it an unqualified success and promised to open more the following year, but only if enough money was raised to buy the sites.

The playground association began an aggressive fundraising campaign in 1909, again hoping to raise at least $1,000 to carry on its work. With the support of the West End Commercial Club and the West Duluth Commercial Club, the association committed to paying the expenses to acquire equipment for two playgrounds, one near the Bryant School (Thirtieth Avenue West and Third Street) and another between Seventeenth and Eighteenth Avenues West on the lower

side of Superior Street. The playgrounds included swings, parallel bars, and other gymnasium apparatus.

The association was, however, unable to raise enough money to purchase property. At this point the park board stepped in and agreed to acquire the necessary land. By the end of 1909, the board announced that it would spend $3,300 for eight lots near Irving School (between Fifty-sixth and Fifty-seventh Avenues West on Nicollet Street) and $10,250 for the two and a half acres on West Third Street near Bryant School, which they named Harrison Park. The board also tried to purchase vacant land north of Wadena Street between Fifty-first and Fifty-third Avenues West, which neighborhood children had long been using as a ball field, but they could not negotiate an acceptable price with the West Duluth Land Company that owned it.

By 1911 the park board had installed playground equipment including swings, sand boxes, and parallel bars at several locations: Lincoln, Fairmount, Chester, Harrison, Lester, Portman, Washington, Portland, Cascade, and Lake Shore parks. A few of these parks also included baseball diamonds, swimming holes, and skating rinks.

In 1912 the park board added land for a playground on West Third Street near Emerson School, which Mayor Prince later agreed to name Observation Park at the suggestion of the Fifth Ward Hillside Improvement Club. But the playground association was unable to raise enough money to provide adult supervisors, which everyone recognized as essential.

In May 1912 playground expert Dr. Henry S. Curtis visited Duluth for a six-day campaign to help build enthusiasm for the movement. Following Curtis's visit, playground association members adopted a resolution urging the Duluth Board of Education to cooperate with the Duluth Board of Park Commissioners and the Duluth Board of Public Welfare to hire a director of public recreation and a play leader.

The revised city charter that took effect in April 1913 eliminated the park board, which stripped the playground association of its main source of support. Responsibility for the city's parks shifted to the mayor, and members soon began lobbying newly elected Mayor William Prince.

THE DARLING OBSERVATORY

In the spring of 1914, the Fifth Ward Improvement Club suggested to Duluth's mayor that the recreation area located on West Third Street between Ninth and Tenth Avenues West should be named Observation Park because "from it is obtained one of the finest views in the city." Mayor William Prince agreed, and the park was officially christened in May 1914.

The name Observation Park took on more significance in 1917 when John H. Darling opened an astronomical observatory in a corner of the park. Born in Michigan in 1847, Darling studied civil engineering at the University of Michigan. Upon graduating in 1873 he took a job as an assistant engineer for the federal government, working on surveys of the Great Lakes and the Mississippi River. He spent two years in St. Paul before coming to Duluth in 1884 to work as a federal assistant engineer for harbor improvements on Lake Superior with the Army Corps of Engineers. Between 1896 and 1902 he and Clarence Coleman supervised the construction of the concrete piers along the Duluth Ship Canal, replacing a crudely engineered wooden pier system first developed in the early 1870s.

Between 1902 and 1903 he mapped magnetic variations in Lake Superior west of the Apostle Islands. His work was published in 1904 in the bulletin of the United States Lake Survey and was used by ship navigators for decades. In 1910 historian Dwight Woodbridge wrote that "astronomy is a science of which Mr. Darling is very fond and he has made frequent contributions of articles on astronomical subjects to the daily press of Duluth."

When Darling retired in 1913, he turned his full attention to his astronomy hobby. Two years later the University of Michigan bestowed on him an honorary doctorate in engineering. That same year Darling approached the Duluth City Council and asked permission to build an observatory in a corner of Observation Park, which was ideally located on the Point of Rocks, roughly 325 feet above the lake. Darling and his wife Addie lived nearby at 532 West Third Street. The facility, he promised, would be built at his own expense and would be "open to the public to allow people to view celestial objects and to educate them in astronomy." He received permission in December 1915 and broke ground the following spring.

The wooden building was covered in stucco; a nineteen-foot dome rose behind what looked like a Greek temple with columns supporting a parapet. The telescope, mounted on solid bedrock, had a nine-inch, 261-pound refracting lens with a focal length of 130 feet; Darling designed some of its components himself. By the time the facility opened in May 1917 Darling had spent over $11,000—$3,500 for the telescope alone—and had a list of people waiting to use the telescope.

The observatory included a lecture room that seated up to twenty people, and about six times a month Darling conducted public sessions lasting as long as three hours. Over sixteen thousand people visited the observatory in 1930. That same year Darling was elected to the Duluth Hall of Fame.

When Darling died in 1942, he willed the observatory to the City of Duluth with a trust fund of $20,000 to continue its operation. Public viewing continued until 1956 under the direction of Darling's assistant, noted UFO enthusiast Frank A. Halstead. In 1965 the University of Minnesota Duluth (UMD) took control of the observatory. The telescope was moved to the UMD campus where it is on display at the Marshall W. Alworth Planetarium. The building at Observation Park, which had been repeatedly vandalized, was demolished in 1972.

Supervised Play becomes Recreation for All Ages

Playground supporters began to see real progress in 1915, including the introduction of the new term *recreation* for the supervised play they were advocating. In February they formed the Duluth Recreation Committee, which included Mayor Prince; Frank A. Brewer, president of the Duluth Board of Education; Robert E. Denfeld, school superintendent; Henry Cleveland, park superintendent; and a number of interested citizens. The committee brought in Mr. T. S. Settle, field secretary of the Playground and Recreation Association of America, to help it create a plan specifically for Duluth. The group's recommendations to the board of education and city council included a minimum expenditure of $3,000 to operate playgrounds from June 1 to December 31, 1915. The group suggested that the money should be provided equally by the city and the board of education.

By May the group announced that a three-month experiment would start on July 1 under direction of the city's welfare board and the board of education. John R. Batchelor, secretary of the local playground association and physical director of the Boys' Department of the YMCA, would be in charge. The board of education provided $80 and Mayor Prince pledged that the city would devote all its recreational funds for the summer to the experiment. The plan would be tried out at three existing playgrounds: Chester Park, Harrison Park, and Fifty-first Avenue West. Daily activities for children included organized games, team races, athletic competitions, and storytelling, alternating with fifteen to thirty minutes of free play.

In July the *News Tribune* reported that four hundred youngsters and grownups were using the playgrounds every day. The supervisors were surprised by the number of adults who participated. According to Batchelor:

> Adults are showing as keen interest as young people and children in supervised recreation, and attendance is increasing so rapidly that directors anticipate trouble in handling crowds. While children frolic in games mapped out for them by qualified supervisors, older folks play quoits, throw horseshoes, vie in athletic contests or bask in the sun observing the young people.... There has never been anything like it before. The sight of mature persons frolicking with children on the same grounds is something new at the Head of the Lakes.

At the end of the successful three-month experiment, the city hired Batchelor as public recreation director at a salary of $75 per month, with half paid by the city and half by the board of education.

For the 1916 summer recreation season, the city opened nine additional playgrounds, all located near schools. On July 23, 1916, the *News Tribune* headline declared, "Duluth Playgrounds are a Moral Force." Reporting attendances of between nine and ten thousand per week, the newspaper claimed that before the "new" way of supervised recreation, boys often ended up forming gangs and going in for some "mild lawlessness" while girls were left to their own devices and mostly played with dolls. Under the new system, "every child has a chance and...the strong characters lose none of their individuality while the more timid ones, who under the old plan of play had to stand back and look on, are given a chance to also participate and thus develop traits and characteristics that might have never come to the surface."

The popularity of recreation continued to grow every year, and the city administration and school board responded by adding more playgrounds and recreation centers. In 1919 the city built a fieldhouse at Harrison Park, and the estate of Duluth pioneer Henry W. Wheeler offered use of about twenty-five acres on West Third Street between Thirty-fourth and Thirty-sixth Avenues West for baseball games.

By the 1920s recreation for adults was just as popular as playgrounds for children. In West Duluth, Memorial Park—at the intersection of Grand Avenue, Elinor Street, and Central Avenue—was created as a memorial to honor those who served in World War I, but West Duluth residents soon requested that the city add a running track for Denfeld High School students to use. In 1927 Park Superintendent F. Rodney Paine opened the golf course at Enger Park, developed Chester Bowl as a center for year-round outdoor activities, and created a plan for the winter sports center at Fond du Lac Park. In 1928 dirt removed to construct Duluth's new city hall was hauled to

Observation Park, doubling the size of its play area. That same year Paine wrote in his annual report that "during the past three years considerable advancement has been made in providing recreational facilities for grown ups."

Duluth's recreation program continued as a cooperative venture between the school board and park department. In 1931 Paine explained that "the Recreation Department of the School Board was in charge of the play activities and games on active recreation areas located within park property, and the Park Department paid the salaries of the supervisors and performed the maintenance work on the grounds and buildings."

Recreation gradually took over the entire city park system, replacing the idealistic vision of Duluth's first park board with a more pragmatic view that recognized how twentieth-century Duluthians were using the parks. In 1911 the park board members had eloquently described their vision when they wrote, "The park system of a modern city not only aims at beauty, but strives to express the concept of the soul of the city. The parks of a modern city bear witness that its people are members of one great family. They are the concrete expression of civic consciousness in its highest visible form."

In 1943 Park Superintendent John Hoene wrote that "recreation, a word which was unheard of a few years ago, has become a very important activity or phase of a person's life. It should be pointed out...that all of the activities carried on by the Park Department are recreational..., whether you enjoy active recreation by participating in some sport... or if you participate in passive recreation by driving along the Skyline Parkway...you still are seeking and obtaining recreation." In 1957 Mayor Eugene Lambert changed the name of the Park Department to the Department of Public Recreation. The playground movement had achieved much more than its original supporters had ever hoped for.

In 2016 the Duluth Parks and Recreation Division maintained dozens of playgrounds at a variety of parks throughout the city,

PAINTERS PUT THE FINAL TOUCHES ON THE FIELDHOUSE AT MEMORIAL PARK IN 1942. LIKE MANY OF THE FIELDHOUSES BUILT FOR DULUTH'S PARKS, THE FACILITY LATER BECAME A COMMUNITY CENTER. IT WAS DEMOLISHED IN 2014.

[IMAGE: UMD MARTIN LIBRARY]

A HIGH DIVER PERFORMS AT ONEOTA PARK, AKA WHEELER RACE TRACK, CA. 1895. THE ESTATE OF HENRY WHEELER LATER DONATED THE PROPERTY, WHICH IS KNOWN TODAY AS THE WHEELER ATHLETIC COMPLEX.

[IMAGE: T. KASPER COLLECTION]

including Birchwood Park, Blackmer Park, Cascade Square, Central Hillside Park, Chester Park, Cobb Park, Como Park, Duluth Heights Park, Endion Park, the Franklin Tot Lot, Grant Park, Harrison Park, Hillside Sport Court, Irving Park, Klang Memorial Park, Lafayette Square, Lester Park, Lincoln Park, Memorial Park, Merritt Park, Minnesota Point Recreation Area, Morgan Park, Munger Park, Norton Park, Observation Park, Piedmont Park, Portland Square, Portman Square, Riverside Park, Smithville Park, Washington Square, and Woodland Park. The newest and largest of these playgrounds, Playfront Park at the Bayfront Festival Park, was created in 1989 as a community project led by the Junior League of Duluth. In 2010 the playground underwent a major renovation, again funded by the Junior League of Duluth.

Sports Facilities

The organized play encouraged at Duluth's playgrounds eventually led to organized sports, especially baseball and hockey. Dozens of neighborhood parks have baseball diamonds, football and soccer fields, basketball and tennis courts, and hockey rinks. Over the years the park department has responded to changes in the popularity of various sports. Duluth's first youth soccer tournament was held in 1977 on the playing field at Chester Park; in 2016 the city had over twenty soccer fields—nine at the Arlington and Lake Park athletic complexes alone. While a complete history of youth and amateur sports in Duluth would fill an entire book, several facilities stand out for their contribution to or reflection of Duluth's history.

Duluth's first municipal sports facility was Recreation Park, a baseball diamond located along Twenty-eighth Avenue West below Superior Street. Athletic Park replaced Recreation Park in 1903. Built for a professional baseball team, the facility hosted all sorts of sporting events, both professional and amateur, from school leagues to industry-related leagues made up of teams of employees. (See page 214.)

Another city-owned sports complex was created on the property that Henry Wheeler's estate allowed the city to use for baseball diamonds in 1919. Known for decades as Oneota Park, the area eventually became the Wheeler Athletic Complex. Wheeler, a pioneer of Oneota, famously walked from St. Paul to the Head of the Lakes in 1855 to establish a sawmill, the first in what is now Duluth. He built a home for his family at 3407 Grand Avenue; the large field behind the Wheeler house was the site of the fifth St. Louis County Fair in 1876 and became the event's home for the next thirty-five years. The facility had just a few buildings and a gravel track for horse racing.

In 1896 new buildings and a race track were constructed for the fair, and the facility became known as the Wheeler Racetrack. After the St. Louis County Fair moved to Hibbing in 1911, Wheeler's property continued to be used as a racetrack and whenever a large space was needed for events such as circuses and carnivals. In 1924 the city began proceedings to condemn Wheeler Racetrack and convert it to a playground. Duluth officially purchased the land in 1926, named it Henry W. Wheeler Field, and over the years developed it into a multiuse sports facility.

In 1971 Wheeler Field became the home of one of Duluth's two new indoor hockey facilities; it was used by high schools as well as neighborhood park teams that belonged to the independent Duluth

Area Hockey Association (DAHA). Prior to that, practices and games had all taken place at outdoor rinks within neighborhood parks. Indoor games were held at the Duluth Curling Club, a privately owned facility at London Road and Twelfth Avenue East that closed in the 1960s.

The arena at the Wheeler complex was named Peterson Arena for Ray Peterson, who had been the director of activities at Wheeler Field since 1941. In the early 1930s, Peterson created and coached some of Duluth's earliest youth hockey teams. Peterson Arena was destroyed by a fire in December 2004 when a propane tank on the facility's Zamboni exploded during a broomball game. The Wheeler Fieldhouse Skate Park now occupies the arena site. In 2016 the

WHEELER FIELD (FOREGROUND) AND A PORTION OF WADE STADIUM (RIGHT, CENTER) CAN BE SEEN IN THIS PHOTOGRAPH CAPTURED SOMETIME DURING WORLD WAR II, AS WITNESSED BY THE ORE BOATS STACKED TWO DEEP, WAITING TO LOAD IRON ORE TO BE SHIPPED TO STEEL MILLS IN THE EAST AS PART OF THE ONGOING WAR EFFORT.

[IMAGE: UMD MARTIN LIBRARY]

ATHLETIC PARK AND WADE STADIUM

Built in 1891, Duluth's first recorded athletic complex was a simple baseball diamond below Superior Street at Twenty-Eighth Avenue West called "Recreation Park." By the time the Duluth Cardinals professional baseball club entered the Northern League in 1903, Recreation Park was a memory and the team needed a place to play, so in April contractors hastily built a wooden ballpark with seating for three thousand in the shadow of Duluth's ore docks at Thirty-fourth Avenue West and Superior Street. Known as Athletic Park, it was a very simple affair: the seats were unadorned boards, and there were no locker rooms for players. The next year the team became the Duluth White Sox (winning pennants in 1904 and 1905). A portion of Athletic Park was converted to a hockey rink as a home for the Northern Hockey Club, but it was late December before the weather turned cold enough for outdoor ice.

While built for Duluth's professional baseball team, Athletic Park doubled as a municipal facility. When not used by the White Sox, Athletic Park hosted baseball and football matches played by children from local elementary and high school teams as well as adult teams made up of employees from various Duluth businesses (Clyde Iron Works fielded a particularly strong baseball squad).

The facility also hosted wrestling matches, and in 1909 two teams representing local Ojibwe and Dakota bands squared off in a lacrosse match. During World War I, shipbuilding firms and other outfits producing materials for the war effort formed a football league that played at the park. That league was where Harry Grant, father of NFL legend Harry "Bud" Grant, learned to play the game he taught to his son.

Athletic Park later became the home field of the National Football League's Duluth Kelleys, who entered the league in 1923. Sportswriter and broadcasting legend Halsey Hall, who later became famous as the radio voice of the Minnesota Twins, reported that Athletic Park had no locker rooms and that the playing field was an "uneven, coal-dust surface." (It was actually iron ore dust.) The Kelleys faced Curly Lambeau and his Green Bay Packers in 1924. Hall performed the referee duties, and the Kelleys beat Green Bay 6–3. (Green Bay played an exhibition game at Athletic Park in 1922, losing 6–2 in a game that featured a safety and an interception returned for a touchdown—neither offense scored a point.)

In 1926 the Kelleys became the Duluth Eskimos, a team that included Hall of Famers Ernie Nevers, Johnny "Blood" McNally, and Walt Kiesling as well as hometown hero Wally Gilbert and players primarily from Duluth, the Iron Range, Two Harbors, and Superior. They only played one game at Athletic Park: because of Nevers's star power, the NFL made the Eskimos play every game except their first on the road in order to sell more tickets.

Professional baseball in Duluth went dormant in 1917 when the United States entered World War I. It returned in 1934 with the revival of the Northern League. The next year Frank Wade fielded the franchise's Duluth team at Athletic Park. The Duluth Dukes—an affiliate of the St. Louis Cardinals—took home the league's 1937 pennant.

According to Duluth baseball researcher Anthony Bush, in 1938 "the call went out for a new stadium to replace dilapidated Athletic Park." The Citywide All-Sports Stadium Committee presented the city with a petition containing over 7,000 signatures supporting a $75,000 bond measure to build "All-Sports Stadium." The bond issue was approved in 1938. Duluth then established a Public Stadium Advisory committee, which included Olaf "Uncle Ole" Haugsrud, the legendary owner of the Eskimos and, later, the Minnesota Vikings. The advisory committee recommended a site adjacent to Athletic Park.

The project was financed with $7,500 from the state and over $80,000 from the Works Progress Administration (WPA). Following some grumbling by local unions, construction began on April 20, 1940. More than 380,000 paving bricks—all salvaged from the reconstruction of Grand Avenue—were used to build the ballpark, dubbed the Duluth Municipal All-Sports Stadium. In the end the project cost $230,880, some of it provided by Mayor Edward H. Hatch from his personal funds. (The photo at left, made in 1940 by L. Perry Gallagher, Jr., shows Athletic Park still standing left of the newly constructed All Sports Stadium.) The Dukes played their first home game in their new digs on July 16, 1941, losing 6–3 to the Superior Blues. (A photograph made during that first game appears on the facing page.)

The Northern League shut down after the 1942 season because of World War II and resumed play in 1946. Two years later five members of the Dukes were killed and most others severely injured when their bus was struck head-on in Roseville, Minnesota, as they drove along Highway 36. Only four members returned to baseball, and four years later Frank Wade sold his beloved team. He acted as adviser to the new owners until a heart attack struck him down in January 1953. The *Duluth News Tribune*, which called him Duluth's "Mr. Baseball," wrote that eighty-year-old Wade, "always vigorous and robust, cracked under the strain" of the 1948 tragedy.

According to Bush, "a year later the old stadium advisory committee came together to propose that the city rename the municipal stadium in Wade's honor." On February 3, 1954, the stadium officially became Wade Municipal Stadium.

The Dukes played without a major league affiliate from 1950 to 1954 when they joined the Cincinnati Redlegs system. The Dukes and Blues merged in 1956 as the Duluth-Superior Dukes. The team became part of Chicago's American League affiliate, bringing the White Sox monicker back to the Zenith City. In 1960 the team changed its name back to Dukes when it hooked its wagon to the Detroit Tigers. Twelve of the players on the Tigers' 1968 World Series Championship team had played for the Duluth-Superior Dukes, including Bill Freehan, Willie Horton, and Denny McLain.

By the end of the 1960s, Duluth's professional baseball team was once again affiliated with the Chicago White Sox. While the Duluth team thrived financially, the Sox struggled. In 1970, as a cost-saving measure, Chicago dropped its affiliation with the Dukes, who could not find another major league sponsor. It was just as well—the league folded the next year.

Wade Stadium continued to host high school baseball, and from 1971 to 1988 the University of Minnesota Duluth baseball team played its home games at Wade. The stadium even hosted rock concerts, with Willie Nelson, the Beach Boys, and Three Dog Night all performing at Duluth's municipal stadium in 1983. Still, the stadium fell into a state of neglect.

At the same time a new, independent Northern League formed in the early 1990s, and a community task force began a fundraising effort called "Save the Wade" to fund the ballpark's renovation. While little money was raised, the promise of a new team and a new league was enough for the city to authorize a $527,000 renovation project. The Duluth-Superior Dukes played at the Wade for ten seasons, taking the league championship in 1997, but failing to turn a profit. The club moved to Kansas City in 2002.

The following year the Duluth Huskies of the Northwoods League, a summer college baseball league, moved into the Wade. (The stadium has also been the home field of the St. Scholastica Saints men's baseball team since 2000 and the longtime home of the Hunters of Duluth's Denfeld High School.) The Huskies worked with the city in 2012 to find funding for much-needed repairs, including bolstering a leaning wall along the first-base line and repointing the building's brickwork. Their efforts to acquire state funding failed in September

2012, but the battle didn't end there. The following March the compromised portion of the facility's right-field wall collapsed, adding more urgency to the project. A 2014 bonding bill provided $2.3 million for the project, less than half of the $5.7 million requested, but enough to get things started. Another $2.3 million was added to the project in February 2015 through a grant from the Minnesota Department of Employment and Economic Development.

The project's finishing touches were completed in May 2015. Much of the work involved installing a new drainage system and artificial turf and reconfiguring the ticket stalls, concession area, and press box. The wall was reconstructed and the entire stadium was spruced up during the effort; some of the work was accomplished by volunteers organized by the Huskies. New lights and a new scoreboard were also installed.

St. Scholastica College athletic director Don Olson gave a lot of credit for the renovation to Mayor Don Ness, City Communications and Policy director Daniel Fanning, and former Huskies general manager Craig Smith for getting the project funded, telling the *News Tribune* that the three "deserved much of the credit for their vision for the project and their perseverance in following through with it." As a result in 2016 Wade Stadium—one of the last brick ballparks built by the WPA—was in better shape than when the Dukes first took the field in 1941. In May 2016 the softball fields adjacent to the stadium were rededicated as Dick Swanson Fields in honor of the longtime varsity softball coach at Denfeld High School.

———— PHOTO: T. KASPER COLLECTION ————

neighborhood, skating on a rink his family maintained on their property. The Frybergers generously opened the ice for the entire neighborhood to use. Growing up on skates, Bob Fryberger started as a hockey player for Duluth Central High School, then played for Dartmouth while in college. He went on to establish the mining company of Rhude & Fryberger, which operated several open-pit mines on the Mesabi Iron Range, but he never lost his love for ice sports. He spearheaded Duluth's emerging youth hockey program in the 1940s and raised the national prominence of the Duluth Curling Club.

Most famously, Fryberger coached youth hockey for the Glen Avon club, which he established in 1947 at Como

athletic complex contained five softball fields, four tennis courts, a bocce ball court, and a historic fieldhouse built in 1919. Wheeler Athletic Complex qualified for the Grand Avenue Parks Fund, part of the St. Louis River Corridor Initiative, and will undergo improvements in 2017.

In 2008 the Duluth Heritage Sports Center was constructed along Michigan Street at Thirtieth Avenue West as a replacement to Peterson Arena. The facility is owned and operated by the Duluth Heritage Sports Center Foundation, a community endowed and managed trust fund, and hosts Duluth high school and youth hockey games; one of its two rinks can be converted for indoor soccer.

Duluth's other city-owned 1972 indoor hockey facility, Fryberger Arena in Woodland Park, was also named in honor of a major contributor to youth hockey in the Zenith City. According to local historian Heidi Bakk-Hansen, Bob Fryberger grew up in Duluth's Hunters Park

Park in Hunters Park. Fryberger's Glen Avon peewees captured the 1951 National Championship of the Amateur Hockey Association of the United States. The championship game was played in New York City, and when they returned to Duluth the players, all either thirteen or fourteen years old, were greeted by thousands of fans and mayor George W. Johnson gave them the key to the city. Fryberger tragically died in a car accident six years later at the age of forty-nine. Fryberger's son Dayton played for the United States on the 1964 Olympic hockey team.

Besides the playgrounds, athletic fields, and other play and sports facilities owned and operated by the city, dozens of similar facilities can be found on the grounds of its schools and colleges. With new amenities such as disc golf, climbing walls, and interconnected trail systems, Duluthians young and old will have plenty of places in which to play and compete long into the foreseeable future.

HERMAN

DULUTH, MINNESOTA

Parks, Landmarks, Neighborhoods & Main Thoroughfares

ALL LOCATIONS APPROXIMATE

T. DIERCKINS 2016

PROCTOR

To Jay Cooke
State Park

Mission Creek

Old Mission Creek Pkwy.

Knowlton Creek

Stewart Creek

Bayview Heights

W. Skyline Pkwy.

Thompson Hill

Cody

Brewer Park

Lincoln Cemetery

Quarry Park

W. Skyline Pkwy.

Magney-Snively Park

W. Skyline Pkwy.

Old W. Skyline Pkwy.

Old Knowlton Creek Pkwy.

Kingsbury Creek

Fairmount

West Duluth ("Spirit Valley")

West En

Pie
H

Merritt

W. Skyline Pkwy.

Sargent Creek

W. Skyline Pkwy.

Braks Road

Spirit Mountain

W. 8th St.

Denfeld

Wheeler Field

Stewart Creek Bridge

Ely's Peak

Fairmount Park

Lake Superior Zoo

Central Ave.

Grand Ave. W.

Raleigh St.

W. 1st St.

Biauswah Bridge

210

Fond du Lac Park

Chambers Grove

Bardon's Peak

Grand Ave.

Spring St.

Norton Park

Fremont St.

23

Irving

W. Superior St.

Wade Stadium

Oneota

13th Ave. W.

Perch Lake

Smithville

Riverside

Clyde Ave.

Tallas Island

Keene Creek

Fond du Lac

Morgan Park

35

Idaho St.

88th Ave. W.

Clough Island (aka Whiteside Island)

St. Louis River

Bong Bridge

2

Ore Docks

St. Louis River

New Duluth

Commonwealth Ave.

USS Steel Plant Creek

Spirit Island

Grassy Point RR Bridge

Gary

Spirit Lake

St. Louis River

McOwn St.

39

Oliver Bridge

WISCONSIN

SUPERIOR, WISCONSIN

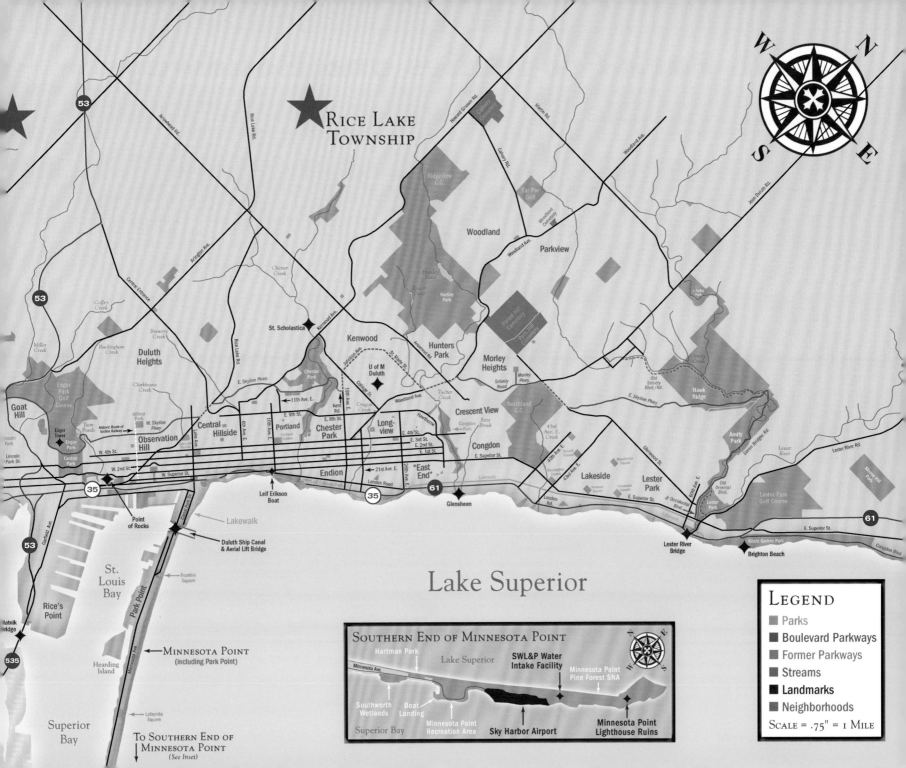

Duluth Park Properties and Roadways

1. Duluth Parks and Recreation Properties

Acreage provided by the Duluth Parks and Recreation Division and may not be 100 percent accurate; n/a = information not available.

Amity Park

LOCATION: Either side of Amity Creek from Skyline Pkwy. to Occidental Blvd.
NEIGHBORHOOD: Lester Park
ESTABLISHED: 1910
SIZE: 222 acres
ACQUIRED: Donations

Amity Park centers on Amity Creek, also known as the west branch of the Lester River. Its central feature is Seven Bridges Road. *See chapter 2, "Skyline Parkway," and chapter 14, "Undeveloped Parks."*

Arena Waterfront Park

LOCATION: Along Harbor Dr. west of the Minnesota Slip to Bayfront Festival Park
NEIGHBORHOOD: Downtown Waterfront
ESTABLISHED: 1966
SIZE: n/a
ACQUIRED: n/a

This park is essentially a pathway that provides access for pedestrian traffic from the Canal Park Business District to Bayfront Festival Park. It also includes a small square behind Amsoil Arena at the junction of Fifth Ave. W. and Harbor Drive, the location of a replica of the Statue of Liberty donated by Ray Bartholdi in 1976 as part of the national Bicentennial celebration.

Arlington Athletic Complex

LOCATION: 601 S. Arlington Ave.
NEIGHBORHOOD: Duluth Heights
ESTABLISHED: 1995
SIZE: 20 acres
ACQUIRED: Tax forfeiture

The land for this sports complex was obtained in the 1970s; three full-sized soccer fields were developed in the mid 1990s.

Bayfront Festival Park

LOCATION: Foot of 7th Ave. E. along the shore of St. Louis Bay
NEIGHBORHOOD: Downtown Waterfront
ESTABLISHED: c. 1990
SIZE: 11 acres
ACQUIRED: Purchase

Since at least the mid-1980s this site has been hosting the Bayfront Blues Festival, although back then it wasn't an official festival park. It became an increasingly popular site for outdoor concerts. In 1999 Lois Paulucci donated two million dollars to improve the park and build a permanent stage that was later named the Lois M. Paulucci Pavilion. Bayfront Festival Park is also home to Playfront Park, a playground. *See chapter 15, "Playgrounds and Sports Facilities."*

Bellevue Park

LOCATION: Skyline Pkwy. between 59th & 62nd Aves. W.
NEIGHBORHOOD: Upper Oneota (West Duluth)
ESTABLISHED: 1889
SIZE: 2.8 acres
ACQUIRED: Plat

See "Oneota Forest Park" in chapter 14, "Undeveloped Parks."

Birchwood Park

LOCATION: South of Heard St. at 102nd Ave. W.
NEIGHBORHOOD: Gary–New Duluth
ESTABLISHED: 1917
SIZE: 2.99 acres
ACQUIRED: Plat

A triangular three-acre park in Gary–New Duluth named for the stand of birch trees that surrounds it; contains some picnic and playground equipment.

Blackmer Park

LOCATION: Beverly St. & 84th Ave. W.
NEIGHBORHOOD: Morgan Park
ESTABLISHED: 1915, 1933
SIZE: 12.3 acres
ACQUIRED: Plat, donation

A sporting facility named for C. F. Blackmer, superintendent of the Minnesota Steel Plant's wire mill. The park was platted in 1915 as part of Morgan Park, a company town for United States Steel (USS). The land became a Duluth park in 1933 when USS gave all of its Morgan Park property to the city.

Brewer Park

LOCATION: Skyline Pkwy. west of 57th Ave. W.
NEIGHBORHOOD: Upper Oneota (West Duluth)
ESTABLISHED: 1926
SIZE: 43 acres (Paine 1936)
ACQUIRED: Donation

See "Oneota Forest Park" in chapter 14, "Undeveloped Parks."

Brighton Beach

Brighton Beach is part of Kitchi Gammi Park. *See chapter 8, "Congdon and Kitchi Gammi Parks."*

Bristol Beach Park

LOCATION: Between Congdon Boulevard & the Lake Superior shore from 87th to 93rd Aves. E.
NEIGHBORHOOD: Lakewood Township
ESTABLISHED: 1922
SIZE: 0.3 acres
ACQUIRED: Plat

Technically within the borders of Lakewood Township, this park is essentially a strip of land between Congdon Boulevard and Lake Superior that was part of the Bristol Beach subdivision platted in 1922. Its name was concocted to reflect its close proximity to Kitchi Gammi Park's Brighton Beach, developed at the same time.

Buffalo Park

LOCATION: Between Wallace Ave. & Vermilion Rd. from Hawthorne Rd. to St. Marie St.
NEIGHBORHOOD: Hunters Park
ESTABLISHED: n/a
SIZE: 3 acres
ACQUIRED: Plat

An undeveloped green space set aside as a park likely because it is too narrow for housing; the origins of its name are unknown. In 1927 Mayor Samuel Snively suggested that the easternmost parcel of this space should be landscaped to create a monument to A. F. McFarlane, whom Snively considered the first resident of Hunters Park. The city also lists this park as "Vermilion Park."

Canal Park

LOCATION: Either side of the Duluth Ship Canal
NEIGHBORHOOD: Canal Park District & Park Point
ESTABLISHED: 1905, 1938
SIZE: 2.81 acres (parking lot)
ACQUIRED: Purchase

Strictly speaking, Canal Park is the green space adjacent to the piers along the Duluth Ship Canal owned by the federal government and a parking lot east of Canal Park Drive owned by the City of Duluth. (The area most people consider "Canal Park" is technically the Canal Park District.) Most of the park is owned and controlled by the federal government, which also owns the canal, the Corps of Engineers Building, and the attached Lake Superior Maritime Visitor Center. In 1938 the city acquired 1.89 acres on the former site of the Wieland Flats tenement, built a parking lot, and named the lot "Canal Park." The city's parking lot/park was later expanded by an additional acre on land that once held King Leo's, Canal Park Inn, and Burger King restaurants.

Carson Park

LOCATION: North of Fond du Lac east of Mission Creek
NEIGHBORHOOD: Fond du Lac
ESTABLISHED: 1912
SIZE: 6.25 acres
ACQUIRED: Donation

Carson Park includes 6.25 acres of undeveloped land; its namesake is not recorded.

Cascade Square (aka Cascade Park)

LOCATION: Above 5th St. between Lake Ave. & 2nd Ave. W.
NEIGHBORHOOD: Central Hillside
ESTABLISHED: 1856, 1870, 1889
SIZE: 2.5 acres (originally 3.16)
ACQUIRED: Plat

See chapter 1, "Nineteenth-Century Squares."

Central Park

LOCATION: Between 14th & 17th Aves. W. from 1st St. to 4th St.
NEIGHBORHOOD: Observation Hill
ESTABLISHED: 1870
SIZE: 30.84 acres
ACQUIRED: Plat

See chapter 9, "Enger Park."

Central Hillside Park

LOCATION: Between Lake Ave. & 1st Ave. E. from E. 3rd St. to E. 4th St.
NEIGHBORHOOD: Central Hillside
ESTABLISHED: c. 1972
SIZE: 2.75 acres
ACQUIRED: Condemnation

A one-block-square park in Central Hillside. The park was created as part of the Duluth Model Cities Administration's effort and today contains basketball courts, playground equipment, and the Central Hillside Community Center. From 1996 to 2012 the center was home to the Duluth Parks and Recreation Department.

Chambers Grove Park

LOCATION: Along the St. Louis River west of Highway 23
NEIGHBORHOOD: Fond du Lac
ESTABLISHED: 1926
SIZE: 13 acres
ACQUIRED: Purchase

See chapter 10, "Chambers Grove and Historical Parks."

Chester Park

LOCATION: Along Chester Creek from E. 4th St. to Kenwood Ave.
NEIGHBORHOOD: Chester Park/East Hillside
ESTABLISHED: 1891 (Lower Chester), 1920 (Upper Chester)
SIZE: 108.2 acres
ACQUIRED: Purchase, donation

See chapter 4, "Chester Park."

Civic Center Plaza

LOCATION: 5th Ave. W. above W. 1st St.
NEIGHBORHOOD: Downtown
ESTABLISHED: 1923–1929
SIZE: 2.28 acres
ACQUIRED: Purchase, condemnation

The Duluth Civic Center is a collection of four buildings: the 1909 St. Louis County Courthouse, the 1923 St. Louis County Jail, the 1928 Duluth City Hall, and the 1929 Gerald W. Heaney Federal Building. The park is essentially the green space between the courthouse, city hall, and federal building. It contains the 1919 Soldiers and Sailors Monument, designed by Minnesota state capitol architect Cass Gilbert. In the 1960s county commissioner Joseph Priley led an effort to beautify the space. Today Priley Drive encircles the monument and a fountain which bears Priley's name.

Cobb Park

LOCATION: West of Woodland Ave. between Faribault & Redwing Sts.
NEIGHBORHOOD: Woodland
ESTABLISHED: 1997
SIZE: 5 acres
ACQUIRED: Purchase

A one-block-square park that originally served as the playground for the Woodland neighborhood's 1913 Cobb Elementary School (currently Woodland Hills Academy), named for civic leader and school board director E. R. Cobb. The school board sold the park to Duluth for one dollar. For many years the city operated a hockey rink and warming house at the park; it now has soccer fields.

Como Park (aka Glen Avon)

LOCATION: 2403 Woodland Ave.
NEIGHBORHOOD: Hunters Park
ESTABLISHED: n/a
SIZE: 2.65 acres
ACQUIRED: n/a

This small park in Hunters Park contains baseball diamonds used by Duluth's Eastern Little League and two hockey rinks for the Glen Avon Hockey Club. The park is a remnant of Hunter's Field, once used as a park by residents of Hunters Park. No records indicate when it officially became a city park or how it was named.

Congdon Park

LOCATION: Along Tischer Creek between Greysolon & Vermilion Rds.
NEIGHBORHOOD: Congdon
ESTABLISHED: 1908
SIZE: 35.86 acres
ACQUIRED: Donation, condemnation

See chapter 8, "Congdon and Kitchi Gammi Parks."

Corner of the Lake Park

See Sister Cities Park.

Downer Park

LOCATION: Between St. Paul Ave. & Vermilion Rd. from Anoka St. to Chisholm St.
NEIGHBORHOOD: Woodland
ESTABLISHED: 1918
SIZE: 17 acres
ACQUIRED: Donation

See chapter 14, "Undeveloped Parks."

Duluth Heights Park

LOCATION: Between Basswood & Arlington Aves. north of Mulberry St.
NEIGHBORHOOD: Duluth Heights
ESTABLISHED: 1928
SIZE: 5.02 acres
ACQUIRED: Purchase

Duluth Heights Park is home to the Duluth Heights Recreation Center and the Helmer I. Carlson Recreational Field.

Endion Ledges Park

LOCATION: Between 24th & 28th Aves. E. from I-35 to the Lake Superior shore

NEIGHBORHOOD: Endion
ESTABLISHED: 2009
SIZE: n/a
ACQUIRED: I-35 Expansion Usage Permit with MNDOT

This greenspace is named in part for the Endion neighborhood, itself named for the Ojibwe word for "my, your, or his home," and in part for the unique geology of the bedrock ledges exposed along the Lake Superior shoreline.

Endion Park

LOCATION: Between 16th and 17th Aves. E. south of E. 2nd St.
NEIGHBORHOOD: Endion
ESTABLISHED: n/a
SIZE: 2 acres
ACQUIRED: n/a

Endion Park occupies the northeast and southwest quarters of the city block located between 16th and 17th Aves. E. south of E. 2nd St.; the northwest quarter is home to Temple Israel and the southeast quarter is occupied by homes. The northeast portion is primarily an open space containing some playground equipment;.

Enger Park

LOCATION: Between Trinity Rd. (Highway 53), Observation Rd. & Skyline Pkwy.
NEIGHBORHOOD: Observation Hill
ESTABLISHED: 1921
SIZE: 129.89 acres
ACQUIRED: Donation, condemnation

See chapter 9, "Enger Park."

Enger Park Golf Course

LOCATION: West of Enger Park along Skyline Pkwy.
NEIGHBORHOOD: Observation Hill
ESTABLISHED: 1927
SIZE: 200 acres
ACQUIRED: Donation, condemnation

See chapter 9, "Enger Park."

Ericson Place

LOCATION: Between 45th & 46th Aves. W. above the CN Railway tracks
NEIGHBORHOOD: Denfeld (West Duluth)
ESTABLISHED: 1890
SIZE: 0.48 acres
ACQUIRED: Donation

See chapter 14, "Undeveloped Parks."

Evergreen Memorial Plaza

Evergreen Memorial Plaza no longer exists; *see "Memorial Park."*

Fairmount Park

LOCATION: Above Grand Ave. between 72nd & 75th Aves. W.
NEIGHBORHOOD: Fairmount
ESTABLISHED: 1901
SIZE: 58 acres (including the Lake Superior Zoo)
ACQUIRED: Purchase

See chapter 6, "Fairmount Park."

Fond du Lac Park

LOCATION: West of 132nd Ave. W. along Highways 23 & 210 & points north
NEIGHBORHOOD: Fond du Lac
ESTABLISHED: 1924
SIZE: 576.66
ACQUIRED: Purchase

See chapter 11, "Fond du Lac Park."

Fond du Lac Square

LOCATION: Between State Highway 23 & 4th St. from 130th to 131st Aves. W.
NEIGHBORHOOD: Fond du Lac
ESTABLISHED: 1856
SIZE: 2.25 acres
ACQUIRED: Plat

See chapter 1, "Nineteenth-Century Squares," and chapter 11, "Fond du Lac Park."

Fortieth Ave. East and Jay Street Park (aka Scott Keenan Park)

LOCATION: Between 40th & 41st Aves. E. from Jay St. to Dodge St.
NEIGHBORHOOD: Lakeside
ESTABLISHED: n/a
SIZE: 5 acres
ACQUIRED: Transferred

A one-block square along Lakeside's western border that features what looks like a circular stone patio. A clue to the formation comes from the property's previous owner, the City of Duluth Water and Light Department. Maps indicate the site was used for gas storage, which means that the circular formation was the base of a gasometer. Designed to hold coal gas, a gasometer was actually a large, cylindrical metal cage that contained an immense bag into which coal gas was pumped and stored. The gas was then piped to local homes, providing gas for lights in the days before electricity. The City of Duluth no longer recognizes this space, briefly called Scott Keenan Park for local runner Scott Keenan, as a park.

Forty-second Ave. East Lake Access

LOCATION: Between 41st & 42nd Aves. E. along the Lake Superior shore
NEIGHBORHOOD: Lakeside
ESTABLISHED: c. 1939
SIZE: 0.89 acres
ACQUIRED: Purchase

Walk down Forty-second Ave. E. below London Rd. to find paths to this small park hidden behind homes, left undeveloped to provide residents of Lakeside access to the lake their community is named for. The property was once part of the John Sebenius estate, most of which is occupied today by the Ecumen Lakeshore senior living facility.

Forty-third Avenue East Lake Access

LOCATION: 43rd Ave. E. along the Lake Superior shore
NEIGHBORHOOD: Lakeside
ESTABLISHED: 1892
SIZE: 0.50 acres
ACQUIRED: Plat

This small park was established by city council action to provide public access to the Lake Superior Shore.

Franklin Square

LOCATION: Between 12th & 13th Sts. S. from St. Louis Ave. to Lake Superior
NEIGHBORHOOD: Park Point
ESTABLISHED: 1856
SIZE: 2 acres
ACQUIRED: Plat

Franklin Square today includes the Franklin Tot Lot and the Franklin Bathing Beach (east of the S-curve). *See chapter 1, "Nineteenth-Century Squares," and chapter 13, "Minnesota Point."*

Fremont Point Park

LOCATION: Between 64th & 65th Aves. W. from Fremont to Natchez Sts.
NEIGHBORHOOD: Fairmount (West Duluth)
ESTABLISHED: 1990
SIZE: 9.48 acres
ACQUIRED: Plat

Fremont Point Park is a small undeveloped park hidden among homes built in the 1990s on Fremont Point east of Indian Point.

Fryberger Arena

LOCATION: 3211 Allendale Ave.
NEIGHBORHOOD: Woodland
ESTABLISHED: 1972
SIZE: n/a
ACQUIRED: Donation

See chapter 15, "Playgrounds and Sports Facilities."

Gary–New Duluth Park

LOCATION: North of Stowe Elementary & west of 101st Ave. W.
NEIGHBORHOOD: Gary–New Duluth
ESTABLISHED: 1890
SIZE: 6.8 acres
ACQUIRED: Plat

Gary–New Duluth Park essentially serves as a baseball diamond and sports field for the adjacent Stowe Elementary school. The park qualifies for the Grand Avenue Parks Fund, part of the St. Louis River Corridor Project, and will undergo improvements in 2017.

Gasser Park

LOCATION: 96th Ave. W. & Gasser St.
NEIGHBORHOOD: Within the Magney-Snively Forest Preserve
ESTABLISHED: 1911
SIZE: 2.08 acres
ACQUIRED: Plat

See chapter 14, "Undeveloped Parks."

Gateway Plaza

LOCATION: Between Superior St. & Michigan St. from Mesaba Ave. to 7th Ave. W.
NEIGHBORHOOD: Downtown
ESTABLISHED: 1979
SIZE: 1 acre

ACQUIRED: I-35 Expansion Usage Permit with MNDOT

Created to put the "Gateway" in the Gateway Urban Renewal Project of the 1960s and early 1970s, this park, originally called Gateway Landscape Plaza, is positioned where traffic exits Interstate 35 and enters downtown Duluth; when conceived, this point was also the northern terminus of I-35, so the site was technically a "gateway" to downtown Duluth. The state paid for 90 percent of the park's cost. According to its landscape designer, Thomas Thorson, the park's thirty-five-foot-tall centralized concrete parapet is meant to invoke a ship's sail or wave motion. The entire "gateway" concept was compromised in the 1980s when the expansion of I-35 allowed drivers to bypass downtown.

Granitoid Memorial Park

See "Clover Hill Triangle" in the "Street Triangles and Mall Drives" section of this appendix.

Grant Park (aka Central Field)

LOCATION: Between 8th & 10th Aves. E. from E. 11th to E. 12th Sts.
NEIGHBORHOOD: East Hillside
ESTABLISHED: 1890, 1918
SIZE: 3.11 acres
ACQUIRED: Plat

This East Hillside park was platted in 1890 but not established until 1918 when it was leased to the school district and named for the adjacent U. S. Grant Elementary school, itself named for the former president and Civil War hero. the school was renamed Myers-Wilkins Elementary in 2013. The park is currently outfitted with a baseball diamond, soccer field, and playground equipment.

Grassy Point Park

LOCATION: Foot of 50th Ave. W. at the St. Louis River
NEIGHBORHOOD: Irving (West Duluth)
ESTABLISHED: c. 1995; expanded 2004
SIZE: 100 acres
ACQUIRED: Purchase

Accessed from Lesure Street, Grassy Point Park is a wedge of land on Grassy Point at the mouth of Keene Creek bookended to the north and south by industrial sites that reflect the point's past, when it was home to Huntress & Brown and Merrill & Ring lumber mills and several coal docks. Lesure Street once led to the Arrowhead Bridge, an eight-hundred-foot drawbridge that connected to Belknap Street in Superior, Wisconsin.

Greysolon Farms Park

LOCATION: Between Heather Ave. & Frederick St. from Claymore St. to Pleasant View Rd.
NEIGHBORHOOD: Parkview
ESTABLISHED: n/a
SIZE: 4.48 acres
ACQUIRED: n/a

This greenspace, also known as Pleasant View Park, was formerly part of Greysolon Farms; *see chapter 14, "Undeveloped Parks."*

Grosvenor Square

LOCATION: Between 49th & 50th Aves. E. from McCulloch St. to Gladstone St.
NEIGHBORHOOD: Lakeside

ESTABLISHED: 1871, 1893

SIZE: 2.75 acres

ACQUIRED: Plat, donation

See chapter 1, "Nineteenth-Century Squares," and chapter 5, "Lester Park."

Harrison Park

LOCATION: Southeast of W. 3rd St. between Winnipeg Ave. & Devonshire St.

NEIGHBORHOOD: West End (aka Lincoln Park)

ESTABLISHED: 1909

SIZE: 2.68 acres

ACQUIRED: Purchase

Sometimes called Harrison Field, this small park in Duluth's West End was named for Henry H. Harrison, a civil engineer who from 1913 to 1920 served as the Washington County representative in the Minnesota State Legislature. Harrison had visited Duluth in the 1890s to consult on the city's water works and, convinced of Duluth's bright future, purchased some property in the Zenith City. A parcel of that property was purchased for Harrison Park. *See chapter 15, "Playgrounds and Sports Facilities."*

Hartley Field

See "Woodland Park" and chapter 12, "Hartley Park."

Hartley Park

LOCATION: Roughly between Woodland Ave. & Howard Gnesen Rd. from Arrowhead Rd. to W. Anoka St.

NEIGHBORHOOD: Woodland

ESTABLISHED: 1941

SIZE: 640 acres

ACQUIRED: Tax forfeiture

See chapter 12, "Hartley Park."

Hartman Park (aka Hartman Tract)

LOCATION: Between Minnesota Ave. & the Lake Superior shore from 43rd to 44th Sts. South

NEIGHBORHOOD: Park Point

ESTABLISHED: 1902

SIZE: 1.5 acres

ACQUIRED: Plat

See chapter 13, "Minnesota Point."

Hawk Ridge

LOCATION: Along Skyline Pkwy. west of Seven Bridges Rd.

NEIGHBORHOOD: Parkview

ESTABLISHED: 1972

SIZE: 235 acres

ACQUIRED: Purchase, conveyance

See chapter 14, "Undeveloped Parks."

Hillside Sport Court

LOCATION: Between 4th & 5th Aves. E. from E. 7th St. to E. 8th St.

NEIGHBORHOOD: Central Hillside

ESTABLISHED: 1973

SIZE: 2.5 acres

ACQUIRED: Purchase

This park occupies the site of the Franklin Elementary School, which was built in 1888 and torn down in 1979. The western portion of the property had served as the school's playground, unofficially called Franklin Park, until the city purchased the property from the school district in 1973. The city held a contest to decide on the park's name, and the winning entry was supplied by thirteen-year-old Cheryl Rock. The paved basketball courts fill a space once occupied by a hockey rink in the upper segment of the park while the lower portion is a mowed lawn.

Hilltop Park

LOCATION: Between 6th & 7th Aves. W. from W. 8th St. to W. 9th St.

NEIGHBORHOOD: Western Hillside

ESTABLISHED: 1907

SIZE: 2.75 acres

ACQUIRED: Purchase

See chapter 2, "Skyline Parkway."

Historical Park

LOCATION: 133rd Ave. W. along the St. Louis River

NEIGHBORHOOD: Fond du Lac

ESTABLISHED: 1927, 2007

SIZE: 0.11 acres

ACQUIRED: Donation

See chapter 10, "Chambers Grove and Historical Parks."

Indian Park

LOCATION: Irwin Ave. & Ash St.

NEIGHBORHOOD: Bayview Heights

ESTABLISHED: 1889

SIZE: 0.76 acres

ACQUIRED: Donation

This rectangular space occupies just three-quarters of an undeveloped acre northeast of the intersection of Irwin Avenue (aka North Seventy-eighth Avenue West) and Ash Street. The origins of its name are not recorded.

Indian Point Campground

LOCATION: Along Kingsbury Creek & the St. Louis River below Grand Ave. between 72nd & 75th Aves. W.

NEIGHBORHOOD: Fairmount Park (West Duluth)

ESTABLISHED: 1901

SIZE: 26.99 acres

ACQUIRED: Purchase

See chapter 6, "Fairmount Park."

Irving Park

LOCATION: Between 57th Ave. W. & Central Ave. S. between Keene Creek & Main St.

NEIGHBORHOOD: Irving Park (West Duluth)

ESTABLISHED: 1910

SIZE: 1.25 acres

ACQUIRED: Purchase

Irving Park was established as a playground for nearby Irving Elementary school; both facilities and the neighborhood that

surround them are named for American author Washington Irving. The park, which once featured two hockey rinks, was severely damaged in the 2012 flood, particularly the fieldhouse that doubled as the Irving Community Center.; the building was razed.

Janette Pollay Park

LOCATION: Along Amity Creek east of Jean Duluth Rd. & north of Evergreen Rd.

NEIGHBORHOOD: Parkview

ESTABLISHED: 1914

SIZE: 60.81 acres

ACQUIRED: Donation

See chapter 14, "Undeveloped Parks."

Jay Cooke Plaza

LOCATION: Between 8th & 9th Aves. E. below Superior St.

NEIGHBORHOOD: Portland

ESTABLISHED: c. 1987

SIZE: 1 acre

ACQUIRED: I-35 Expansion Usage Permit with MNDOT

This park was created by the construction of I-35 through eastern Duluth in the 1980s and and sits over the highway on top of Jay Cooke Tunnel. Its central feature is a statue of Jay Cooke erected in 1921. *See "Jay Cooke Triangle" in the "Street Triangles and Mall Drives" section of this appendix for a history of the statue.*

Johnson Park

LOCATION: North of Acre St. west of the convergence of Kenwood Ave. and Howard Gnesen Rd.

NEIGHBORHOOD: Kenwood

ESTABLISHED: 1927

SIZE: 0.52 acres

ACQUIRED: Plat

The City of Duluth lists the location of Johnson Park at Kenwood Avenue and St. Marie Street, but the two roads do not intersect. They once did—or were planned to—but the construction of Arrowhead Road changed the area considerably. The park is undeveloped and well hidden. The park's name came from the area surrounding it, which was platted as Johnson's Addition.

Jollystone Park

LOCATION: 717 W. 5th St.

NEIGHBORHOOD: Central Hillside

ESTABLISHED: 1971, 1999

SIZE: 0.49 acres

ACQUIRED: Donation

This small square greenspace is surrounded by homes and occupied by a large rock outcrop, which is likely why a house was not built on the site. Its name is a take on Jellystone Park, the fictional park (itself a take on Yellowstone Park) that was the home of Yogi Bear, who first appeared in Hanna-Barbera cartoons in 1958. The park once featured a picnic area, playground equipment, and a basketball court. The park was created as part of the Duluth Model Cities Administration's effort in the early 1970s to create two "kiddie parks" or "vest pocket parks" intended to serve children under ten years old on vacant lots within urban neighborhoods.

Keene Creek Park

LOCATION: Under the I-35 overpass between Grand Ave. & 63rd Ave. W.

NEIGHBORHOOD: Irving (West Duluth)

ESTABLISHED: 1985

SIZE: 10.6 acres

ACQUIRED: I-35 Expansion Usage Permit with MNDOT

Named for the waterway that winds through it, Keene Creek Park occupies a wedge-shaped space created when Interstate 35 was built in the 1970s. In 1975 the park placed second in the Federal Highway Administration's "Highway and Its Environment" contest. A portion of the green-space became Duluth's first dog park in 2006. The creek is named for Freeman Keen, built a homestead near its banks in the 1850s (the final "e" was later mistakenly added to his surname). Online maps label a greenspace north of Brewer Park along Keene Creek "Keene Creek Park." That park is located in Hermantown; it is not a Duluth park.

Kelso Park

LOCATION: 45th Ave. E. & Cambridge St.

NEIGHBORHOOD: Lakeside

ESTABLISHED: 1938

SIZE: 0.99

ACQUIRED: Plat

This triangular greenspace in Lakeside rests within a larger triangle bordered by Forty-fifth Avenue East, Cambridge Street, and an alley above London Road. Although listed as a city park, it is essentially the backyard of Lakeland Shores, a senior housing facility. Its namesake has not been identified.

Klang Memorial Park

LOCATION: South of Orchard St. between Boundary Ave. & Terminal Ave.

NEIGHBORHOOD: Bayview Heights

ESTABLISHED: 1945

SIZE: 9.8 acres

ACQUIRED: Purchase

A roughly one-block square outfitted with with two baseball diamonds, running track, picnic grounds, and playground equipment. While this park is technically within Duluth city limits, it serves as the official Little League field for the town of Proctor, Minnesota, located directly across Boundary Ave. from the park. Originally named Missabe Park and owned by the Duluth, Missabe & Iron Range Railroad, the space was purchased by the Bayview Heights Community Club, which in September 1945 renamed it in honor of Sergeant Lawrence C. Klang, the first soldier from Bayview Heights to be killed in action during World War II. The Proctor School District has maintained the park since 1955.

Kitchi Gammi Park

LOCATION: Along Congdon Boulevard from 61st Ave. E. east to roughly 76th Ave. E.

NEIGHBORHOOD: Lester Park & Lakeview Township

ESTABLISHED: 1922

SIZE: 153.24 acres

ACQUIRED: Donation, condemnation

See chapter 8, "Congdon and Kitchi Gammi Parks."

Lafayette Square

LOCATION: Between 30th & 31st Sts. S. east of Minnesota Ave.

NEIGHBORHOOD: Park Point

ESTABLISHED: 1856

SIZE: 1.83 acres

ACQUIRED: Plat

See chapter 1, "Nineteenth-Century Squares," and chapter 13, "Minnesota Point."

Lake Park Athletic Complex

LOCATION: Riley & Jean Duluth Rds.

NEIGHBORHOOD: Parkview

ESTABLISHED: 1995

SIZE: 20 acres

ACQUIRED: Donation

Also known as the Jean Duluth Soccer Fields, this sports facility includes five soccer fields used by the Arrowhead Youth Soccer Association, six baseball diamonds, and a pavilion dedicated in 2012 in the name of Bob Pratt, a longtime soccer organizer and volunteer who died in 2011. The land was donated by the University of Minnesota Duluth in 1972; the city operated a tree nursery on the site from 1972 to 2000.

Lake Place Park

LOCATION: Between 1st & 4th Aves. E. from Michigan St. to the Lakewalk

NEIGHBORHOOD: Downtown

ESTABLISHED: 1992

SIZE: 1.9 acres

ACQUIRED: I-35 Expansion Usage Permit with MNDOT

Lake Place Park was built over a tunnel carrying Interstate 35 through eastern Duluth when the highway was extended in the 1980s, creating a link from downtown to the waterfront. It contains several sculptures, including *Green Bear*, a gift from Duluth's sister city of Petrozavodsk, Russia, *The Stone* from sister city Växjö, Sweden, and *Arising*, a bronze by former Duluth sculptor Carla Stetson. In 1994 Lake Place Park, designed by Kent Worley as simply "Lake Place," won the Federal Highway Administration's Award of Excellence, its top honor, "bestowed on highways and related projects that move people and goods in the safest and most efficient way while maintaining respect for the environment and community." In 2016 the city was considering changing the park's name.

Lake Place Plaza

LOCATION: Southeast corner of Lake Ave. & Superior St.

NEIGHBORHOOD: Downtown

ESTABLISHED: 1979

SIZE: Less than one acre

ACQUIRED: Condemnation

This small space was created when Lake Ave. was widened in 1979 and today serves as an entrance to Lake Place Park. At its center is the Lake Superior Fountain, designed by local artist Ben Effinger.

Lake Superior Plaza (aka Minnesota Power Plaza)

LOCATION: Southwest corner of Lake Ave. & Superior St.

NEIGHBORHOOD: Downtown

ESTABLISHED: 1985

SIZE: Less than one acre

ACQUIRED: Owned by Minnesota Power

Although this public plaza sits on property technically owned by Minnesota Power, the city and power company have a joint ownership agreement governing it use. Each holiday season it becomes home to Duluth's community Christmas tree.

Lake Superior Zoo

See chapter 6, "Fairmount Park."

Lakeside Court Park

LOCATION: 55th Ave. E. from London Rd. to the Lake Superior shore

NEIGHBORHOOD: Lester Park

ESTABLISHED: 1920

SIZE: 0.42 acres

ACQUIRED: Donation

This tiny rectangular park is the center of Lakeside Court, a small development of eight houses established in 1920. Although it is listed as a public park, Lakeside Court includes no public access to the park or lake and essentially serves as backyards for the private homes that surround it.

Lakeview Park

LOCATION: Between 12th & 14th Aves. E. below Skyline Pkwy.

NEIGHBORHOOD: East Hillside

ESTABLISHED: 1891–1892

SIZE: 2.75 acres

ACQUIRED: Purchase

A rectangular portion of greenspace below Skyline Parkway that is both too narrow and too steep to support development, this park was likely acquired along with other property to create the original segment of Skyline Parkway (Rogers Boulevard).

Lakeview Manor Park

LOCATION: Centered on 53rd Ave. E. from Avondale to Oakley Sts.

NEIGHBORHOOD: Lester Park

ESTABLISHED: 1924

SIZE: 0.5 acres

ACQUIRED: Donation

This half-acre park in Lakeside is essentially a common backyard for residents living along the streets surrounding the block.

Lakewalk

LOCATION: From Bayfront Festival Park to Kitchi Gammi Park

NEIGHBORHOOD: Downtown, Endion, East End, Congdon, Lakeside, Lester Park.

ESTABLISHED: 1986

SIZE: 7.3 miles

ACQUIRED: Various methods

While Duluth's Lakewalk was conceived in the 1980s as part of the expansion of I-35 through eastern Duluth, it helps realize a dream of the visionaries of Duluth's park system for public access to the shores of Lake Superior. The multiuse trail began with a less-than-half-mile section of pathway in 1986 and has been expanded over the years to extend from Bayfront Park to Kitchi Gammi Park. From Bayfront Park to Canal Park the Lakewalk connects via Arena Waterfront Park to the Minnesota Slip Bridge and follows a sidewalk along the waterfront to Canal Park. From Canal Park it follows the Lake Superior shore to Twenty-first Avenue East, where the trail diverts inland to pass through Endion Ledges Park at Twenty-fourth Avenue East before heading under I-35 at Twenty-seventh Avenue East. From there it runs adjacent to the tracks of the North Shore Scenic Railroad to Sixty-first Avenue East. It then follows the avenue south to Congdon Boulevard and along the lakeshore to Brighton Beach in Kitchi Gammi Park.

Leif Erikson Park

LOCATION: From the Lake Superior Shore to London Rd. between 9th & 14th Aves. E.
NEIGHBORHOOD: Endion/East Hillside
ESTABLISHED: 1907 (as Cullum Park), 1909 (as Lake Shore Park), 1927 (Leif Erikson Park)
SIZE: 14.69 acres
ACQUIRED: Donation, purchase
See chapter 7, "Leif Erikson Park."

Lester-Amity Chalet Winter Sports Complex

LOCATION: Along Seven Bridges Road within Amity Park
NEIGHBORHOOD: Lester Park
ESTABLISHED: 1960
SIZE: 59 acres within Amity Park
ACQUIRED: Donation, tax forfeiture

Essentially a fieldhouse, the chalet was first constructed as the "Lakeview Sports Chalet" to serve as a warming house for hockey rinks used by the now defunct Lester Park Hockey Association of the Duluth Area Hockey Association. For many years the site was popular for snow sledding. The chalet and fifty-nine acres within Amity Park adjacent to it are currently operated by the Duluth Cross-Country Ski Club, which restored the chalet in 2014.

Lester Park

LOCATION: Between Lester River Rd. & Occidental Blvd. from Superior St. to Oakley St.
NEIGHBORHOOD: Lester Park
ESTABLISHED: 1889, 1894
SIZE: 46 acres (Paine 1936)
ACQUIRED: Plat, purchase
See chapter 5, "Lester Park."

Lester Park Golf Course

LOCATION: East of Lester River Rd. north of E. Superior St.
NEIGHBORHOOD: Lester Park
ESTABLISHED: 1931, 1978
SIZE: 152.65 acres
ACQUIRED: Purchase, tax forfeiture
See chapter 5, "Lester Park."

Lilliput Park

LOCATION: Above E. 5th St. between 3rd & 4th Aves. E.
NEIGHBORHOOD: Central Hillside
ESTABLISHED: 1971
SIZE: 0.49 acres
ACQUIRED: Donation

Lilliput Park was created as part of the Duluth Model Cities Administration's effort in the early 1970s to create two "kiddie parks" or "vest pocket parks" on vacant lots within urban neighborhoods (the other became Jollystone Park). Originally called Lilliput Land (for the fictional island populated by tiny people in Jonathan Swift's *Gulliver's Travels*), the park occupies the space where a house once stood at 215 East Fifth Street and was intended to serve children under ten years old. In 1978 the neighbors asked that the park be leveled, as it had become a magnet for vandalism and litter. The city considered removing it from its parks inventory, but in 1998 several community groups came together to give it a makeover with new sod, playground equipment, and a modest community garden.

Lincoln Park

LOCATION: Along Miller Creek between W. 3rd St. & Skyline Pkwy.
NEIGHBORHOOD: West End (aka "Lincoln Park")
ESTABLISHED: 1889
SIZE: 37.41 acres
ACQUIRED: Condemnation, purchase
See chapter 3, "Lincoln Park."

Longview Tennis Courts

LOCATION: 326 N. 25th Ave. E.
NEIGHBORHOOD: Longview
ESTABLISHED: 1907, 1931
SIZE: 64 acres
ACQUIRED: Purchase

In 1907 A. L. Agatin and four other Duluthians organized the Longview Lawn Tennis Club of Duluth in anticipation of the demise of the Endion Tennis Club, whose courts were being replaced by a housing development. The founders were concerned that with the loss of the Endion facility the only tennis courts in the city would be for the exclusive use of members of the private Northland Country Club and Duluth Boat Club. The following year the group secured the location and began making clay courts and building its clubhouse. The club reorganized under the same name as an exclusive club led by president Frederic W. Paine, who served on Duluth's first park board. The new club held its first tournament on July 2, 1912. In 1931 park superintendent F. Rodney Paine—Frederic's son—acquired the tennis courts on behalf of the city as the club was struggling financially due to the Great Depression. Today the Duluth Friends of Tennis, a non-profit community tennis association dedicated to promoting tennis in Duluth, maintains the Longview courts and clubhouse.

Lost Park

LOCATION: Below Skyline Pkwy. between 18th & 22nd Aves. W.
NEIGHBORHOOD: Goat Hill (West Hillside)
ESTABLISHED: c. 1890s
SIZE: 0.64 acres
ACQUIRED: Purchase

Lost Park appears to be essentially an extension of Enger Park south of the Enger Park Golf Course; in fact, the course's driving range abuts with the northeast portion of Lost Park. However, the property was purchased for park purposes nearly thirty years before Enger Park was established. According to retired park director

Kathy Bergen, the name Lost Park comes from the fact that there is no public access. Local residents led by Jimmy Padowski once partially developed the greenspace, constructing a tennis court and a baseball diamond, but those facilities are now abandoned. Today the Superior Hiking Trail passes through the park.

Lower Chester Park Playground

Lower Chester Park Playground, found between East Fifth and Sixth Streets west of Fifteenth Avenue East, is a segment of what is technically known as Lower Chester Park, the portion of Chester Park below Skyline Parkway to Fourth Street. A hockey rink was first installed at the playground in 1915. It later became the home of the Lower Chester Hockey Association, which in 1990 built the Rip Williams Memorial Rink, an outdoor rink with a compressor system that keeps the ice frozen when the temperature is above freezing. The rink is named for Rip Williams who learned how to skate and later coached at Lower Chester. His sons Tommy and Butch were the first brothers to ever play in the National Hockey League. See chapter 4, "Chester Park," and chapter 15, "Playgrounds and Sports Facilities."

Lyman Park

LOCATION: Below Skyline Pkwy. west of 29th Ave. W.
NEIGHBORHOOD: West End
ESTABLISHED: 1911
SIZE: 2.72 acres
ACQUIRED: Plat

Lyman Park in Duluth's West End was developed as a residential neighborhood in the early years of the twentieth century, named for its developers, brothers Ceylon E. and George N. Lyman Jr. Several streets were platted, but only a handful of homes were ever built along Lyman Street.

Magney-Snively Park

LOCATION: Roughly south of I-35 above Morgan Park, Smithville & Gary–New Duluth
NEIGHBORHOOD: West Duluth
ESTABLISHED: 1921, 1923, 1926
SIZE: 728 acres (Magney, 328.05; Snively 400.13)
ACQUIRED: Donation, purchase
See chapter 14, "Undeveloped Parks."

Manchester Square

LOCATION: Between 46th & 47th Aves. E. from Peabody St. to Colorado St.
NEIGHBORHOOD: Lakeside
ESTABLISHED: 1871, 1893
SIZE: 2.75 acres
ACQUIRED: Plat
See chapter 1, "Nineteenth-Century Squares," and chapter 5, "Lester Park."

Memorial Park

LOCATION: Between Grand Ave., Central Ave., & Elinor St.
NEIGHBORHOOD: Oneota (West Duluth)
ESTABLISHED: 1917
SIZE: 2.87 acres
ACQUIRED: Purchase, condemnation

A triangle of land originally less than three acres in size, Memorial Park was conceived as a memorial to Duluthians who died in World War I. It almost immediately also became a neighborhood playground. In 1928 twenty-two trees were planted in Memorial Park, and markers, each bearing the name of a West Duluthian who had served and died in World War I, were placed beneath each tree. One marker was for the unknown war dead, and in 1971 a marker was placed at the base of a flagpole in memory of Harold C. High, who died in service in 1959. Today only a handful of the markers—and the trees—still remain in Memorial Park. In 1935 the Works Progress Administration built a fieldhouse within the park that also served as the Memorial Park Community Center. From 1960 until 1996 a Lockheed F-94C Starfire jet once used by the Minnesota Air National Guard (and owned by the West Duluth American Legion) stood on a pedestal within the park. In 1984 a 0.37-acre triangle of land below Cody Street that once contained a used car lot (at one time named Crazy Carl's) was acquired and named Evergreen Memorial Plaza. In 1998 this new park became part of Memorial Park, expanding its footprint. The fieldhouse, damaged in the flood of 2012, was razed in April 2014. In November 2015 the city announced plans for $7 to $10 million in improvements that include a new community center. Financing for the project will come from the Grand Avenue Parks Fund, part of the St. Louis River Corridor Project. The work is scheduled for 2017.

Merritt Park

LOCATION: Between 40th & 41st Aves. W. from W. 7th St. to W. 8th St.

NEIGHBORHOOD: Denfeld (West Duluth)

ESTABLISHED: 1913

SIZE: 2.56 acres

ACQUIRED: Condemnation

First called Merritt Playground, this 2.5-acre square contains a fieldhouse, hockey rink, baseball diamond, and playground equipment. The park is named for Duluth's Merritt family, founders of Oneota Township, a predecessor to West Duluth. Brothers Alfred and Andrus Merritt both owned homes near the park. *See chapter 14, "Undeveloped Parks," for more about the Merritts.*

Michael Colalillo Medal of Honor Park

LOCATION: Michael Colalillo Dr. & Wadena St.

NEIGHBORHOOD: Oneota (West Duluth)

ESTABLISHED: 1990

SIZE: Less than one-quarter acre

ACQUIRED: Condemnation

This small triangular park and the road adjacent to it are named in honor of Michael Colalillo (1925–2011), a native of West Duluth who was awarded the Medal of Honor for his heroic actions of April 7, 1945, in the vicinity of Untergriesheim, Germany, during World War II. Both the street and park were created with the expansion of I-35.

Midtowne Park

LOCATION: Between Piedmont & 20th Aves. W. from 1st St. to 5th St.

NEIGHBORHOOD: West End (Lincoln Park)

ESTABLISHED: 1981

SIZE: 1.20 acres

ACQUIRED: Purchase & Usage Permit with MNDOT

This park is essentially made up of the nondevelopable space below elevated Highway 53 where it passes through the West End. It is named for nearby Midtowne Manor, an apartment building constructed to serve senior citizens. The park originally contained a children's sand pit, slides and swings, a tennis court, a basketball court, a bocce court, and a horseshoe pit.

Miller Creek Disc Golf Course

LOCATION: West of Trinity Rd. south of Lake Superior College

NEIGHBORHOOD: Piedmont Heights

ESTABLISHED: 2007

SIZE: 40 acres

ACQUIRED: Likely purchased along with the property that became Enger Park Golf Course.

This nine-hole disc golf course sits on property once used by the city as a gravel pit and is accessed via the parking lot of Lake Superior College.

Minnesota Point Pine Forest Scientific and Natural Area

LOCATION: South of the Minnesota Point Recreation Area

NEIGHBORHOOD: Minnesota Point

ESTABLISHED: 1938, 1990s

SIZE: 18 acres

ACQUIRED: Purchase, donation

See chapter 13, "Minnesota Point."

Minnesota Point Recreation Area

LOCATION: Southern terminus of Minnesota Avenue

NEIGHBORHOOD: Minnesota Point

ESTABLISHED: 1938

SIZE: 203.95 acres (including the beachfront from the Duluth Ship Canal to the end of the Pine Forest SNA)

ACQUIRED: Purchase

See chapter 13, "Minnesota Point."

Mira M. Southworth Lake Superior Wetlands Preserve

LOCATION: Bayside of Minnesota Point at South 41st Street & Minnesota Avenue

NEIGHBORHOOD: Minnesota Point

ESTABLISHED: 1999

SIZE: 10.3 acres

ACQUIRED: Plat

Known informally as Southworth Marsh, this parcel of land was created by dumping sand dredged from the bottom of the bay to maintain a channel deep enough to be navigable by ore boats and oceangoing vessels. The wetlands preserve was established at the request of Park Point residents and named for Mira M. Southworth, a longtime teacher at Duluth Central High School who spent many hours walking in the marsh and taking photographs.

Moose Hill Park

LOCATION: Northeast of Lester Park Golf Course

NEIGHBORHOOD: Lester Park

ESTABLISHED: 1941

SIZE: 80 acres

ACQUIRED: Tax forfeiture

Moose Hill Park is an undeveloped rectangle of land within a larger undeveloped space east of the Lester River Road and north of Highway 61. It is not the same as the Moose Mountain Scientific and Natural Area, which is 177 acres of hardwood forest owned by the Minnesota Department of Natural Resources found east of the Lester River Road 3.5 miles north of Highway 61.

Morgan Park

LOCATION: Between 88th Ave. W., Hilton St. & Falcon St.

NEIGHBORHOOD: Morgan Park

ESTABLISHED: 1915, 1933

SIZE: 8.95 acres

ACQUIRED: Donation

The land that makes up the park was originally home to the community's 1917 Good Fellowship Club. It became part of the Duluth park system in 1933 when United States Steel, which built the "company town" of Morgan Park in 1915, gave all of its Morgan Park property to the city, but was maintained by USS until the 1970s. The club was demolished in 1981. Today the park contains hockey rinks, playground equipment, and the Goodfellowship Community Center.

Morley Heights Park

LOCATION: Between the east & west segments of Morley Pkwy. from Leicester to Spear Aves.

NEIGHBORHOOD: Morley Heights

ESTABLISHED: 1922

SIZE: 1.17 acres

ACQUIRED: Plat, donation

Morley Heights Park is the center of the Morley Heights neighborhood, established by the Marshall-Wells Hardware Company as a community for its executives and named for the company's founder, Albert Morley Marshall. In 1921 the company purchased over eighty houses from the DuPont Company in Barksdale, Wisconsin. The houses were dismantled, placed on packing freighters, and shipped to Duluth over Lake Superior. They were then hauled up Woodland Avenue on sleds and reassembled. The park, donated to the city by the company, is essentially a town square and today contains picnic tables and playground equipment.

Morningside Park

LOCATION: East of Livingston Ave. between Rose & Everett Sts.

NEIGHBORHOOD: Morley Heights

ESTABLISHED: 1922

SIZE: 0.70 acres

ACQUIRED: Plat, donation

This tiny square in Morley Heights, named for a nearby street, contains a soccer field.

Munger Park

LOCATION: South of E. 8th St. between Munger Apartments (12th Ave. E.) & Trinity Lutheran Church (11th Ave. E.)

NEIGHBORHOOD: East Hillside

ESTABLISHED: 1973

SIZE: 0.5 acres

ACQUIRED: Transfer (from school district)

This tiny East Hillside park, outfitted with some playground equipment, originally served as the playground of the 1914

Munger School, which closed in 1973 and is now an apartment building. Both the school and the park were named for Duluth pioneer Roger S. Munger.

New Park

LOCATION: Between 51st & 54th Aves. E. south of Skyline Pkwy.
NEIGHBORHOOD: Parkview/Lester Park
ESTABLISHED: 2007
SIZE: 5.6 acres
ACQUIRED: Plat

This unimaginatively named undeveloped park is one of the newest pieces of Duluth's park system, created as part of the Hawk Ridge Estates housing development.

Norton Park

LOCATION: Between 81st & 82nd Aves. W. from Caldwell to Coleman Sts.
NEIGHBORHOOD: Norton Park
ESTABLISHED: 1912, 1944
SIZE: 2.71 acres
ACQUIRED: Plat

Norton Park was established in 1912 as part of the platting of the neighborhood that surrounds it. In 1920 the park became the home of Norton Park Elementary school, which served the neighborhood from 1920 to 1944; when the school closed, the property reverted to park land. The park once had a hockey rink and today has some playground equipment and the 1965 Norton Park Community Center. The park, like the neighborhood that surrounds it, is named for real estate developer James W. Norton, one of the founders of New Duluth.

Oatka Park

Oatka Park was the unofficial name of private property used as a public picnic and bathing area in the 1870s–1890s and later the site of White City/Joyland Amusement Park (1905–1909). It became known as the Oatka Beach Addition in 1902. *See chapter 13, "Minnesota Point."*

Observation Park

LOCATION: Below W. 3rd St. between 9th & 10th Aves. E.
NEIGHBORHOOD: Observation Hill
ESTABLISHED: 1912
SIZE: 5.52 acres
ACQUIRED: Purchase

In 2014 a portion of Observation Park was converted to a dog park. *See chapter 15, "Playgrounds and Sports Facilities."*

Old Main Park

LOCATION: Above E. 5th St. between 22nd & 23rd Aves. E.
NEIGHBORHOOD: Longview
ESTABLISHED: 1994
SIZE: 5.55 acres
ACQUIRED: Donation

Old Main Park occupies the site of the original main building of the Duluth Normal School, first built in 1902. The Normal School, later the Duluth State Teacher's College, evolved into today's University of Minnesota Duluth (UMD); the central campus was moved to its present location in the 1950s. The building was torched by arsonists in 1993, after which UMD donated the property to the city. Three of the building's exterior walls were bolstered in place while the rest of the building was demolished.

Oneota Park

LOCATION: West of Oneota Cemetery along Skyline Pkwy.
NEIGHBORHOOD: Oneota (West Duluth)
ESTABLISHED: 1913
SIZE: 23.53 acres
ACQUIRED: Purchased

See chapter 14, "Undeveloped Parks."

Ordean Park

LOCATION: Site of today's Duluth East High School
NEIGHBORHOOD: Congdon
ESTABLISHED: 1928
SIZE: n/a
ACQUIRED: Donation

Ordean Park no longer exists. Located between Thirty-ninth and Fortieth Avenues East south of Superior Street, prior to 1912 Northland Country Club owned the land, part of the former Howell estate. Five of the golf courses' original holes were located on this property—the fifth and ninth holes crossed the street. In 1912 the course was expanded and redesigned, and the club sold the land below Superior Street to Albert Ordean. When Ordean died in 1928 his will gave the property to the city to be used exclusively as "a recreational field" or ownership would revert back to Northland Country Club. In March 1954 the Duluth School Board asked permission to build a junior high school on a section of Ordean Park. Northland Country Club executed a quit claim deed and the city council voted to donate Ordean Park to the school board. Ordean Junior High School was completed in 1956; sporting fields and Ordean Stadium were later built on the site. In 2011 the school was expanded and renovated into the new Duluth East High School.

Ordean Court

LOCATION: Southeast corner of 5th Ave. W. & Superior St.
NEIGHBORHOOD: Downtown
ESTABLISHED: n/a
SIZE: 0.26 acres
ACQUIRED: n/a

Ordean Court (not to be confused with Ordean Court on the University of Minnesota Duluth campus) is a small plaza outside the Ordean Building in downtown Duluth. The space is owned by the owners of the Ordean Building, but it is used as a public space, much like Lake Superior Plaza.

Pennell Park

LOCATION: Between Arlington Ave. & Myrtle Pl. from Central Entrance Myrtle St.
NEIGHBORHOOD: Duluth Heights
ESTABLISHED: 1911, 1929
SIZE: 1 acre
ACQUIRED: Purchase

This small square in Duluth Heights, originally five acres known as Arlington Park, was first established in 1911. In 1929 the Duluth City Council renamed the park after receiving a petition from area residents who wanted to honor Minnie R. Pennell, "an active worker in the interests of her community." Pennell Park is also the home of the Duluth Heights Garden Club, Duluth's oldest garden club, established in 1927 by Pennell and others. In 1978 the city sold most of the park to a developer who built the Pennell Park Commons apartment complex on the property.

Piedmont Heights Park

LOCATION: Centered on W. 23rd St. between Piedmont Ave. & Springvale Rd.
NEIGHBORHOOD: Piedmont Heights
ESTABLISHED: c. 1975
SIZE: 12.25 acres
ACQUIRED: Purchase, tax forfeiture

This playground facility in Piedmont Heights was created to expand recreational facilities in the neighborhood beyond the small playground at Piedmont Heights Elementary. It contains a fieldhouse, hockey rinks, baseball diamond, and playground equipment. In 2016 the park was being considered as the site of a dog park.

Playfront Park

Playfront is actually part of Bayfront Festival Park; *See chapter 15, "Playgrounds and Sports Facilities," and "Bayfront Festival Park" in this appendix.*

Pleasant View Park

See Greysolon Farms Park.

Point of Rocks Park

LOCATION: Between 8th & 14th Aves. W. from Superior St. to W. 1st St.
NEIGHBORHOOD: Point of Rocks (West Hillside)
ESTABLISHED: 1964
SIZE: 11.95 acres
ACQUIRED: Plat

From the 1880s through the 1950s this property was part of an impoverished neighborhood first known as The Glen and later Little Italy (and, derogatorily, Skunk Hollow). Humble, haphazardly placed houses occupied this space until the 1950s when they were torn down as part of the urban renewal effort. In 1964 the Project Duluth Committee worked with the Duluth Women's Institute to turn the vacant land into a park. The women's institute offered money from a bequest left by the late Raymond W. Higgins, once the president of Duluth hardware wholesaler Kelley-How-Thomson; the bequest and additional funds donated by the Higgins family paid for landscaping improvements to the property. The family and the women's institute requested that the park be named Ray Higgins Observation Point. Although the park was dedicated under that name in 1965, the city calls it Point of Rocks Park. The park parcel surrounds Glenn Place Apartments and other private property, which splits the park into two halves.

Portland Square

LOCATION: Between 10th & 11th Aves. E. from E. 4th St. to E. 5th St.
NEIGHBORHOOD: Portland (East Hillside)
ESTABLISHED: 1871

SIZE: 2.75 acres
ACQUIRED: Plat

See chapter 1, "Nineteenth-Century Squares."

Portman Square
LOCATION: Between 46th & 47th Aves. E. from McCulloch St. to Gladstone St.
NEIGHBORHOOD: Lakeside
ESTABLISHED: 1871, 1893
SIZE: 2.75 acres
ACQUIRED: Plat

See chapter 1, "Nineteenth-Century Squares," and chapter 5, "Lester Park."

Quarry Park
LOCATION: East of Oneota Cemetery below Skyline Pkwy.
NEIGHBORHOOD: Upper Oneota (West Duluth)
ESTABLISHED: 2016
SIZE: 30 acres
ACQUIRED: Purchase, tax forfeiture

See "Oneota Forest Park" in chapter 14, "Undeveloped Parks."

Rail Park
LOCATION: Below Michigan St. between 7th Ave. W. & 11th Ave. W.
NEIGHBORHOOD: Downtown
ESTABLISHED: c. 1979
SIZE: 0.5 acres
ACQUIRED: I-35 Expansion Usage Permit with MNDOT

Rail Park was created as a result of the expansion of Interstate 35 through Duluth; much of it lies below the elevated highway. It contains tracks leading to the historic Duluth Depot, which serves today as the St. Louis County Heritage and Arts Center. A ramp in the western portion of this green space leads to a pedestrian walkway that crosses above I-35 along the path of Eleventh Avenue West.

Ray Higgins Observation Point
See "Point of Rocks Park."

Scott Keenan Park
See "Fortieth Ave. East and Jay Street Park."

Reverend L. F. Merritt Memorial Park
LOCATION: East of 46th Ave. W. between Michigan & 1st Sts.
NEIGHBORHOOD: Oneota (West Duluth)
ESTABLISHED: 1924
SIZE: 0.5 acres
ACQUIRED: Donation

In 1924 a park was established on a half-acre of this rectangle, a gift from the Merritt family, located adjacent to the L. F. Merritt Memorial Methodist Episcopal Church. The church was razed in 1992 and the park expanded at that time.

Riverside Park
LOCATION: West of Riverside Dr. above Industrial Ave.
NEIGHBORHOOD: Riverside
ESTABLISHED: 1936

SIZE: 1.3 acres
ACQUIRED: Donation

Riverside residents use this space for community garden plots and like most Duluthians may not be aware it is a public park.

Riverside Playground
LOCATION: Manitou St. and Cato Ave.
NEIGHBORHOOD: Riverside
ESTABLISHED: 1930
SIZE: 3 acres
ACQUIRED: Donation

A triangle of land outfitted with some playground equipment adjacent to the Riverside neighborhood that was developed in 1918 as a company town for the McDougall-Duluth Shipbuilding Company. The park land was donated to the city in 1930.

Rose Garden
Duluth's rose garden is a 4.4-acre section of Leif Erikson Park; *See chapter 7, "Leif Erikson Park."*

Rose Park
See "Morningside Park."

Russell Square
LOCATION: Between 42nd & 43rd Aves. E. from Pitt St. to Jay St.
NEIGHBORHOOD: Lakeside
ESTABLISHED: 1871, 1893
SIZE: 2.75 acres
ACQUIRED: Plat

See chapter 1, "Nineteenth-Century Squares," and chapter 5, "Lester Park."

Short Line Park
Those using online maps have encountered a greenspace labelled Short Line Park southwest of Magney-Snively State Park along Becks Road. The map is incorrect; this area is not a Duluth city park but rather a small housing development named Short Line Park after a railway that once passed near the location.

Sister Cities Park (aka Corner of the Lake Park)
LOCATION: East of Lake Ave. between I-35 & Lake Superior
NEIGHBORHOOD: Downtown
ESTABLISHED: 2012
SIZE: n/a
ACQUIRED: I-35 Expansion Usage Permit with MNDOT

Originally—and unofficially—named Corner of the Lake Park, this greenspace was created after the construction of a large sanitary sewer overflow storage facility at the same location; the park sits atop the tank. (Duluth has four other similar holding tanks at Sixtieth, Fifty-second, Twenty-first, and Eighteenth Avenues East.) Because of its location the park serves as an extension of the connection between the Lakewalk and Lake Place Park. Its location also provides its former name: the park is perched at the very southwest corner of Lake Superior. Today the park contains artistic elements designed as representations of Duluth's four sister cities—Växjö, Sweden; Petrozavodsk, Russia; Ohara-Isumi City, Japan; and Thunder Bay, Canada—as well as a signpost

showing the direction and distance to each sister city. Monuments to Duluth's sister cities also exist within Lake Place Park and Enger Park.

Smithville Park
LOCATION: South of Clyde Ave. between 89th & 91st Aves. W.
NEIGHBORHOOD: Smithville
ESTABLISHED: n/a
SIZE: 6.09 acres
ACQUIRED: n/a

Sometimes called Smithville Playground, this wooded, undeveloped rectangular park in the southeast portion of the Smithville neighborhood is roughly one square block in size and bisected diagonally by Stewart Creek. It once contained a baseball diamond.

Southworth Marsh
See Mira M. Southworth Lake Superior Wetlands Preserve.

Spirit Mountain Recreation Area
LOCATION: Between I-35 & Grand Ave. above Norton Park & Riverside
NEIGHBORHOOD: West Duluth (Norton Park/Riverside)
ESTABLISHED: 1973
SIZE: 1,038 acres
ACQUIRED: State legislation

See chapter 14, "Undeveloped Parks."

Stanley Park
LOCATION: Blackman Ave. & Englewood Dr.
NEIGHBORHOOD: Kenwood
ESTABLISHED: 1926
SIZE: 1.11 acres
ACQUIRED: Donation

This small rectangle of undeveloped land rests among a handful of homes north of Arrowhead Road; the surrounding homeowners may not even be aware it is a park. Its namesake is Stanislaus Swapinski, who changed his name to Stanley Spencer after emigrating from Poland. Spencer donated the property in 1926. The *Duluth News Tribune* explained that "a stone brought from Poland, Mr. Spencer's native land, in 1907 was placed in the center of several stones located in a hole dug in the park property."

Stoney Point
NEIGHBORHOOD: Duluth Township
LOCATION: North end of Congdon Blvd. along Lake Superior
ESTABLISHED: ca. 1925
SIZE: n/a
ACQUIRED: Donation

While this rocky stretch of beach is technically within Duluth Township, it sits on property donated to the City of Duluth by Chester Congdon. *See chapter 8, "Congdon and Kitchi Gammi Park."*

Strickland Park
LOCATION: Between Mesaba Ave., 4th Ave. W. & W. 4th St.
NEIGHBORHOOD: Central Hillside

ESTABLISHED: 1925
SIZE: 0.36 acres
ACQUIRED: Donation

A triangle of undevelopable land positioned where Mesaba Avenue intersects with two streets, Strickland Park was named to honor William P. Strickland, a veteran of the Civil War who fought at Gettysburg. Strickland settled in Duluth in 1874, later becoming an assistant state weighmaster. His family donated the land eleven years after his death.

Twin Ponds
LOCATION: Buckingham Creek along Skyline Pkwy.
NEIGHBORHOOD: Observation Hill
ESTABLISHED: c. 1895
SIZE: 14.89 acres
ACQUIRED: Purchase

Originally called Gem Lakes, Twin Ponds were created in the 1890s along with the first section of Skyline Parkway by damming Buckingham Creek; the site was designed as a picnic area for those taking horse-and-carriage drives along the parkway. Today the ponds are primarily used as swimming and fishing holes. Buckingham Creek is named for Frederick A. Buckingham, a surveyor who established a homestead along the creek in the 1850s.

Unnamed Dog Park
LOCATION: Riley Rd. west of Jean Duluth Rd.
NEIGHBORHOOD: Parkview
ESTABLISHED: 2015
SIZE: 3.5 acres
ACQUIRED: n/a

Duluth's newest dog park is located roughly one quarter of a mile north of the Lake Park Athletic Complex. As of fall 2016 officials were considering naming the facility Jean Duluth Dog Park.

Unnamed Park
LOCATION: North of MacFarlane Rd. along the east branch of Chester Creek
NEIGHBORHOOD: Kenwood
ESTABLISHED: 2002
SIZE: 17 acres
ACQUIRED: Trade

The land that makes up this yet-to-be-named park became city property in 2002 when developer John Hovland asked the city to swap this area with land he had given to Duluth in 1974 to be used as a park for a housing development that never developed.

Unity Park
LOCATION: Southwest corner of Gary St. & Commonwealth Ave.
NEIGHBORHOOD: Gary–New Duluth
ESTABLISHED: 1992
SIZE: 0.25 acres
ACQUIRED: Plat

This three-thousand-square-foot park in Gary–New Duluth was developed on city property by the Gary–New Duluth Community Club and, according to the *Duluth News Tribune*, was named Unity Park to ease "lingering conflicts over zoning and a controversial landfill in the area." Unity Park does not appear on the city's list of park properties.

University Park
LOCATION: Above London Rd. at 60th Ave. E.
NEIGHBORHOOD: Lester Park
ESTABLISHED: Unknown
SIZE: 2.75 acres
ACQUIRED: Donation

The property that makes up University Park was part of a parcel of land purchased for the 1889 Lester River Fish Hatchery. The property was purchased by the University of Minnesota Duluth after the hatchery closed in 1946. The original hatchery building remains on the south side of London Road. University Park, on the north side of the road, is a half-block square of groomed lawn.

Vermilion Park
See Buffalo Park.

Wade Stadium Athletic Complex
LOCATION: 101 N. 34th Ave. W.
NEIGHBORHOOD: Oneota (West Duluth)
ESTABLISHED: 1941
SIZE: 22 acres
ACQUIRED: Purchase
See chapter 15, "Playgrounds and Sports Facilities."

Wallbank's Park
LOCATION: Centered on Exeter St. west of Pacific Ave.
NEIGHBORHOOD: West End (aka "Lincoln Park")
ESTABLISHED: 1918
SIZE: 0.91 acres
ACQUIRED: Donation

This little-known park sits in the center of eighty acres once owned by Dr. Samuel Seddon Walbank, Duluth's first, and at one time only, physician. The family donated the land to the city as a memorial to Dr. Walbank in 1918, nearly thirty years after his death. According to researcher Heidi Bakk-Hansen, the space was supposed to be called Walbank Memorial Park, though the "memorial" part has fallen away and Walbank's name is misspelled.

Washington Park
LOCATION: 310 N. 1st Ave. W.
NEIGHBORHOOD: Central Hillside
ESTABLISHED: Unknown
SIZE: .25 acres
ACQUIRED: n/a

Washington Park is a tiny greenspace at the northeast corner of Third Street and First Avenue West, which once contained the playground of the adjacent Washington Junior High School. After the school closed, the building was acquired by Artspace, a nonprofit real estate developer, which transformed it into an affordable space for artists to live and work, known today as the Washington Studios Artists Cooperative.

Washington Square
LOCATION: Between 42nd & 43rd Aves. E. from Superior St. to Regent St.

NEIGHBORHOOD: Lakeside
ESTABLISHED: 1871, 1893
SIZE: 2.75 acres
ACQUIRED: Plat
See chapter 1, "Nineteenth-Century Squares," and chapter 5, "Lester Park."

Waterfront Park
See Endion Ledges Park.

Waverly Park
LOCATION: Below Snively Rd. between Laurie St. & Lakeview Dr.
NEIGHBORHOOD: Hunters Park
ESTABLISHED: 1926
SIZE: 2.21 acres
ACQUIRED: n/a

This small island of greenspace in Hunters Park is named for a neighborhood that once spanned today's Hunters Park and Chester Park–UMD neighborhoods from Snively Road to St. Marie Street between Lakeview Drive and Woodland Avenue. Today's park was the old neighborhood's northeast corner. Today's Hunters Park neighborhood includes Waverly Park, Kenilworth Park, and Glen Avon, all once considered individual neighborhoods.

Web Woods
LOCATION: Between Blackman Ave. & Pecan Ave. from North Oak Bend to Boulder Dr.
NEIGHBORHOOD: Duluth Heights
ESTABLISHED: 2012
SIZE: 18 acres
ACQUIRED: Tax forfeiture

For over thirty years author and Marshall School science teacher Larry Weber used this greenspace in Duluth Heights—once a sixty-acre mix of hardwood forest and wetlands—as an outdoor classroom, taking his seventh-grade students to the site twice a week for hands-on learning. Before Weber, generations of Duluth Heights residents used the site as an unofficial park, which at the time was tax-forfeited property. In 2004, despite citizen protests, the city sold half the site to Summit Management, which built the Boulder Ridge and Summit Ridge luxury apartment complexes. Within a few years, another twenty acres were sold to the Miller Dwan Foundation for the Solvay Hospice House and the Amberwing Center for Youth and Family Well-Being. The remaining eighteen acres of forested land were set aside as a park; it was dedicated in honor of Weber when he retired in 2012. The pond within its borders is called Marshall Pond, named for the nearby school.

Wheeler Athletic Complex
LOCATION: 3500 Grand Ave.
NEIGHBORHOOD: Oneota (West Duluth)
ESTABLISHED: 1926
SIZE: 29.11 acres
ACQUIRED: Purchase
See chapter 15, "Playgrounds and Sports Facilities."

Winnipeg Park
LOCATION: 27th Ave. W. & Winnipeg Ave.
NEIGHBORHOOD: West End

ESTABLISHED: n/a

SIZE: 0.02 acres

ACQUIRED: n/a

Little is known about this small triangle of greenspace in an otherwise residential neighborhood.

Woodland Park

LOCATION: Between Woodland & Allendale Aves. south of Anoka St.

NEIGHBORHOOD: Woodland

ESTABLISHED: 1929

SIZE: 10 acres

ACQUIRED: Donation

Donated by the Hartley family and originally called Hartley Field, today Woodland Park is the home of Fryberger Arena, the Woodland Community Club, the John Baggs Memorial Field (Duluth Eastern Little League), the Tony Emanuel Memorial Field, three tennis courts, and two outdoor hockey rinks. *See chapter 12, "Hartley Park."*

Zenith Park

Zenith Park was an early name of today's Enger Park, not including the property that is now the Enger Park Golf Course. *See chapter 9, "Enger Park," for the history of Zenith Park.* Zenith Park was also the name of an amusement park owned by real estate developer E. P. Alexander that operated on Whiteside (aka Clough) Island in the St. Louis River during the 1890s.

---

2. Street Triangles and Mall Drives

One often overlooked aspect of Duluth's park system is its street triangles, most often formed where three roads converge, creating a triangular island of undevelopable land. A few have been turned into greenspaces tended by neighborhood garden clubs. Most are identified simply by the names of the streets that surround them. (See also Strickland Park and Winnipeg Park.) Acreage provided by the Duluth Parks and Recreation Division; n/a = information not available.

Central Entrance Triangle

NEIGHBORHOOD: Hillside

ESTABLISHED: n/a

SIZE: 0.48 acres

Also known as the "Fifth Avenue East and Ninth Street Triangle," this triangle sits adjacent to a parking lot on the same parcel of property occupied by Udac, a nonprofit organization licensed and regulated by the State of Minnesota Department of Human Services. The triangle contains a public orchard/garden.

Clover Hill Triangle

NEIGHBORHOOD: Longview

ESTABLISHED: 1890, 1959

SIZE: 0.05 acres

This triangle is also known as "Twenty-fifth Avenue East and Seventh Street Triangle" and Granitoid Memorial Park for the streets that surround it, made of a particularly strong concrete formed with horizontal grooves to allow better traction for horses. Duluth's

granitoid streets were the first in Minnesota (1909) and are among the few that remain in the nation. Many historians consider them the oldest surviving concrete-paved roadways in the United States. The Longview Garden Club maintains the garden within the triangle.

Fairmount Park Triangle

NEIGHBORHOOD: Fairmount

ESTABLISHED: n/a

SIZE: 0.11 acres

Also called "Seventy-First Avenue West & Grand Avenue Triangle"

Fifth Ave. W. Mall

LOCATION: Along 5th Ave. W. from Michigan St. to W. 1st St.

NEIGHBORHOOD: Downtown

ESTABLISHED: 1969

SIZE: 2.89 acres

ACQUIRED: Plat

The mall is a greenspace between two lanes of divided Fifth Ave. W., developed in the mid-1960s to create a dramatic entrance to Duluth's Civic Center as part of the Gateway Urban Renewal Project.

Fifty-ninth Ave. W. Mall

LOCATION: Along 59th Ave. W. from Main St. to W. 8th St.

NEIGHBORHOOD: Spirit Valley (West Duluth)

ESTABLISHED: 1920

SIZE: 2.9 acres

ACQUIRED: Plat

This "park" is actually a tree-lined median that divides Fifty-ninth Avenue West.

Forty-seventh Ave. E. & London Rd. & Regent St. Triangle

NEIGHBORHOOD: Lakeside

ESTABLISHED: 1892

SIZE: 0.14 acres

ACQUIRED: Plat

Greysolon Block Triangle

LOCATION: The convergence of Greysolon Rd., Jefferson St. & 23rd Ave. E.

NEIGHBORHOOD: East End

ESTABLISHED: 1922

SIZE: 0.69 acres

ACQUIRED: Plat

Hazelwood Triangle

LOCATION: Southeast corner of 39th Ave. W. & Traverse St.

NEIGHBORHOOD: Oneota

ESTABLISHED: 1870

SIZE: 0.12 acres

ACQUIRED: Plat

Also known as the "Thirty-ninth Ave W. and Traverse St. Triangle," this triangle gets its name because it sits within a subdivision originally named Hazelwood Park. Traverse Street, which ran adjacent to railroad tracks, no longer exists—and neither does this triangle. The property now belongs to St. Germain's Glass, which

long owned the adjacent property. Traverse Street ran essentially along the same path as today's West Second Street.

Heritage Park

LOCATION: The convergence of Woodland Ave., E. 4th St. & 20th Ave. E.

NEIGHBORHOOD: Endion

ESTABLISHED: 1910

SIZE: 0.12 acres

ACQUIRED: Plat

Heritage Park, sometimes called Heritage Garden, was first known as the "Woodland Avenue and Fourth Street Triangle" and was later named Dickerman Square, likely after Gilbert and Charles Dickerman, two brothers who took over their father's real estate development firm, Dickerman Investment Co. Plans to reconstruct East Fourth Street may alter or eliminate this park.

Jay Cooke Triangle

LOCATION: At the convergence of Superior St., London Rd. & 9th Ave. E

NEIGHBORHOOD: East Hillside

ESTABLISHED: 1870

SIZE: 0.01 acres

Jay Cooke Triangle, originally "London Road and Superior Street Triangle," was eliminated when Interstate 35 was extended through Duluth. When the park was originally platted in 1870, Superior Street and London Road converged at Ninth Avenue East. The triangle, directly in front of the Kitchi Gammi Club, became Jay Cooke Triangle in 1921 when a statue of Jay Cooke, who invested heavily in Duluth in the 1860s, was installed at the site. Following the highway expansion the statue was relocated to Jay Cooke Plaza, a new park along the south side of Superior Street between Eighth and Ninth Avenues East above the Jay Cooke Tunnel. *See chapter 7, "Leif Erikson Park."*

Lester Park Library Triangle

NEIGHBORHOOD: Lester Park

ESTABLISHED: 1892

SIZE: 1.17 acres

Also called the "Fifty-fourth Avenue East and Tioga Street Triangle," this greenspace is home to the Lester Park Community Center, which occupies the building that originally served as the Lester Park Branch of the Duluth Public Library.

Mesaba Ave. & Central Entrance Triangle

NEIGHBORHOOD: Central Hillside/Duluth Heights

ESTABLISHED: 1930

SIZE: 0.01 acres

The actual size of this park is difficult to identify, as today, thanks to reconfigurations of roadways, there are now three triangles at the convergence of Central Entrance and Mesaba Avenue.

Second Ave. E. & Tenth St. Triangle

NEIGHBORHOOD: Hillside

ESTABLISHED: n/a

SIZE: .01 acres

This triangle no longer exists and its former location is now the property of St. Luke's Hospital.

Thirtieth Ave. E. & Greysolon Rd. Triangle
NEIGHBORHOOD: Congdon
ESTABLISHED: 1913
SIZE: 0.08 acres (in two triangles)

Thirty-first Ave. E. & Greysolon Rd. Triangle
NEIGHBORHOOD: Congdon
ESTABLISHED: 1908
SIZE: 0.21 acres (in two triangles)

Thirty-eighth Ave. E. & Greysolon Rd. Triangle
NEIGHBORHOOD: Congdon
ESTABLISHED: 1908
SIZE: 0.02 acres

This "park" is not accessible to the public and was set aside by the city in order to access underground utilities for maintenance.

Twenty-seventh Ave. W. & Winnipeg Ave. Triangle
NEIGHBORHOOD: West End
ESTABLISHED: 1925
SIZE: 0.20 acres

Little is known about this small triangle of greenspace in an otherwise residential neighborhood.

Vermilion Trail Triangle
NEIGHBORHOOD: Downtown/Hillside
ESTABLISHED: 1870
SIZE: 0.02 acres

Also called the "Seventh Avenue East and First Street Triangle," the eastern side of this triangle is a sidewalk that runs along the former path of Washington Avenue. The spot marks the beginning of the Vermilion Road, built in 1868 to allow prospectors to reach Lake Vermilion during a short-lived "gold rush." The triangle once held a historic marker donated by the Daughters of the American Revolution; in the 1990s Mayor Gary Doty had the plaque moved to the Lakewalk.

Wallace Triangle
NEIGHBORHOOD: Longview (East End)
ESTABLISHED: 1926
SIZE: 0.04 acres

Also called the "Wallace Avenue and East Fifth Street Triangle," this triangle lies south of the intersection.

Wallace Ave. & Vermilion Rd. Triangle
NEIGHBORHOO: Longview (East End)
ESTABLISHED: 1911
SIZE: 0.12 acres

This triangle lies at the northeast corner of the intersection.

Woodland Ave. & Eighth St. Triangle
NEIGHBORHOOD: Chester Park/Longview (East End)
ESTABLISHED: 1911
SIZE: 0.05 acres

This triangle lies at the northwest corner of the intersection and contains a garden maintained by the Oregon Creek Garden Club.

Woodland Ave. & Fifth St. Triangle
NEIGHBORHOOD: Endion
ESTABLISHED: 1911
SIZE: 0.09 acres

This triangle lies at the southwest corner of the intersection.

Woodland Ave., Wallace Ave. & Victoria St. Triangle
NEIGHBORHOOD: Hunters Park
ESTABLISHED: 1911
SIZE: 0.14 acres

This triangle is formed by the convergence of Woodland Avenue, Wallace Avenue, and Arrowhead Road (originally Victoria Street).

---

3. Boulevards

Old West Skyline Parkway
A short segment of Skyline Parkway west of Knowlton Creek which was abandoned when the Spirit Mountain Recreation Area was created. *See chapter 2, "Skyline Parkway."*

Congdon Boulevard
A sixteen-mile stretch of road from the Lester River to Stoney Point along the north shore of Lake Superior that is also a portion of Scenic Highway 61. *See chapter 8, "Congdon and Kitchi Gammi Parks."*

Knowlton Creek Boulevard
A 1.7-mile roadway within Bardon's Peak Forest Park that originally connected Fairmount Park to Skyline Parkway. It is now a hiking trail. *See chapter 2, "Skyline Parkway."*

Lincoln Park Drive
A roadway within Lincoln Park stretching from Third Street to Skyline Parkway. *See chapter 3, "Lincoln Park."*

Mission Creek Boulevard
A 2.3-mile stretch of roadway within Fond du Lac Park that once connected Skyline Parkway to Jay Cooke State Park; it is now a hiking trail. *See chapter 2, "Skyline Parkway," and chapter 11, "Fond du Lac Park."*

Occidental Boulevard
A short (less than a mile long) road originally built as a bridle path along the west side of Amity Creek (aka the western branch of the Lester River) in Lester Park. *See chapter 5, "Lester Park."*

Oriental Boulevard
Originally a bridle path that paralleled Occidental Boulevard along the east side of Amity Creek within Lester Park, Oriental Boulevard no longer exists; its path is now part of the park's cross-country ski trail system. *See chapter 5, "Lester Park."*

Seven Bridges Road
Originally "Snively Boulevard" this road runs along and over Amity Creek within Amity Park from the eastern end of Skyline Parkway to the border of Lester Park, where it becomes Occidental Boulevard. *See chapter 2, "Skyline Parkway."*

Skyline Parkway
A 27-mile roadway built mostly along a hillside terrace that was once the beach of ancient Glacial Lake Duluth, from Becks Road in Gary–New Duluth to Seven Bridges Road in Lester Park. *See chapter 2, "Skyline Parkway."*

---

4. Public Boat Launches

Boy Scout Landing
This boat launch facility, at the foot of Commonwealth Avenue at the St. Louis River in Gary–New Duluth, is so named because Troop 13 of the Boy Scouts of America Voyageurs Area Council—sponsored by the Gary–New Duluth Community Club—maintained the dock, landing, and surrounding area from the late 1950s until the boat landing became city property in the early 1980s. Troop 13, led by Jerome A Blazevic, worked with the city to ensure that the area remained free for public use. Troop 13 still pitches in to maintain and clean the area when city funds don't allow for regular upkeep.

Minnesota Point Recreation Area Landing
A 2.25-acre boat launch facility at the foot of Minnesota Avenue at the entrance to the Minnesota Point Recreation Area.

Munger Landing
This 6.75-acre boat launch facility in the Smithville neighborhood is named for former Duluth legislator and environmentalist Willard Munger, who owned the nearby Munger Inn and whose efforts helped clean up the St. Louis River. Willard Munger is also the namesake of the nearby Munger Trail.

Rice's Point Landing
Also known as the Garfield Boat Launch, this two-acre boat landing facility at the southern tip of Rice's Point is adjacent to the remains of the northern span of the Interstate Bridge, a swing-arm bridge that connected Duluth and Superior from 1889 to 1961. The bridge's remaining span is used today as a fishing dock. The city technically does not own this property, but has an agreement with the Minnesota Department of Natural Resources to maintain it.

---

5. Trail Systems

Most of Duluth's larger parks contain trail systems used for a variety of activities, many of which are connected via the Duluth Traverse (a mountain bike trail built and maintained by the Cyclists of Gitchee Gumee Shores) and the Superior Hiking Trail, which is built and maintained by the non-profit Superior Hiking Trail Association. Since these trails are constantly undergoing expansion and reconfiguration, visit the Duluth's Parks and Recreation Division's website for up-to-date information on location, access, distance, and uses allowed on each trail.

Index

LITHOGRAPHIC POSTCARD MADE FROM A PHOTOGRAPH OF CONGDON PARK BY HUGH MCKENZIE SHOWING A RUSTIC BRIDGE AND STAIRS DESIGNED BY LANDSCAPE ARCHITECTS MORELL & NICHOLS, CA. 1910.

[IMAGE: ZENITH CITY PRESS]

7572 RUSTIC BRIDGE IN CONDON PARK
© MCKENZIE
DULUTH MINN

References

Publications

Alanen, Arnold R. *Morgan Park: Duluth, U.S. Steel, and the Forging of a Company Town*. Minneapolis: University of Minnesota Press, 2007.

Andrews, C. C., ed. *Minnesota in the Civil and Indian Wars 1861-1865*. St. Paul, Minn.: Printed for the state by the Pioneer Press Co., 1891.

Board of Realtors Atlas of the City of Duluth. Duluth, Minn.: Duluth Board of Realtors, 1924.

Brown, Curt. *So Terrible a Storm: A Tale of Fury on Lake Superior*. Minneapolis, Minn.: Voyageur Press, 2008.

Carlson, Christine. "*Wa ye kwaa gichi gamiing*: Fond du Lac, End of A Great Body of Water & a Visual Feast." A collection of newspaper clippings and other research materials regarding Fond du Lac, Minnesota. Nickerson, Minn.: Self published by the author, n.d.

Coventry, William D. *Duluth's Age of Brownstone*. Duluth, Minn.: St. Louis County Historical Society, 1987.

Cranz, Galen. "Changing Roles of Urban Parks: from Pleasure Garden to Open Space." *The Urbanist*. June 1, 2000.

Darling, J. H. "Private Observatory in Duluth." *Popular Astronomy*. October 1917.

"Darling Observatory 1917–1972." *Reference@Duluth*. https://dplreference.wordpress.com/2011/04/04/the-darling-observatory-1917-1972/. First published April 4, 2011.

Dierckins, Tony, and Maryanne C. Norton. *Lost Duluth: Landmarks, Industries, Buildings, Homes, and the Neighborhoods in Which They Stood*. Duluth, Minn.: Zenith City Press, 2012.

Dierckins, Tony. *Crossing the Canal: An Illustrated History of Duluth's Aerial Bridge*. Duluth, Minn.: Zenith City Press, 2009.

——. *Historic Glensheen*. Duluth, Minn.: Zenith City Press, 2015.

——. *Zenith: A Postcard Perspective of Historic Duluth*. Duluth, Minn.: Zenith City Press, 2007.

Denny, Jim J. Interview via email with Tony Dierckins, December 31, 2015–January 2, 2016.

Dregni, Eric. *Vikings in the Attic: In Search of Nordic America*. Minneapolis, Minn.: University of Minnesota Press, 2011.

Duluth Archaeological Society. "Archaeological Phase I Survey for the Historical Park." Duluth, Minn.: City of Duluth Department of Parks and Recreation, December 2015.

"Duluth zoo planning upgrades a year after flood drowned animals, damaged facilities" *MPR Updraft Blog*. http://blogs.mprnews.org/updraft/2013/06. Posted June 20, 2013.

Ellestad, Randy A. "Introduction to Gerhard Folgero's 'Across the North Atlantic in an Open Boat.'" Leif Erikson Viking Ship Restoration Project. http://leiferiksonvikingship.com/folgeros_voyage.htm. Accessed January 12, 2016.

"Existing Land Use Profile." Duluth, Minn.: City of Duluth Parks and Recreation Division, 2009.

Federal Writer's Project. *Minnesota: A State Guide*. New York: The Viking Press, 1938.

Federal Writer's Project. *The WPA Guide to the Minnesota Arrowhead Country: 1930s Minnesota*. St. Paul, Minn.: Minnesota Historical Society Press, 1988.

"Flood Recovery at the Lake Superior Zoo." *Lake Superior Zoo*. http://www.lszooduluth.org/about-the-zoo/flood-recovery/. Accessed January 6, 2016.

Folgero, Gearhard. "Across the North Atlantic in an Open Boat." Leif Erikson Viking Ship Restoration Project. http://leiferiksonvikingship.com/folgeros_voyage.htm. Accessed January 12, 2016.

——. "Viking Ship 'Leif Erikson'." Self published booklet, 1926.

Frederick, Chuck. *Leatherheads of the North: The True Story of Ernie Nevers and the Duluth Eskimos*. Zenith City Press. Duluth, Minn. 2007.

Fritzen, John. *The History of Fond du Lac and Jay Cooke Park*. Duluth, Minn.: St. Louis County Historical Society, 1978.

Granger, Susan, with Scott Kelly and Kay Grossman. "Lester River Bridge (Bridge #5772)." National Register of Historic Places Nomination Form. St. Paul: Minnesota Historical Society, September 6, 2002.

Grant v. Vollman. U.S. District Court D. Minnesota. No. Civ. 5-78-60.; 526 F.Supp. 15 (1981). February 11, 1981. Handy, Ray D. *The News Tribune Cartoon Book: Containing a Carefully Selected Collection of Our Best Cartoons*. Duluth, Minn.: Duluth News Tribune, Undated (ca. 1905).

Handy, Ray D. *The News Tribune Cartoon Book: Containing a Carefully Selected Collection of Our best Cartoons*. Duluth, Minn.: Duluth News Tribune, Undated (ca. 1903–06).

Hartman, Daniel. Interviews with Tony Dierckins, December 2015.

"Hawk Ridge Mission & History." Hawk Ridge Bird Observatory. http://www.hawkridge.org/about-us/mission-history/. Accessed February 23, 2016.

Helberg, Davis, ed. *Esko's Corner: An Illustrated History of Esko and Thomson Township*. Esko, Minn.: Esko Historical Society, 2013.

Hess, Jeffrey A. "Stewart Creek Bridge (Bridge #L6007)." National Register of Historic Places. Nomination Form. St. Paul: Minnesota Historical Society, May 30, 1990.

"Historic Timeline." *Chester Bowl*. http://www.chesterbowl.org/history/people/historical-timeline/. Accessed December 24, 2015.

Hoover, Roy. *A Lake Superior Lawyer*. Castro Valley, Calif.: Kutenai Press, 2013.

House, Ronald. Interview via email with Tony Dierckins, January 8–9, 2016.

"ICRI 2011 Project Award Winners." *International Concrete Repair Institute*. http://www.icri.org/AWARDS/2011/lesterriverbridge.asp. Accessed December 29, 2015.

Isaacs, Aaron. *Twin Ports by Trolley: The Streetcar Era in Duluth–Superior*. Mpls., Minn.: University of Minnesota Press, 2014.

Insbell, Jim. "Hagbert J. Enger." http://www.findagrave.com/cgi-bin/fg.cgi?page=gr&GRid=15531826. Accessed August 27, 2006.

Kenny, Edwin. "Associate Justice Clarence R. Magney." *Minnesota Reports*. Vol. 273. St. Paul, Minn.: Minnesota Supreme Court, January–April 1965.

Kopischke, Gregory. "Morell & Nichols." *Pioneers of American Landscape Design: An Annotated Bibliography*. Edited by Charles A. Birnbaum and Julie K. Fix. Washington, DC: U.S. Department of the Interior, 1995.

Kraker, Dan. "Norway's royalty rededicates Enger Tower in Duluth." *Minnesota Public Radio*. http://www.mprnews.org/story/2011/10/17/norway-royalty-dedicate-enger-tower. Accessed October 17, 2011.

"Lincoln Park Bridge (Bridge L8477)." Minnesota Architecture–History Inventory Form. Minnesota Department of Transportation. May 4, 2011.

"Lake Superior Zoo Regains Accreditation." Northland News Center. http://www.northlandsnewscenter.com/news/local/Lake-Superior-Zoo-Back-in-Action-129723203.html. Posted September 13, 2011.

Ly, Pakou. "City and Zoological Society Reach Consensus on Zoo/Fairmount Park Concept." City of Duluth Communications Office press release. November 4, 2015.

Lundeen, Lauren. "The race that meant more near Duluth's Hartley Nature Center." *Lake Voice News*. http://www.d.umn.edu/writ/jour/lakevoice/?p=199. Posted February 25, 2010.

Mackety, Dawn, and John Scott. "2014 Annual Report of Lake Superior Zoo Activities." Duluth, Minn.: Lake Superior Zoological Society. April 23, 2015.

"Merritt Family (1809–1996)." Merritt Family Papers. http://sandbox.archon.org/latest/?p=creators/creator&id=5528. Accessed January 17, 2016.

Merritt, Grant. Interview via email with Tony Dierckins, January 17–18, 2016.

Michols, J. M., ed., with Coleman F. Naughton and Ray D. Handy, illustrators. *As We See 'Em; Duluthians in Cartoon: Being a Most Successful Attempt at Portraying Representative Business Men of Duluth, Minnesota, in their Respective Professions and Trades*.

Duluth, Minn.: Duluth News Tribune and Duluth Herald, undated (ca. 1909).

Mirza, Madiha. "Duluth's statue of Leif Ericsson shouldn't have horns." *UMD Statesman*. http://theumdstatesman. com/2012/03/08/duluths-statue-of-leif-ericsson-shouldnt-have-horns/. Posted March 8, 2012.

Morell, Anthony U. and Arthur R. Nichols. *Landscape Architecture*. Minneapolis, Minn.: Morell & Nichols, 1911.

Morell and Nichols Collection. Northwest Architectural Archives. University of Minnesota Libraries, Minneapolis.

Mullholand, Susan C., et al. "Final Technical Report, Archaeological Phase I Survey for the Historical Park." Duluth, Minn.: Duluth Archaeological Center, LLC: 2015.

Nunnally, Patrick D. "Jewel of the North: Duluth's Parkway System." Prepared for the Duluth Heritage Preservation Commission. July 1997.

O'Hara, Dennis and Tony Dierckins. *Glensheen: The Official Guide to Duluth's Historic Congdon Estate*. Duluth, Minn.: Zenith City Press, 2016.

"Parks, Recreation, and Open Space Profile." Duluth, Minn.: City of Duluth, 2006.

R. L. Polk's & Co.'s Duluth City Directories. Duluth, Minn.: Duluth Directory Co., 1932–2015.

Roe, Frederick B. *Atlas of the City of Duluth, St. Louis Co., Minn., and Vicinity*. Philadelphia: F. B. Roe, 1890.

"St. Louis River Corridor Vision." City of Duluth. http://www. duluthmn.gov/st-louis-river-corridor/. Accessed January–February, 2016.

Sanborn Fire Insurance Maps: City of Duluth. Pelham, New York: Sanborn Map Company, 1883–1954.

Simplot, Alex. *Souvenir of Duluth*. No publisher, no date. (Ca. 1893.)

Slabodnik, Robert J. "The Evolution of Landscape: Allandale Farm-Hartley Park, 1890 to 1990." 1990. Research project. University of Minnesota Duluth Kathryn A. Martin Library Archives and Special Collections.

"Station Duluth, Minnesota." *United States Coast Guard Website*. https://www.uscg.mil/history/stations/DULUTH.pdf. Accessed February 1, 2016.

Storm, Thom. Interview via email with Tony Dierckins, December 31, 2015–January 2, 2016.

"Timeline of Human History in Hartley Park." *Hartley Nature Center*. https://www.hartleynature.org/explore/timeline.html. Accessed January 18, 2016.

Trefousse, Hans L. *Rutherford B. Hayes*. New York, NY: Henry Holt, 2002.

Upham, Warren. *Minnesota Geographic Names: Their Original and Historic Significance*. St. Paul, Minn.: Minnesota Historical Society Press, 1920.

Van Brunt, Walter. *Duluth and St. Louis County, Minnesota: Their Story and People. Vols. 1–3*. New York: The American Historical Society, 1921.

Warshaw, Shirley Anne. *Guide to White House Staff*. Thousand Oaks, Calif.: CQ Press, 2013.

"William King Rogers and Duluth, Minnesota's Skyline Parkway." *Ohio's Yesterdays*. http://ohiosyesterdays.blogspot. com/2009/12/william-king-rogers-and-duluth.html. Accessed December 31, 2009.

"William King Rogers." *Rutherford B. Hayes Presidential Center*. http://www.rbhayes.org/hayes/mssfind/487/ RogersWKwebpage.htm. Accessed February 8, 2016.

Woodbridge, Dwight E., and John S. Pardee, eds. *History of Duluth and St. Louis County. Volumes 1 and 2*. Chicago: C. F. Cooper & Company, 1910.

Reports by the City of Duluth

Published by the Board of Park Commissioners: "An Act of the Legislature of the State of Minnesota Providing for a System of Public Grounds for the City of Duluth," August 1, 1889; "First Annual Report of the Board of Park Commissioners of the City of Duluth for the Period from April 22, 1891 to December 31, 1891"; "Third Annual Report of the Board of Park Commissioners of the City of Duluth for the Year 1894"; "Fifth Annual Report of the Board of Park Commissioners of the City of Duluth for the Year 1896"; "Annual Report of Park Commissioners, 1900"; "Annual Report of Park Commissioners, 1901"; "Annual Report of Park Commissioners, 1902"; "Annual Report of Park Commissioners, 1903"; "Annual Report of Park Commissioners, 1905"; "Annual Report of Park Commission, 1906"; "Annual Report of Park Commission, 1907"; "Annual Report of Park Commission, 1908"; "Annual Report of Park Commission, 1909"; "Annual Report of Park Commission, 1910"; "Annual Report of Park Commission, 1911"; "Duluth's Parks: Report of the Board of Park Commissioners, Duluth Minnesota, 1911"; "Annual Report of Park Commission, 1912"; "Minutes of the Board of Park Commissioners of the City of Duluth, May 1889 through April 1913." Published by the City of Duluth: "Annual Report of the Park Superintendent (Division of Public Works), 1913"; "Annual Report of the Park Superintendent (Division of Public Works), 1914"; "Annual Report of the Park Department (Division of Public Works)," 1915; "Annual Report, Park Department, City of Duluth (F. Rodney Paine, Superintendent of Parks)," 1928–1936; "Annual Report, Park Department, City of Duluth (Earl H. Sherman, Superintendent of Parks)," 1937–1940; "Annual Report, Park Department, City of Duluth (John V. Hoene, Superintendent of Parks), 1941–1944"; "Annual Report, Park Department, City of Duluth (Gust A. Johnson, Superintendent of Parks), 1945–1952"; "Annual Report, Park Department, City of Duluth (S. I. Duclett, Acting Superintendent of Parks), 1956"; "Annual Report, Recreation Department, City of Duluth (Lauren J. Ogsten, Director, Department of Public Recreation), 1958"; "Annual Report. Department of Parks and Recreation, City of Duluth (Harry W. Nash, Director), 1970–1971"; "Annual Report, Parks & Recreation Department (Carl Seehus, Director of Parks & Recreation), 1989–1992"; "Annual Report, Parks & Recreation Department (Suzanne Moyer, Director of Parks & Recreation), 1992–1999"; "Annual Report, Parks & Recreation Department (Carl Seehus, Director of Parks & Recreation), 1999–2006"; "Annual Report, Parks & Recreation Division, City of Duluth (Kathleen Bergen, Division Manager), 2006–2011"; "Duluth Parks & Recreation Master Plan (City of Duluth Parks and Recreation Division), 2009."

From *Zenith City Online*

The following reference sources were all originally published on *Zenith City Online* (zenithcity.com).

By Heidi Bakk-Hansen: "Calling Dr. Walbank," April 11, 2013; "E. P. Alexander: Son of the Confederacy, Grandfather to Watergate," December 12, 2012; "From Patriarch to Neighborhood Namesake: John C. Hunter and His Family's Influence on Duluth," November 17, 2014; "The Lawyer and the Forlorn Two-Acre Wood," July 15, 2013; "Living in a Tartan Paradise: A Brief History of Hunters Park," February 1, 2015; "Lyman Park: A Lost Neighborhood of the West End," July 14, 2014.

By Anthony Bush: "1911: White Sox Build New Field on Minnesota Point, Never Use It," May 19, 2014; "Frank Wade's Legacy: Beyond the Brick Walls," October 1, 2012.

By Jim Heffernan. "Remembering Bessie, Duluth's Elephant," March 6, 2014.

By Mark Ryan: "The Sad, Troubled Life of William K. Rogers," May 1, 2012; "Sam Snively: Duluth's Grand Old Dad," November 1, 2012. "The Day Mr. Jackson Came to Town," March, 2015.

Newspapers

Research for this book included thousands of newspaper articles found in the following newspapers:

Chicago Inter-Ocean, Chicago, Illinois

Duluth Budgeteer, Duluth, Minnesota

Duluth Evening Herald, Duluth, Minnesota

Duluth Herald, Duluth, Minnesota

Duluth Minnesotian, Duluth, Minnesota

Duluth Morning Call, Duluth, Minnesota

Duluth News Tribune, Duluth, Minnesota

Duluth Weekly Herald, Duluth, Minnesota

Duluth Weekly Tribune, Duluth, Minnesota

Lake Superior News, Duluth, Minnesota

Lake Superior Review & Weekly Tribune, Duluth, Minnesota

Minneapolis Star Tribune, Minneapolis, Minnesota

Previously Published Material

This book's introduction and chapters were previously published as serialized articles in earlier versions on *Zenith City Online* (zenithcity.com) as listed below and have been updated and expanded for this book.

By Nancy S. Nelson: "A 'Good Place to Go!': A History of Chambers Grove Park," June 15, 2015; "A Man of Far-Reaching Vision: F. Rodney Paine and Duluth's Parks," September 17, 2015; "Cascade Square in the 'Heart of the City," September 13, 2012; "Chester Park, Part 1: A Primeval Forest in the Heart of the City," February 21, 2013; "Chester Park, Part 2: Chester Bowl / Upper Chester," March 21, 2013; "Chester Park, Part 3: The City Takes Control of Chester Bowl," April 22, 2013; "Congdon Park: A 'Most Picturesque Sylvan District'," June 24, 2013; "Duluth Park

A LITHOGRAPHIC POSTCARD MADE CA. 1920 SHOWING A CAR DRIVING ALONG ROGERS BOULEVARD (SKYLINE PARKWAY TODAY) AS IT PASSES OVER CHESTER CREEK IN CHESTER PARK.

[IMAGE: ZENITH CITY PRESS]

Board Eliminated with Change in Government," May 27, 2013; "Duluth: The Homecroft City," April 1, 2013 ; "Duluth's Park System, Part 1: Getting Started," June 6, 2012; "Duluth's Park System, Part 2: Parks Board Spends Wildly," June 14, 2012; "Duluth's Park System, Part 3: The Parkway and Five Parks," July 16, 2012; "Duluth's Park System, Part 4: Citizens Help Build Parks," August 15, 2012; "Duluth's Undeveloped Central Park," March 24, 2014; "Enger Park: A Gift from a Furniture Salesman," April 24, 2014; "Fairmount Park, Part 1: A Breathing Spot for West Duluth," November 25, 2013; "Fairmount Park, Part 2: Indian Point Bathing Beach," December 23, 2013; "Fairmount Park, Part 3: Indian Point Tourist Camp," January 27, 2014; "Fairmount Park, Part 4: Fairmount Park becomes Home to a Zoo," February 24, 2014; "Fond du Lac Park, Part 1: Mission Creek Parkway, the (Missing) Link to Jay Cooke State Park," July 16, 2015; "Fond Du Lac Park, Part 2: Winter Sports and a Summer Nursery," August 17, 2015; "From Park to Lifesaving Station Back to Park: Park Point's Franklin Square," August 12, 2016; "Hartley Park, Part 1: From Lettuce Fields to Hartley Field," April 16, 2015; "Hartley Park, Part 2: From Lettuce to Learning," May 14, 2015; "Hilltop Park: A Small Space Occupied by Big Memories," February 8, 2016; "Janette Pollay Park, Part 1: 'An Exquisite Specimen of Nature's Handiwork'," September 22, 2014; "Janette Pollay Park, Part 2: 'Forever Available for... All the Inhabitants of the City'," October 20, 2014; "Kitchi Gammi Park and Congdon Boulevard: Preserving Public Access to the Lakeshore," October 24, 2013; "Leif Erikson Park, Part 1: A Park Along Superior's Shore," May 22, 2014; "Leif Erikson Park, Part 2: Lake Shore Park," June 23, 2014; "Leif Erikson Park, Part 3: Unrealized Dreams," July 21, 2014; "Leif Erikson Park, Part 4: A Viking Vessel Inspires a Name Change," August 21, 2014; "Lester Park, Part 1: An 'Enchanted Land of Fairy-Like Beauty'," July 25, 2013; "Lester Park, Part 2: 'You are Invited'," August 22, 2013; "Lester Park, Part 3: Pushing the Boundaries," September 23, 2013; "Lincoln Park, Part 1: So Rich in Beauty," November 19, 2012; "Lincoln Park, Part 2: Home of Duluth's First Playground," December 13, 2012; "Lincoln Park, Part 3: A Community Gathering Place," January 24, 2013; "Magney-Snively Park, Part 1: A Panoramic View of the St. Louis River," December 22, 2014; "Magney-Snively Park, Part 2: Duluth's Finest Virgin Hardwood Forest," February 19, 2015; "Minnesota Point, Duluth's Summer Resort, Part 1: The Parks of Minnesota Point," October 19, 2015; "Minnesota Point, Duluth's Summer Resort, Part 2: Basking on the Beach," November 16, 2015; "Something New at the Head of the Lakes: The Playground Movement in Duluth," December 17, 2015; "The Cheerful, Creative and Practical Henry Cleveland, Duluth's Superintendent of Parks 1909–1925," March 19, 2015.

By Tony Dierckins: "Leif Erikson Park's Rose Garden," May 23, 2016; "Morell & Nichols: Minnesota's Premier Landscape Architects Left Their Mark on Duluth," March 8, 2016; "Policing the Parks," January 11, 2016; "Thornton's Kiddieland," July 11, 2016; "The Zenith City's Public Squares," April 18, 2016.

By Nancy S. Nelson And Tony Dierckins: "Hilltop Park: Small Park, Big Memories," February 8, 2016; "Meet Duluth's First Park Board," September 9, 2016; "Park Point's Franklin Square: From Park to Lifesaving Station Back to Park," August 12, 2016.

Books by Zenith City Press: Several sidebar stories accompanying the chapters of this book have been adapted and expanded from similar stories that have appeared in the following books written by Tony Dierckins: *Crossing the Canal: An Illustrated History of Duluth's Aerial Bridge* (Zenith City Press, 2009). *Lost Duluth: Landmarks, Industries, Buildings, Homes, and the Neighborhoods in Which They Stood* (with Maryanne C. Norton, Zenith City Press, 2012), *Glensheen: The Official Guide to the Historic Congdon Estate* (Zenith City Press, 2016).

About the Images

Digital Correction

Most of the historic photographs found in this book have been digitally enhanced in some way. We've adjusted the contrast and lightness, corrected the tone of those that have faded with age, cleaned up scratches and other blemishes that have marred prints, and made other minor alterations intended to make the subjects of the photographs more visible to the reader; nearly all have been cropped to fit the book's design. Likewise, the historic sketches found in this book, several from newspapers originally published in black and white, have been colorized for this publication, and lithographic postcards faded with age have been color corrected to restore their original appearance. If you seek these images from the sources listed below, you will not find them in the same condition as they appear in this book.

Major Duluth Photographers

While myriad individuals have photographed Duluth since the 1860s, four have made a major contribution and you will find many of their photos in this book. Paul B. Gaylord (ca. 1847–1903), a native of Ohio, was active in Duluth from the late 1860s to the 1890s and took dozens of stereoscopic images of Duluth's early years. Born in Oshkosh, Wisconsin, Hugh McKenzie (1879–1957) worked in Winona and Litchfield, Minnesota, prior to arriving in Duluth in 1900, and he worked for J. R. Zweifel before establishing his own studio. He specialized in commercial, architectural, and landscape photography and retired in 1947. Several of the images made by McKenzie were used to create color lithographic postcards between 1900 and 1939. Duluth had two photographers named Louis Perry Gallagher, father and son. L. Perry Gallagher Sr. (1875–1945) was born in Saginaw, Michigan, and came to Duluth in 1894 to work for Herman Brown. He left Brown to photograph for the Zenith View Company before establishing his own studio in 1898. L. Perry Gallagher Jr. (1912–1988) apprenticed with his father and eventually inherited Gallagher Studios. Anecdotal evidence indicates that the senior Gallagher had retired by ca. 1935 and that his son worked until shortly before his death. While the Gallaghers, like McKenzie, took a great deal of architectural and landscape photographs, they also recorded dozens of historic events and specialized in aerial photography.

The F. Rodney Paine Collection

Nearly forty of the photographs found in this book were made by F. Rodney Paine between 1926 and 1938, the years he served as Duluth's park superintendent under Mayor Sam Snively. Those images belong to the Duluth Public Library and are archived at the University of Minnesota Duluth Kathryn A. Martin Library Archives and Special Collections, as part of the Northeast Minnesota Historical Collection. The Paine collection contains over 950 negatives, of which have been digitized. You can find the digitized images, along with many other images that appear in this book (including those of Paul B. Gaylord, Hugh McKenzie, and Gallagher Studios), at reflections.mndigital.org, where they can be viewed in their original archived condition and in great detail.

The Detroit Publishing Company

Several images published in this book were originally made by photographers working for the Detroit Publishing Company, started in 1897 by William A. Livingstone and photographer Edwin H. Husher and active through 1923. In all, the company produced 25,000 glass negatives and transparencies, most of which were donated to the United States Library of Congress in 1949. The Library of Congress has digitized the majority of these images and has made them—and thousands more from other sources—available for online viewing at http://www.loc.gov/pictures/.

The Zenith City Press Collection

Since 2002 Zenith City Press and its parent company, X-Communication, have been collecting digital images in the public domain for use in its books and on *Zenith City Online* (zenithcity.com), including postcards made between 1895 and 1940. The majority of these cards were donated to Zenith City Press by individuals. Together Herb Dillon, Tom Kasper, Jerry Paulson, and Bob Swanson contributed more than 1,500 images between 2002 and 2012. Images from that effort used in this book are credited herein to Zenith City Press. In the past year Herb Dillon has provided even more postcard images, and we have credited them to the H. Dillon Collection. Zenith City Press has also worked with the Reference Staff of the Duluth Public Library to digitize images from books in the public domain and slides within its collection at the library's main branch. Images from this effort are credited herein to the Duluth Public Library; digital files are archived by Zenith City Press.

Contributing Individuals

Some of the images in this book come from the private collections of individuals. In particular, many images used herein were acquired by Tom Kasper, who originally dreamed up the idea of this book. The following individuals provided images for this book:

- Herb Dillon (credited herein as H. Dillon Collection)
- Andy Ebling
- Jerry Fryberger
- Tom Kasper (credited herein as T. Kasper Collection)
- Jeff Lemke
- Ryan Marshik
- Maryanne C. Norton
- Mark Ryan (credited herein as M. Ryan Collection)
- Walter N. Trennery
- Robert Rodriguez
- Erin Walsburg
- Gary Wildung

Contributing Organizations

The following organizations provided images for this book:

- Chester Bowl Improvement Club
- Climb Duluth
- Duluth Facilities Management (credited herein as City of Duluth)
- Duluth News Tribune
- Duluth Public Library
- Glensheen Historic Estate
- Hartley Nature Center
- Hayes Presidential Library and Museum
- Minnesota Historical Society (credited herein as MN Historical Society)
- Provincetown History Preservation Project
- United States Library of Congress
- University of Minnesota Duluth Kathryn A. Martin Library Archives and Special Collections (credited herein as UMD Martin Library)
- University of Minnesota Morris (credited herein as UM Morris)
- Zenith City Press

About the Authors

Nancy S. Nelson

Nancy S. Nelson has worked as a freelance technical writer, geologist, and educator in the Duluth area for over twenty years, writing and editing for a variety of nonprofit and grassroots organizations, political campaigns, newspapers, government agencies, and environmental consulting firms. She has also taught at Lake Superior College, University of Wisconsin–Superior, and Wisconsin Indianhead Technical College. She moved to Duluth from northern Illinois in 1987 to live near Lake Superior and attend the University of Minnesota Duluth where she earned a master's degree in geology. One of the founders of Duluth's Skyline Planning and Preservation Alliance, she continues to advocate for the protection of our historic greenspaces and enjoys exploring local parks and trails, always seeking to better understand the ways in which we are influenced by the landscape.

Tony Dierckins

Duluth author (and St. Paul native) Tony Dierckins has written or co-written more than two dozen books, from the ridiculous *Duct Tape* books and calendars to the fun and informative *Mosquito Book*. His regional history books include *Crossing the Canal: An Illustrated History of Duluth's Aerial Bridge* and, with Maryanne C. Norton, *Lost Duluth: Landmarks, Industries, Buildings, Homes, and the Neighborhoods in which They Stood*—both finalists for the Minnesota Book Award—and *Glensheen: The Official Guide to Duluth's Historic Congdon Estate*. Dierckins is the 2012 recipient of the Duluth Depot Foundation's Historic Preservation and Interpretation Award and the publisher of Zenith City Press, celebrating historic Duluth and the Western Lake Superior region at www.zenithcity.com.

THE COVER OF THE JUNE 1911 *ZENITH* MAGAZINE (A PUBLICATION OF DULUTH'S MARSHALL-WELLS HARDWARE CO.) DEPICTING PICNICKERS, INCLUDING A MAN CARVING A MARSHALL-WELLS "ZENITH TOOLS" LOGO INTO A TREE IN AN UNIDENTIFIED PARK.

[IMAGE: ZENITH CITY PRESS]